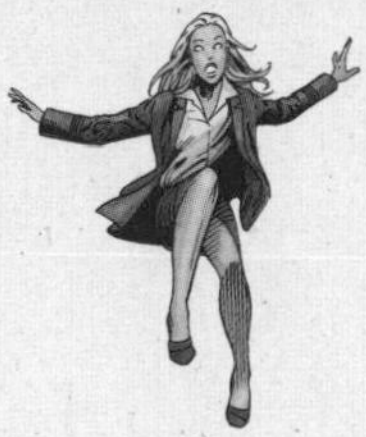

air

PURELAND

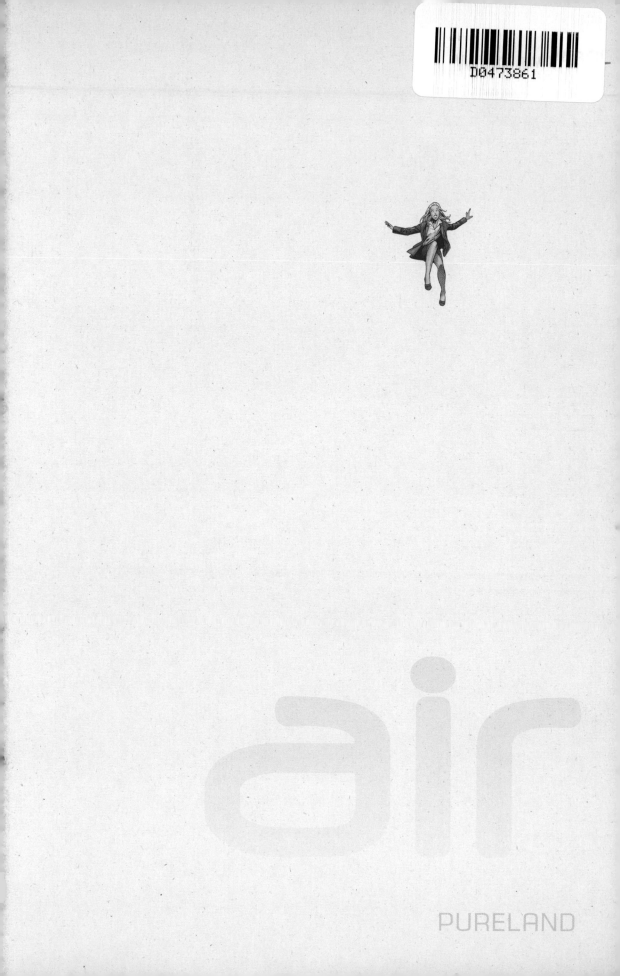

PURELAND

G. Willow Wilson Writer

M. K. Perker Artist

Chris Chuckry Colorist

Jared K. Fletcher Letterer

AIR created by Wilson and Perker

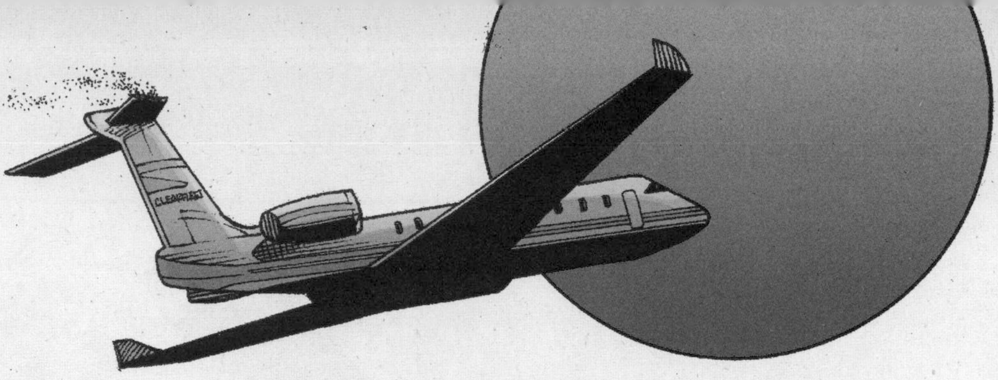

Karen Berger SVP-Executive Editor & Editor-original series
Pornsak Pichetshote Associate Editor-original series
Brandon Montclare Sarah Litt Assistant Editors-original series
Georg Brewer VP-Design & DC Direct Creative
Bob Harras Group Editor-Collected Editions & Editor
Robbin Brosterman Design Director-Books
Louis Prandi Art Director

DC COMICS
Diane Nelson President
Dan DiDio and Jim Lee Co-Publishers
Geoff Johns Chief Creative Officer
Patrick Caldon EVP-Finance and Administration
John Rood EVP-Sales, Marketing and Business Development
Amy Genkins SVP-Business and Legal Affairs
Steve Rotterdam SVP-Sales and Marketing
John Cunningham VP-Marketing
Terri Cunningham VP-Managing Editor
Alison Gill VP-Manufacturing
David Hyde VP-Publicity
Sue Pohja VP-Book Trade Sales
Alysse Soll VP-Advertising and Custom Publishing
Bob Wayne VP-Sales
Mark Chiarello Art Director

Cover by M.K. Perker

AIR: PURELAND

Published by DC Comics. Cover and compilation
Copyright © 2010 DC Comics. All Rights Reserved.

Originally published in single magazine form as
AIR #11-17. Copyright © 2009, 2010 G. Willow
Wilson and M.K. Perker. All Rights Reserved.
All characters, their distinctive likenesses and
related elements featured in this publication
are trademarks of DC Comics. VERTIGO is a
trademark of DC Comics. The stories, characters
and incidents featured in this publication are
entirely fictional. DC Comics does not read or
accept unsolicited submissions of ideas, stories
or artwork.

DC Comics, 1700 Broadway, New York, NY 10019
A Warner Bros. Entertainment Company
Printed in Dubuque, IA, USA. First Printing. 4/28/10.
ISBN: 978-1-4012-2706-7

SWEET ON THE TONGUE

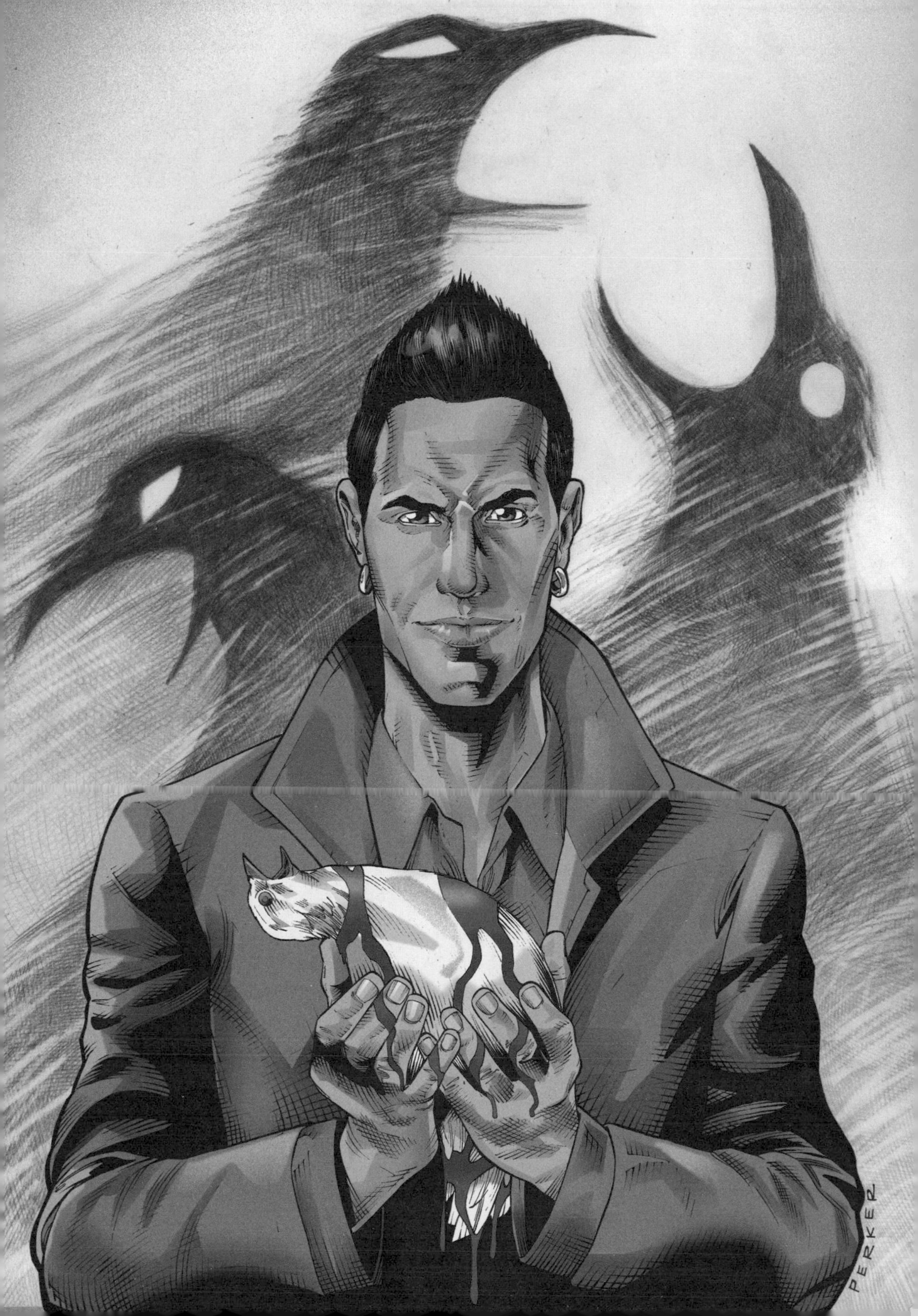

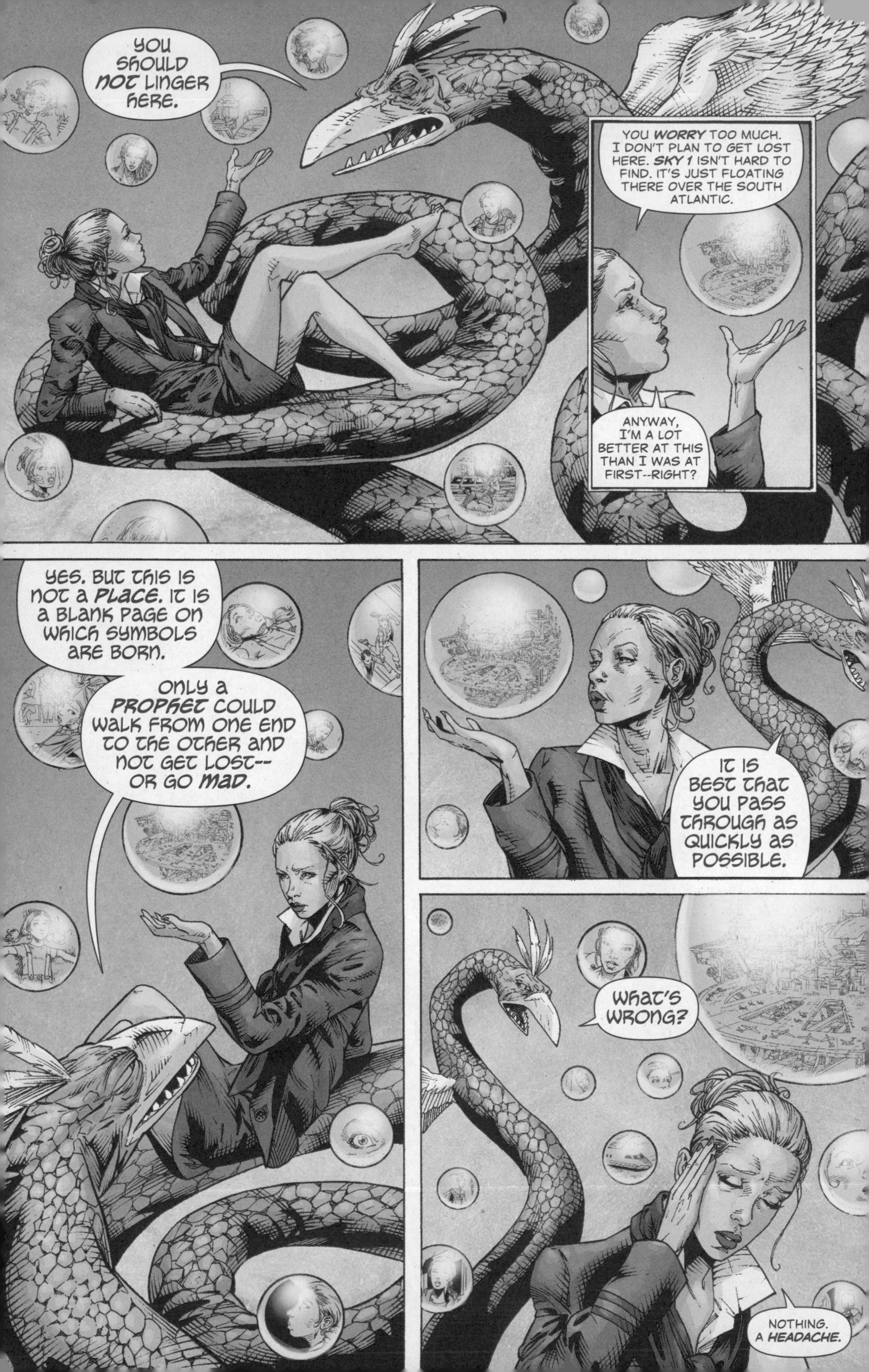
YOU SHOULD NOT LINGER HERE.
YOU WORRY TOO MUCH. I DON'T PLAN TO GET LOST HERE. SKY 1 ISN'T HARD TO FIND. IT'S JUST FLOATING THERE OVER THE SOUTH ATLANTIC.
ANYWAY, I'M A LOT BETTER AT THIS THAN I WAS AT FIRST--RIGHT?
YES. BUT THIS IS NOT A PLACE. IT IS A BLANK PAGE ON WHICH SYMBOLS ARE BORN.
ONLY A PROPHET COULD WALK FROM ONE END TO THE OTHER AND NOT GET LOST-- OR GO MAD.
IT IS BEST THAT YOU PASS THROUGH AS QUICKLY AS POSSIBLE.
WHAT'S WRONG?
NOTHING. A HEADACHE.

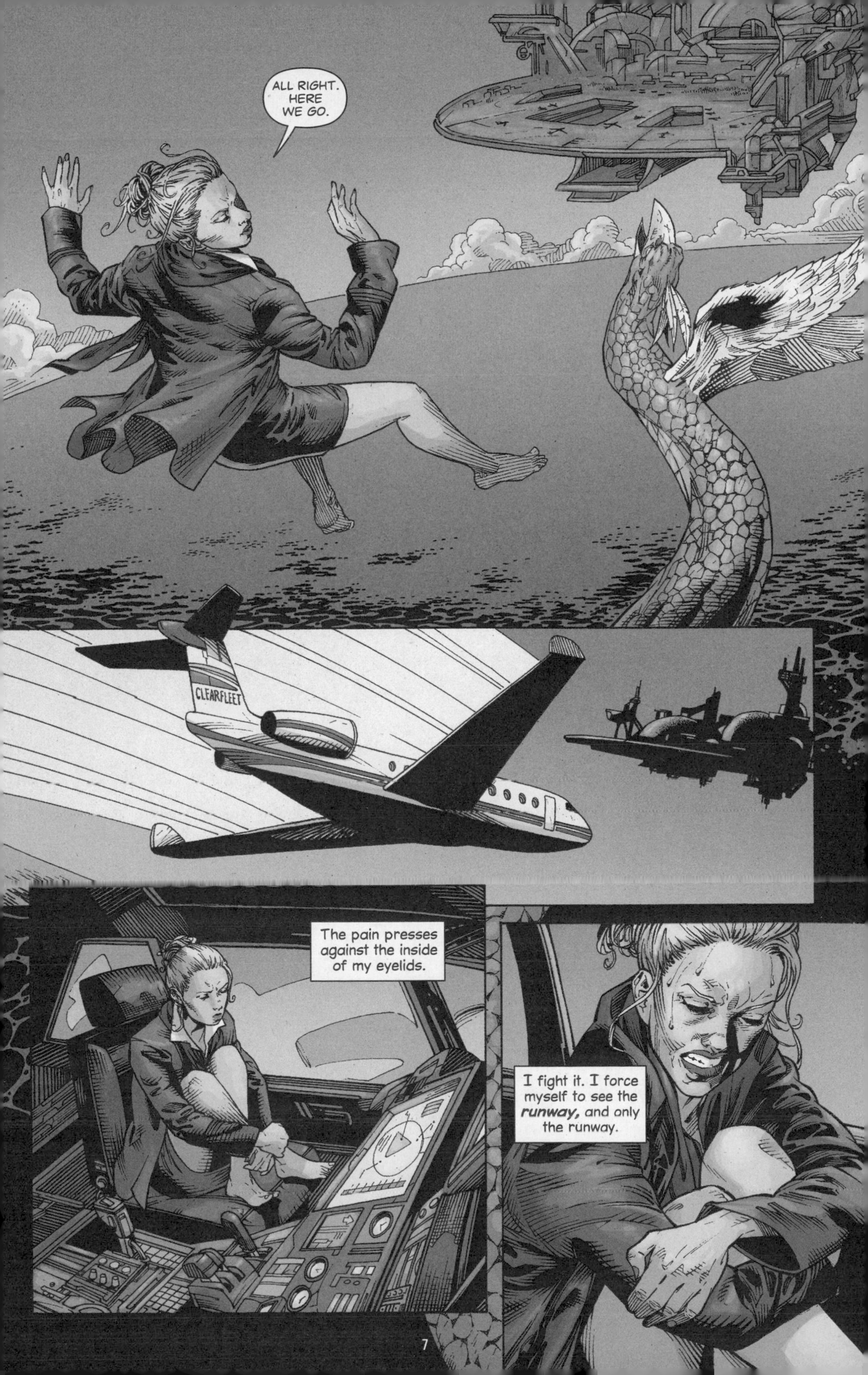
ALL RIGHT. HERE WE GO.
CLEARFLEET
The pain presses against the inside of my eyelids.
I fight it. I force myself to see the *runway,* and only the runway.

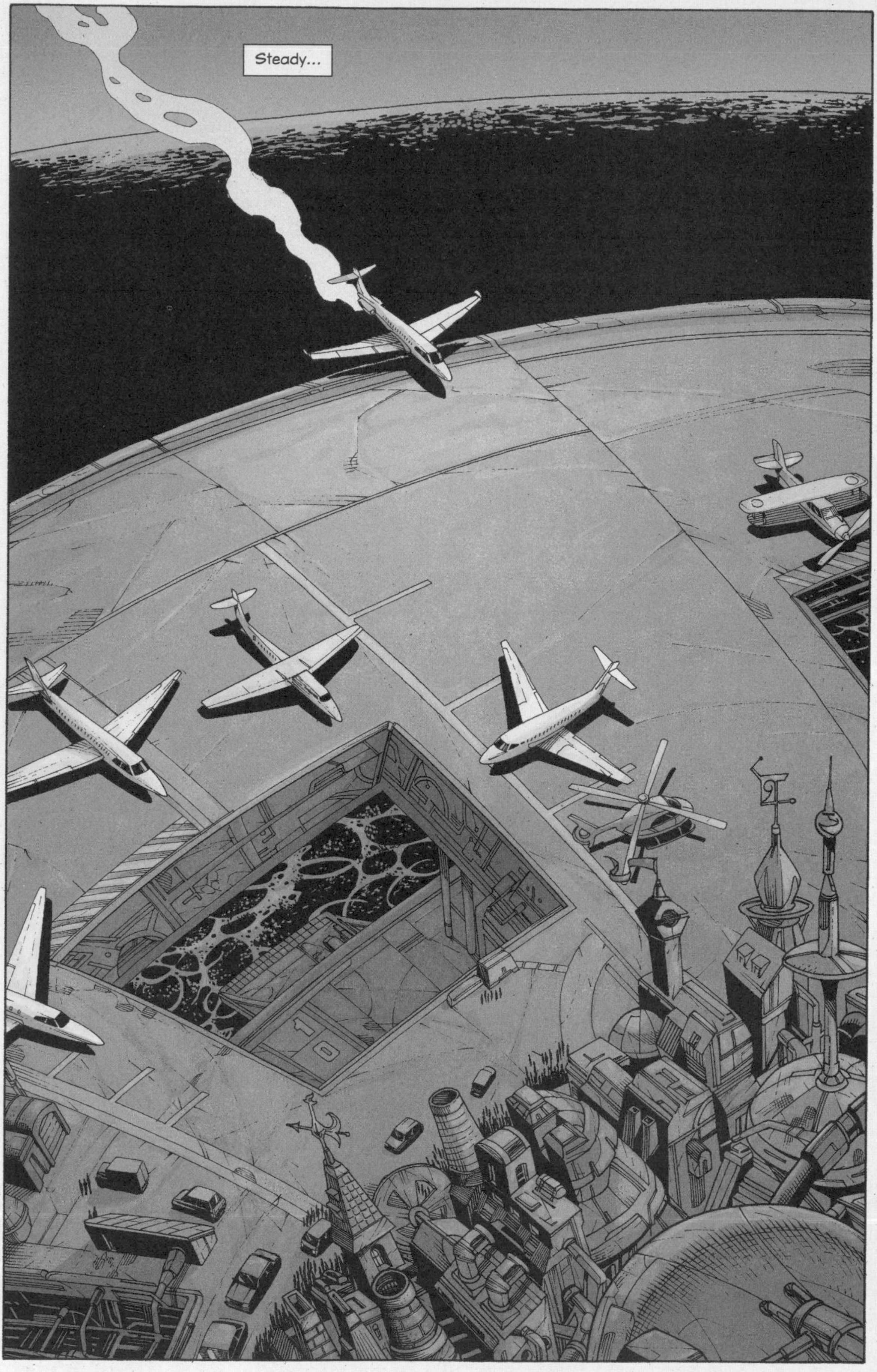
Steady...

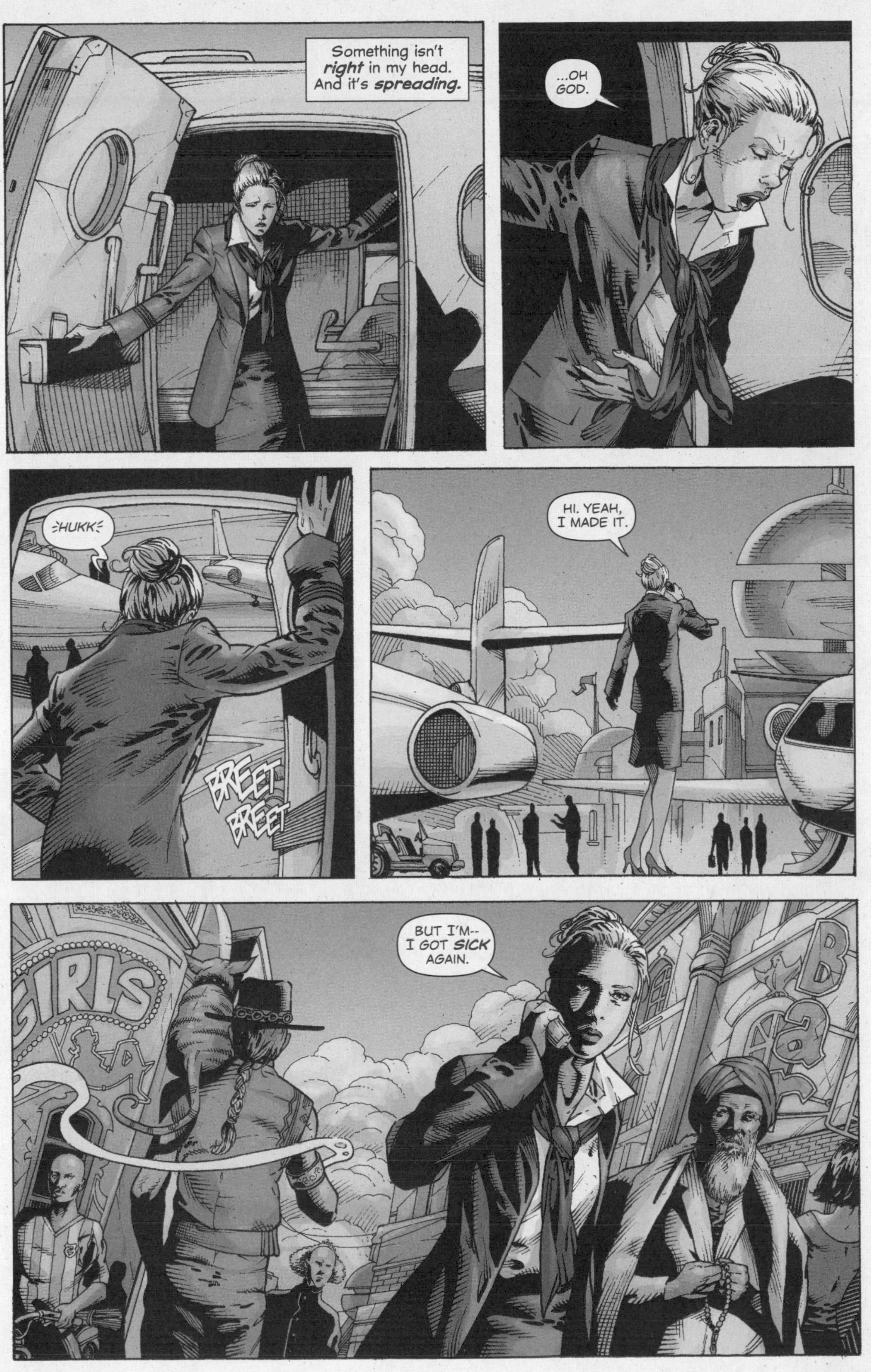
Something isn't right in my head. And it's spreading.
...OH GOD.
HUKK
BREET BREET
HI. YEAH, I MADE IT.
BUT I'M-- I GOT SICK AGAIN.
GIRLS

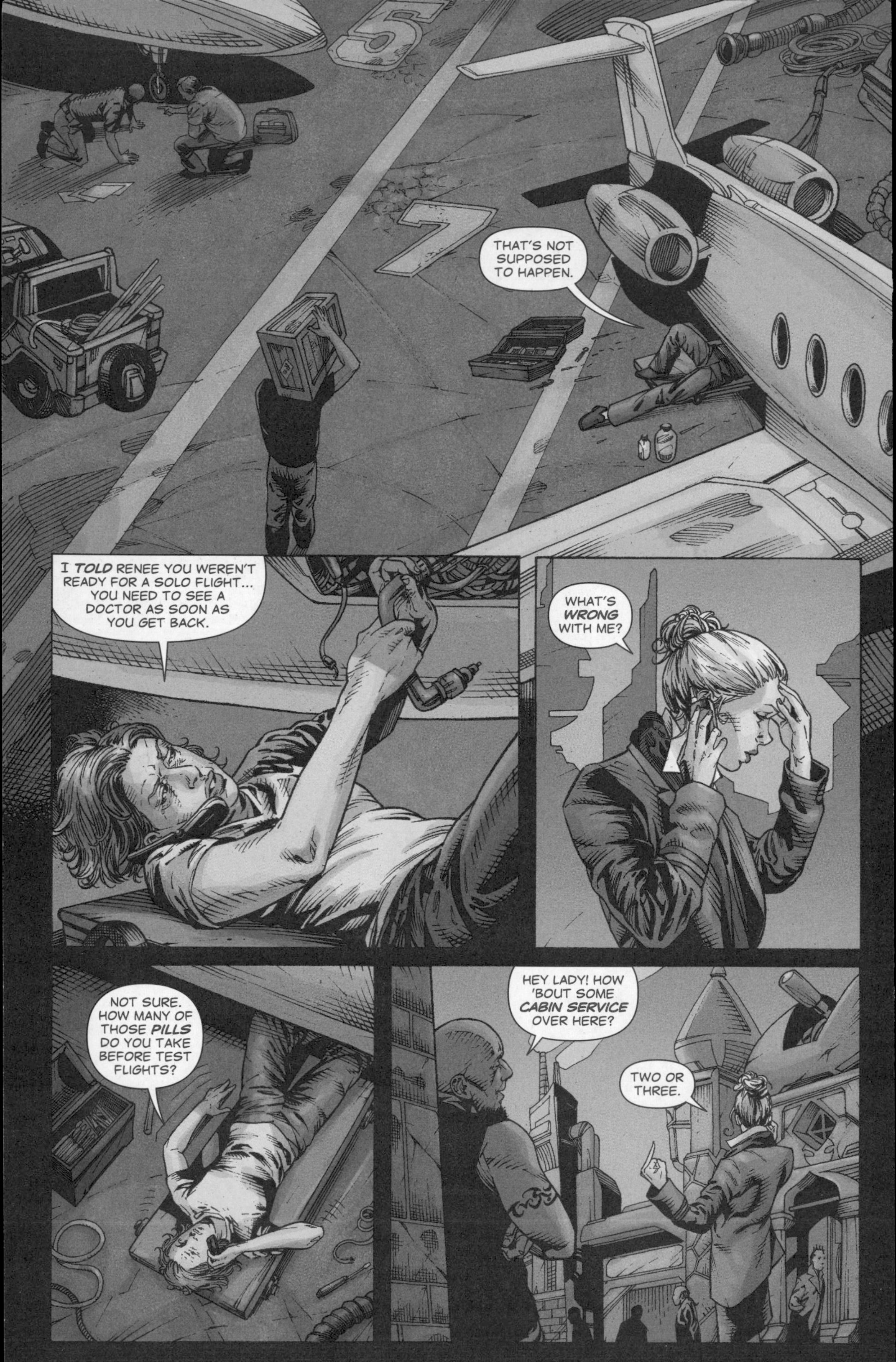
THAT'S NOT SUPPOSED TO HAPPEN.
I TOLD RENEE YOU WEREN'T READY FOR A SOLO FLIGHT... YOU NEED TO SEE A DOCTOR AS SOON AS YOU GET BACK.
WHAT'S WRONG WITH ME?
NOT SURE. HOW MANY OF THOSE PILLS DO YOU TAKE BEFORE TEST FLIGHTS?
HEY LADY! HOW 'BOUT SOME CABIN SERVICE OVER HERE?
TWO OR THREE.

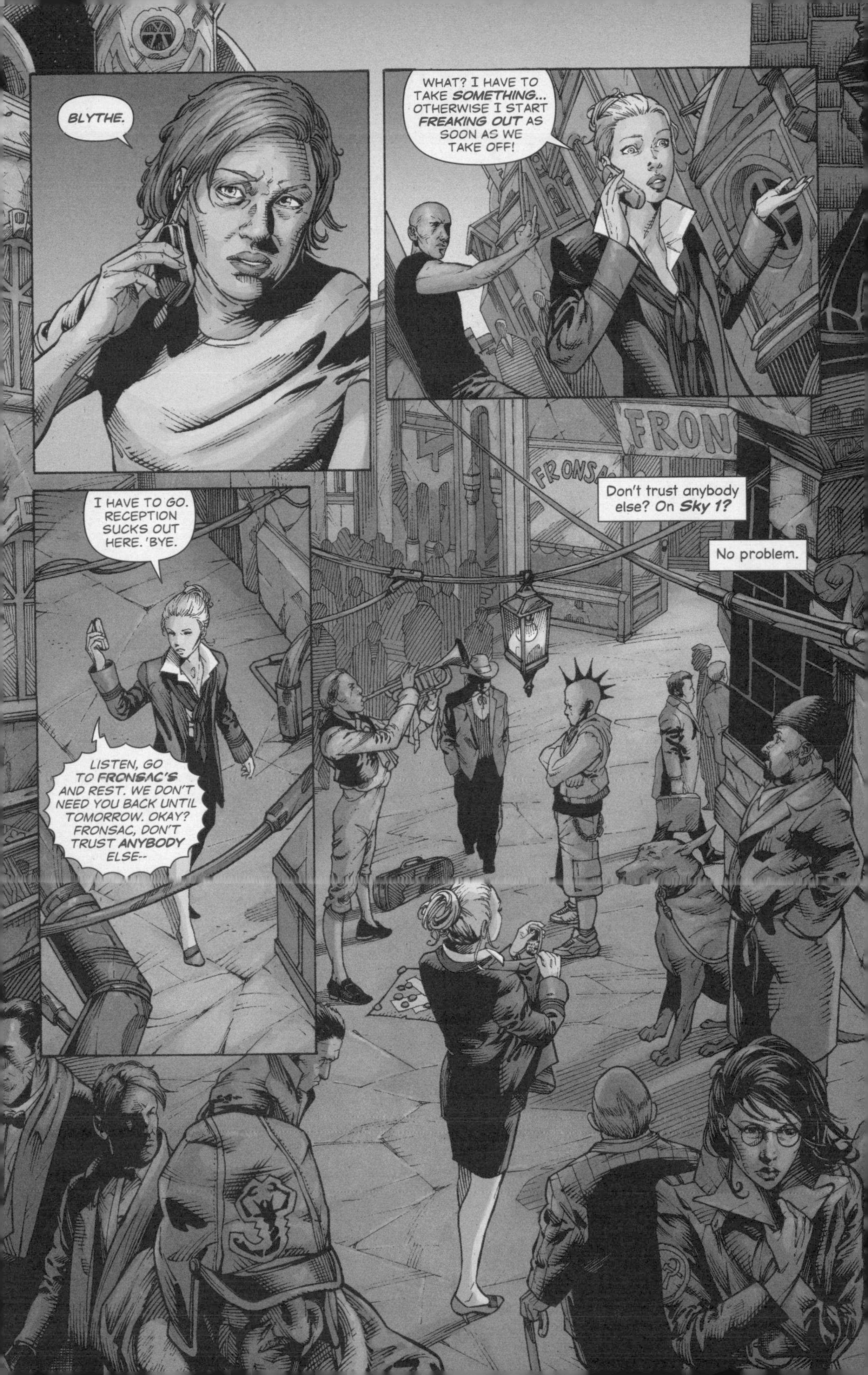
BLYTHE.
WHAT? I HAVE TO TAKE SOMETHING... OTHERWISE I START FREAKING OUT AS SOON AS WE TAKE OFF!
I HAVE TO GO. RECEPTION SUCKS OUT HERE. 'BYE.
LISTEN, GO TO FRONSAC'S AND REST. WE DON'T NEED YOU BACK UNTIL TOMORROW. OKAY? FRONSAC, DON'T TRUST ANYBODY ELSE--
FRON
FRONSA
Don't trust anybody else? On Sky 1?
No problem.

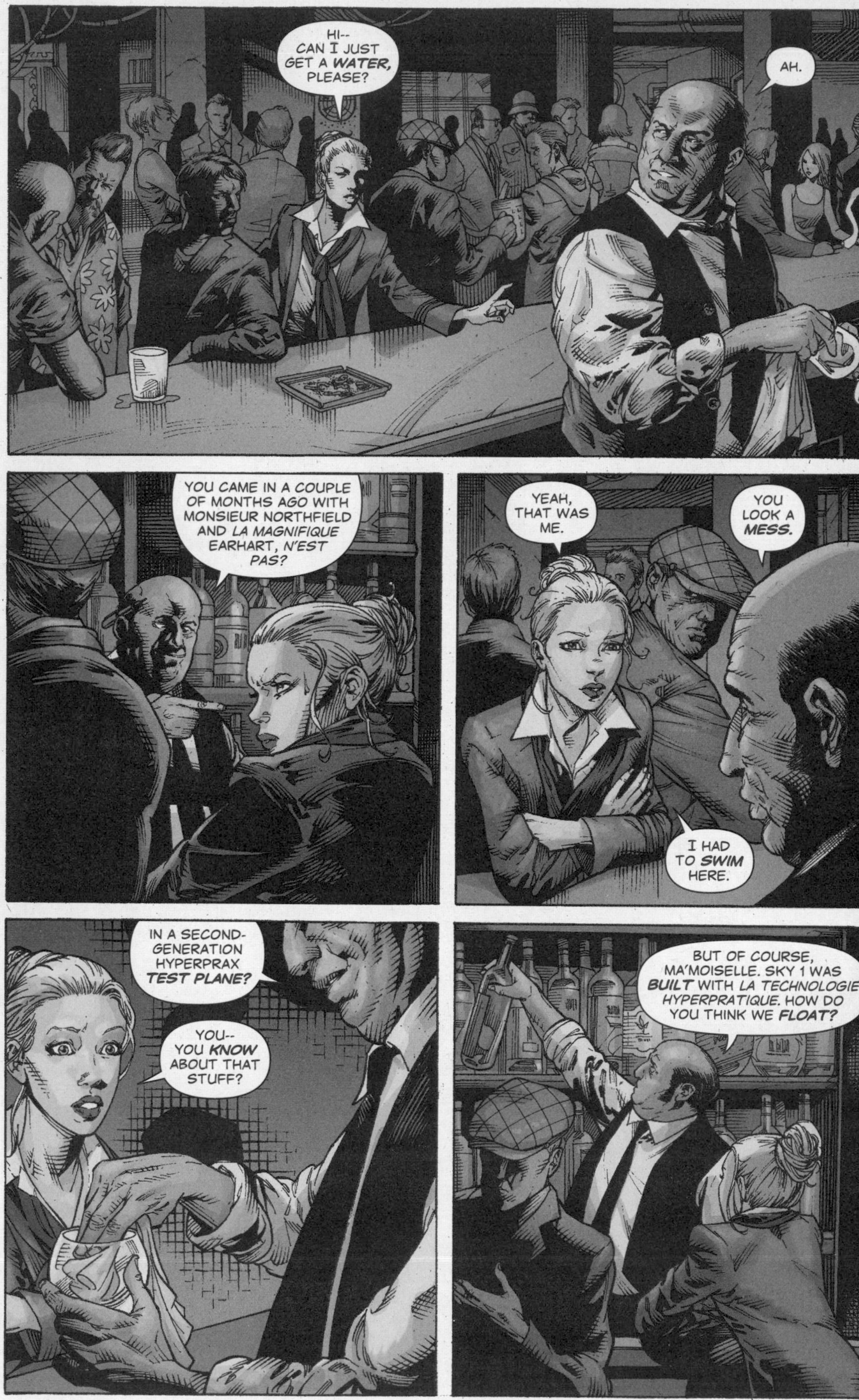
HI-- CAN I JUST GET A WATER, PLEASE?
AH.
YOU CAME IN A COUPLE OF MONTHS AGO WITH MONSIEUR NORTHFIELD AND LA MAGNIFIQUE EARHART, N'EST PAS?
YEAH, THAT WAS ME.
YOU LOOK A MESS.
I HAD TO SWIM HERE.
IN A SECOND-GENERATION HYPERPRAX TEST PLANE?
YOU-- YOU KNOW ABOUT THAT STUFF?
BUT OF COURSE, MA'MOISELLE. SKY 1 WAS BUILT WITH LA TECHNOLOGIE HYPERPRATIQUE. HOW DO YOU THINK WE FLOAT?

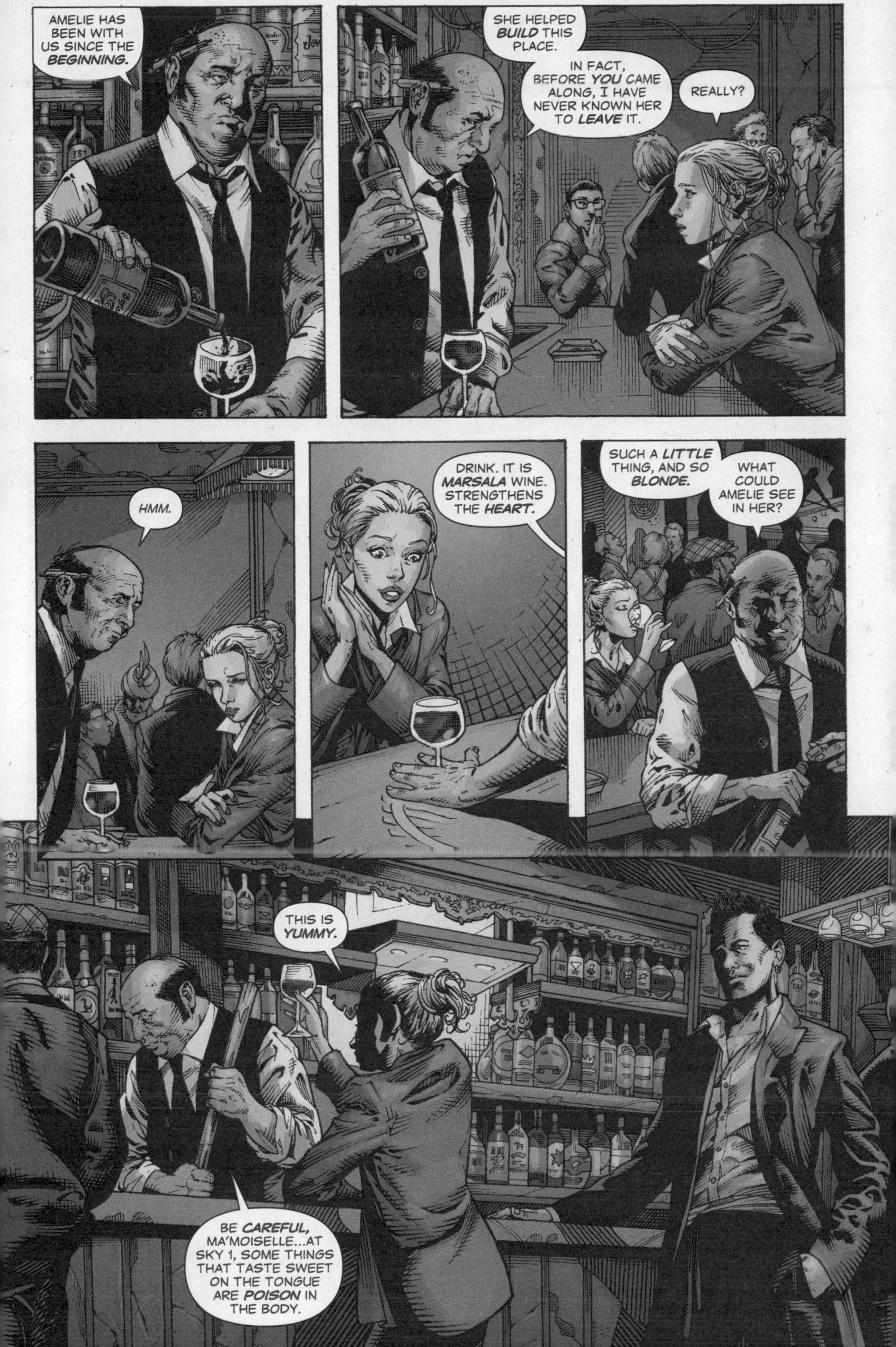
AMELIE HAS BEEN WITH US SINCE THE BEGINNING.
SHE HELPED BUILD THIS PLACE.
IN FACT, BEFORE YOU CAME ALONG, I HAVE NEVER KNOWN HER TO LEAVE IT.
REALLY?
HMM.
DRINK. IT IS MARSALA WINE. STRENGTHENS THE HEART.
SUCH A LITTLE THING, AND SO BLONDE.
WHAT COULD AMELIE SEE IN HER?
THIS IS YUMMY.
BE CAREFUL, MA'MOISELLE...AT SKY 1, SOME THINGS THAT TASTE SWEET ON THE TONGUE ARE POISON IN THE BODY.

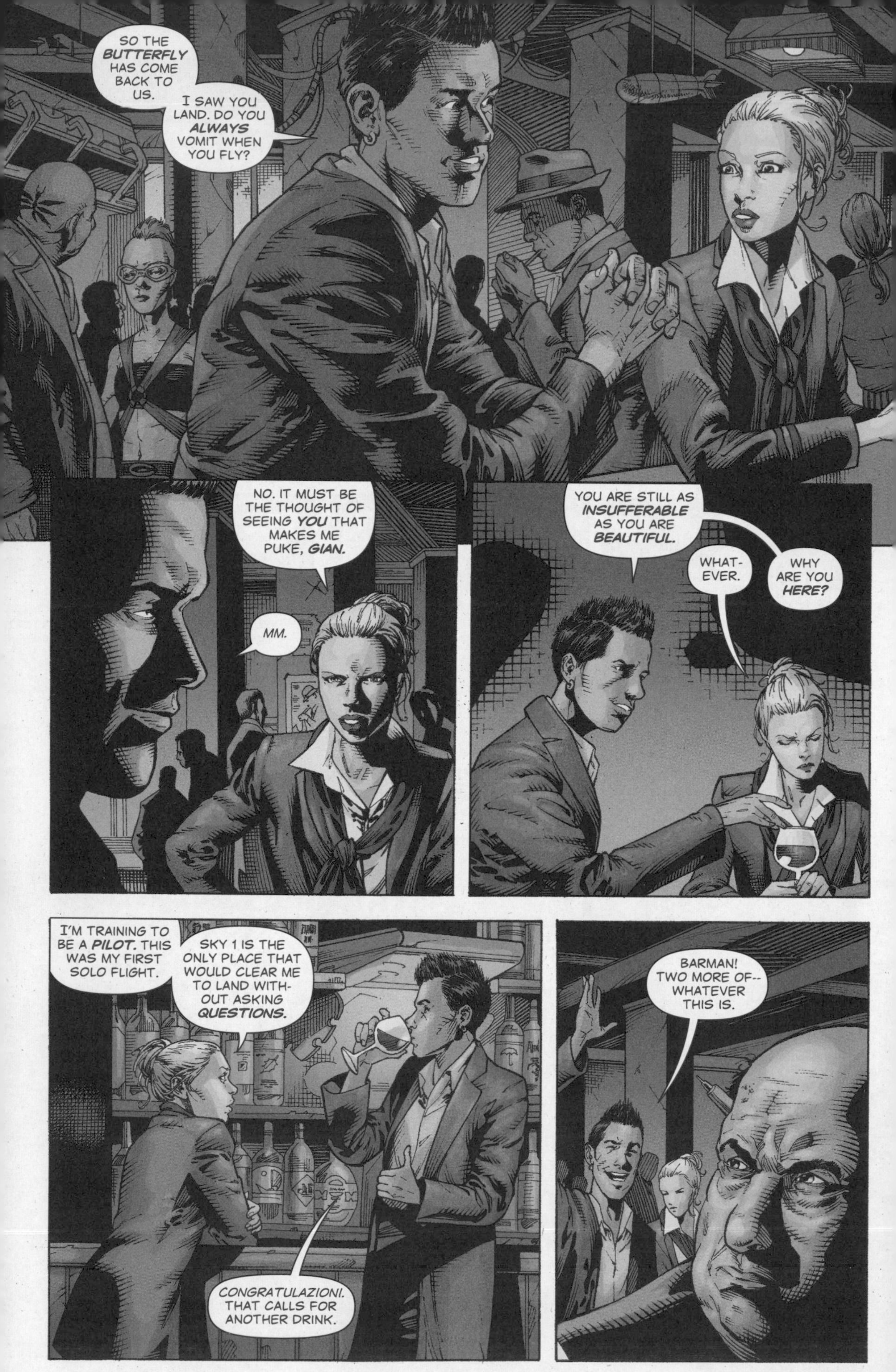

SO THE ***BUTTERFLY*** HAS COME BACK TO US.
I SAW YOU LAND. DO YOU ***ALWAYS*** VOMIT WHEN YOU FLY?
NO. IT MUST BE THE THOUGHT OF SEEING ***YOU*** THAT MAKES ME PUKE, ***GIAN.***
MM.
YOU ARE STILL AS ***INSUFFERABLE*** AS YOU ARE ***BEAUTIFUL.***
WHAT-EVER.
WHY ARE YOU ***HERE?***
I'M TRAINING TO BE A ***PILOT.*** THIS WAS MY FIRST SOLO FLIGHT.
SKY 1 IS THE ONLY PLACE THAT WOULD CLEAR ME TO LAND WITH-OUT ASKING ***QUESTIONS.***
CONGRATULAZIONI. THAT CALLS FOR ANOTHER DRINK.
BARMAN! TWO MORE OF-- WHATEVER THIS IS.

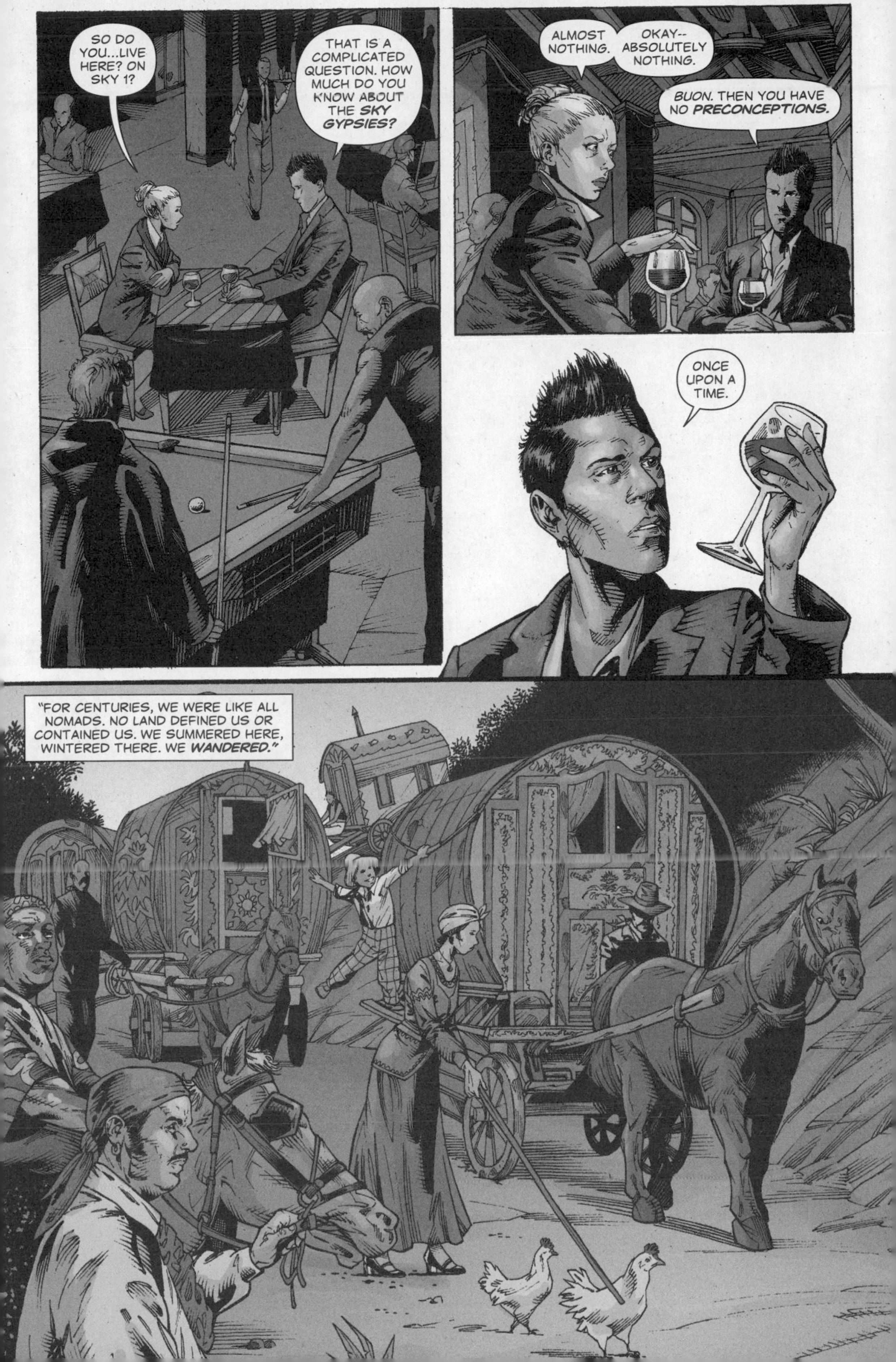
SO DO YOU...LIVE HERE? ON SKY 1?
THAT IS A COMPLICATED QUESTION. HOW MUCH DO YOU KNOW ABOUT THE SKY GYPSIES?
ALMOST NOTHING.
OKAY-- ABSOLUTELY NOTHING.
BUON. THEN YOU HAVE NO PRECONCEPTIONS.
ONCE UPON A TIME.
"FOR CENTURIES, WE WERE LIKE ALL NOMADS. NO LAND DEFINED US OR CONTAINED US. WE SUMMERED HERE, WINTERED THERE. WE WANDERED."

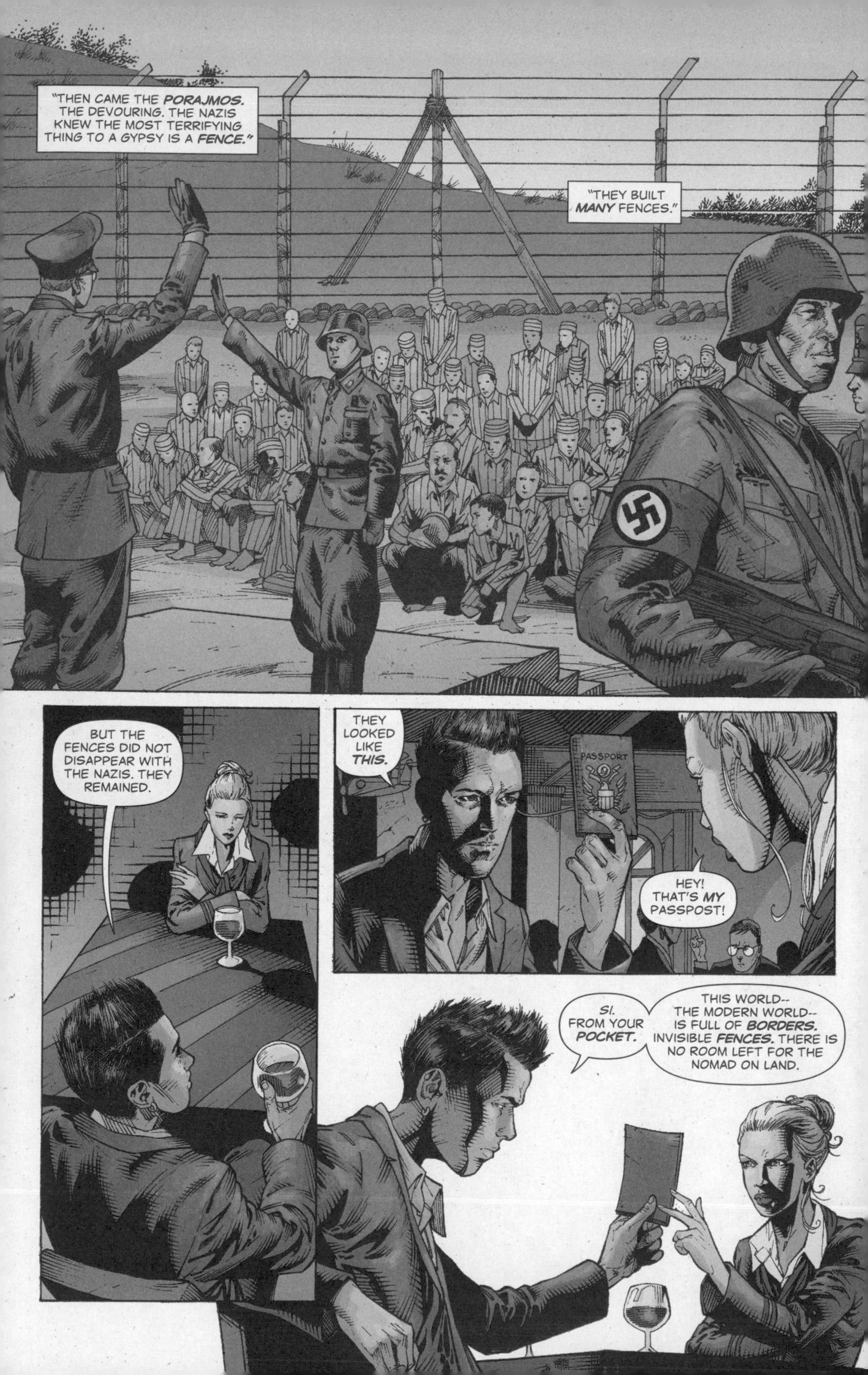
"THEN CAME THE PORAJMOS. THE DEVOURING. THE NAZIS KNEW THE MOST TERRIFYING THING TO A GYPSY IS A FENCE."
"THEY BUILT MANY FENCES."
BUT THE FENCES DID NOT DISAPPEAR WITH THE NAZIS. THEY REMAINED.
THEY LOOKED LIKE THIS.
PASSPORT
HEY! THAT'S MY PASSPOST!
SI. FROM YOUR POCKET.
THIS WORLD-- THE MODERN WORLD-- IS FULL OF BORDERS. INVISIBLE FENCES. THERE IS NO ROOM LEFT FOR THE NOMAD ON LAND.

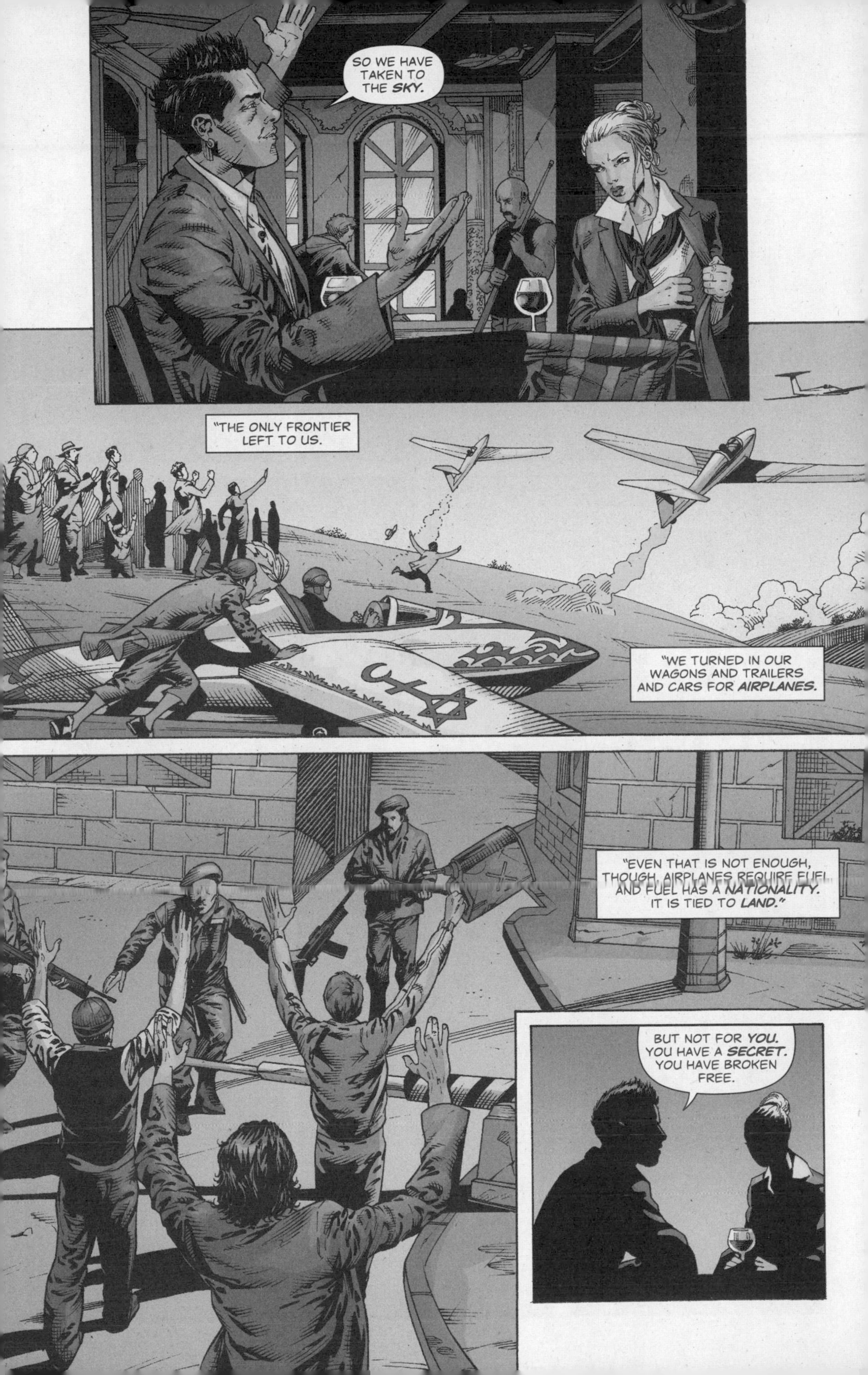
SO WE HAVE TAKEN TO THE SKY.
"THE ONLY FRONTIER LEFT TO US.
"WE TURNED IN OUR WAGONS AND TRAILERS AND CARS FOR AIRPLANES.
"EVEN THAT IS NOT ENOUGH, THOUGH. AIRPLANES REQUIRE FUEL AND FUEL HAS A NATIONALITY. IT IS TIED TO LAND."
BUT NOT FOR YOU. YOU HAVE A SECRET. YOU HAVE BROKEN FREE.

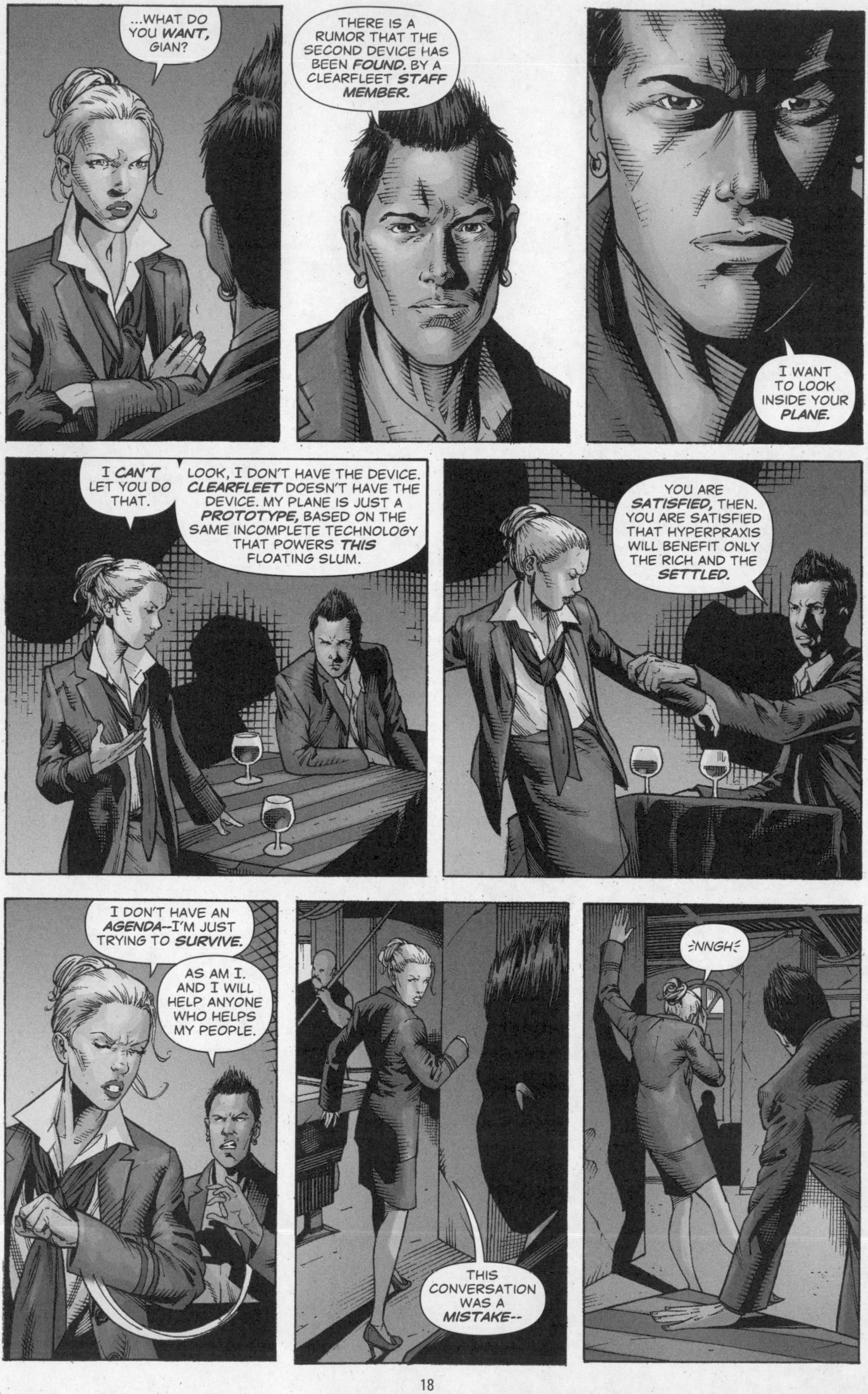
...WHAT DO YOU WANT, GIAN?
THERE IS A RUMOR THAT THE SECOND DEVICE HAS BEEN FOUND. BY A CLEARFLEET STAFF MEMBER.
I WANT TO LOOK INSIDE YOUR PLANE.
I CAN'T LET YOU DO THAT.
LOOK, I DON'T HAVE THE DEVICE. CLEARFLEET DOESN'T HAVE THE DEVICE. MY PLANE IS JUST A PROTOTYPE, BASED ON THE SAME INCOMPLETE TECHNOLOGY THAT POWERS THIS FLOATING SLUM.
YOU ARE SATISFIED, THEN. YOU ARE SATISFIED THAT HYPERPRAXIS WILL BENEFIT ONLY THE RICH AND THE SETTLED.
I DON'T HAVE AN AGENDA--I'M JUST TRYING TO SURVIVE.
AS AM I. AND I WILL HELP ANYONE WHO HELPS MY PEOPLE.
THIS CONVERSATION WAS A MISTAKE--
NNGH

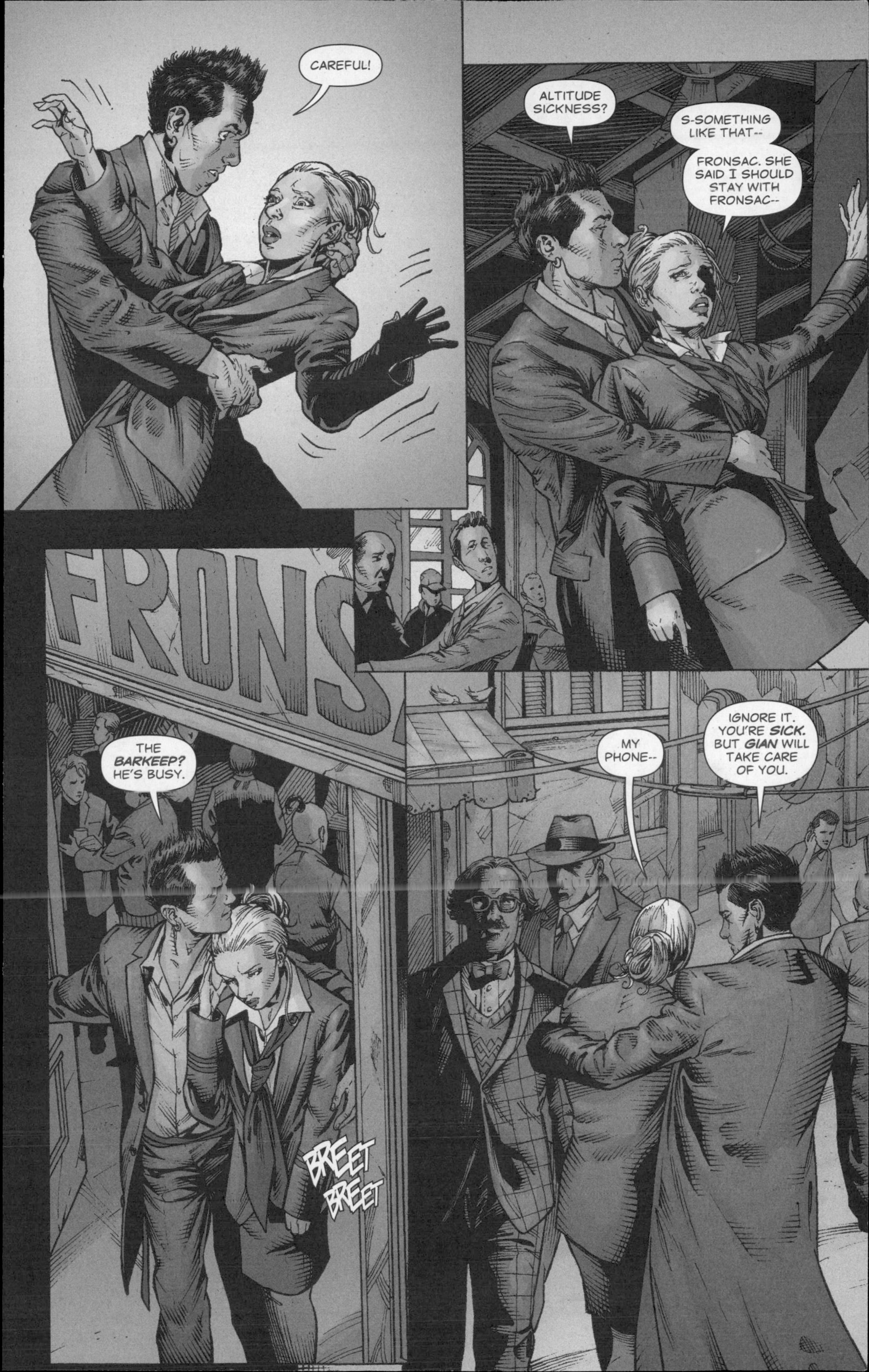
CAREFUL!
ALTITUDE SICKNESS?
S-SOMETHING LIKE THAT--
FRONSAC. SHE SAID I SHOULD STAY WITH FRONSAC--
FRONS
THE BARKEEP? HE'S BUSY.
BREEET BREEET
MY PHONE--
IGNORE IT. YOU'RE SICK. BUT GIAN WILL TAKE CARE OF YOU.

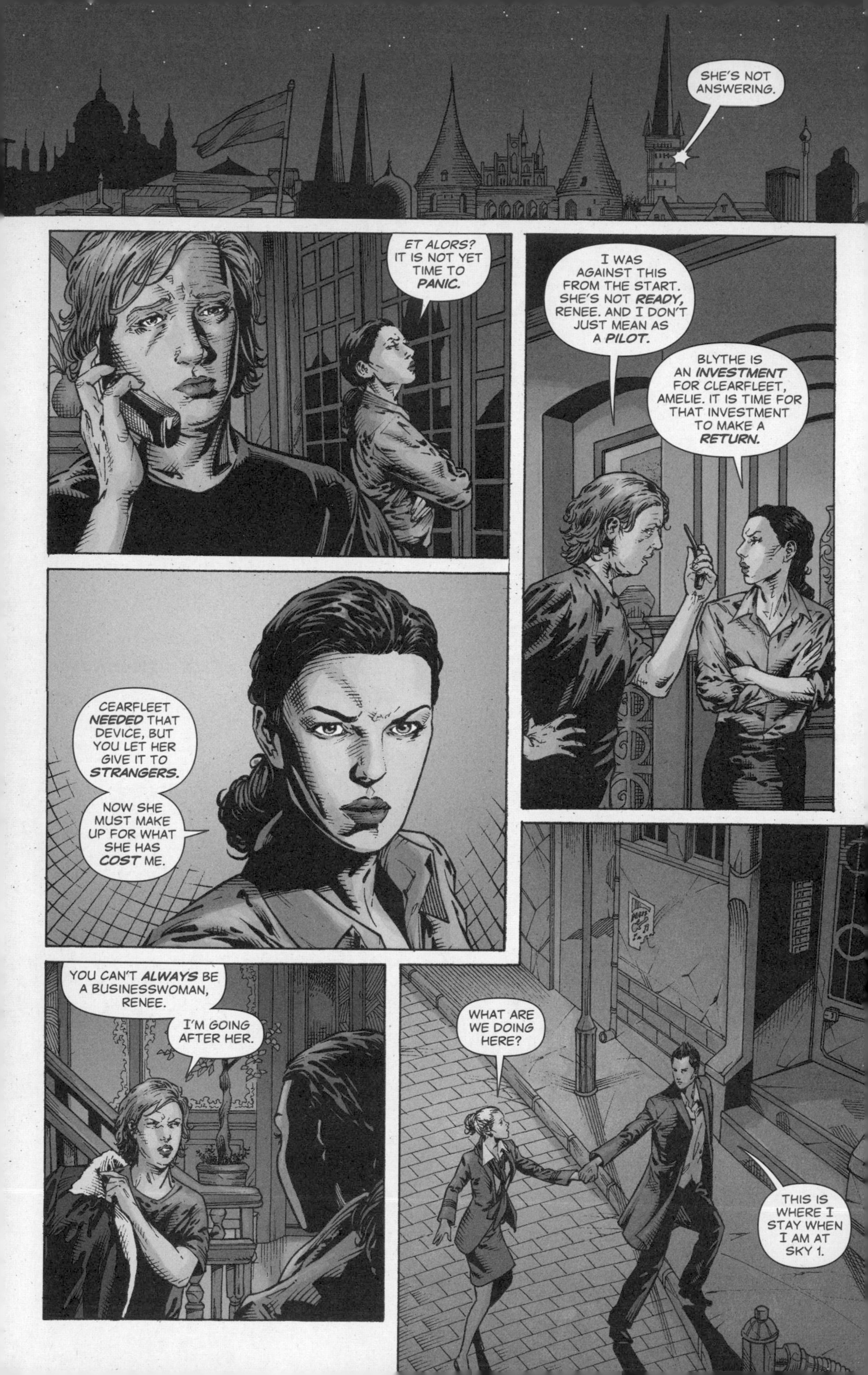

SHE'S NOT ANSWERING.
ET ALORS? IT IS NOT YET TIME TO PANIC.
I WAS AGAINST THIS FROM THE START. SHE'S NOT READY, RENEE. AND I DON'T JUST MEAN AS A PILOT.
BLYTHE IS AN INVESTMENT FOR CLEARFLEET, AMELIE. IT IS TIME FOR THAT INVESTMENT TO MAKE A RETURN.
CEARFLEET NEEDED THAT DEVICE, BUT YOU LET HER GIVE IT TO STRANGERS.
NOW SHE MUST MAKE UP FOR WHAT SHE HAS COST ME.
YOU CAN'T ALWAYS BE A BUSINESSWOMAN, RENEE.
I'M GOING AFTER HER.
WHAT ARE WE DOING HERE?
THIS IS WHERE I STAY WHEN I AM AT SKY 1.

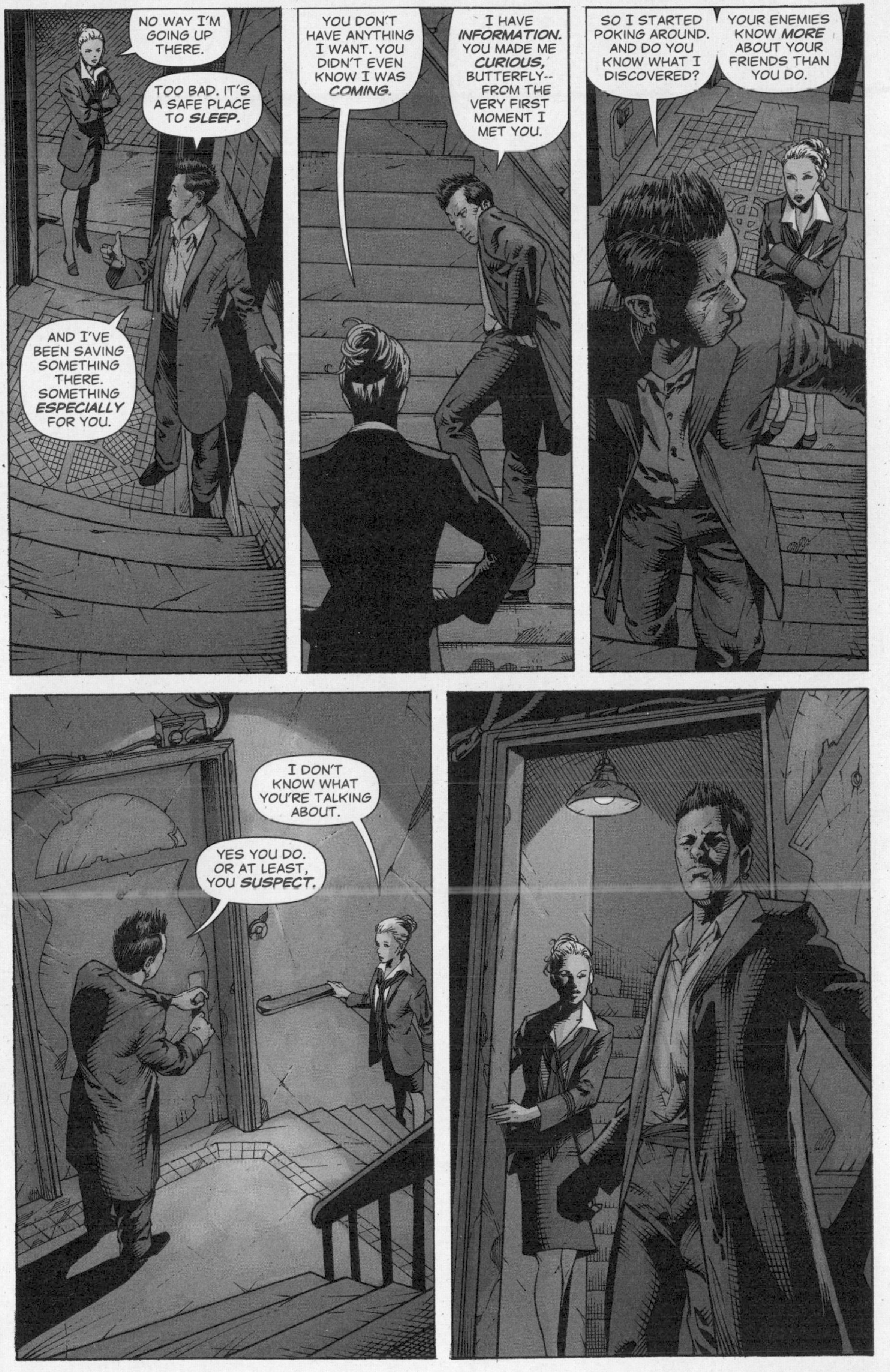
NO WAY I'M GOING UP THERE.
TOO BAD. IT'S A SAFE PLACE TO *SLEEP.*
AND I'VE BEEN SAVING SOMETHING THERE. SOMETHING *ESPECIALLY* FOR YOU.
YOU DON'T HAVE ANYTHING I WANT. YOU DIDN'T EVEN KNOW I WAS *COMING.*
I HAVE *INFORMATION.* YOU MADE ME *CURIOUS,* BUTTERFLY-- FROM THE VERY FIRST MOMENT I MET YOU.
SO I STARTED POKING AROUND. AND DO YOU KNOW WHAT I DISCOVERED?
YOUR ENEMIES KNOW *MORE* ABOUT YOUR FRIENDS THAN YOU DO.
I DON'T KNOW WHAT YOU'RE TALKING ABOUT.
YES YOU DO. OR AT LEAST, YOU *SUSPECT.*

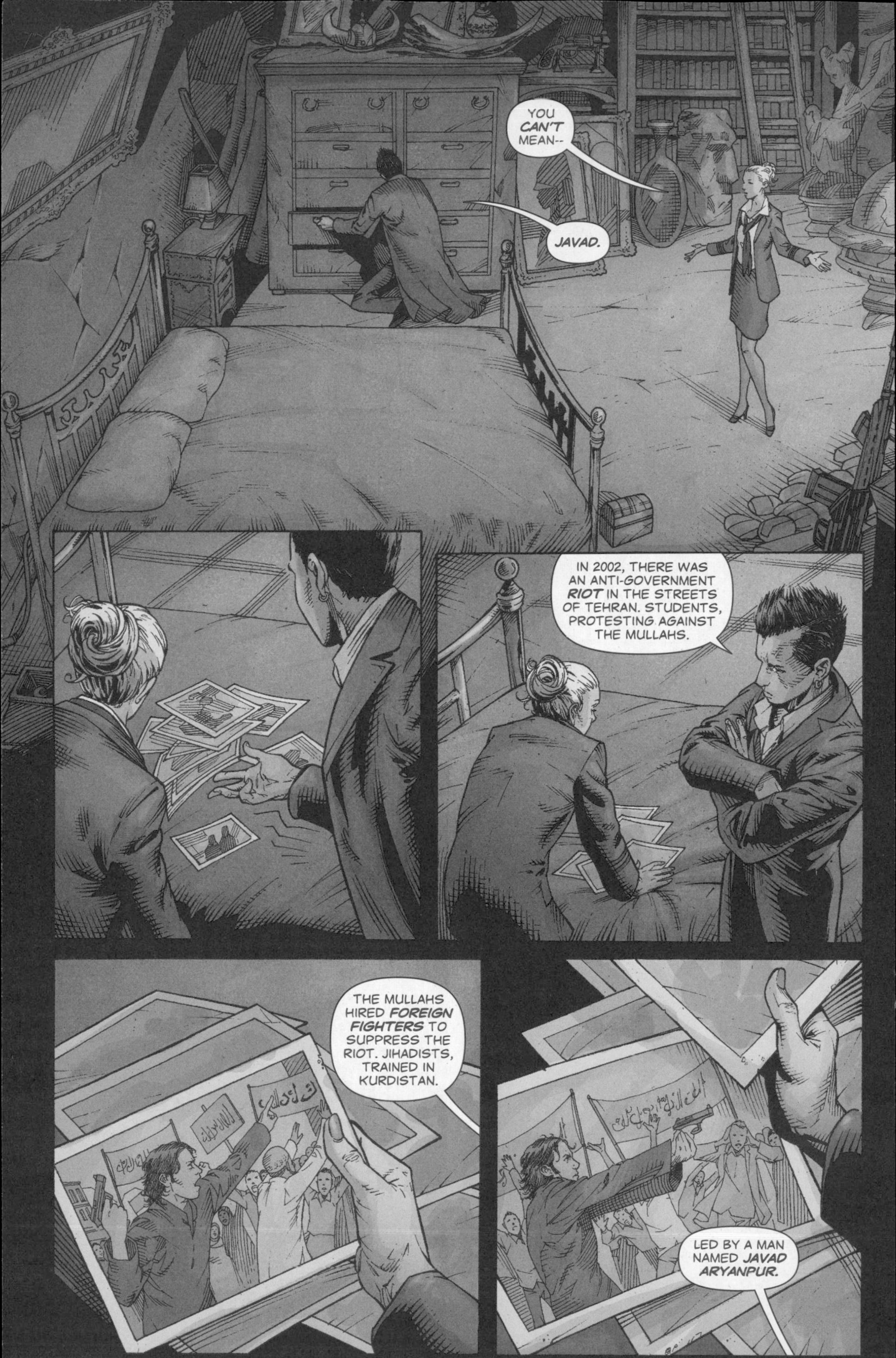
YOU CAN'T MEAN--
JAVAD.
IN 2002, THERE WAS AN ANTI-GOVERNMENT RIOT IN THE STREETS OF TEHRAN. STUDENTS, PROTESTING AGAINST THE MULLAHS.
THE MULLAHS HIRED FOREIGN FIGHTERS TO SUPPRESS THE RIOT. JIHADISTS, TRAINED IN KURDISTAN.
LED BY A MAN NAMED JAVAD ARYANPUR.

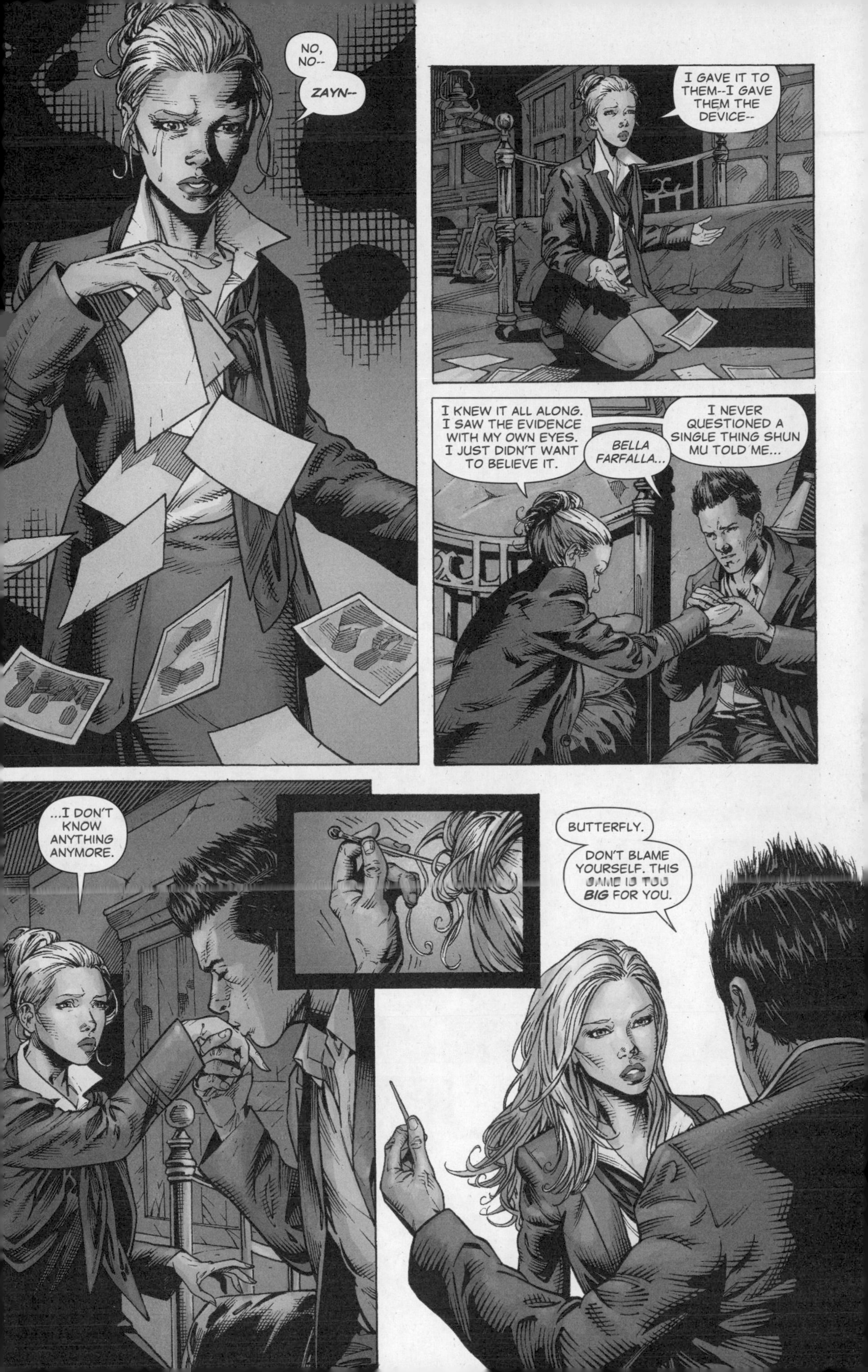
NO, NO--
ZAYN--
I GAVE IT TO THEM--I GAVE THEM THE DEVICE--
I KNEW IT ALL ALONG. I SAW THE EVIDENCE WITH MY OWN EYES. I JUST DIDN'T WANT TO BELIEVE IT.
I NEVER QUESTIONED A SINGLE THING SHUN MU TOLD ME...
BELLA FARFALLA...
...I DON'T KNOW ANYTHING ANYMORE.
BUTTERFLY.
DON'T BLAME YOURSELF. THIS GAME IS TOO BIG FOR YOU.

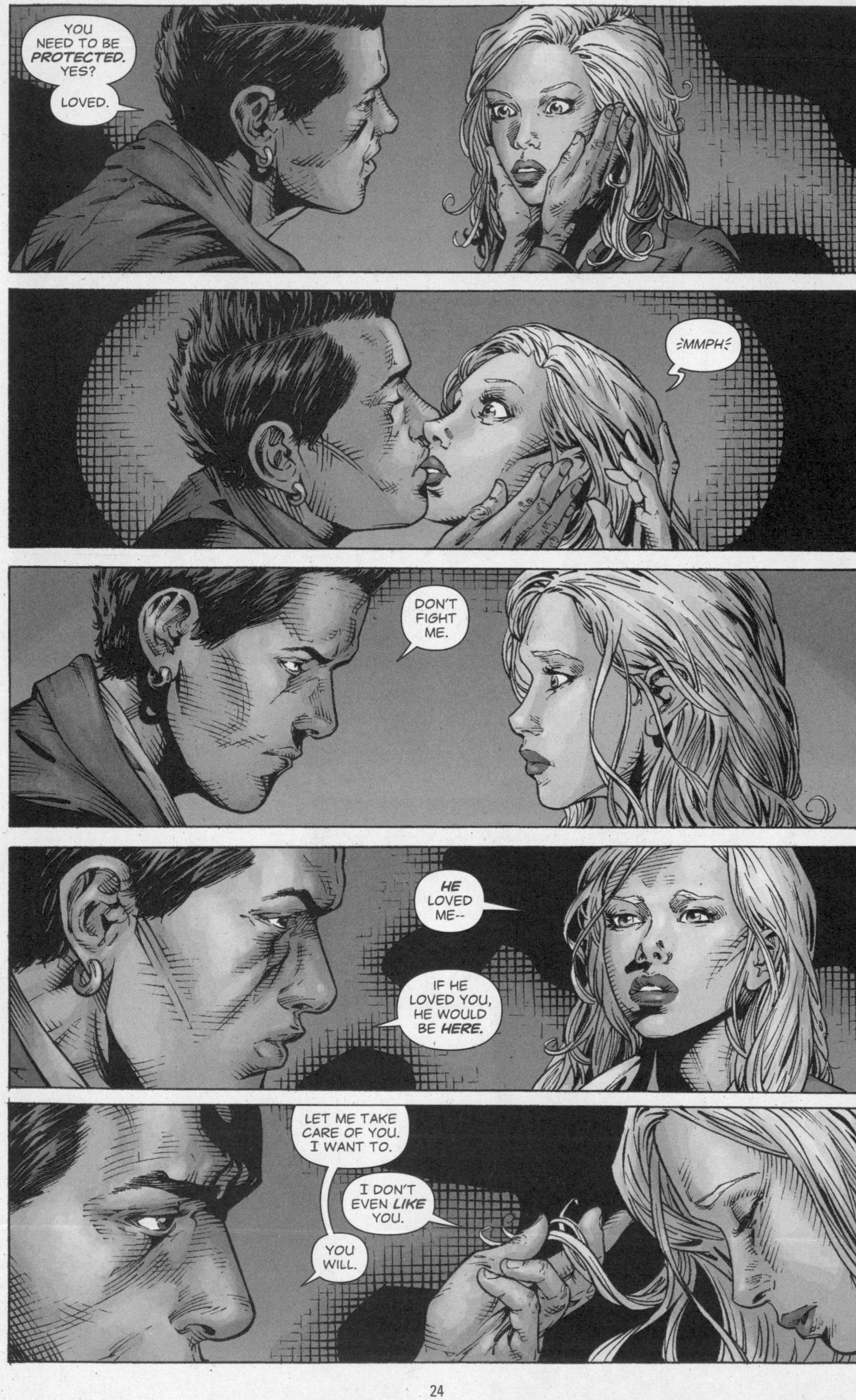
YOU NEED TO BE *PROTECTED.* YES?
LOVED.
MMPH
DON'T FIGHT ME.
HE LOVED ME--
IF HE LOVED YOU, HE WOULD BE *HERE.*
LET ME TAKE CARE OF YOU. I WANT TO.
I DON'T EVEN *LIKE* YOU.
YOU WILL.

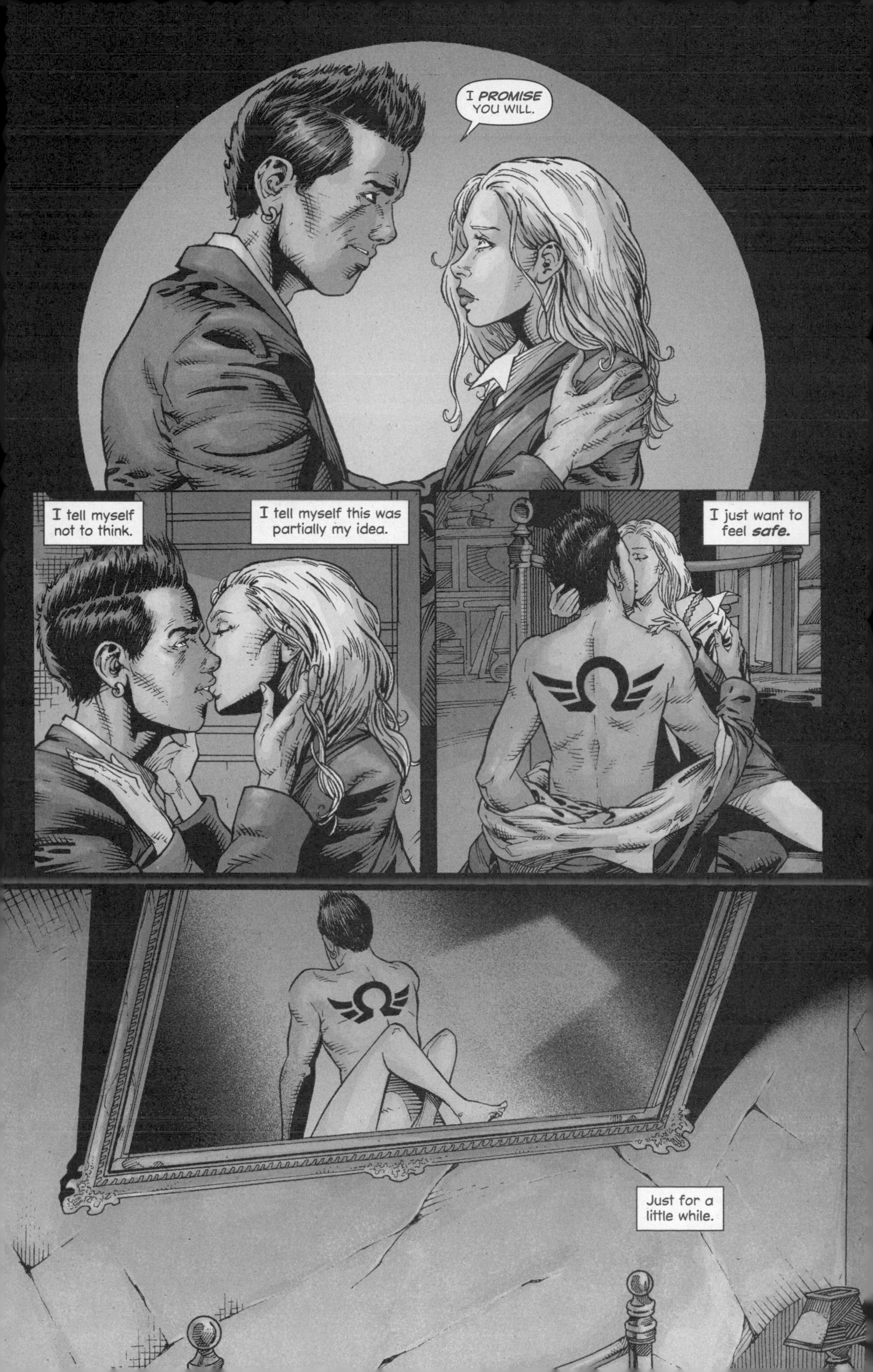
I *PROMISE* YOU WILL.
I tell myself not to think.
I tell myself this was partially my idea.
I just want to feel *safe.*
Just for a little while.

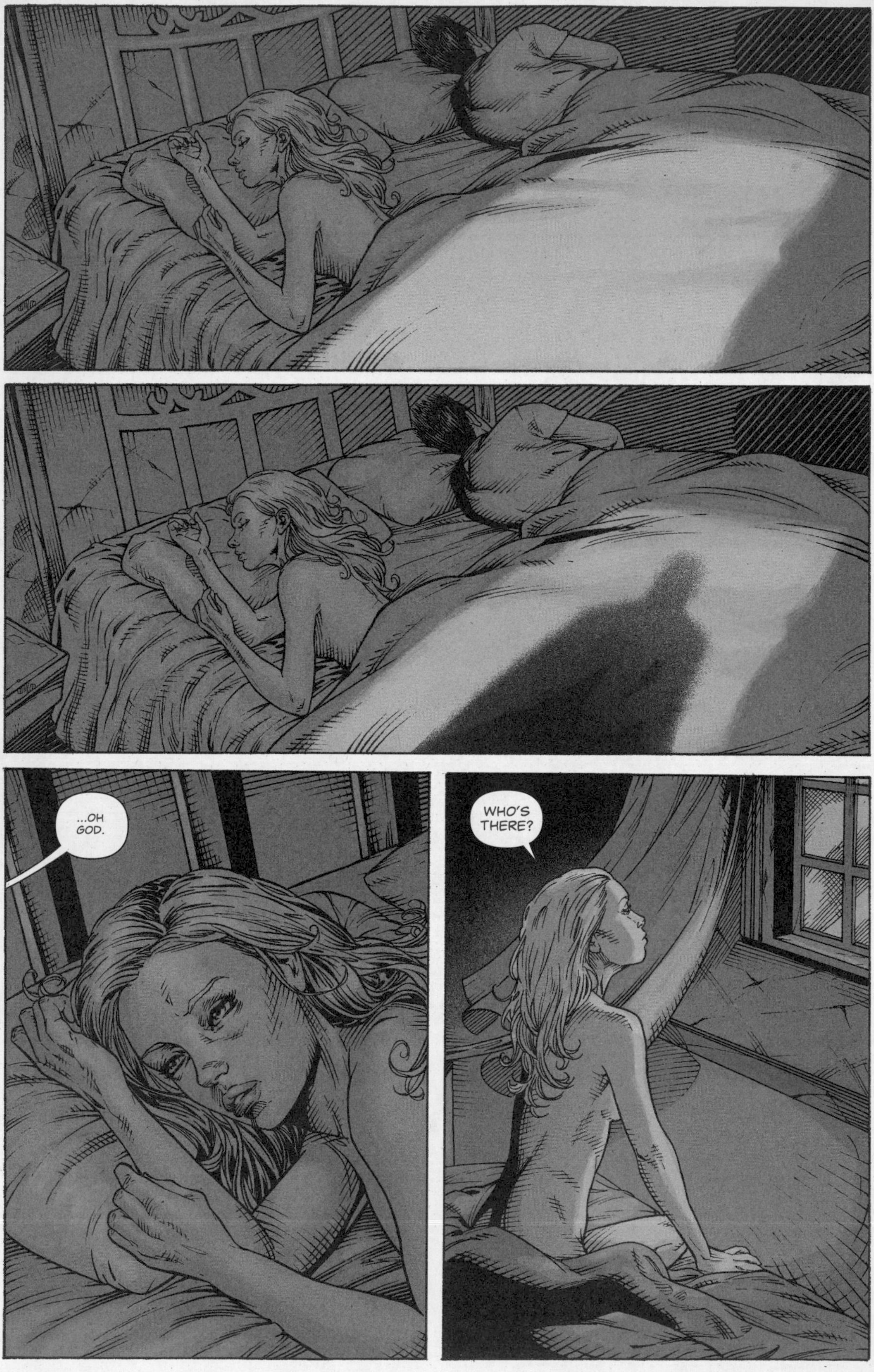
...OH GOD.
WHO'S THERE?

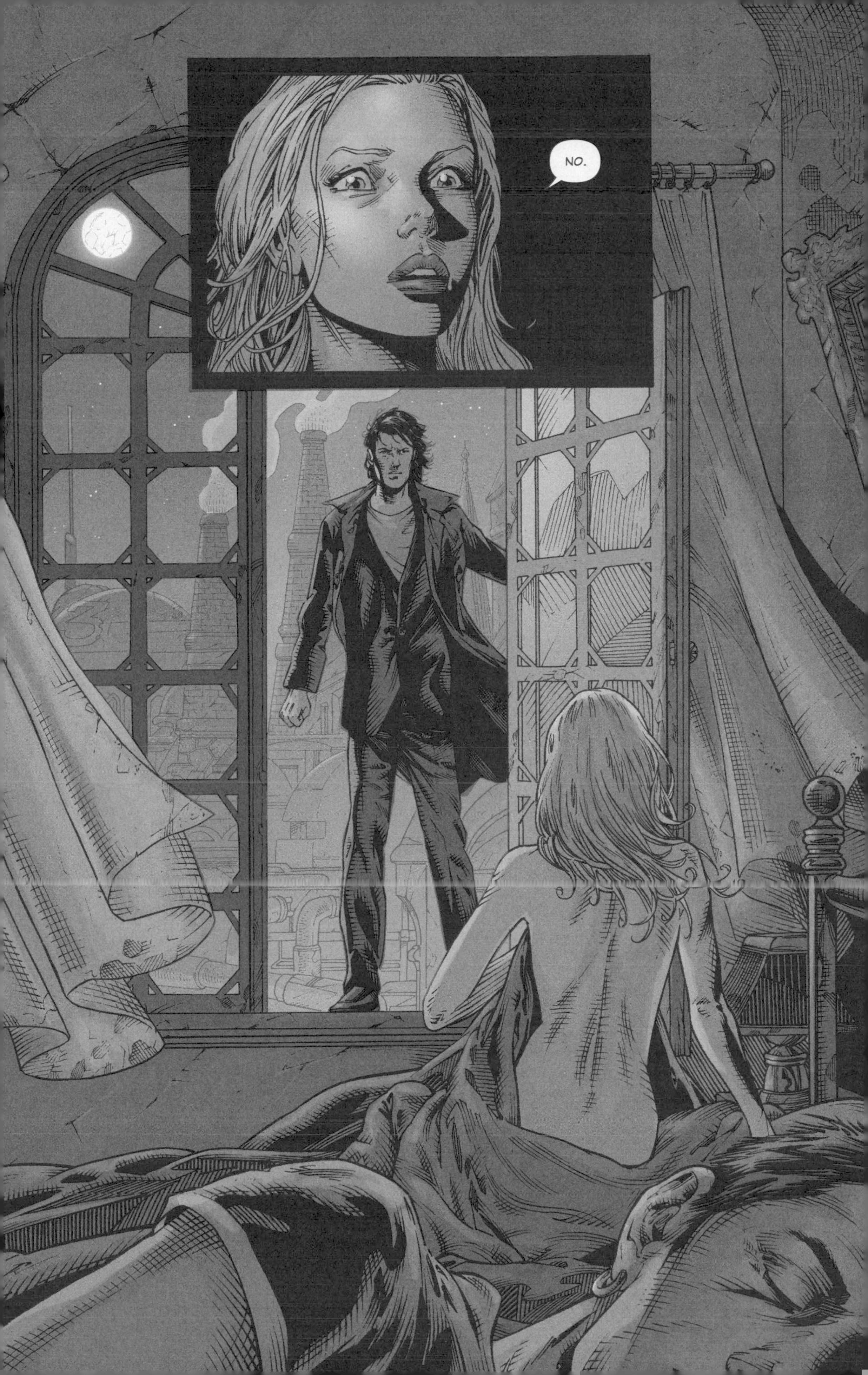
NO.

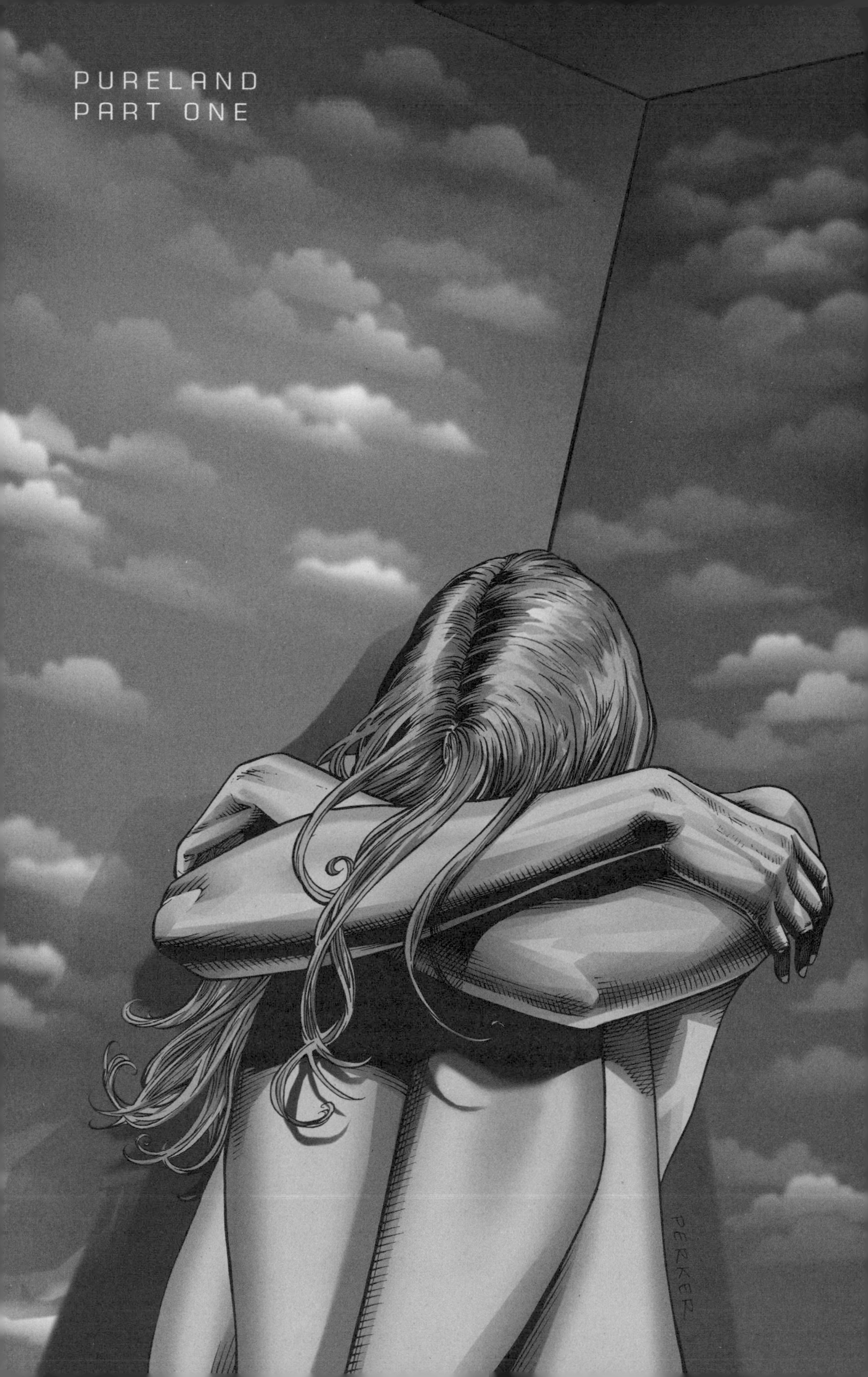
PURELAND
PART ONE
PERKER

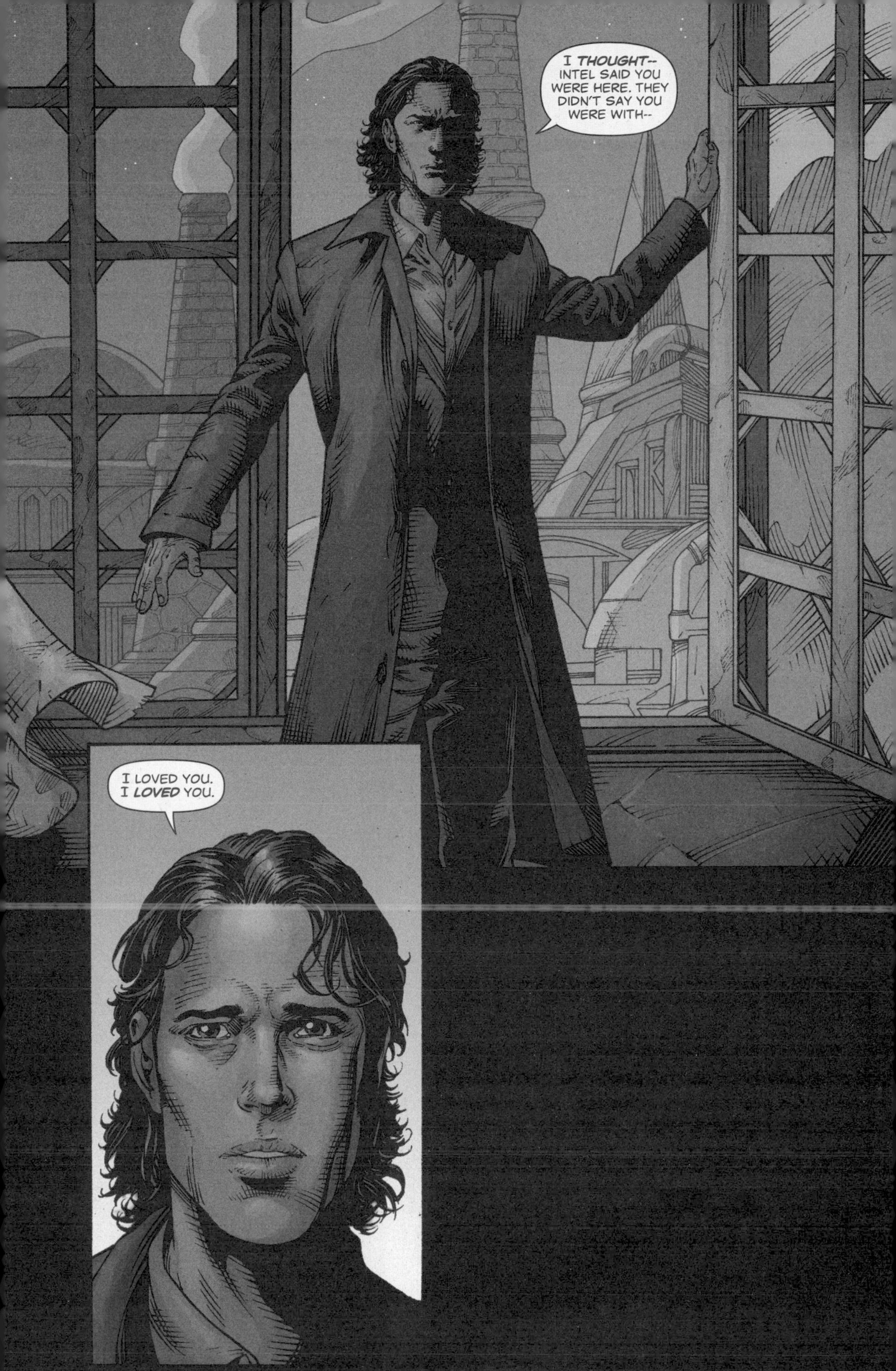
I *THOUGHT*-- INTEL SAID YOU WERE HERE. THEY DIDN'T SAY YOU WERE WITH--
I LOVED YOU. I *LOVED* YOU.

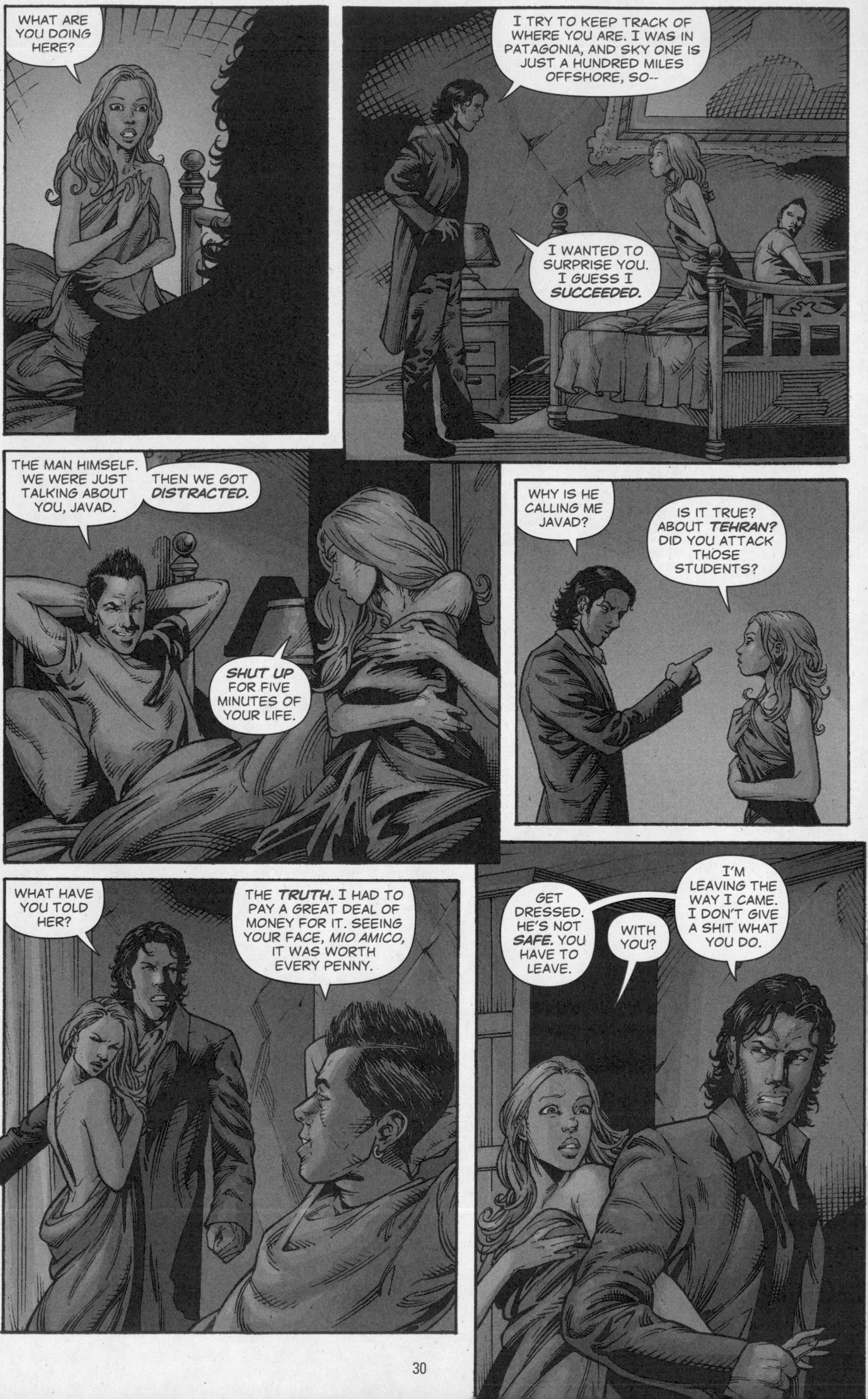
WHAT ARE YOU DOING HERE?
I TRY TO KEEP TRACK OF WHERE YOU ARE. I WAS IN PATAGONIA, AND SKY ONE IS JUST A HUNDRED MILES OFFSHORE, SO--
I WANTED TO SURPRISE YOU. I GUESS I SUCCEEDED.
THE MAN HIMSELF. WE WERE JUST TALKING ABOUT YOU, JAVAD.
THEN WE GOT DISTRACTED.
SHUT UP FOR FIVE MINUTES OF YOUR LIFE.
WHY IS HE CALLING ME JAVAD?
IS IT TRUE? ABOUT TEHRAN? DID YOU ATTACK THOSE STUDENTS?
WHAT HAVE YOU TOLD HER?
THE TRUTH. I HAD TO PAY A GREAT DEAL OF MONEY FOR IT. SEEING YOUR FACE, MIO AMICO, IT WAS WORTH EVERY PENNY.
GET DRESSED. HE'S NOT SAFE. YOU HAVE TO LEAVE.
WITH YOU?
I'M LEAVING THE WAY I CAME. I DON'T GIVE A SHIT WHAT YOU DO.

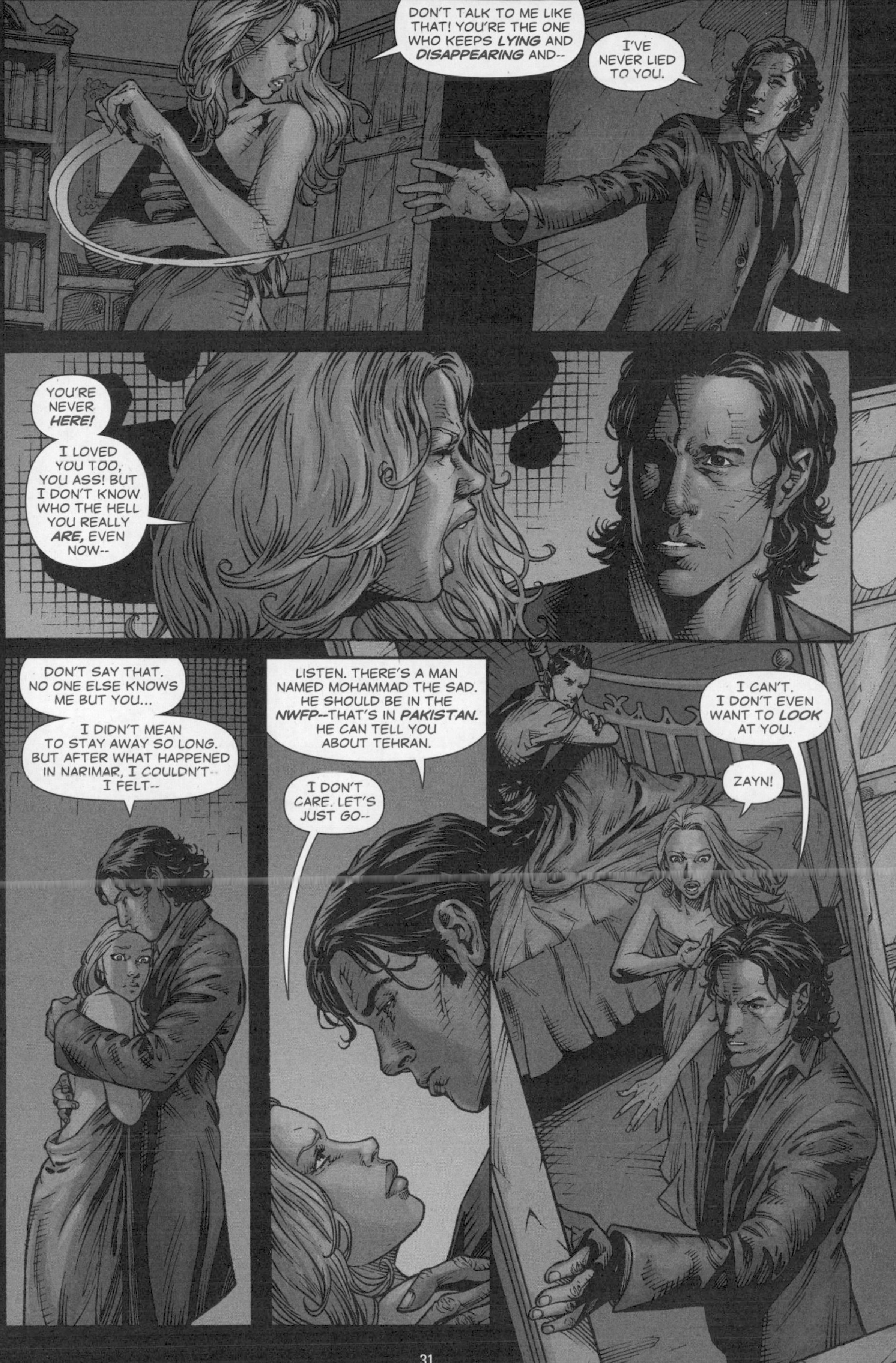
DON'T TALK TO ME LIKE THAT! YOU'RE THE ONE WHO KEEPS LYING AND DISAPPEARING AND--
I'VE NEVER LIED TO YOU.
YOU'RE NEVER HERE!
I LOVED YOU TOO, YOU ASS! BUT I DON'T KNOW WHO THE HELL YOU REALLY ARE, EVEN NOW--
DON'T SAY THAT. NO ONE ELSE KNOWS ME BUT YOU...
I DIDN'T MEAN TO STAY AWAY SO LONG. BUT AFTER WHAT HAPPENED IN NARIMAR, I COULDN'T-- I FELT--
LISTEN. THERE'S A MAN NAMED MOHAMMAD THE SAD. HE SHOULD BE IN THE NWFP--THAT'S IN PAKISTAN. HE CAN TELL YOU ABOUT TEHRAN.
I DON'T CARE. LET'S JUST GO--
I CAN'T. I DON'T EVEN WANT TO LOOK AT YOU.
ZAYN!

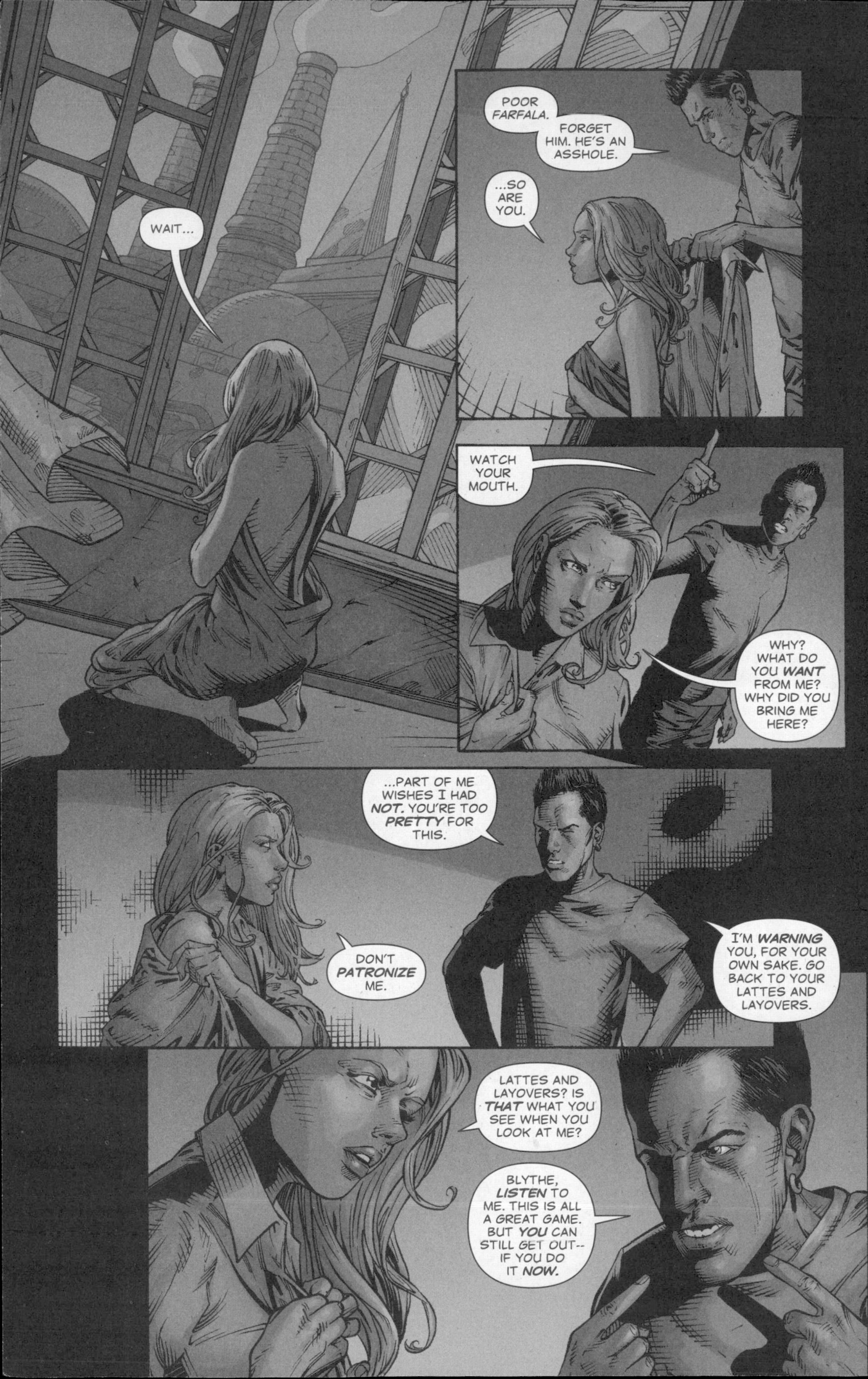
WAIT...
POOR FARFALA.
FORGET HIM. HE'S AN ASSHOLE.
...SO ARE YOU.
WATCH YOUR MOUTH.
WHY? WHAT DO YOU WANT FROM ME? WHY DID YOU BRING ME HERE?
...PART OF ME WISHES I HAD NOT. YOU'RE TOO PRETTY FOR THIS.
DON'T PATRONIZE ME.
I'M WARNING YOU, FOR YOUR OWN SAKE. GO BACK TO YOUR LATTES AND LAYOVERS.
LATTES AND LAYOVERS? IS THAT WHAT YOU SEE WHEN YOU LOOK AT ME?
BLYTHE, LISTEN TO ME. THIS IS ALL A GREAT GAME. BUT YOU CAN STILL GET OUT-- IF YOU DO IT NOW.

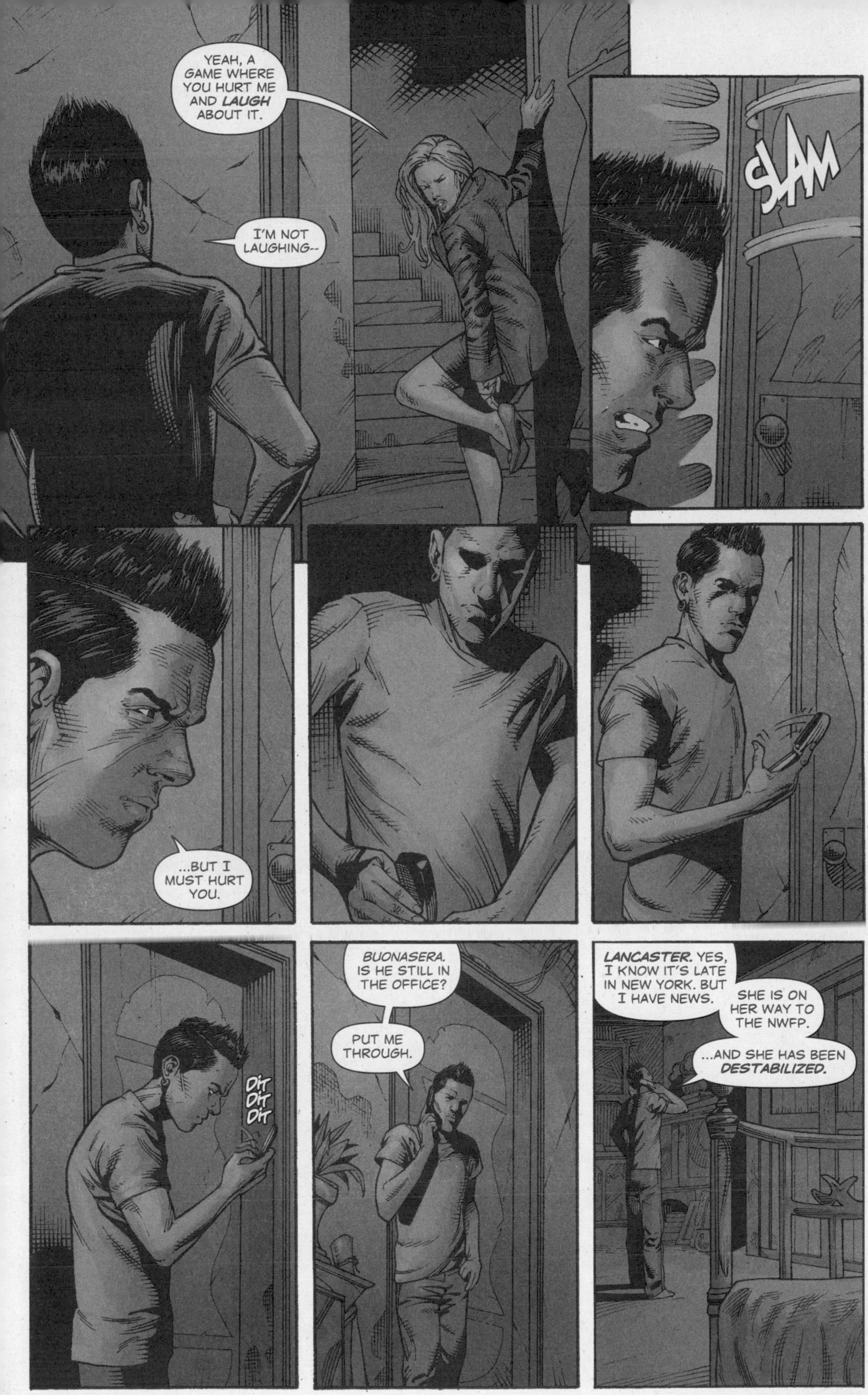
YEAH, A GAME WHERE YOU HURT ME AND LAUGH ABOUT IT.
I'M NOT LAUGHING--
SLAM
...BUT I MUST HURT YOU.
DIT DIT DIT
BUONASERA. IS HE STILL IN THE OFFICE?
PUT ME THROUGH.
LANCASTER. YES, I KNOW IT'S LATE IN NEW YORK. BUT I HAVE NEWS.
SHE IS ON HER WAY TO THE NWFP.
...AND SHE HAS BEEN DESTABILIZED.

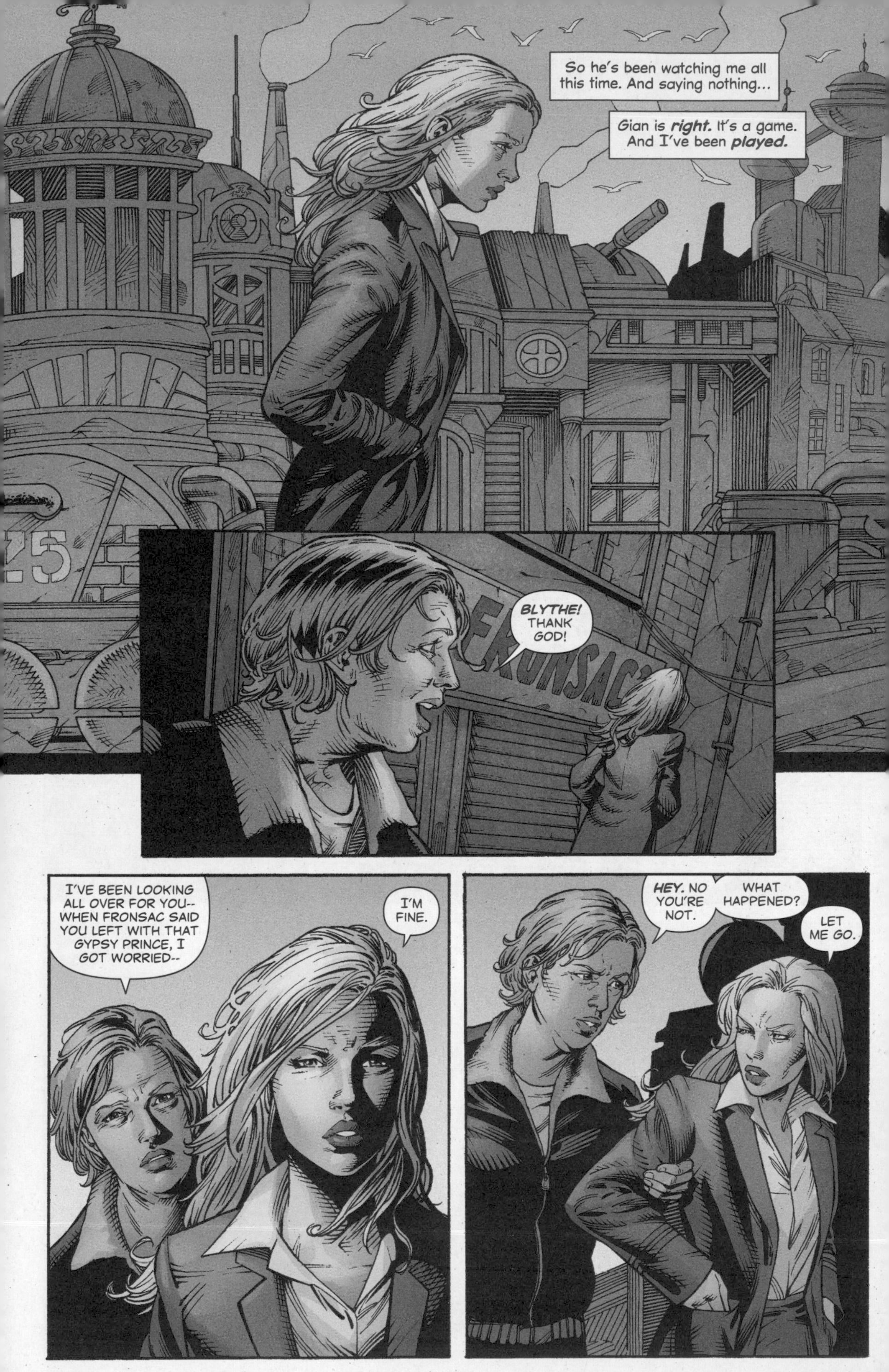

So he's been watching me all this time. And saying nothing...
Gian is right. It's a game. And I've been played.
FRONSAC
BLYTHE! THANK GOD!
I'VE BEEN LOOKING ALL OVER FOR YOU-- WHEN FRONSAC SAID YOU LEFT WITH THAT GYPSY PRINCE, I GOT WORRIED--
I'M FINE.
HEY. NO YOU'RE NOT.
WHAT HAPPENED?
LET ME GO.

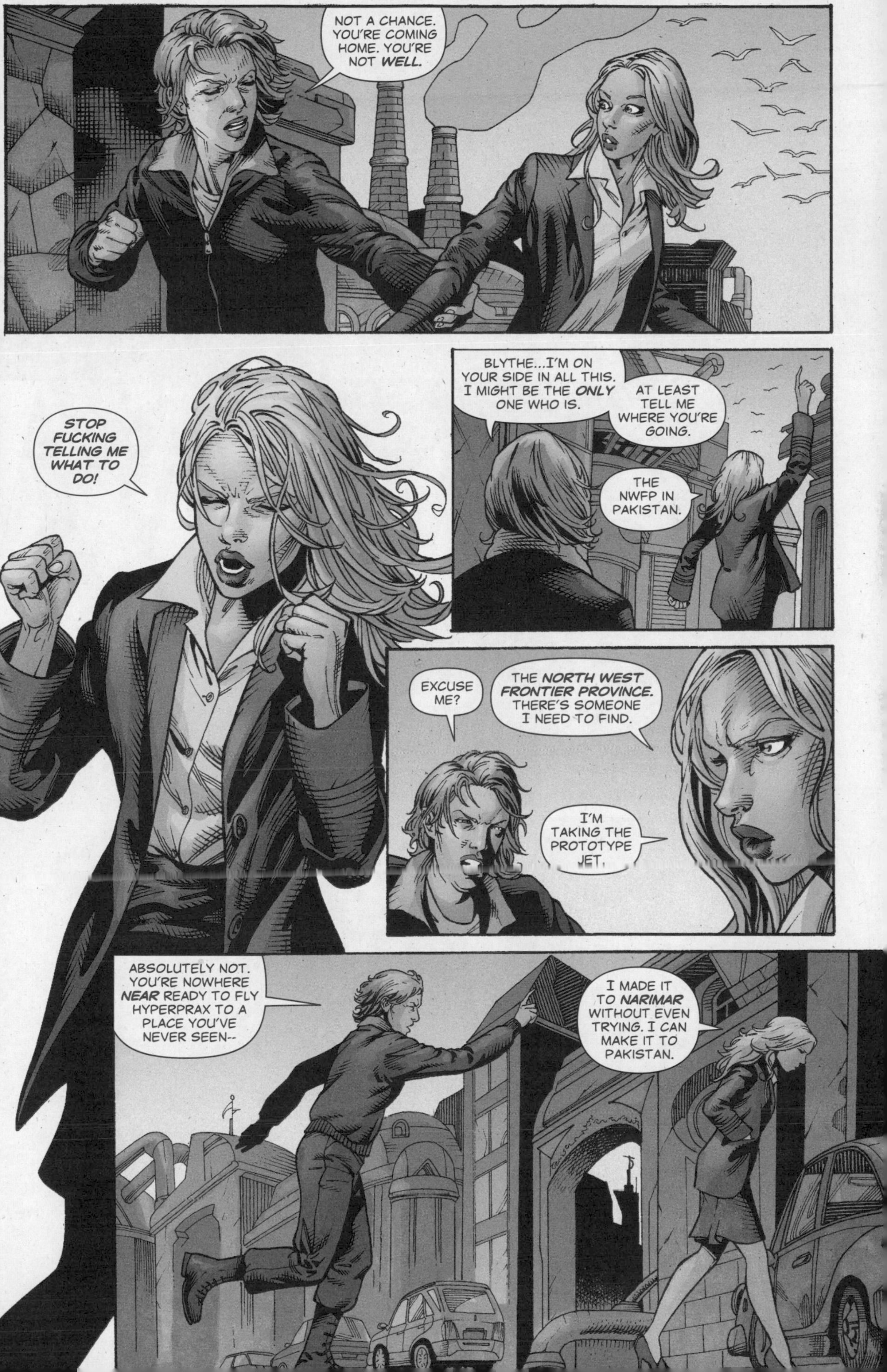

NOT A CHANCE. YOU'RE COMING HOME. YOU'RE NOT WELL.
STOP FUCKING TELLING ME WHAT TO DO!
BLYTHE...I'M ON YOUR SIDE IN ALL THIS. I MIGHT BE THE ONLY ONE WHO IS.
AT LEAST TELL ME WHERE YOU'RE GOING.
THE NWFP IN PAKISTAN.
EXCUSE ME?
THE NORTH WEST FRONTIER PROVINCE. THERE'S SOMEONE I NEED TO FIND.
I'M TAKING THE PROTOTYPE JET.
ABSOLUTELY NOT. YOU'RE NOWHERE NEAR READY TO FLY HYPERPRAX TO A PLACE YOU'VE NEVER SEEN--
I MADE IT TO NARIMAR WITHOUT EVEN TRYING. I CAN MAKE IT TO PAKISTAN.

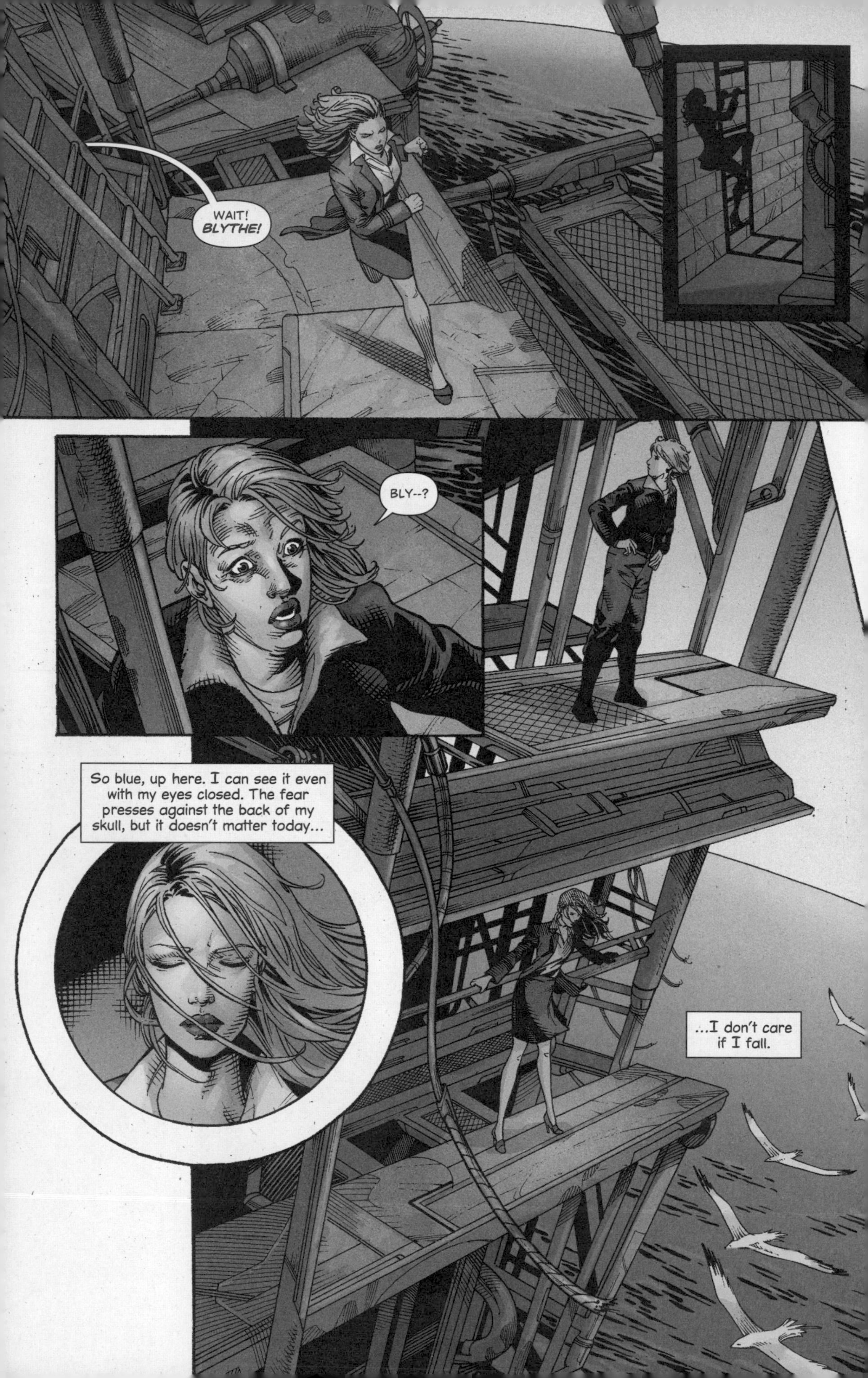
WAIT! BLYTHE!
BLY--?
So blue, up here. I can see it even with my eyes closed. The fear presses against the back of my skull, but it doesn't matter today...
...I don't care if I fall.

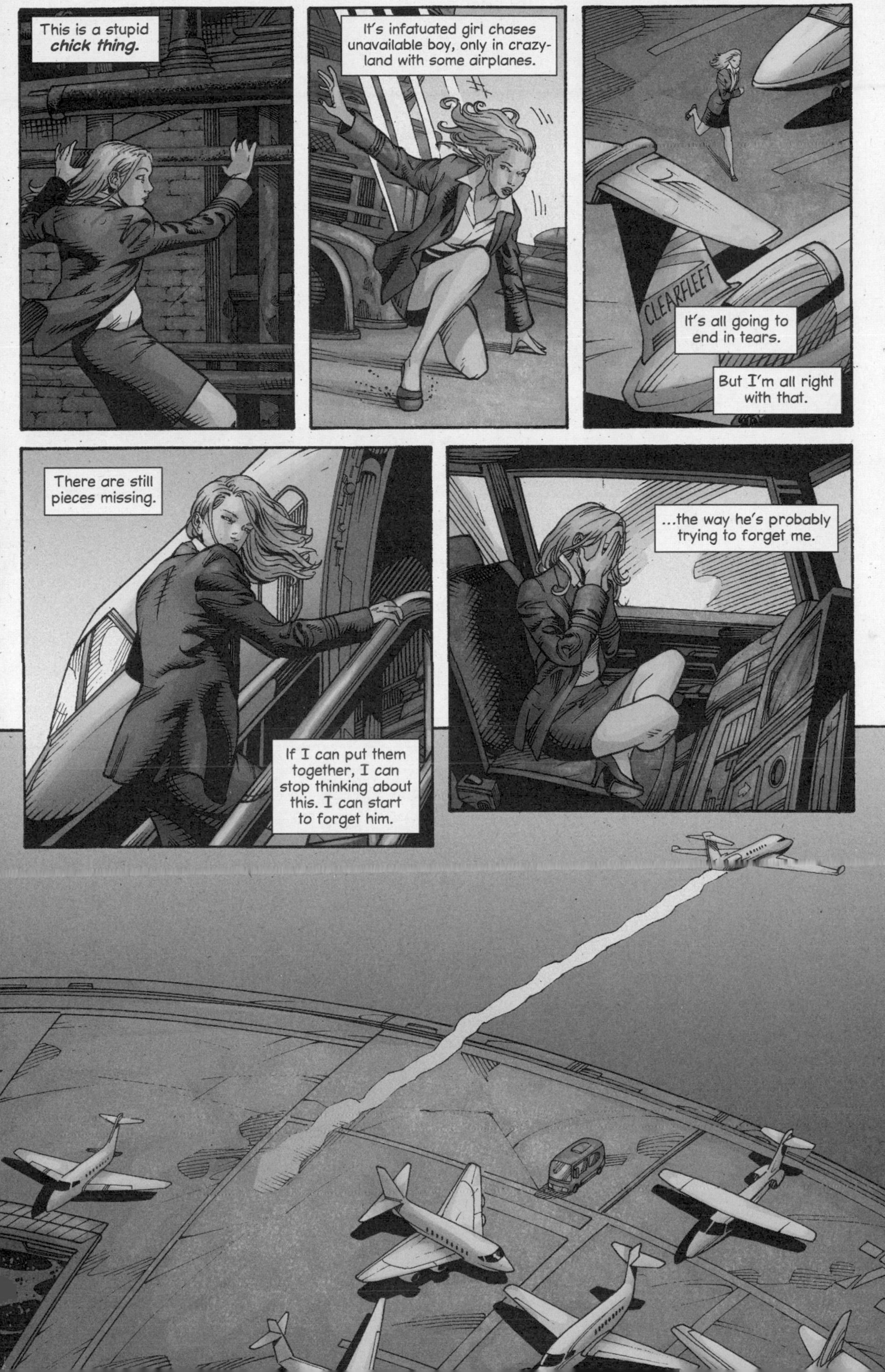

This is a stupid **chick thing.**
It's infatuated girl chases unavailable boy, only in crazy-land with some airplanes.
CLEARFLEET
It's all going to end in tears.
But I'm all right with that.
There are still pieces missing.
If I can put them together, I can stop thinking about this. I can start to forget him.
...the way he's probably trying to forget me.

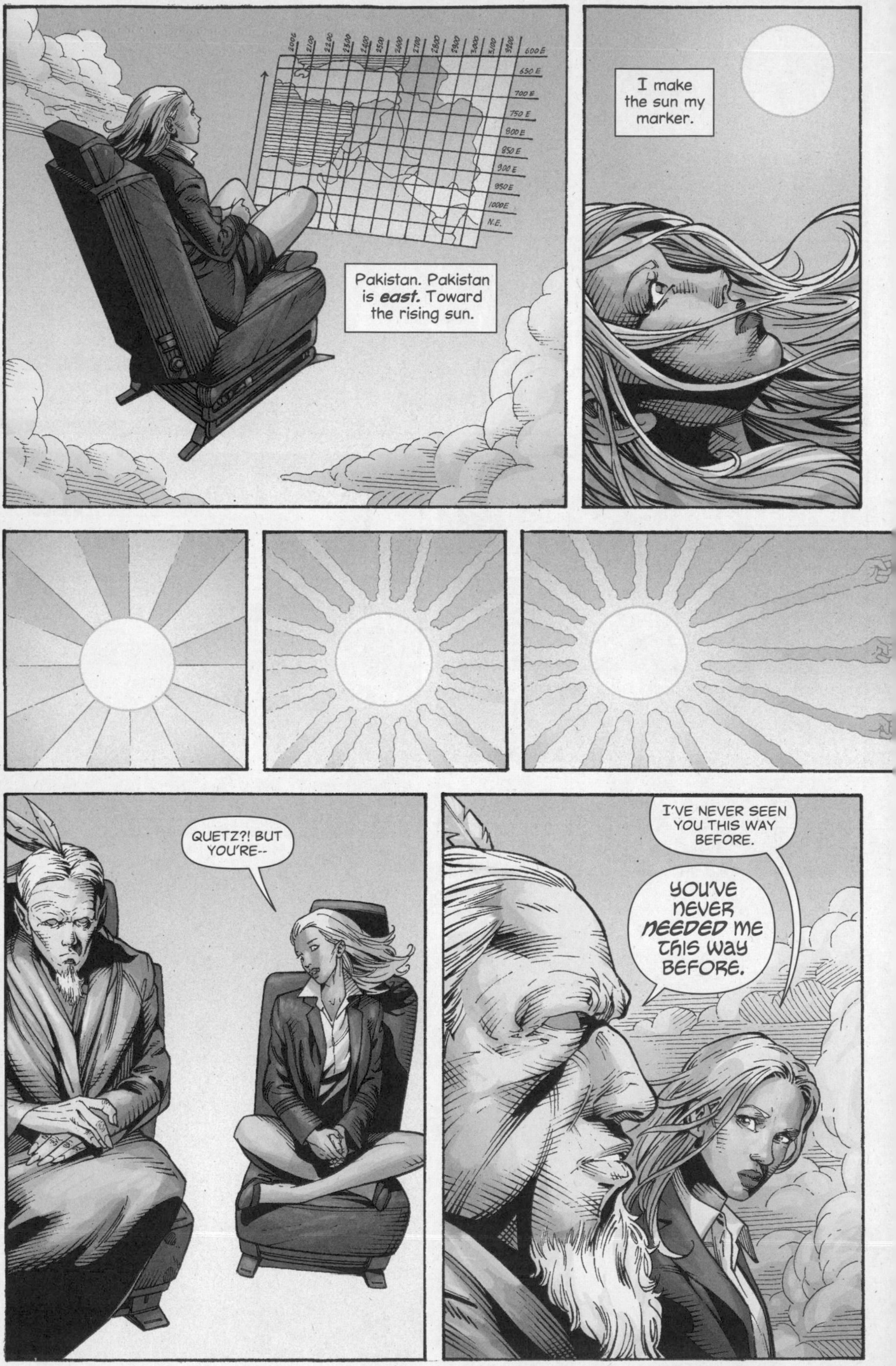
Pakistan. Pakistan is *east.* Toward the rising sun.
I make the sun my marker.
QUETZ?! BUT YOU'RE--
I'VE NEVER SEEN YOU THIS WAY BEFORE.
YOU'VE NEVER *NEEDED* ME THIS WAY BEFORE.

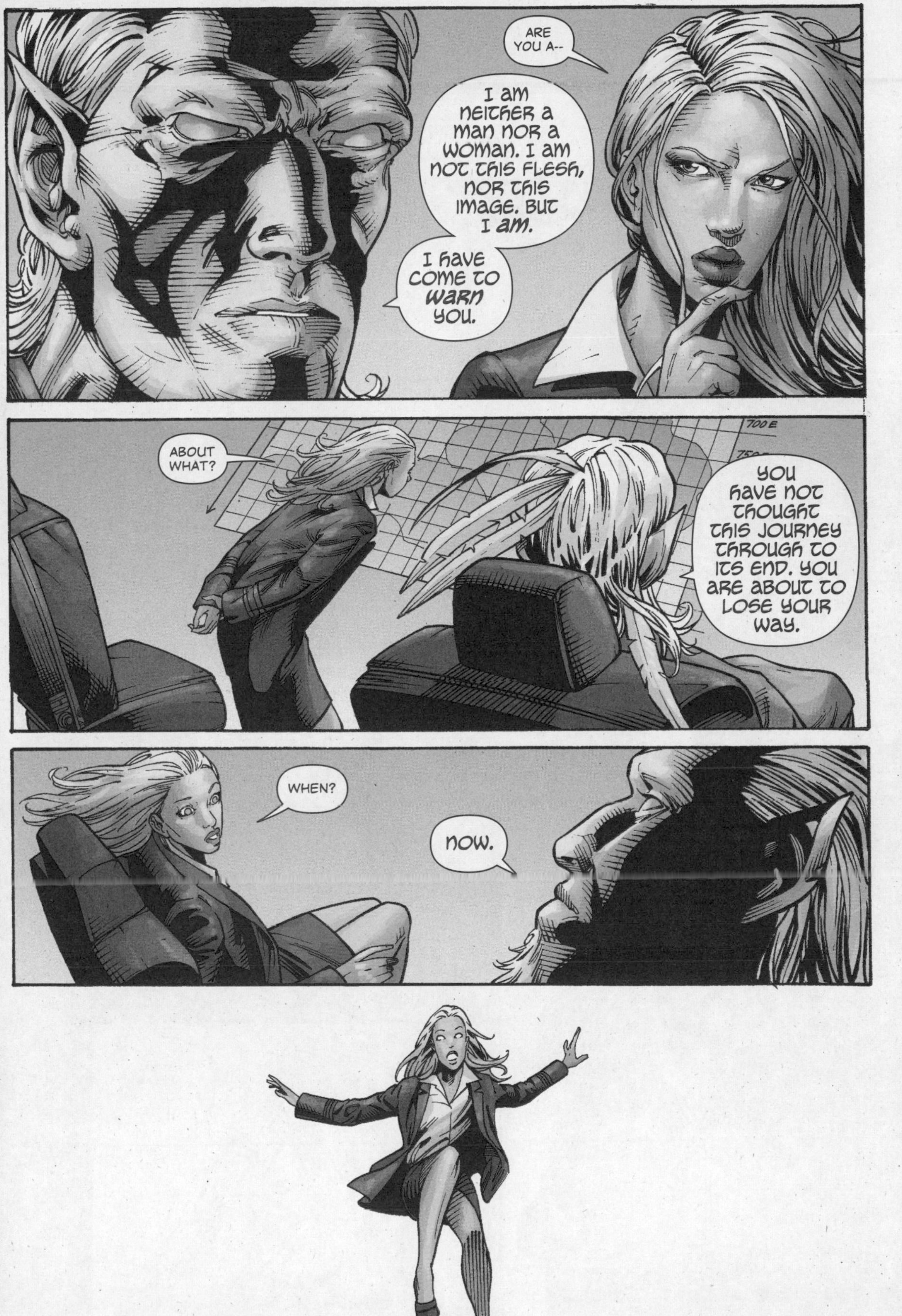
ARE YOU A--
I AM NEITHER A MAN NOR A WOMAN. I AM NOT THIS FLESH, NOR THIS IMAGE. BUT I AM.
I HAVE COME TO WARN YOU.
ABOUT WHAT?
YOU HAVE NOT THOUGHT THIS JOURNEY THROUGH TO ITS END. YOU ARE ABOUT TO LOSE YOUR WAY.
WHEN?
NOW.

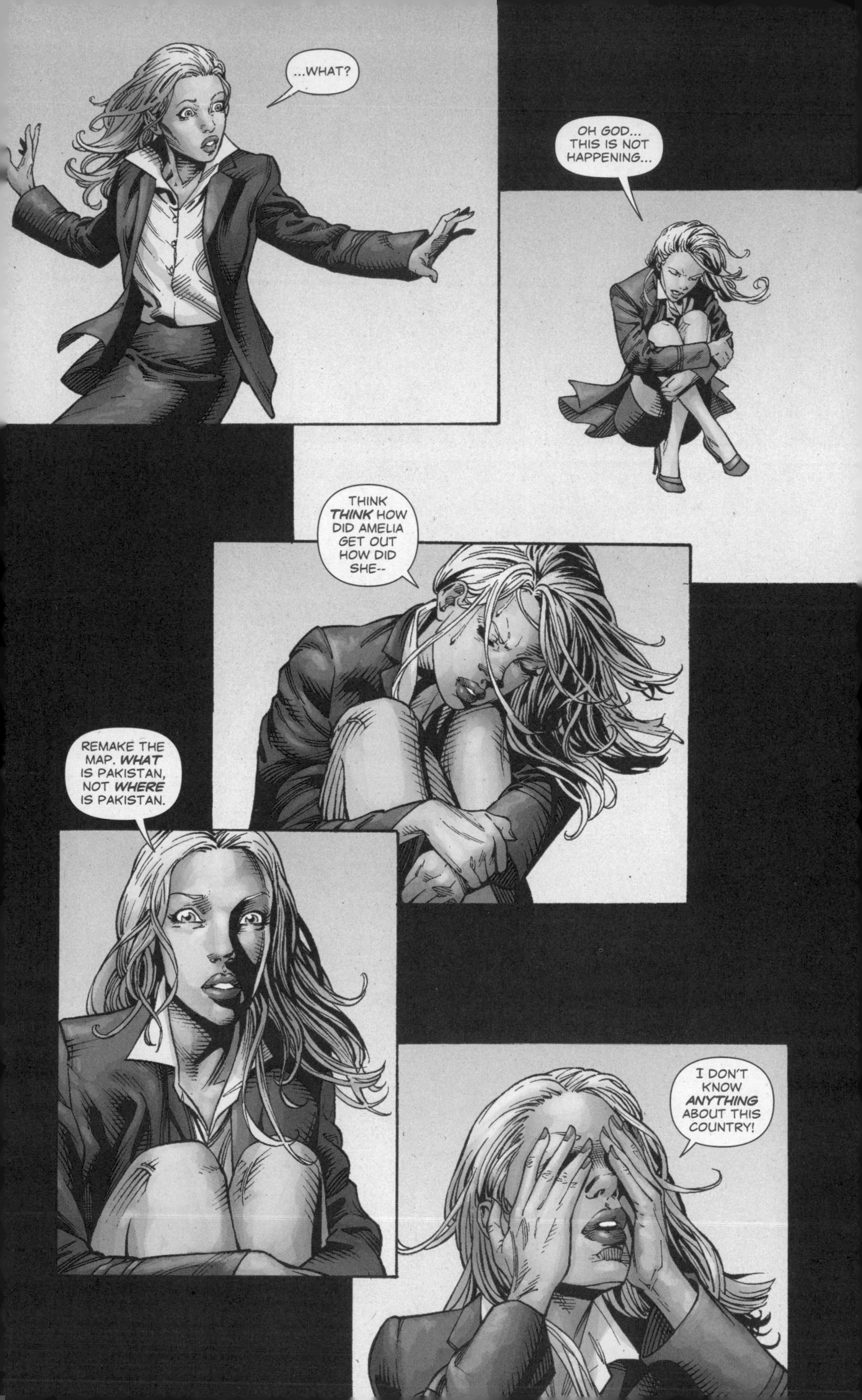
...WHAT?
OH GOD... THIS IS NOT HAPPENING...
THINK **THINK** HOW DID AMELIA GET OUT HOW DID SHE--
REMAKE THE MAP. **WHAT** IS PAKISTAN, NOT **WHERE** IS PAKISTAN.
I DON'T KNOW **ANYTHING** ABOUT THIS COUNTRY!

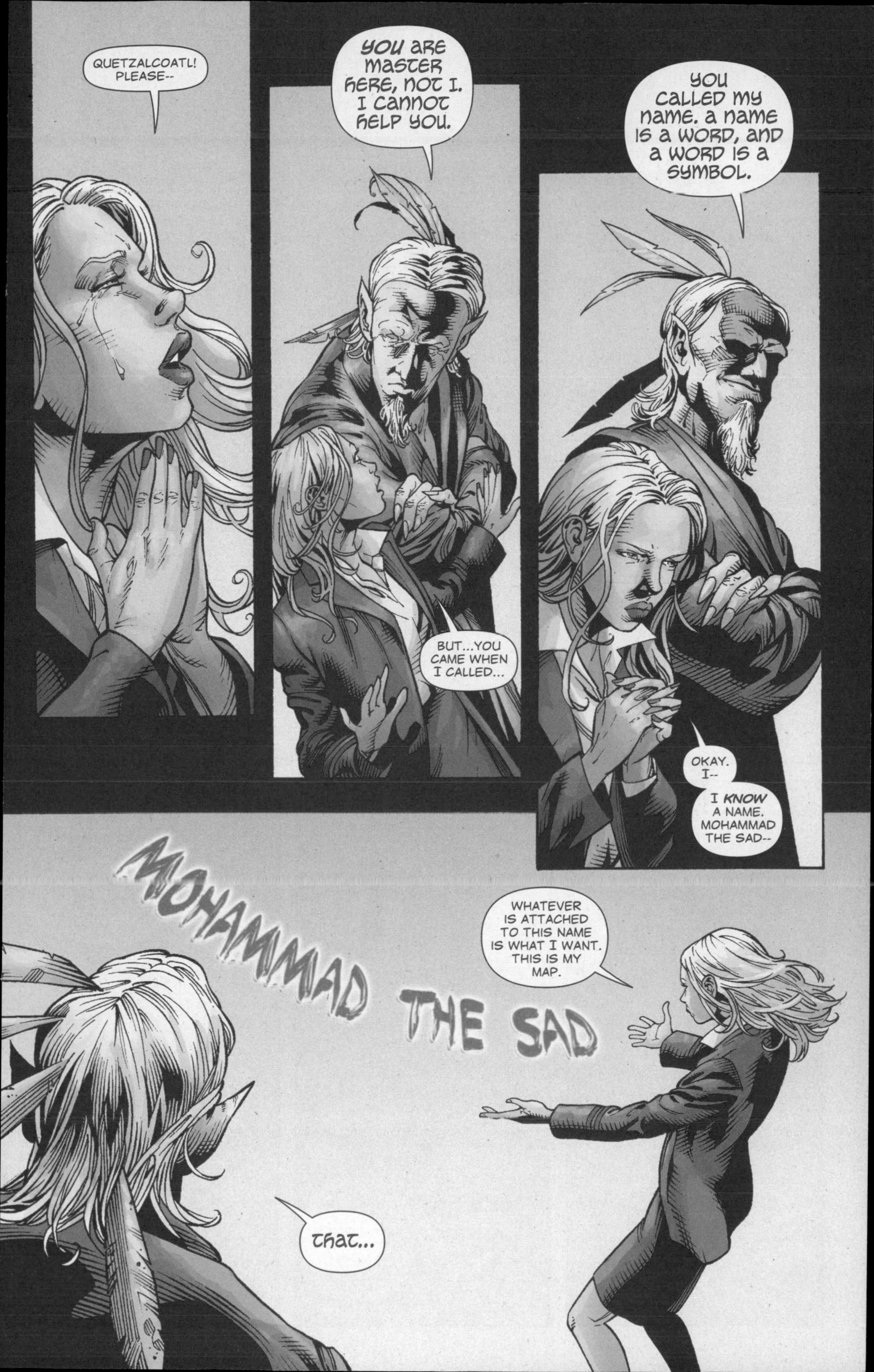
QUETZALCOATL! PLEASE--
YOU ARE MASTER HERE, NOT I. I CANNOT HELP YOU.
BUT...YOU CAME WHEN I CALLED...
YOU CALLED MY NAME. A NAME IS A WORD, AND A WORD IS A SYMBOL.
OKAY. I--
I KNOW A NAME. MOHAMMAD THE SAD--
MOHAMMAD THE SAD
WHATEVER IS ATTACHED TO THIS NAME IS WHAT I WANT. THIS IS MY MAP.
THAT...

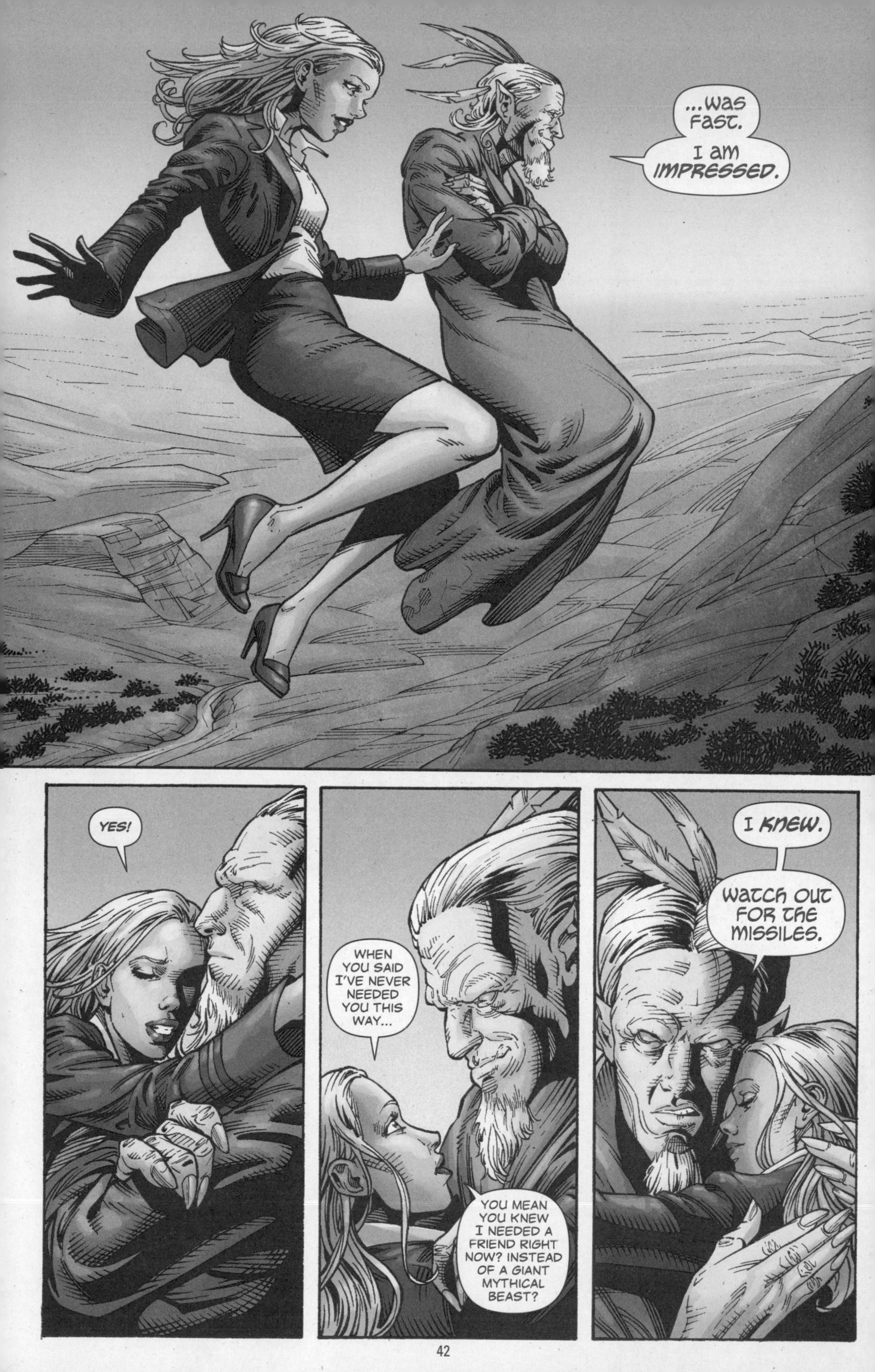
...was fast.
I am IMPRESSED.
YES!
WHEN YOU SAID I'VE NEVER NEEDED YOU THIS WAY...
YOU MEAN YOU KNEW I NEEDED A FRIEND RIGHT NOW? INSTEAD OF A GIANT MYTHICAL BEAST?
I KNEW.
Watch out for the missiles.

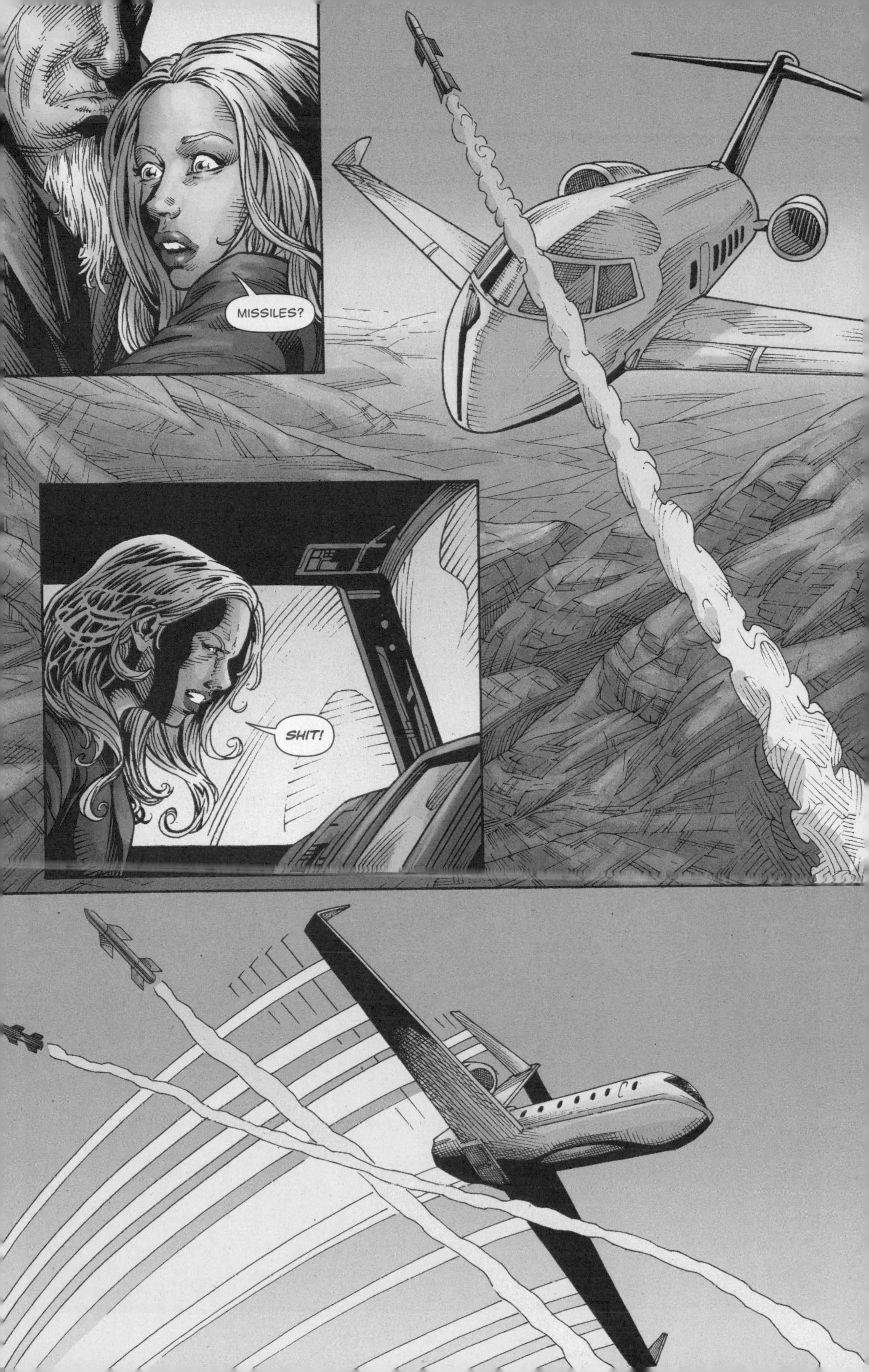
MISSILES?
SHIT!

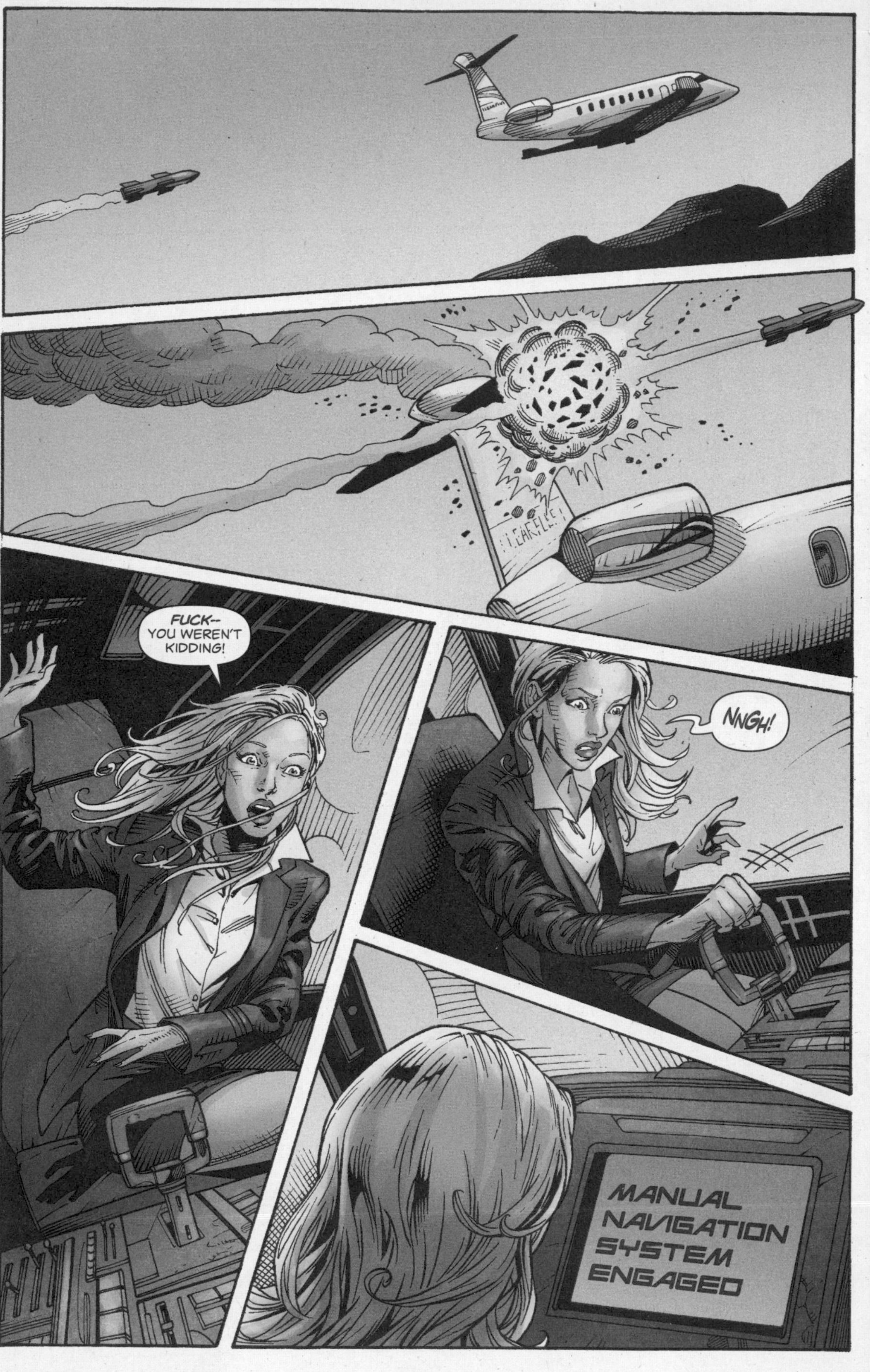
FUCK-- YOU WEREN'T KIDDING!
NNGH!
MANUAL NAVIGATION SYSTEM ENGAGED

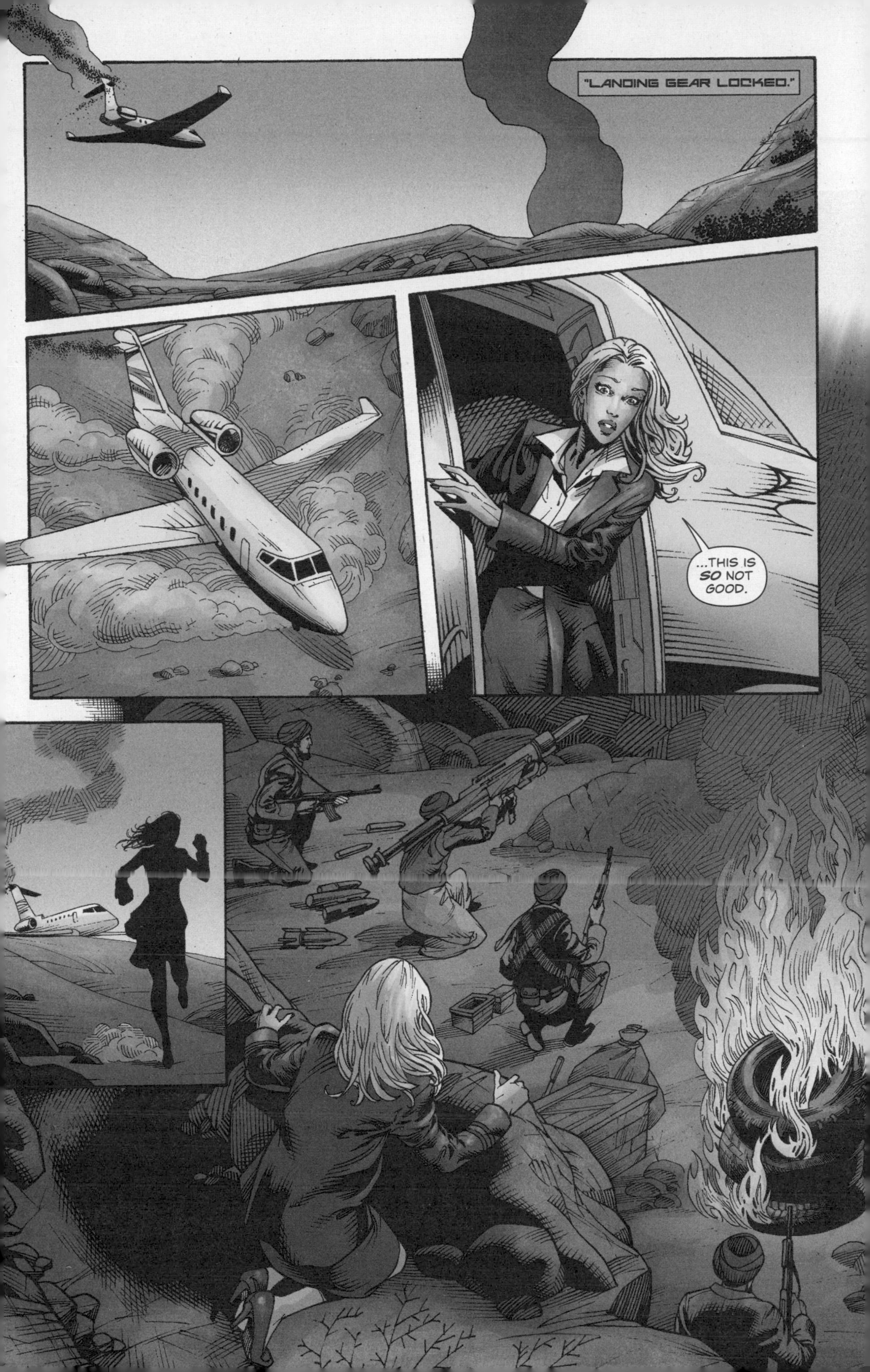
"LANDING GEAR LOCKED."
...THIS IS SO NOT GOOD.

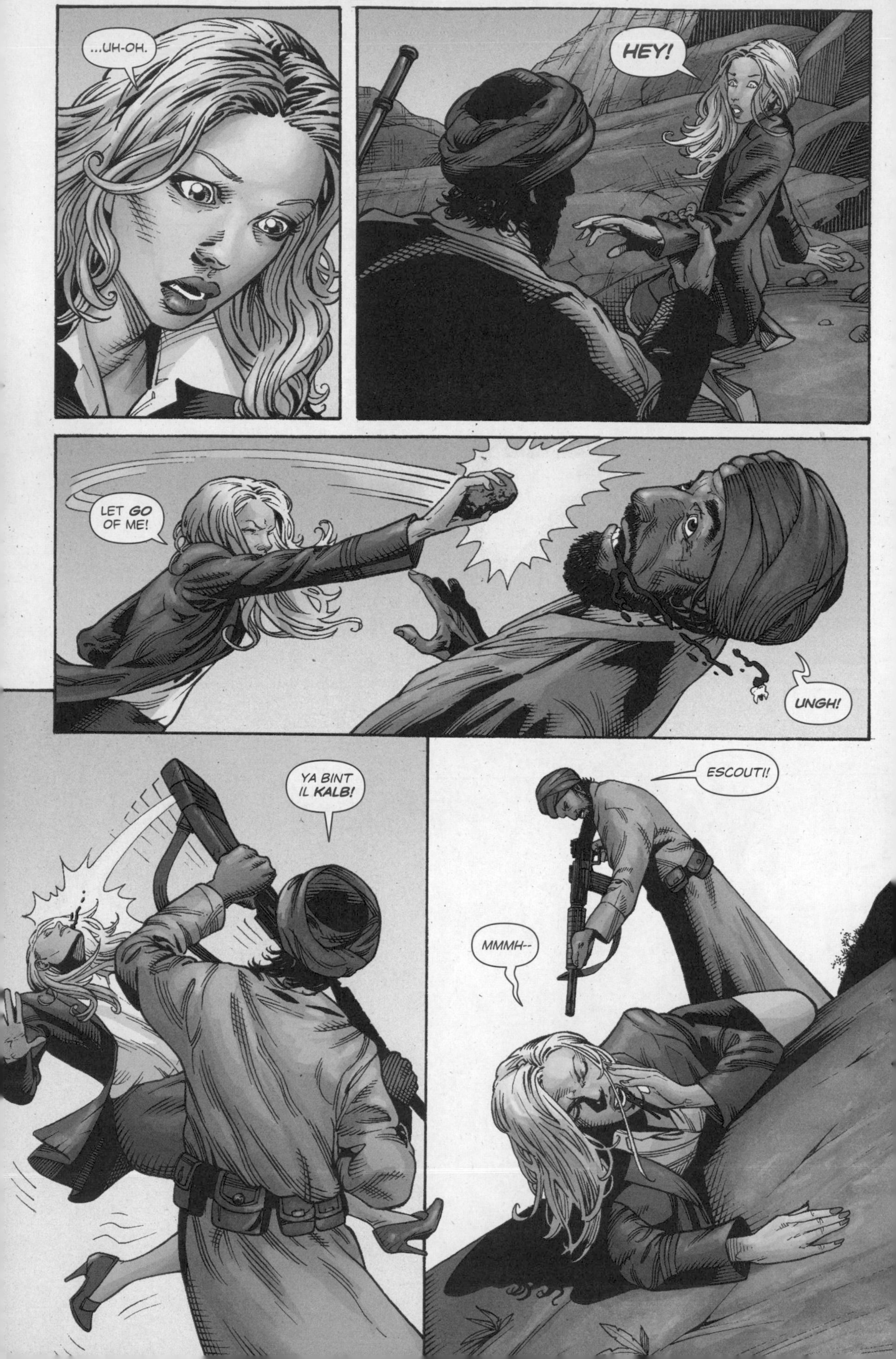
...UH-OH.
HEY!
LET GO OF ME!
UNGH!
YA BINT IL KALB!
ESCOUTI!
MMMH--

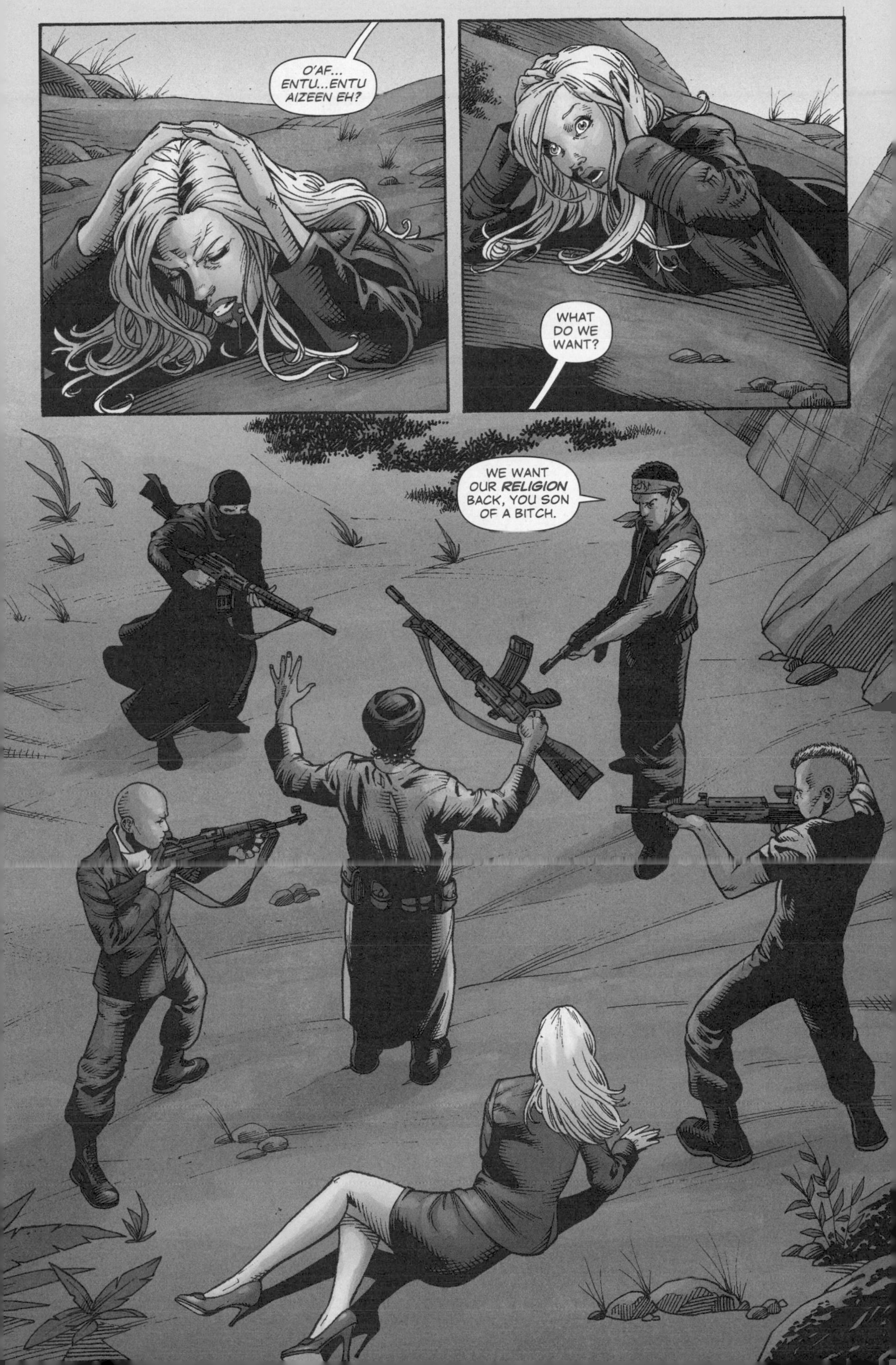
O'AF... ENTU...ENTU AIZEEN EH?
WHAT DO WE WANT?
WE WANT OUR **RELIGION** BACK, YOU SON OF A BITCH.

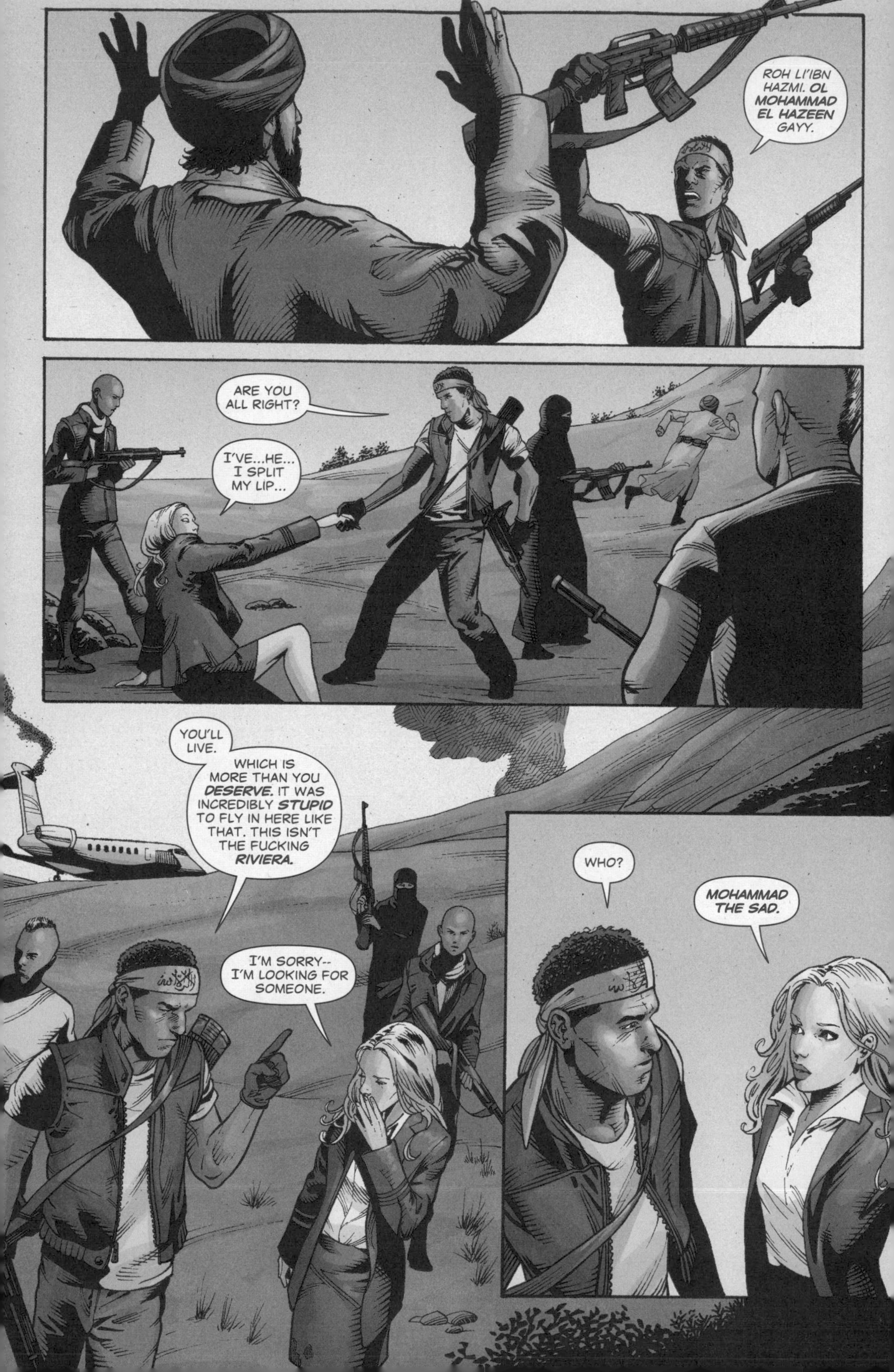
ROH LI'IBN HAZMI. OL MOHAMMAD EL HAZEEN GAYY.
ARE YOU ALL RIGHT?
I'VE...HE... I SPLIT MY LIP...
YOU'LL LIVE.
WHICH IS MORE THAN YOU DESERVE. IT WAS INCREDIBLY STUPID TO FLY IN HERE LIKE THAT. THIS ISN'T THE FUCKING RIVIERA.
I'M SORRY-- I'M LOOKING FOR SOMEONE.
WHO?
MOHAMMAD THE SAD.

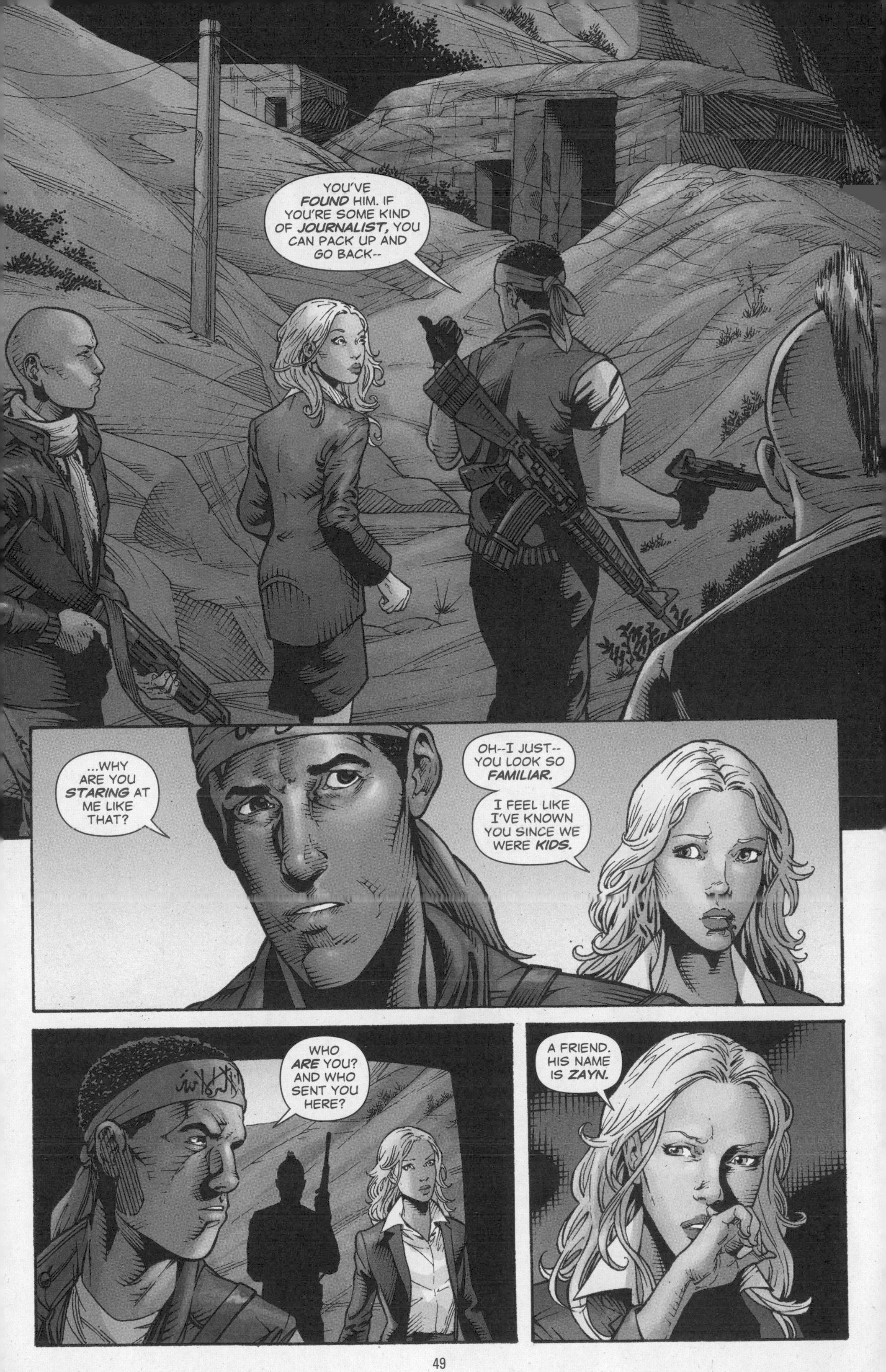
YOU'VE FOUND HIM. IF YOU'RE SOME KIND OF JOURNALIST, YOU CAN PACK UP AND GO BACK--
...WHY ARE YOU STARING AT ME LIKE THAT?
OH--I JUST-- YOU LOOK SO FAMILIAR.
I FEEL LIKE I'VE KNOWN YOU SINCE WE WERE KIDS.
WHO ARE YOU? AND WHO SENT YOU HERE?
A FRIEND. HIS NAME IS ZAYN.

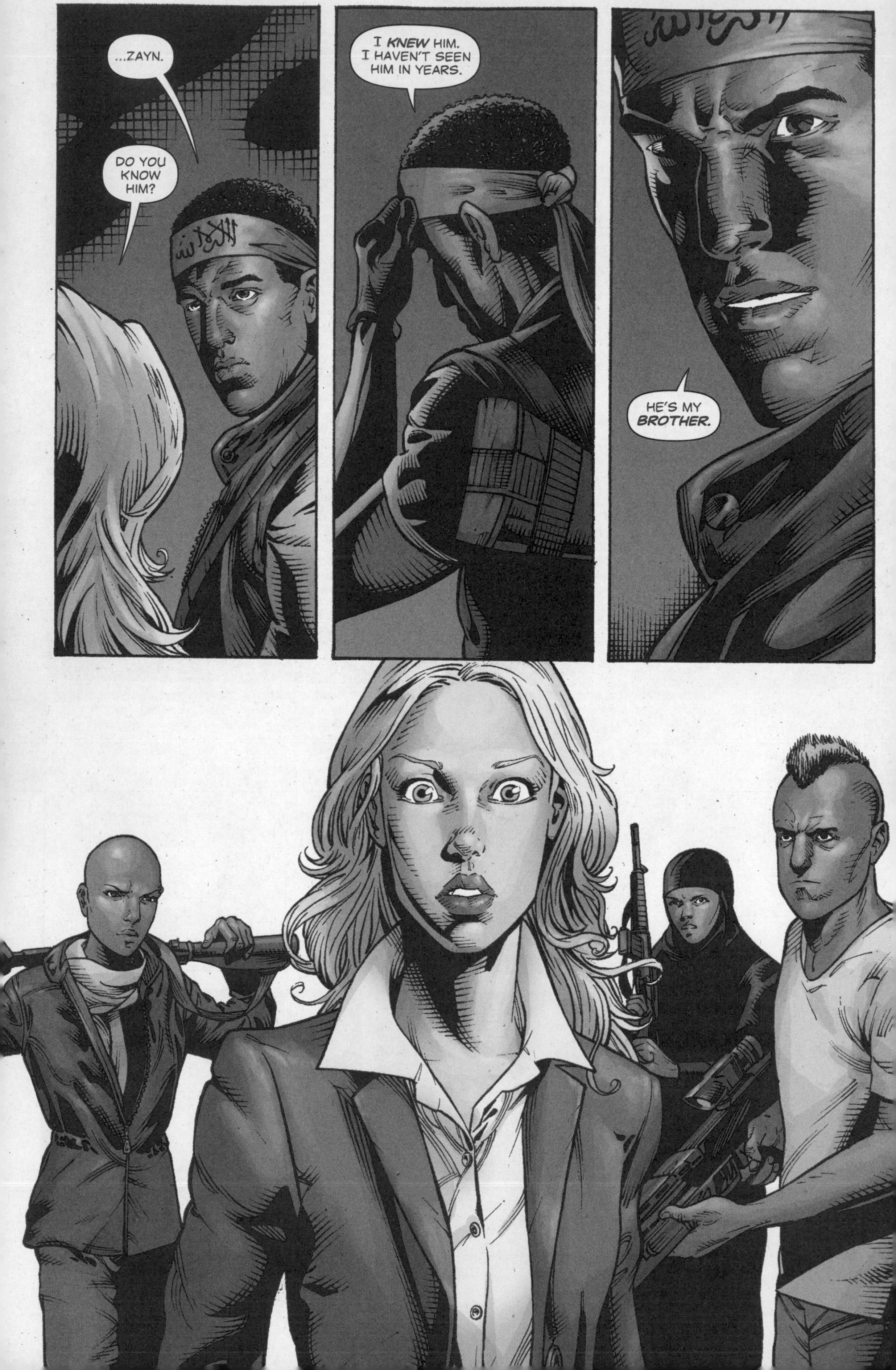
...ZAYN.
DO YOU KNOW HIM?
I KNEW HIM. I HAVEN'T SEEN HIM IN YEARS.
HE'S MY BROTHER.

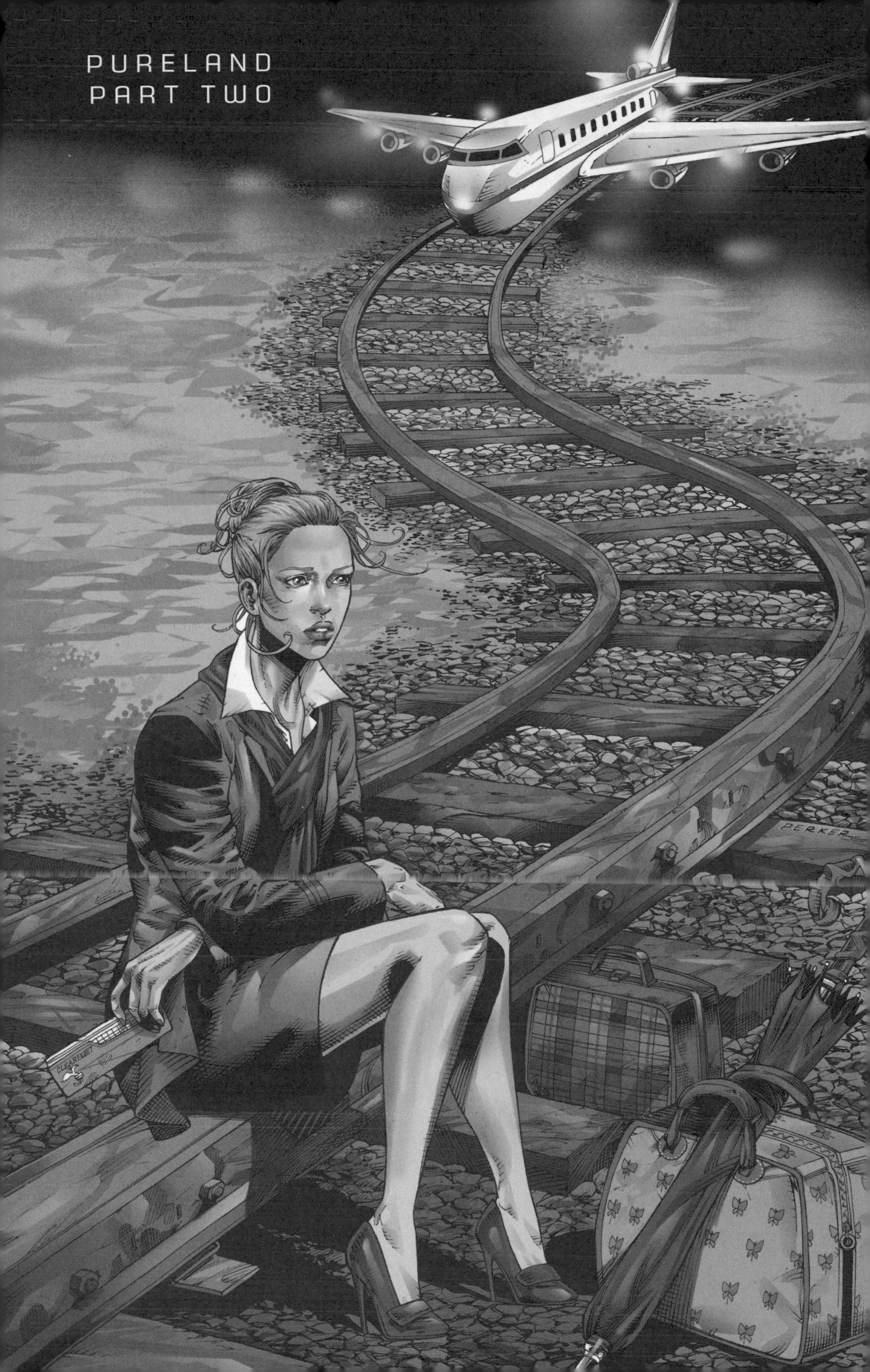
PURELAND
PART TWO
PERKER

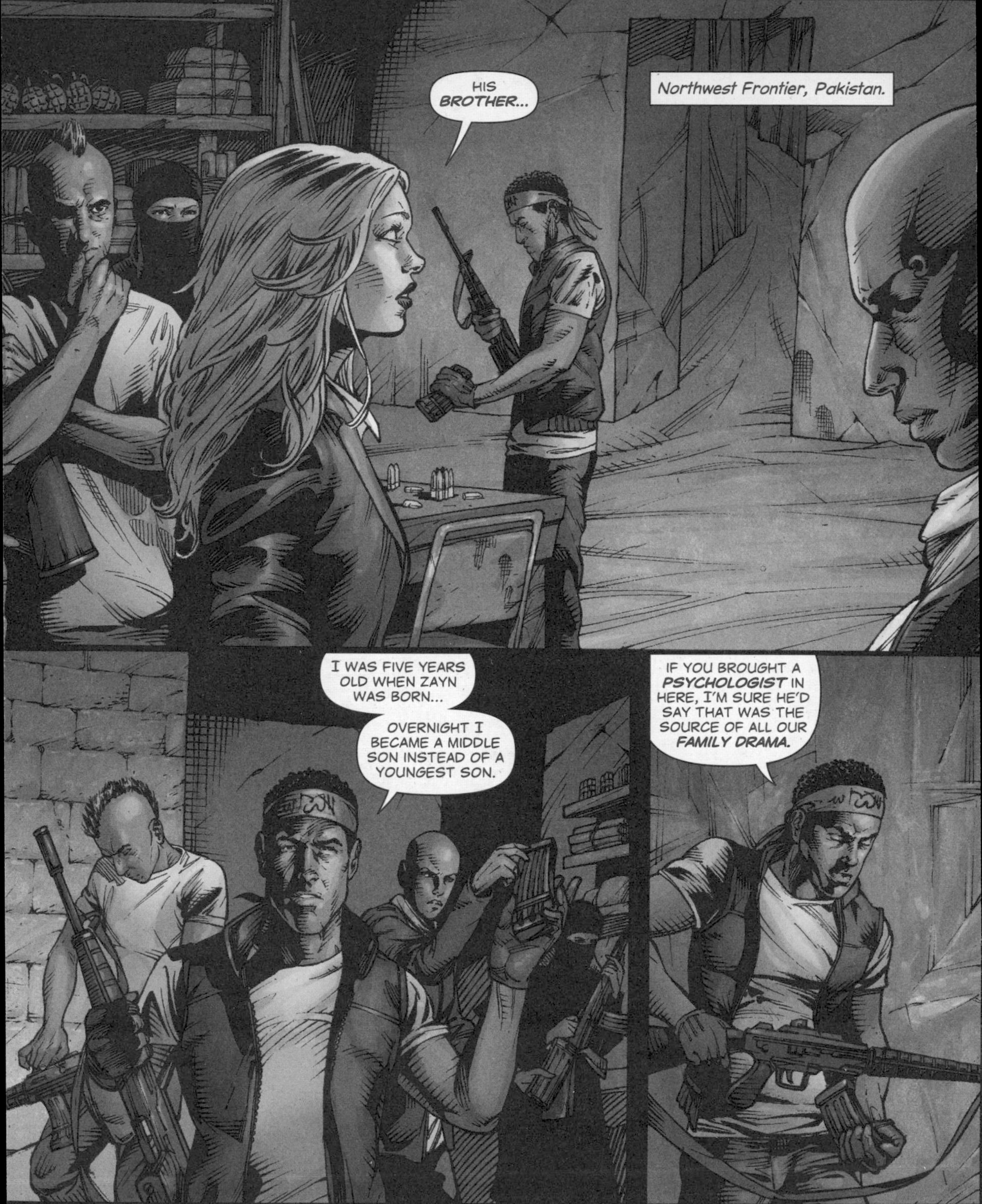
Northwest Frontier, Pakistan.
HIS BROTHER...
I WAS FIVE YEARS OLD WHEN ZAYN WAS BORN...
OVERNIGHT I BECAME A MIDDLE SON INSTEAD OF A YOUNGEST SON.
IF YOU BROUGHT A PSYCHOLOGIST IN HERE, I'M SURE HE'D SAY THAT WAS THE SOURCE OF ALL OUR FAMILY DRAMA.

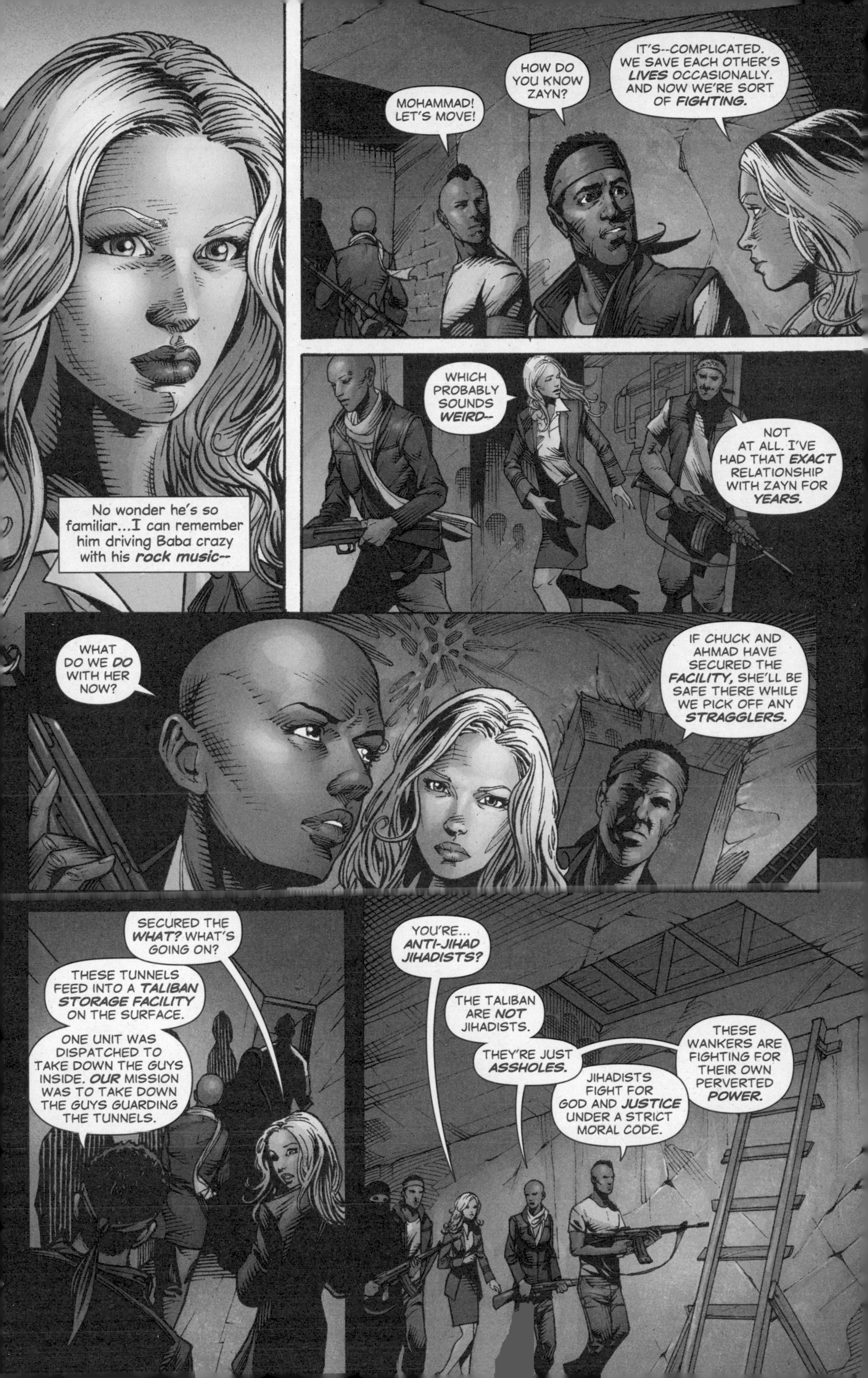
No wonder he's so familiar...I can remember him driving Baba crazy with his rock music--
MOHAMMAD! LET'S MOVE!
HOW DO YOU KNOW ZAYN?
IT'S--COMPLICATED. WE SAVE EACH OTHER'S LIVES OCCASIONALLY. AND NOW WE'RE SORT OF FIGHTING.
WHICH PROBABLY SOUNDS WEIRD--
NOT AT ALL. I'VE HAD THAT EXACT RELATIONSHIP WITH ZAYN FOR YEARS.
WHAT DO WE DO WITH HER NOW?
IF CHUCK AND AHMAD HAVE SECURED THE FACILITY, SHE'LL BE SAFE THERE WHILE WE PICK OFF ANY STRAGGLERS.
SECURED THE WHAT? WHAT'S GOING ON?
THESE TUNNELS FEED INTO A TALIBAN STORAGE FACILITY ON THE SURFACE.
ONE UNIT WAS DISPATCHED TO TAKE DOWN THE GUYS INSIDE. OUR MISSION WAS TO TAKE DOWN THE GUYS GUARDING THE TUNNELS.
YOU'RE... ANTI-JIHAD JIHADISTS?
THE TALIBAN ARE NOT JIHADISTS.
THEY'RE JUST ASSHOLES.
JIHADISTS FIGHT FOR GOD AND JUSTICE UNDER A STRICT MORAL CODE.
THESE WANKERS ARE FIGHTING FOR THEIR OWN PERVERTED POWER.

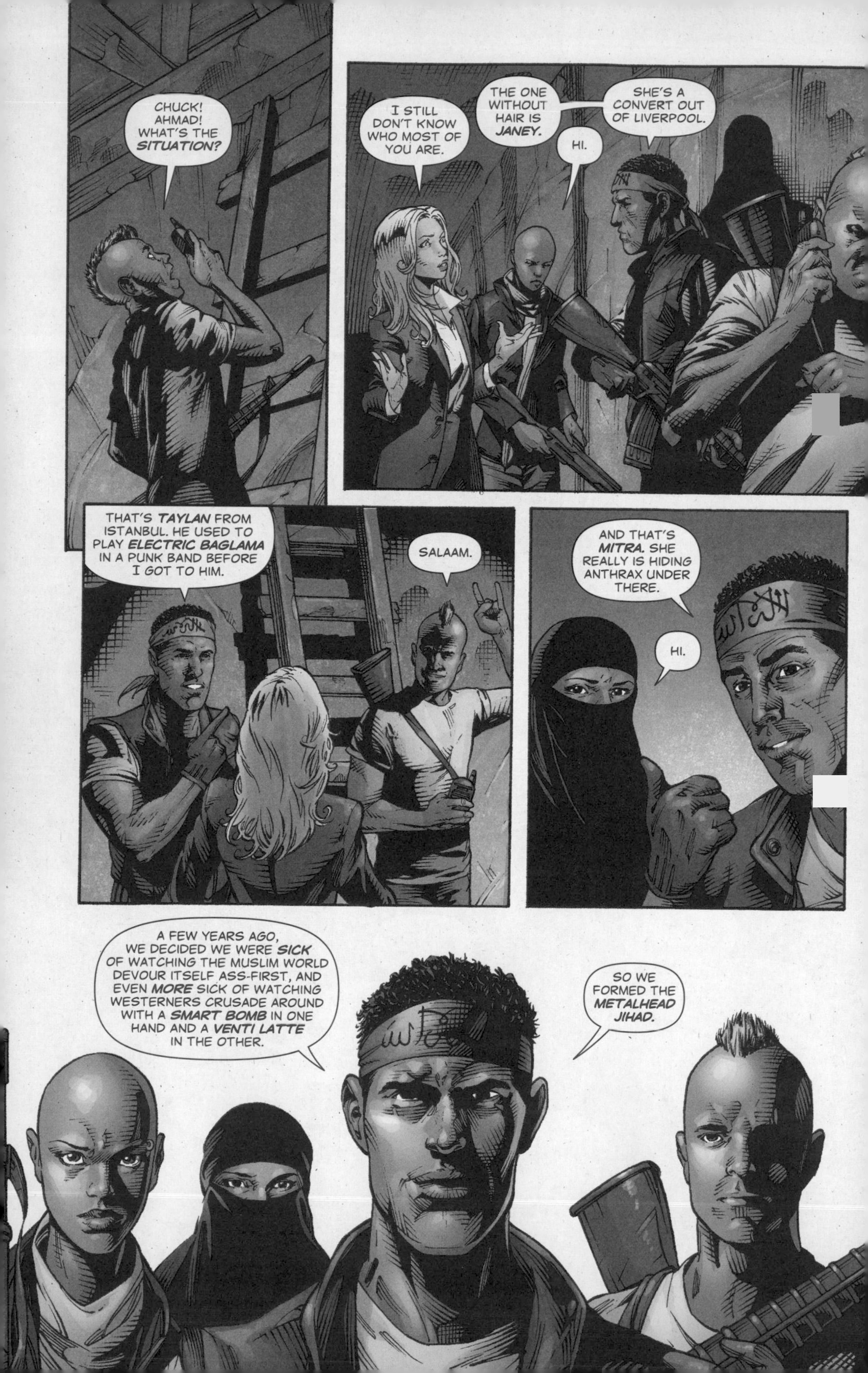
CHUCK! AHMAD! WHAT'S THE SITUATION?
I STILL DON'T KNOW WHO MOST OF YOU ARE.
THE ONE WITHOUT HAIR IS JANEY.
SHE'S A CONVERT OUT OF LIVERPOOL.
HI.
THAT'S TAYLAN FROM ISTANBUL. HE USED TO PLAY ELECTRIC BAGLAMA IN A PUNK BAND BEFORE I GOT TO HIM.
SALAAM.
AND THAT'S MITRA. SHE REALLY IS HIDING ANTHRAX UNDER THERE.
HI.
A FEW YEARS AGO, WE DECIDED WE WERE SICK OF WATCHING THE MUSLIM WORLD DEVOUR ITSELF ASS-FIRST, AND EVEN MORE SICK OF WATCHING WESTERNERS CRUSADE AROUND WITH A SMART BOMB IN ONE HAND AND A VENTI LATTE IN THE OTHER.
SO WE FORMED THE METALHEAD JIHAD.

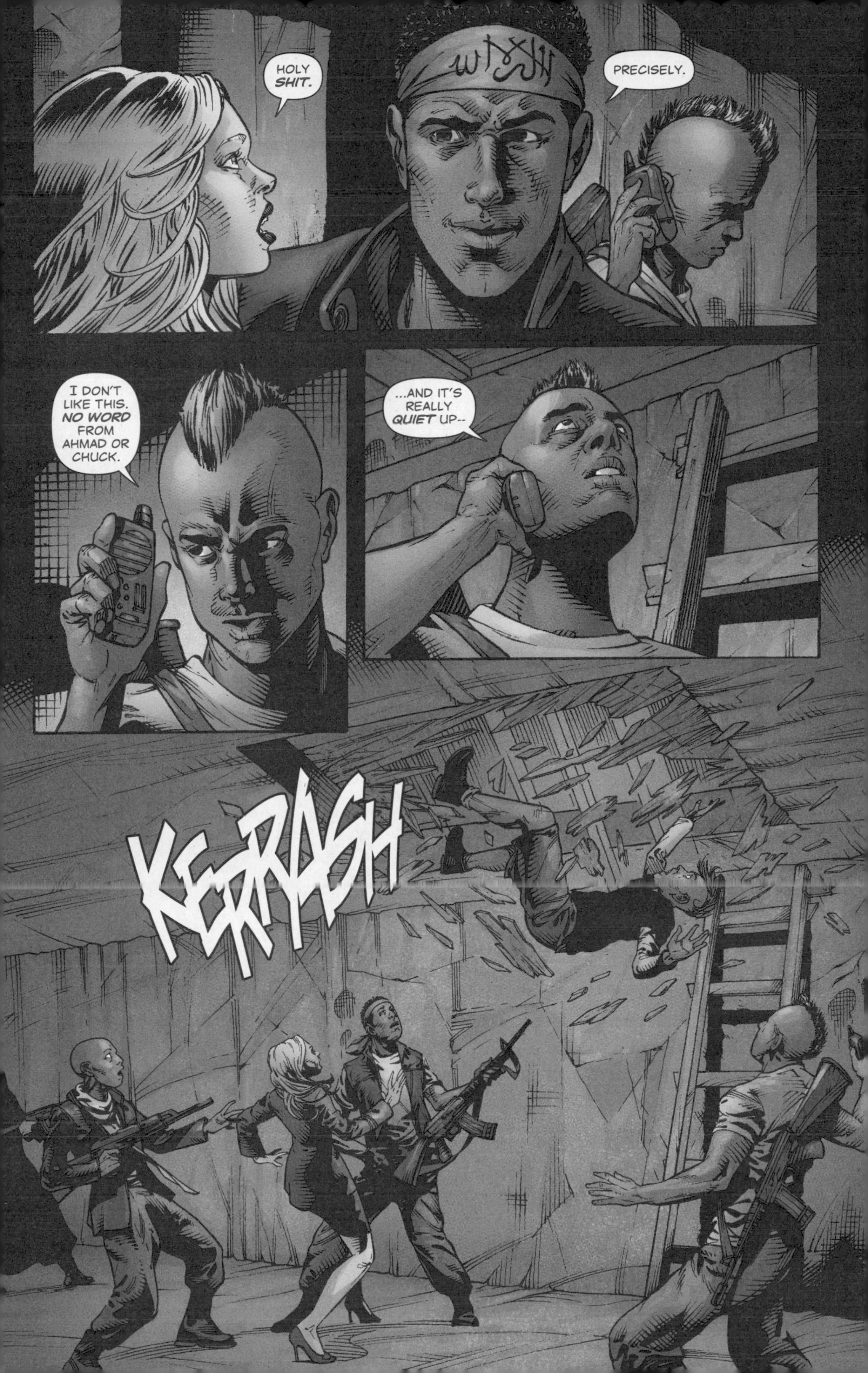
HOLY SHIT.
PRECISELY.
I DON'T LIKE THIS. NO WORD FROM AHMAD OR CHUCK.
...AND IT'S REALLY QUIET UP--
KERASH

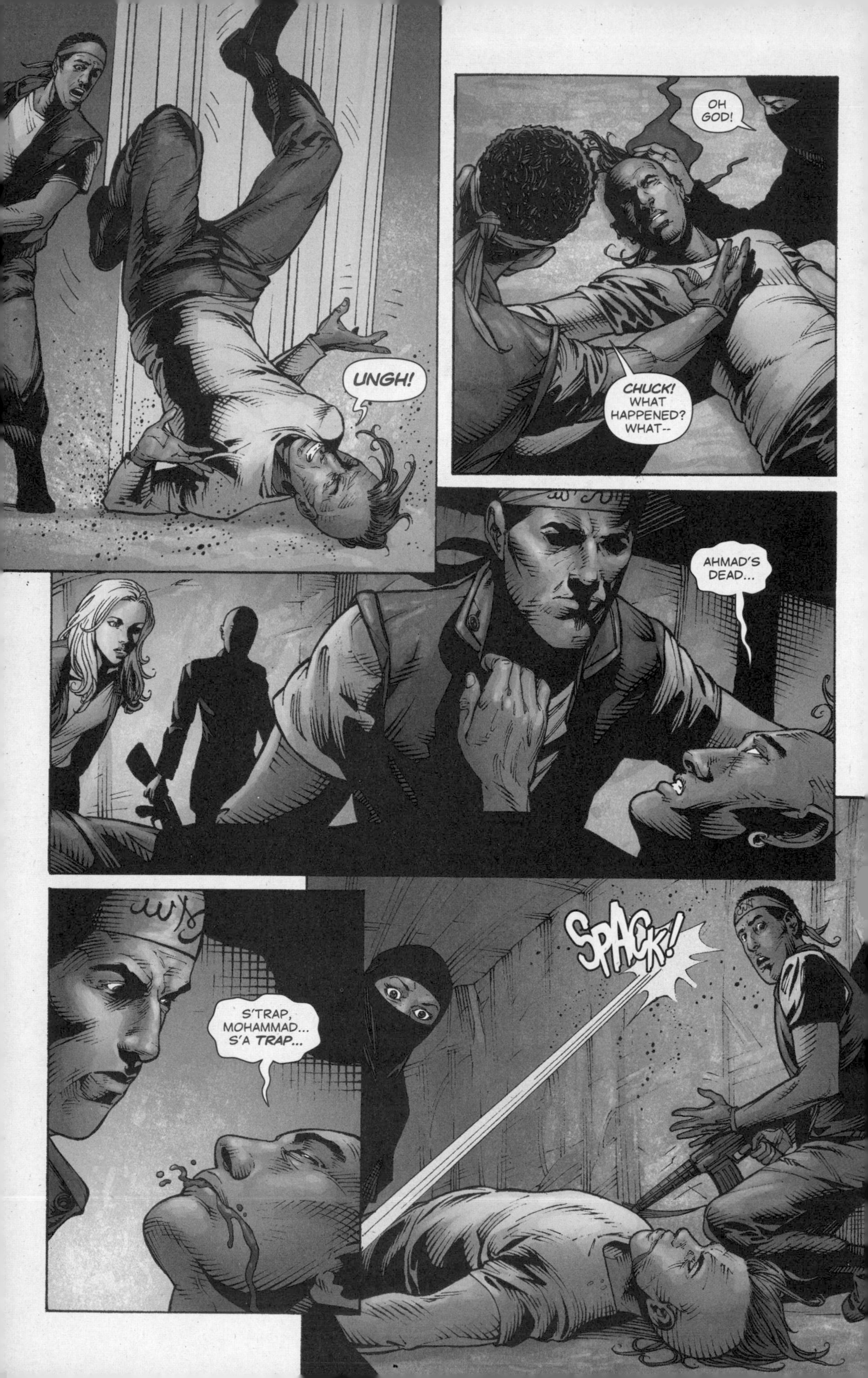
UNGH!
OH GOD!
CHUCK! WHAT HAPPENED? WHAT--
AHMAD'S DEAD...
S'TRAP, MOHAMMAD... S'A TRAP...
SPACK!

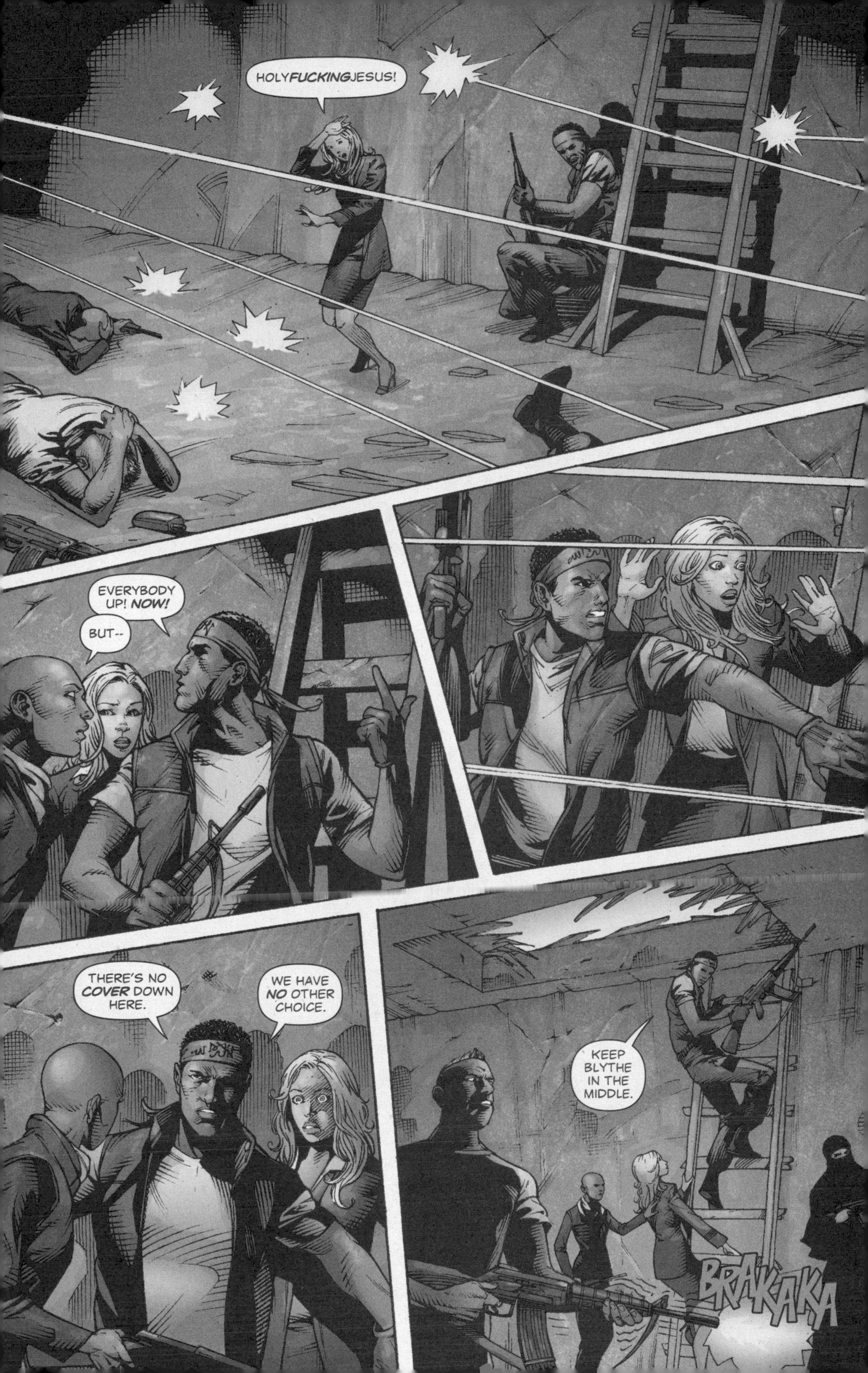
HOLY**FUCKING**JESUS!
EVERYBODY UP! **NOW!**
BUT--
THERE'S NO **COVER** DOWN HERE.
WE HAVE **NO** OTHER CHOICE.
KEEP BLYTHE IN THE MIDDLE.
BRAKAKA

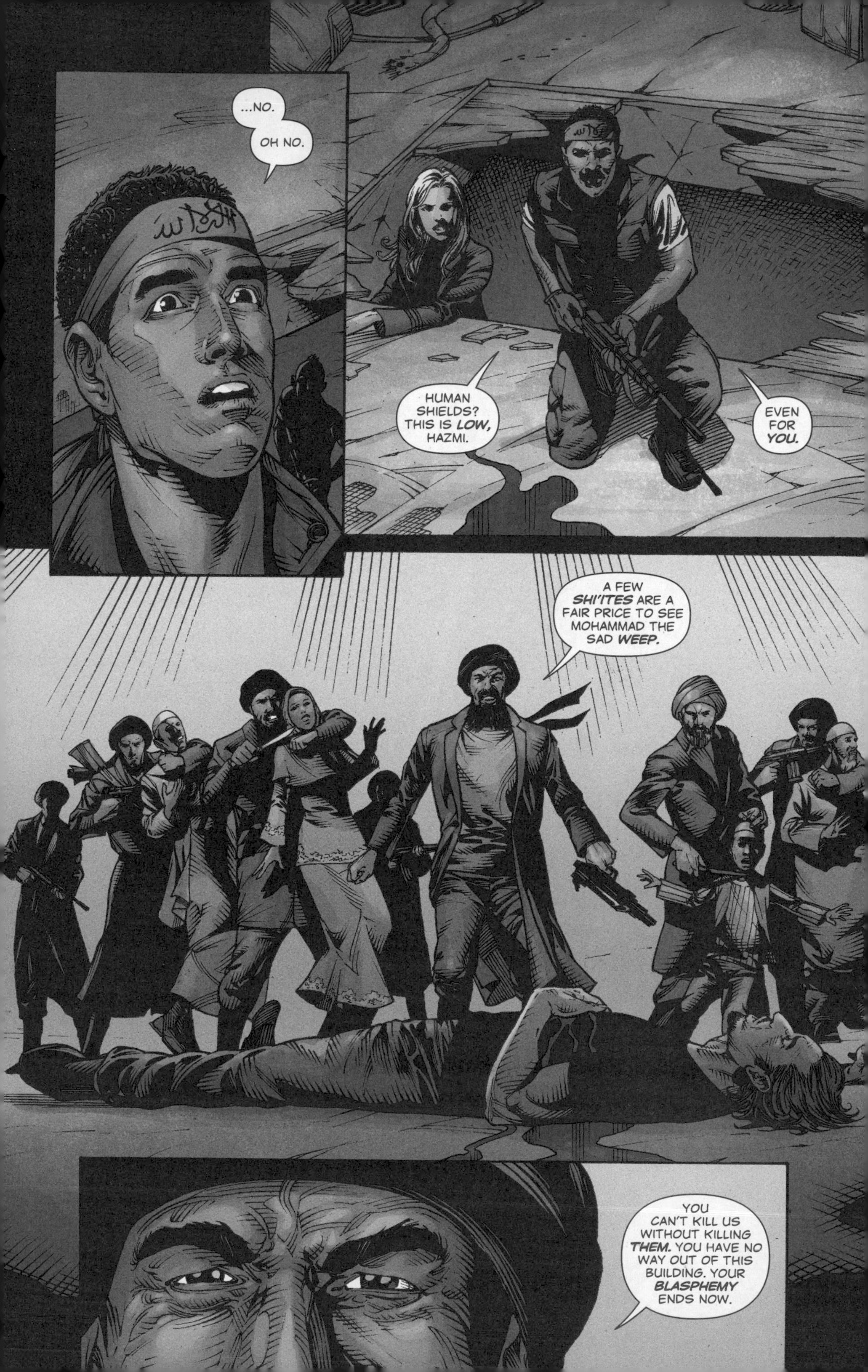
...NO.
OH NO.
HUMAN SHIELDS? THIS IS LOW, HAZMI.
EVEN FOR YOU.
A FEW SHI'ITES ARE A FAIR PRICE TO SEE MOHAMMAD THE SAD WEEP.
YOU CAN'T KILL US WITHOUT KILLING THEM. YOU HAVE NO WAY OUT OF THIS BUILDING. YOUR BLASPHEMY ENDS NOW.

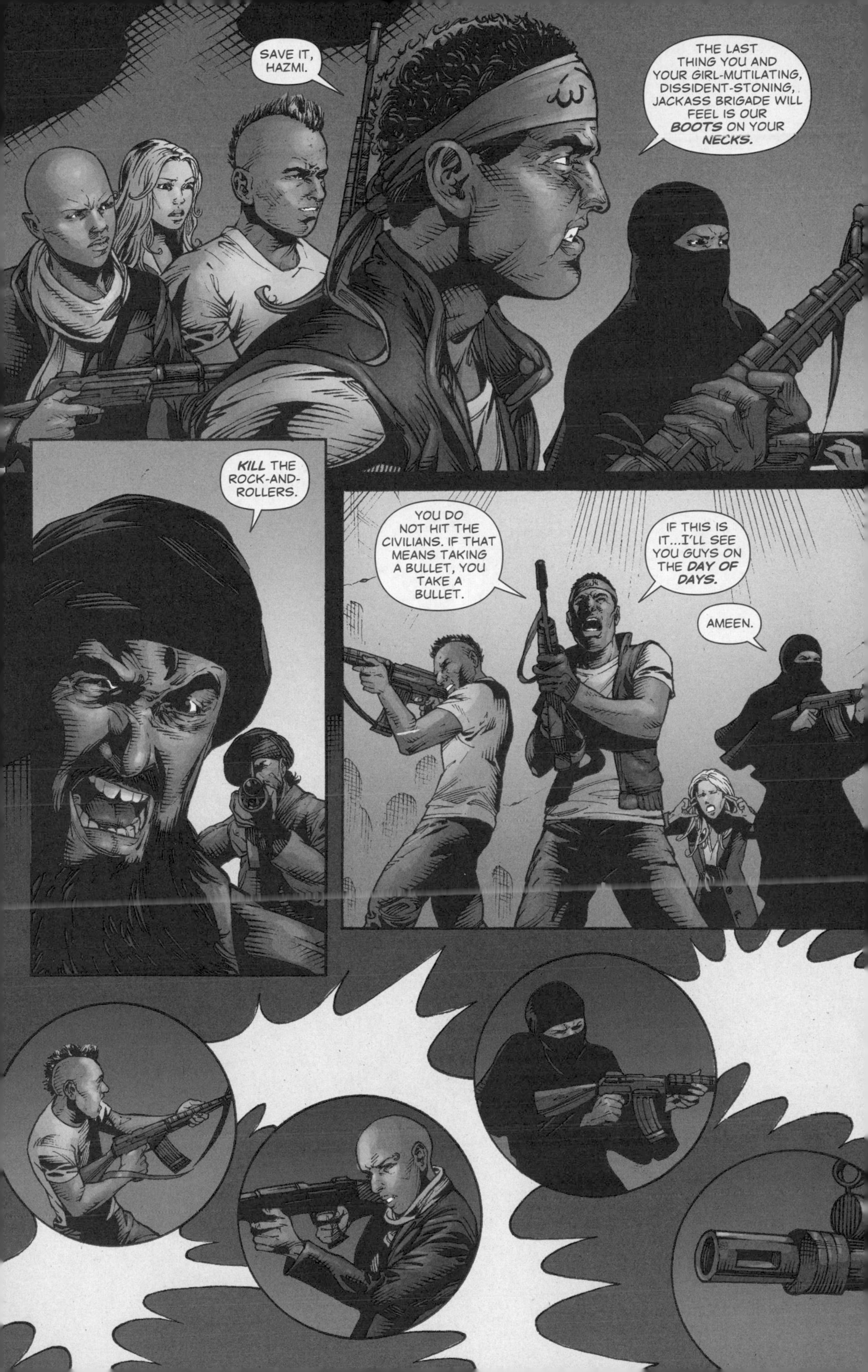
SAVE IT, HAZMI.
THE LAST THING YOU AND YOUR GIRL-MUTILATING, DISSIDENT-STONING, JACKASS BRIGADE WILL FEEL IS OUR BOOTS ON YOUR NECKS.
KILL THE ROCK-AND-ROLLERS.
YOU DO NOT HIT THE CIVILIANS. IF THAT MEANS TAKING A BULLET, YOU TAKE A BULLET.
IF THIS IS IT...I'LL SEE YOU GUYS ON THE DAY OF DAYS.
AMEEN.

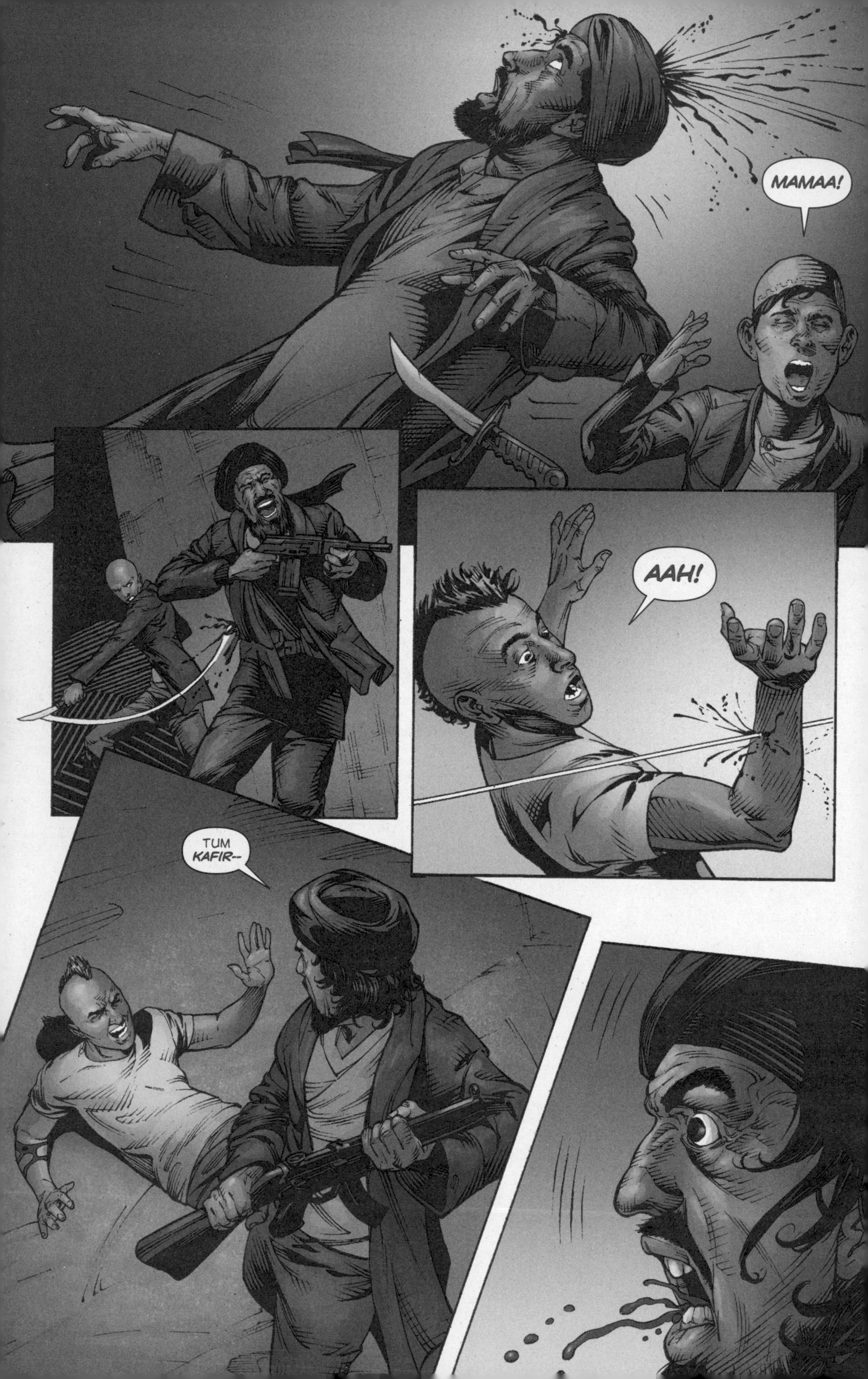
MAMAA!
AAH!
TUM KAFIR--

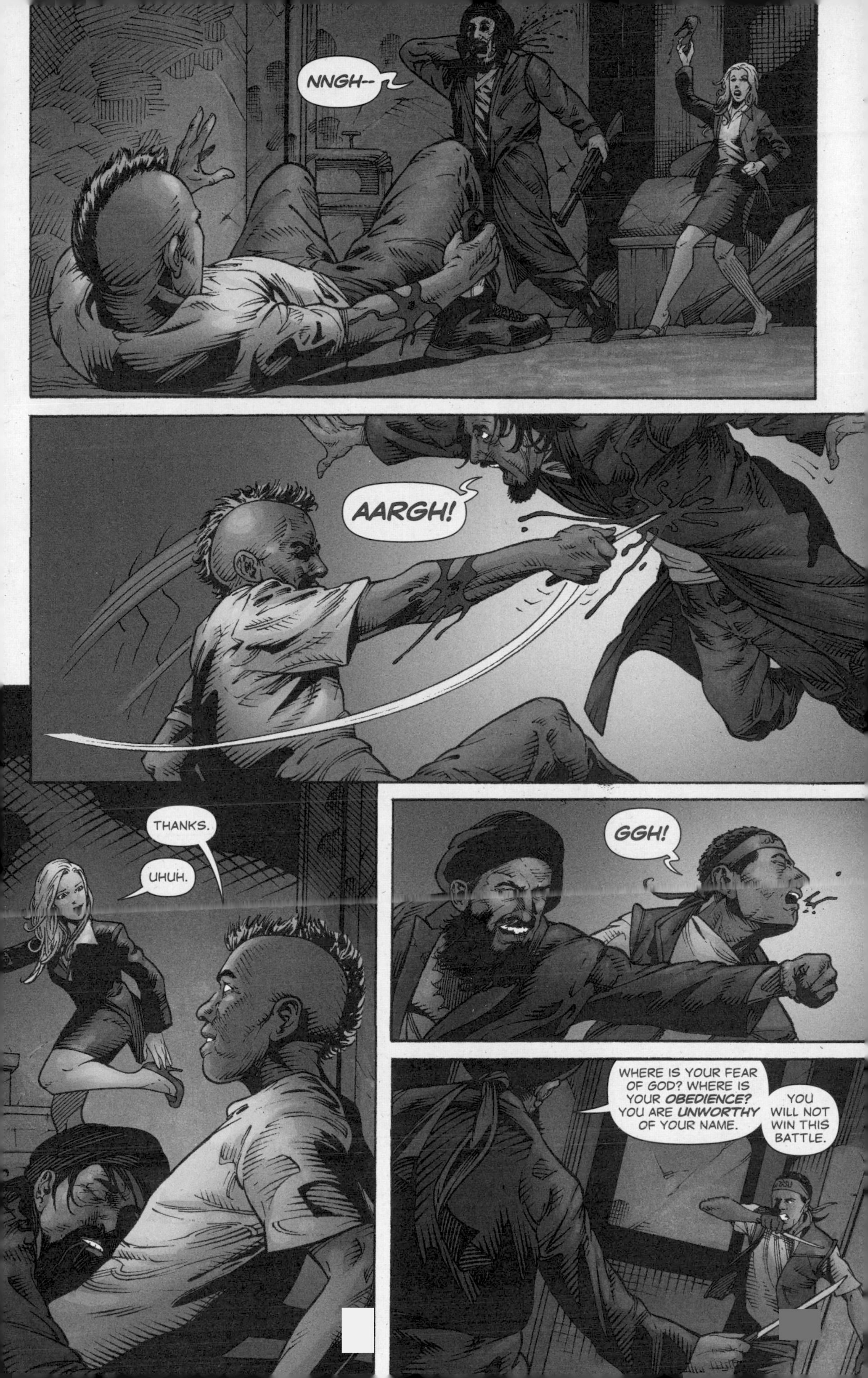
NNGH--
AARGH!
THANKS.
UHUH.
GGH!
WHERE IS YOUR FEAR OF GOD? WHERE IS YOUR OBEDIENCE? YOU ARE UNWORTHY OF YOUR NAME.
YOU WILL NOT WIN THIS BATTLE.

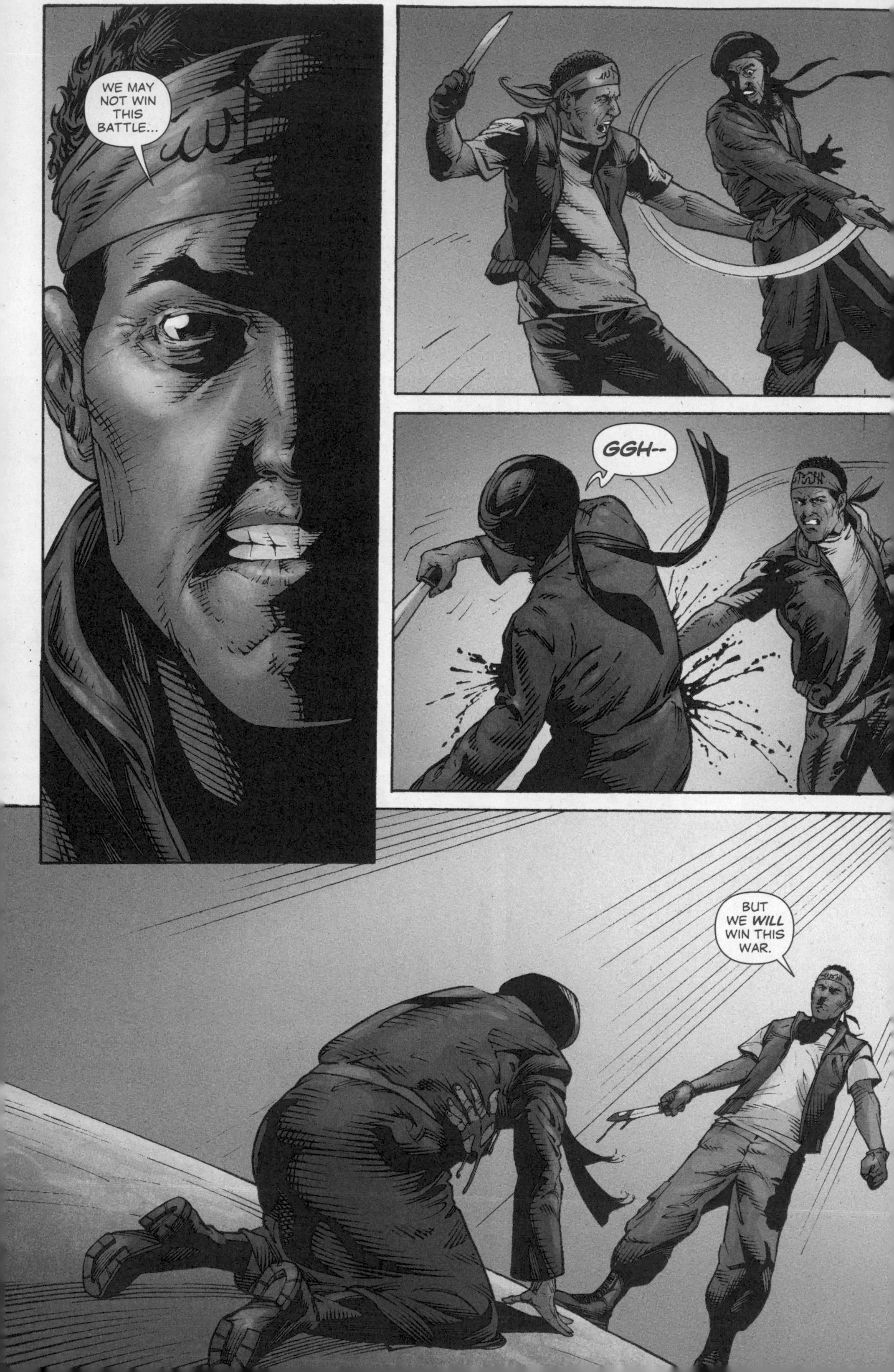
WE MAY NOT WIN THIS BATTLE...
GGH--
BUT WE WILL WIN THIS WAR.

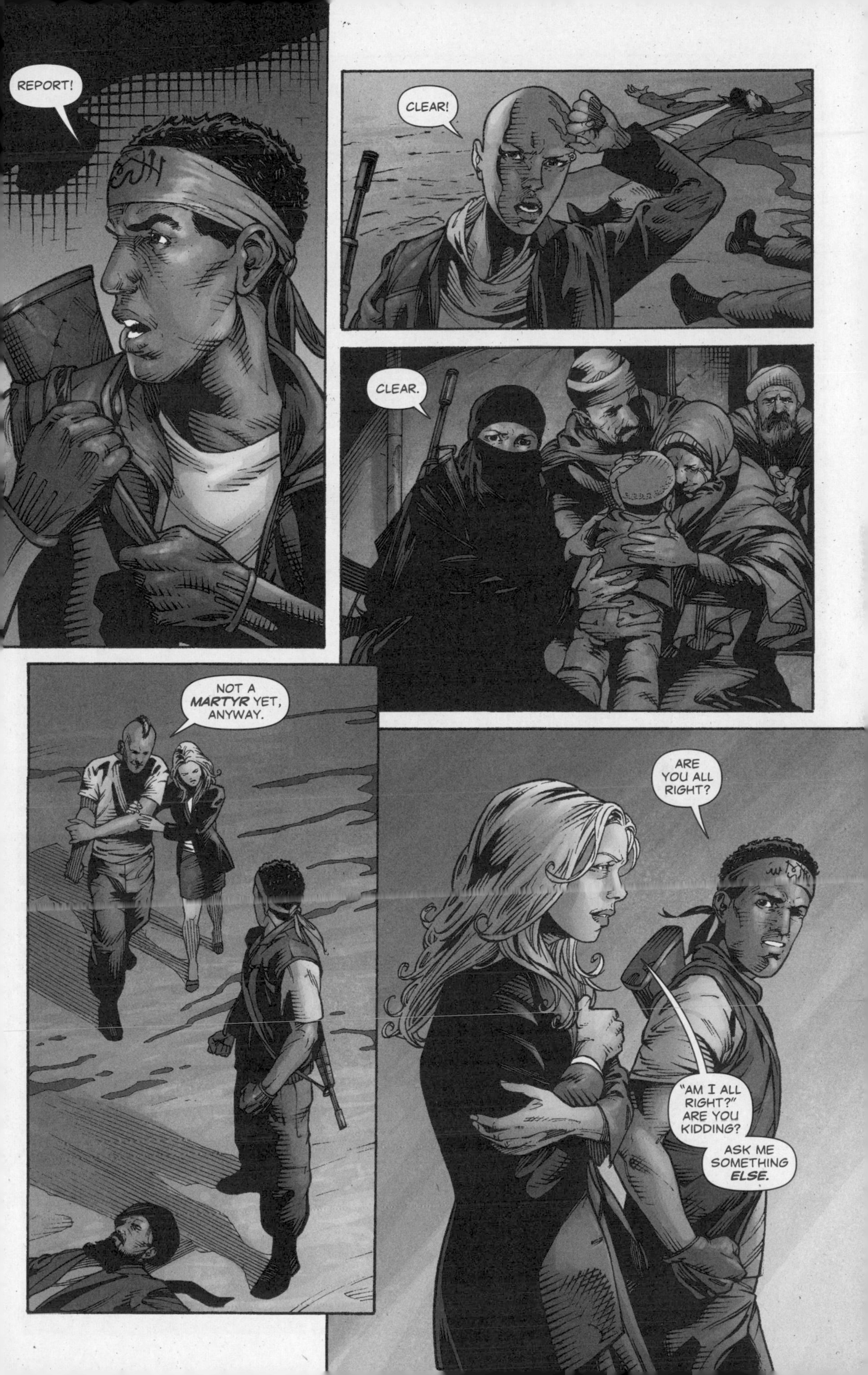
REPORT!
CLEAR!
CLEAR.
NOT A MARTYR YET, ANYWAY.
ARE YOU ALL RIGHT?
"AM I ALL RIGHT?" ARE YOU KIDDING?
ASK ME SOMETHING ELSE.

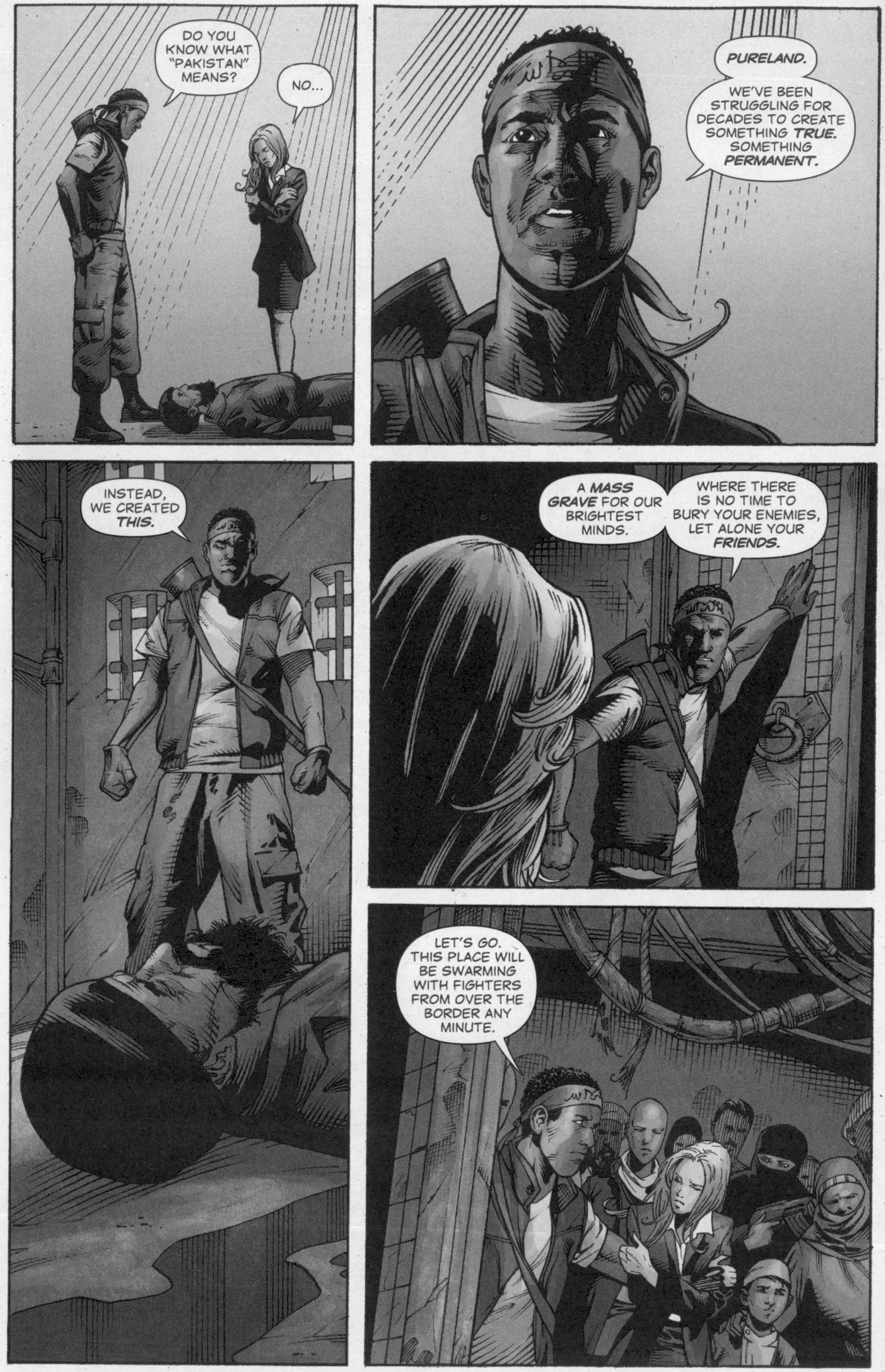
DO YOU KNOW WHAT "PAKISTAN" MEANS?
NO...
PURELAND.
WE'VE BEEN STRUGGLING FOR DECADES TO CREATE SOMETHING TRUE. SOMETHING PERMANENT.
INSTEAD, WE CREATED THIS.
A MASS GRAVE FOR OUR BRIGHTEST MINDS.
WHERE THERE IS NO TIME TO BURY YOUR ENEMIES, LET ALONE YOUR FRIENDS.
LET'S GO. THIS PLACE WILL BE SWARMING WITH FIGHTERS FROM OVER THE BORDER ANY MINUTE.

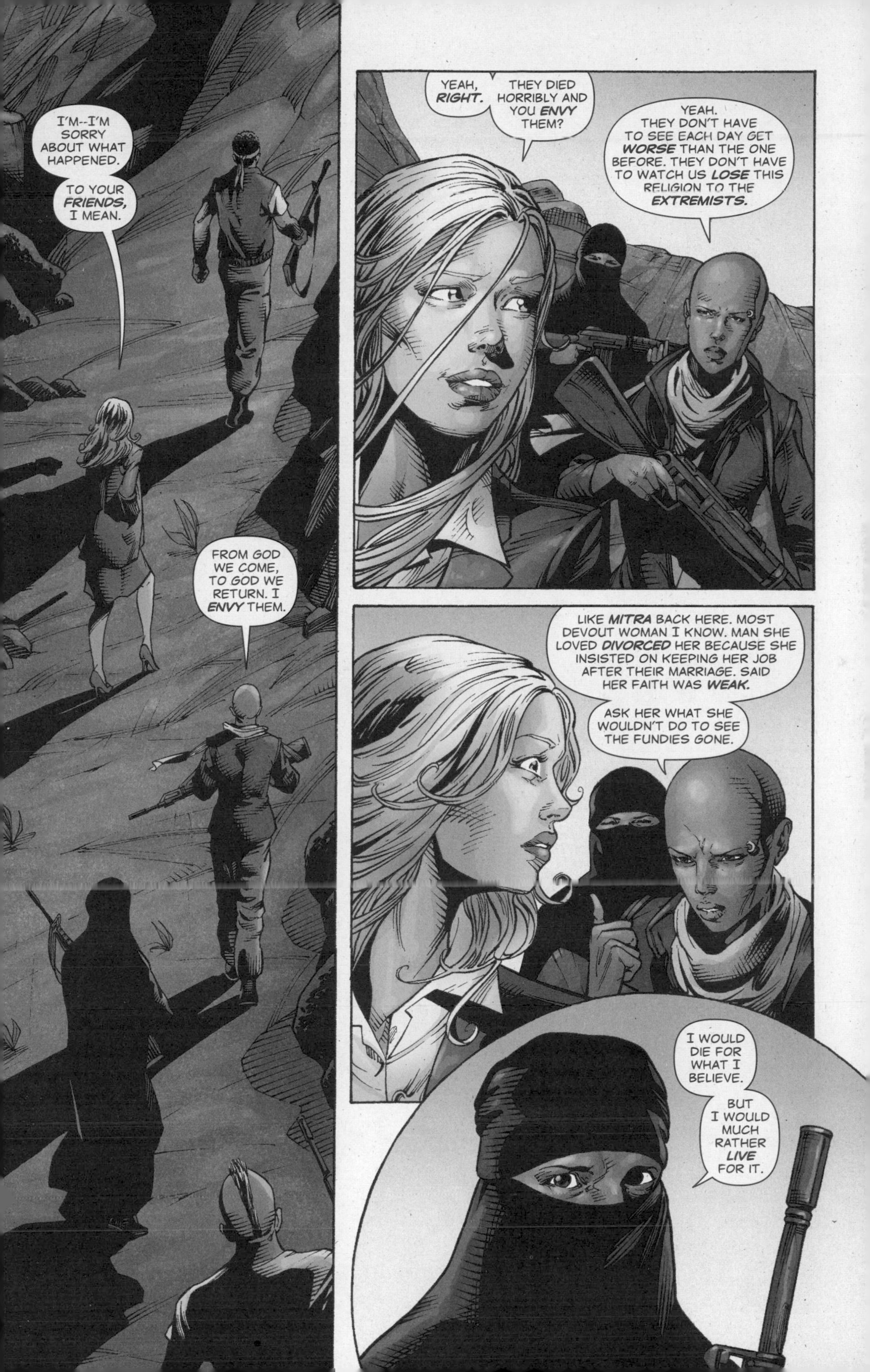

I'M--I'M SORRY ABOUT WHAT HAPPENED.
TO YOUR FRIENDS, I MEAN.
FROM GOD WE COME, TO GOD WE RETURN. I ENVY THEM.
YEAH, RIGHT.
THEY DIED HORRIBLY AND YOU ENVY THEM?
YEAH. THEY DON'T HAVE TO SEE EACH DAY GET WORSE THAN THE ONE BEFORE. THEY DON'T HAVE TO WATCH US LOSE THIS RELIGION TO THE EXTREMISTS.
LIKE MITRA BACK HERE. MOST DEVOUT WOMAN I KNOW. MAN SHE LOVED DIVORCED HER BECAUSE SHE INSISTED ON KEEPING HER JOB AFTER THEIR MARRIAGE. SAID HER FAITH WAS WEAK.
ASK HER WHAT SHE WOULDN'T DO TO SEE THE FUNDIES GONE.
I WOULD DIE FOR WHAT I BELIEVE.
BUT I WOULD MUCH RATHER LIVE FOR IT.

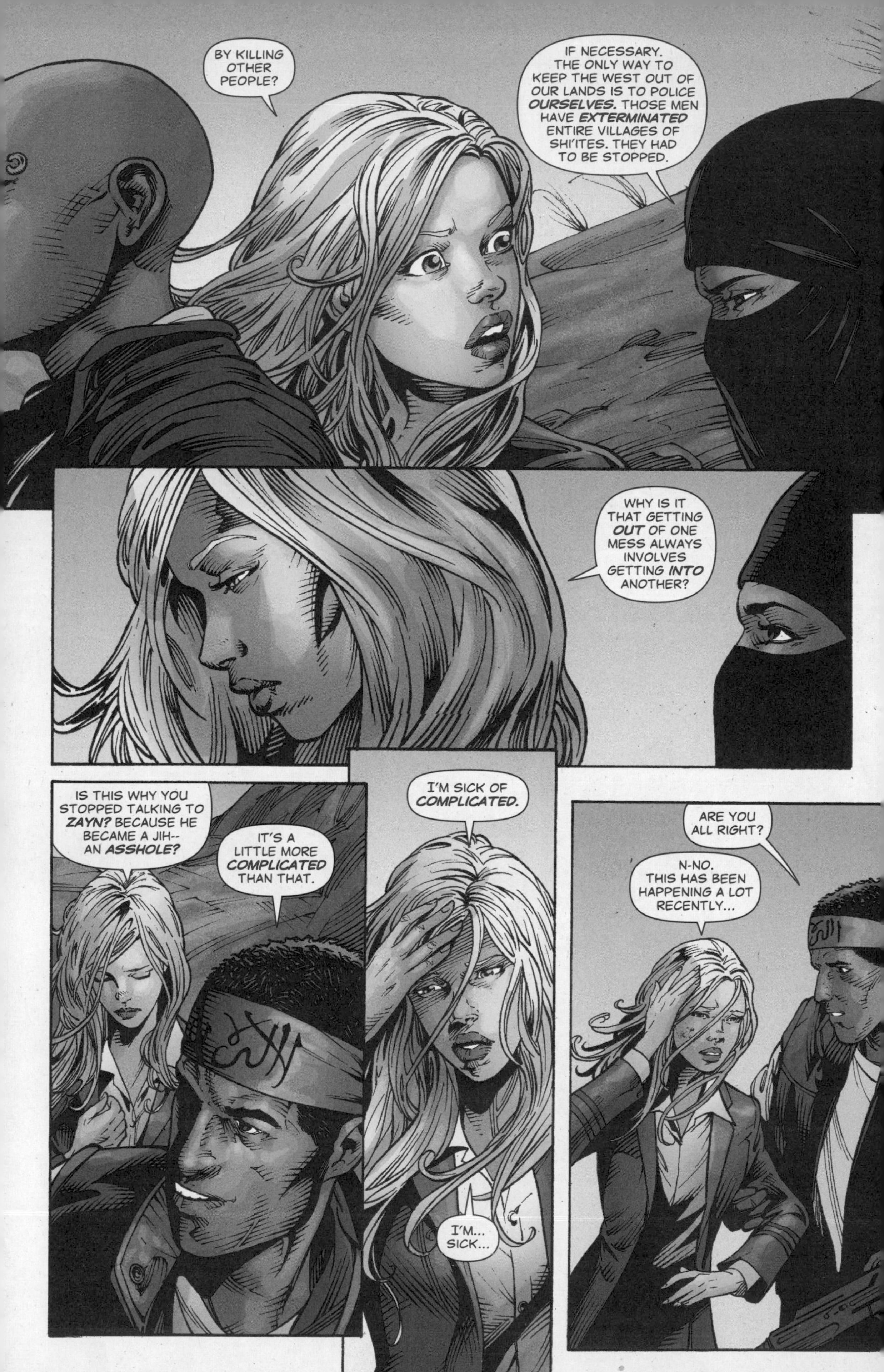
BY KILLING OTHER PEOPLE?
IF NECESSARY. THE ONLY WAY TO KEEP THE WEST OUT OF OUR LANDS IS TO POLICE OURSELVES. THOSE MEN HAVE EXTERMINATED ENTIRE VILLAGES OF SHI'ITES. THEY HAD TO BE STOPPED.
WHY IS IT THAT GETTING OUT OF ONE MESS ALWAYS INVOLVES GETTING INTO ANOTHER?
IS THIS WHY YOU STOPPED TALKING TO ZAYN? BECAUSE HE BECAME A JIH-- AN ASSHOLE?
IT'S A LITTLE MORE COMPLICATED THAN THAT.
I'M SICK OF COMPLICATED.
I'M... SICK...
ARE YOU ALL RIGHT?
N-NO. THIS HAS BEEN HAPPENING A LOT RECENTLY...

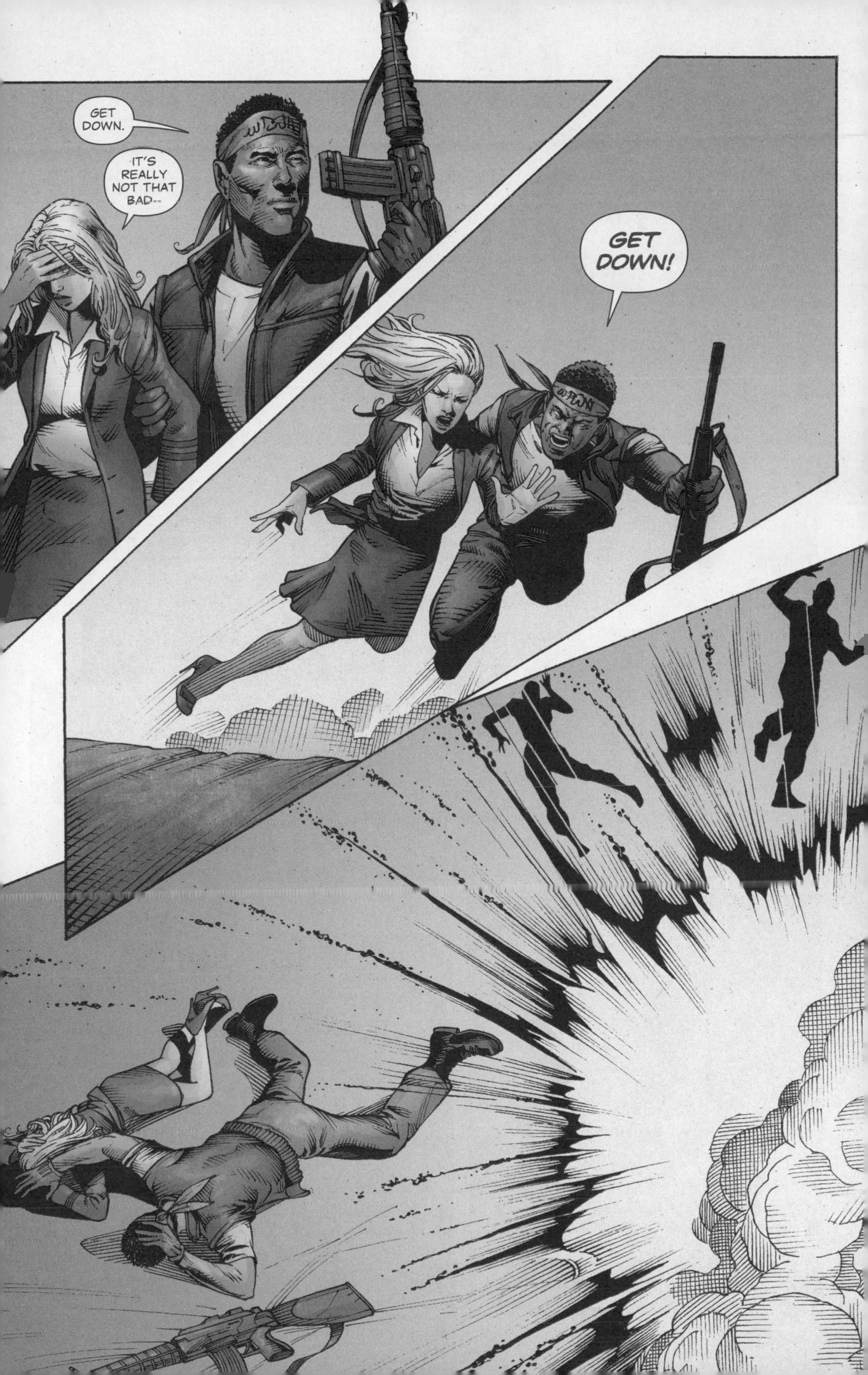
GET DOWN.
IT'S REALLY NOT THAT BAD--
GET DOWN!

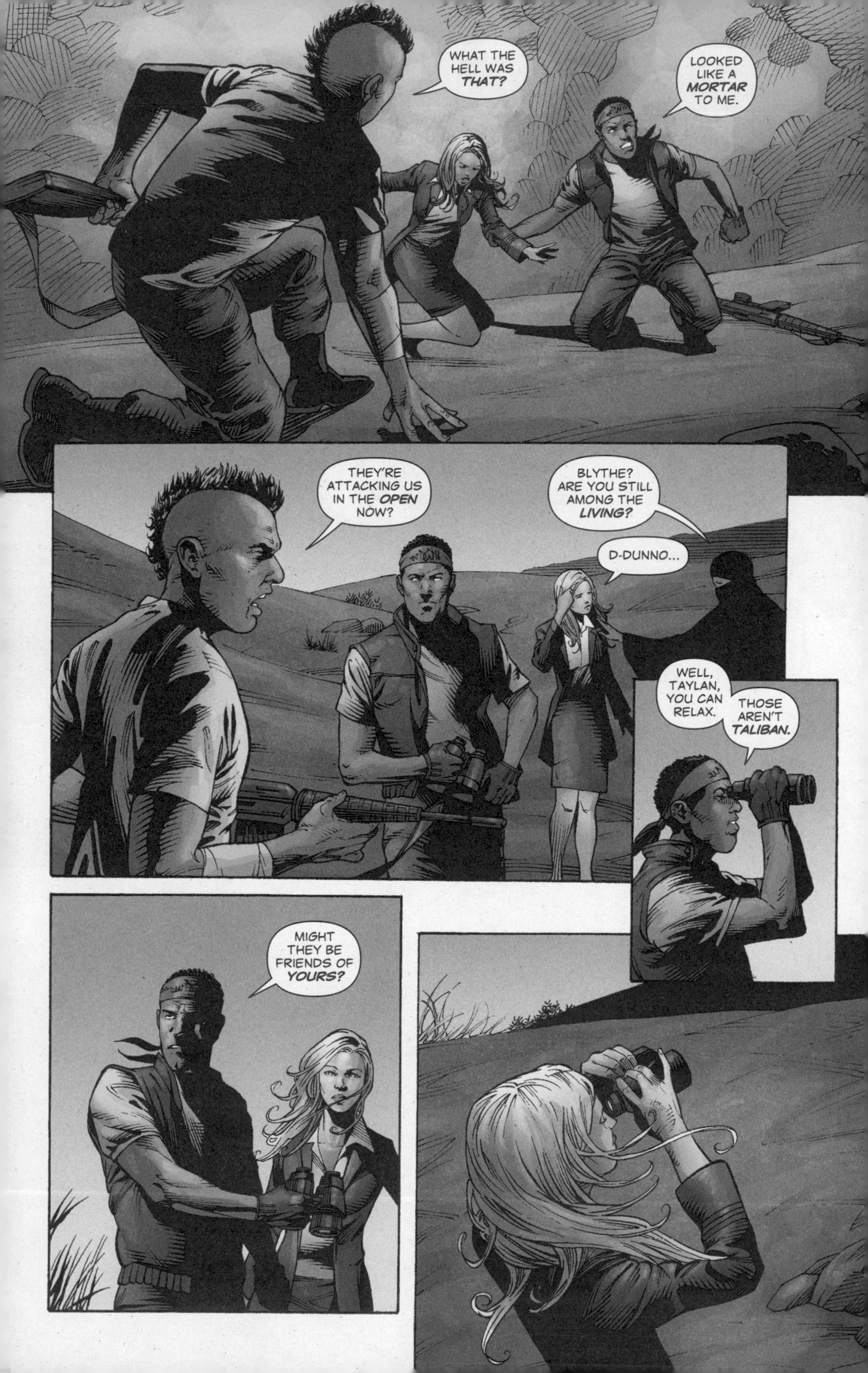
WHAT THE HELL WAS THAT?
LOOKED LIKE A MORTAR TO ME.
THEY'RE ATTACKING US IN THE OPEN NOW?
BLYTHE? ARE YOU STILL AMONG THE LIVING?
D-DUNNO...
WELL, TAYLAN, YOU CAN RELAX.
THOSE AREN'T TALIBAN.
MIGHT THEY BE FRIENDS OF YOURS?

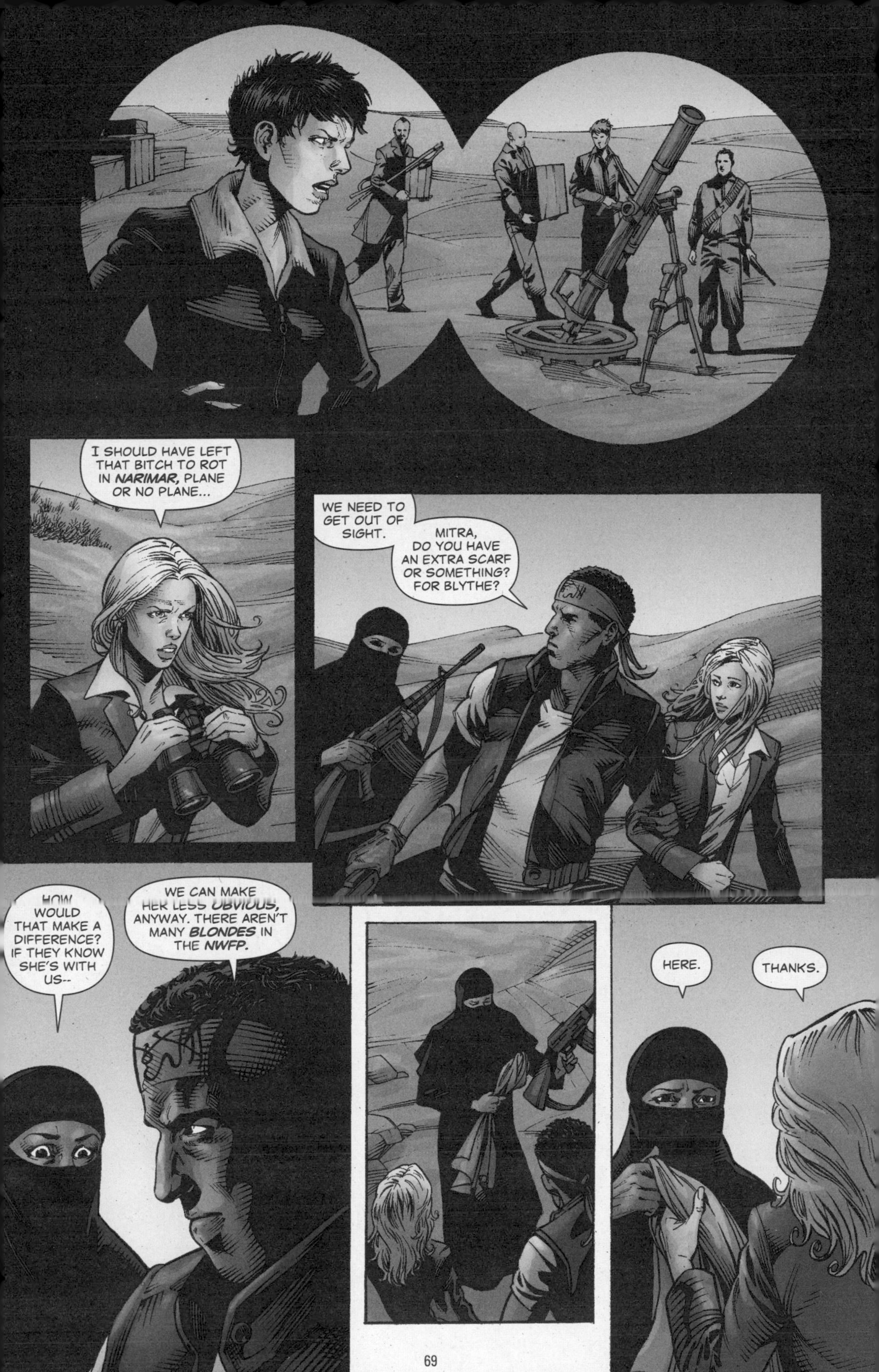
I SHOULD HAVE LEFT THAT BITCH TO ROT IN NARIMAR, PLANE OR NO PLANE...
WE NEED TO GET OUT OF SIGHT.
MITRA, DO YOU HAVE AN EXTRA SCARF OR SOMETHING? FOR BLYTHE?
HOW WOULD THAT MAKE A DIFFERENCE? IF THEY KNOW SHE'S WITH US--
WE CAN MAKE HER LESS OBVIOUS, ANYWAY. THERE AREN'T MANY BLONDES IN THE NWFP.
HERE.
THANKS.

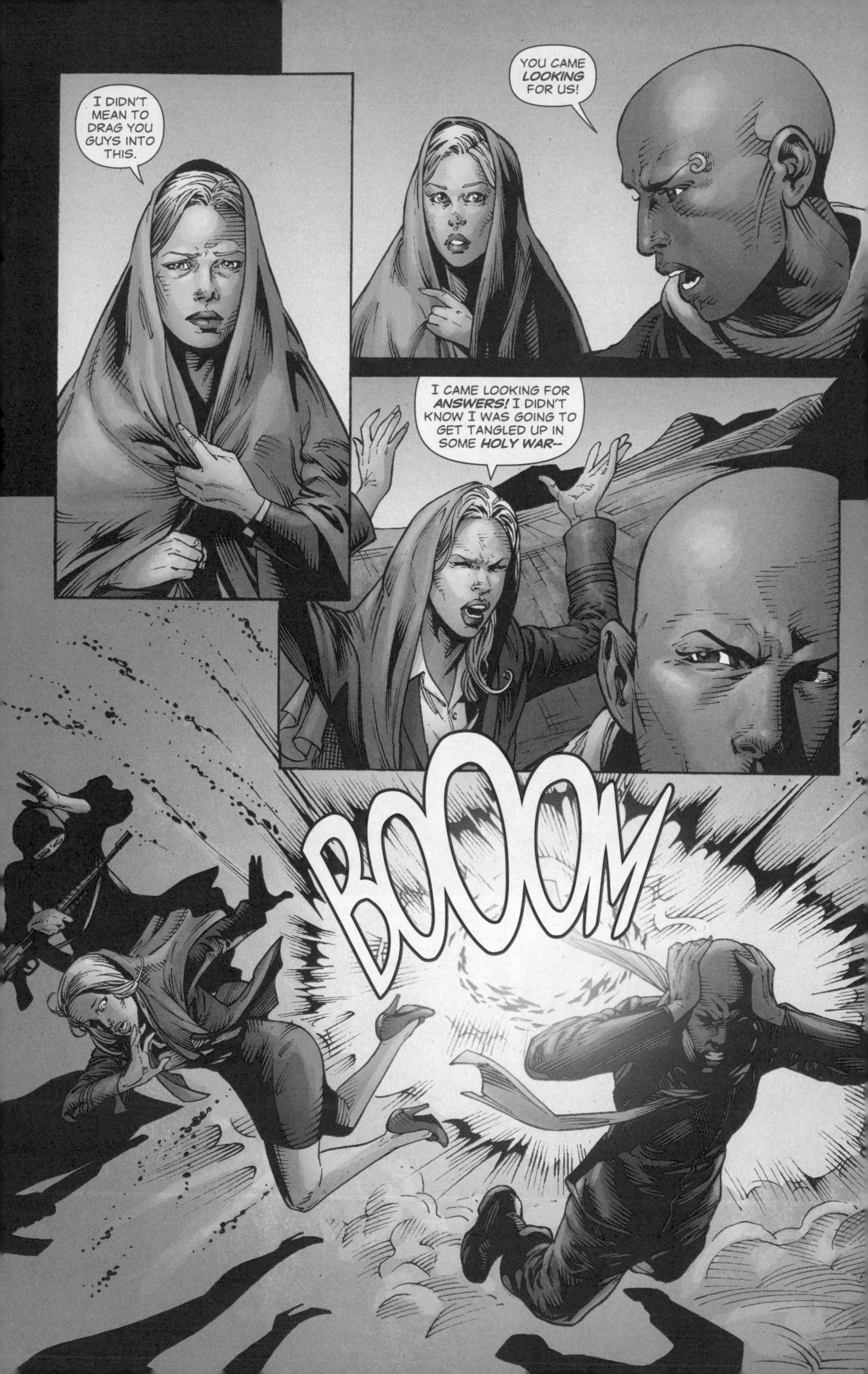
I DIDN'T MEAN TO DRAG YOU GUYS INTO THIS.
YOU CAME LOOKING FOR US!
I CAME LOOKING FOR ANSWERS! I DIDN'T KNOW I WAS GOING TO GET TANGLED UP IN SOME HOLY WAR--
BOOOM

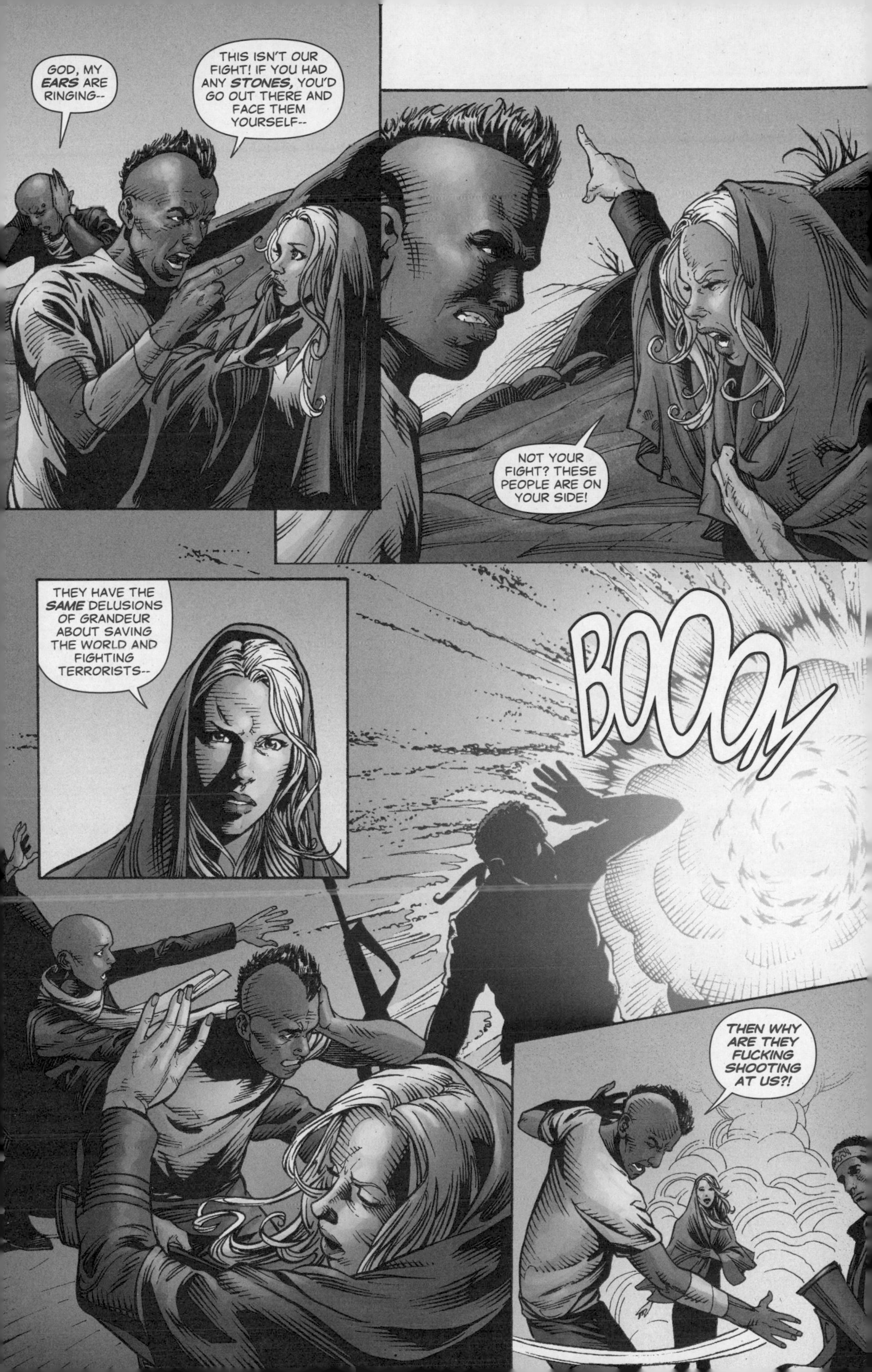
GOD, MY EARS ARE RINGING--
THIS ISN'T OUR FIGHT! IF YOU HAD ANY STONES, YOU'D GO OUT THERE AND FACE THEM YOURSELF--
NOT YOUR FIGHT? THESE PEOPLE ARE ON YOUR SIDE!
THEY HAVE THE SAME DELUSIONS OF GRANDEUR ABOUT SAVING THE WORLD AND FIGHTING TERRORISTS--
BOOOM
THEN WHY ARE THEY FUCKING SHOOTING AT US?!

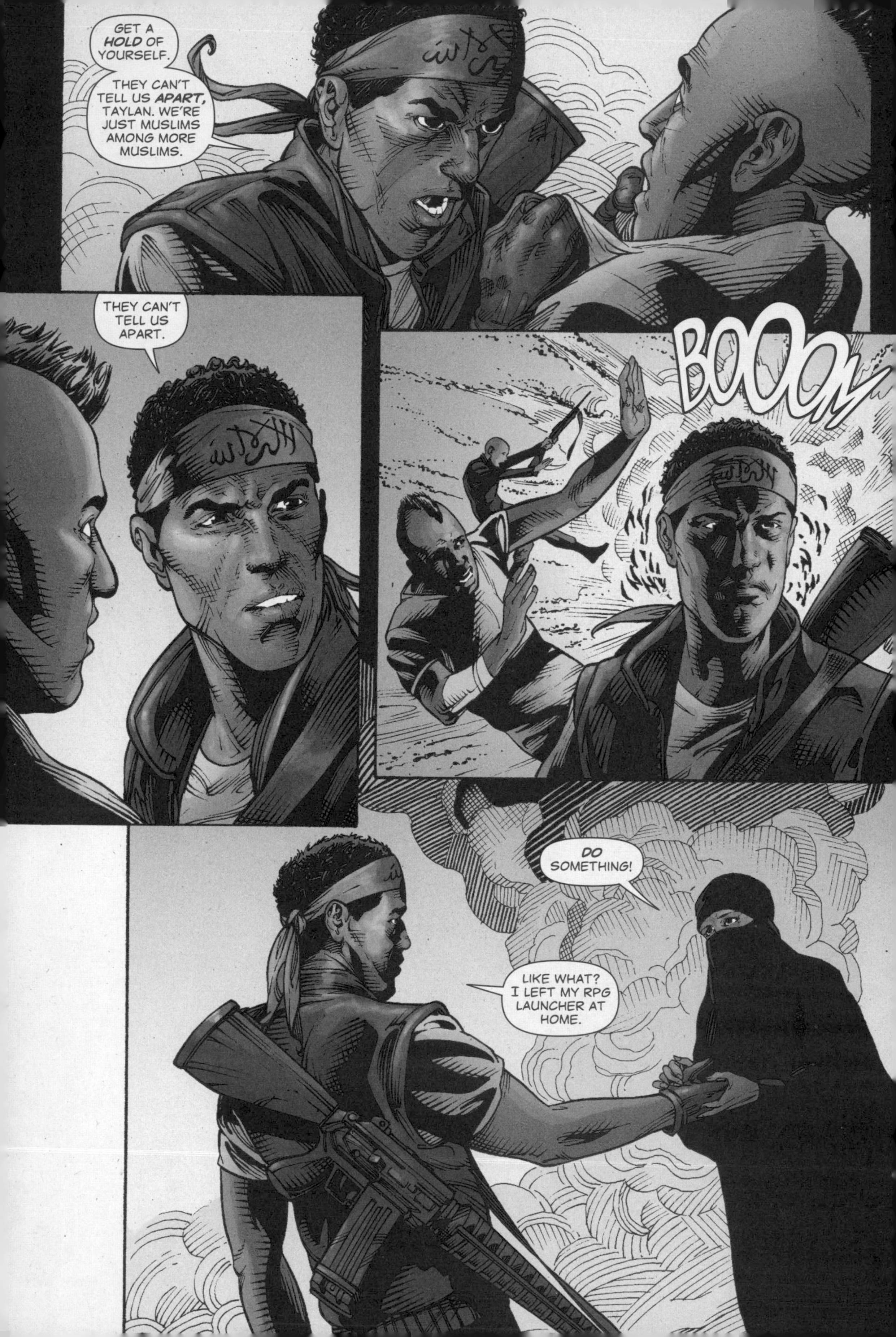
GET A HOLD OF YOURSELF.
THEY CAN'T TELL US APART, TAYLAN. WE'RE JUST MUSLIMS AMONG MORE MUSLIMS.
THEY CAN'T TELL US APART.
BOOOOM
DO SOMETHING!
LIKE WHAT? I LEFT MY RPG LAUNCHER AT HOME.

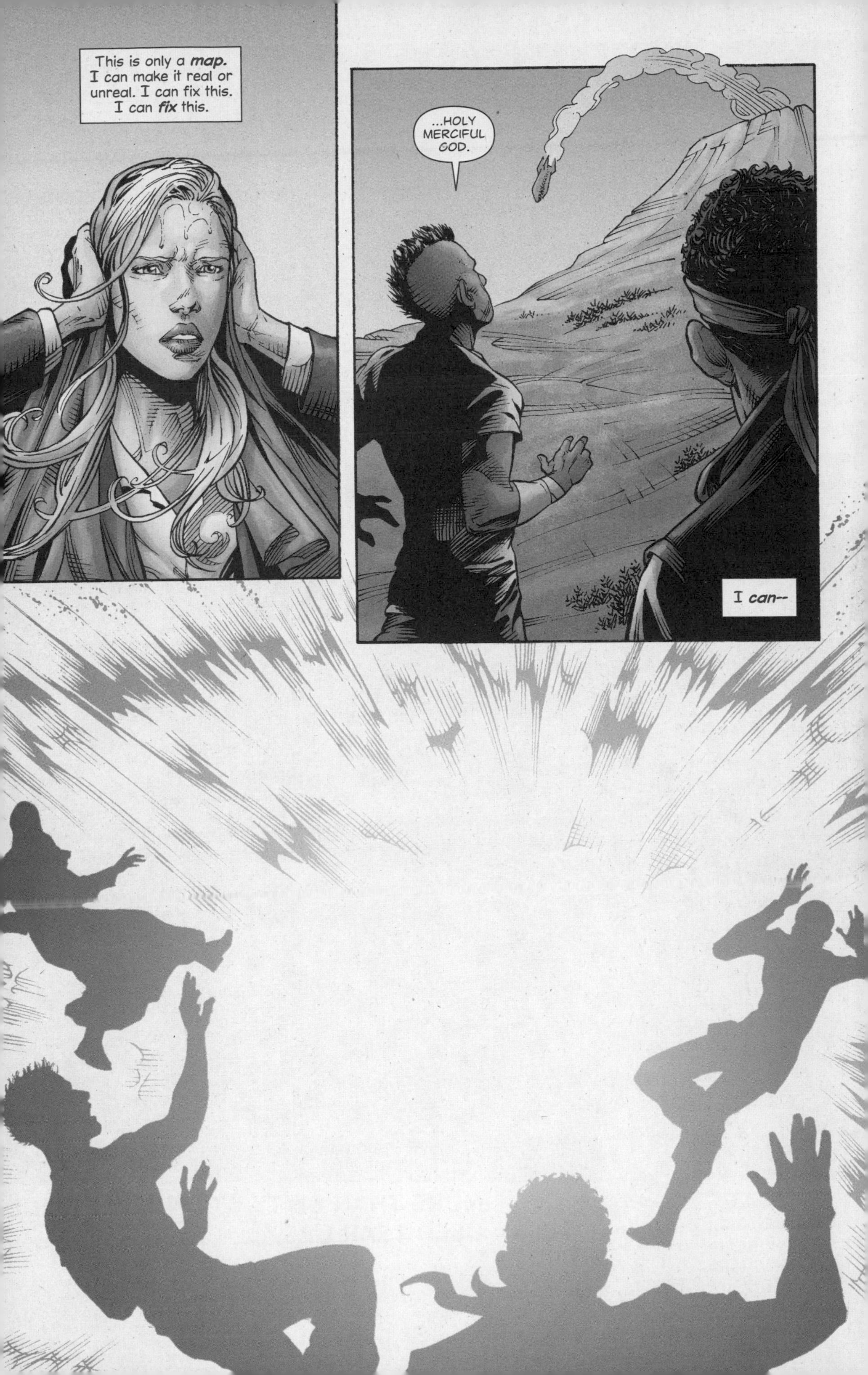
This is only a *map.* I can make it real or unreal. I can fix this. I can *fix* this.
...HOLY MERCIFUL GOD.
I *can*--

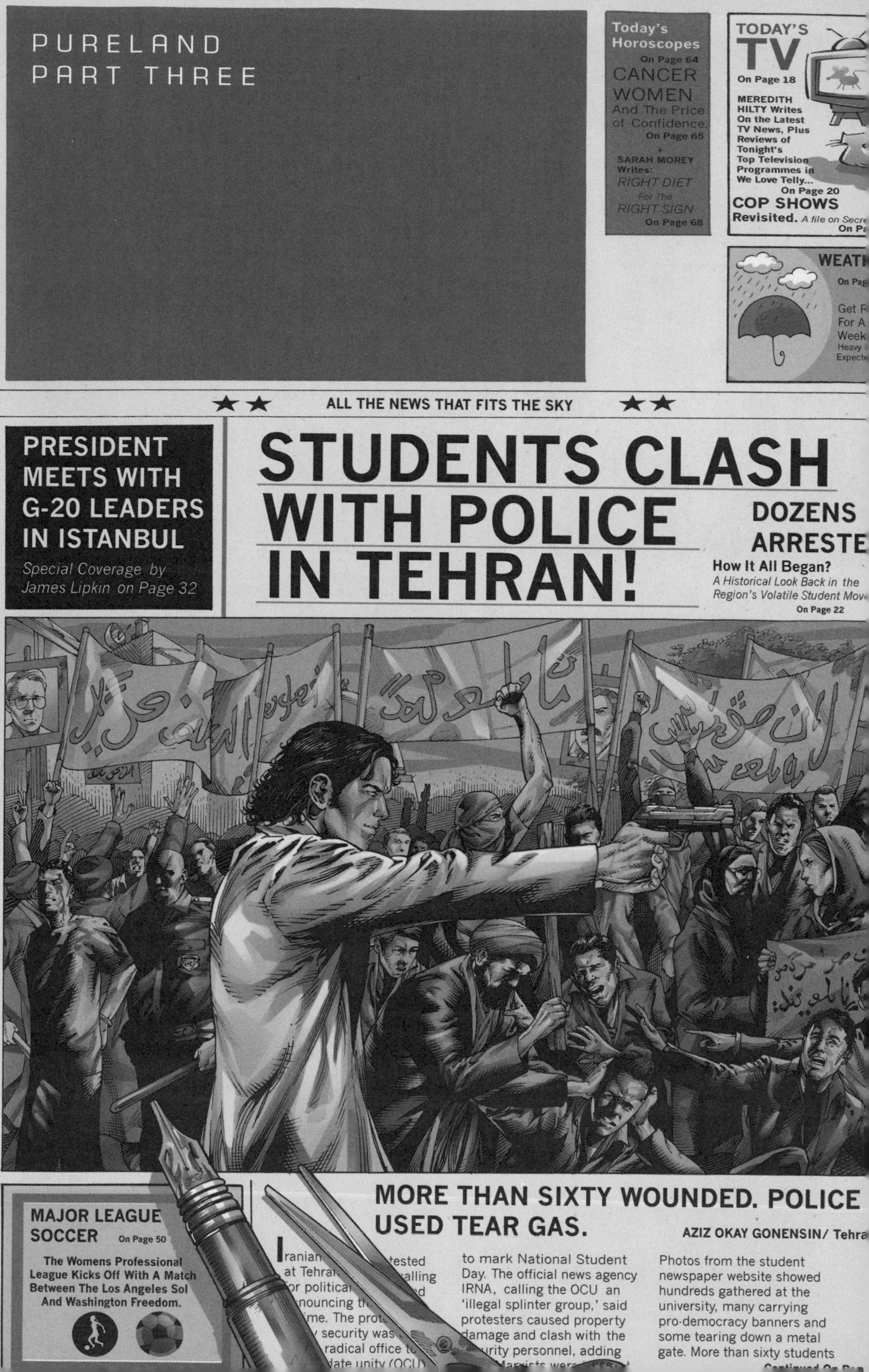

PURELAND
PART THREE
Today's Horoscopes
On Page 64
CANCER WOMEN
And The Price of Confidence.
On Page 65
+
SARAH MOREY Writes:
RIGHT DIET For The RIGHT SIGN
On Page 68
TODAY'S TV
On Page 18
MEREDITH HILTY Writes On the Latest TV News, Plus Reviews of Tonight's Top Television Programmes in We Love Telly...
On Page 20
COP SHOWS Revisited.
ALL THE NEWS THAT FITS THE SKY
PRESIDENT MEETS WITH G-20 LEADERS IN ISTANBUL
Special Coverage by James Lipkin on Page 32
STUDENTS CLASH WITH POLICE IN TEHRAN!
DOZENS
How It All Began?
A Historical Look Back in the
On Page 22
MAJOR LEAGUE SOCCER
On Page 50
The Womens Professional League Kicks Off With A Match Between The Los Angeles Sol And Washington Freedom.
MORE THAN SIXTY WOUNDED. POLICE USED TEAR GAS.
to mark National Student Day. The official news agency IRNA, calling the OCU an 'illegal splinter group,' said protesters caused property damage and clash with the
Photos from the student newspaper website showed hundreds gathered at the university, many carrying pro-democracy banners and some tearing down a metal gate. More than sixty students

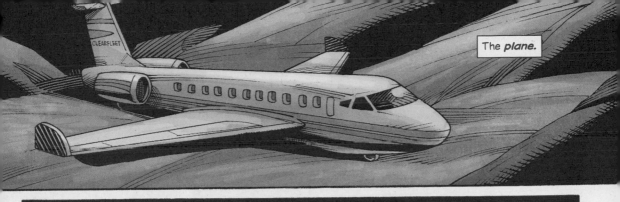

The *plane.*

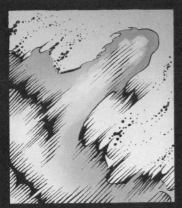

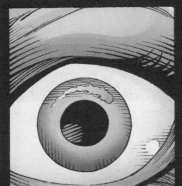

I make myself *see* it.

The *engine* is huddled inside, sleeping--

But if I can wake it up--

Fast--

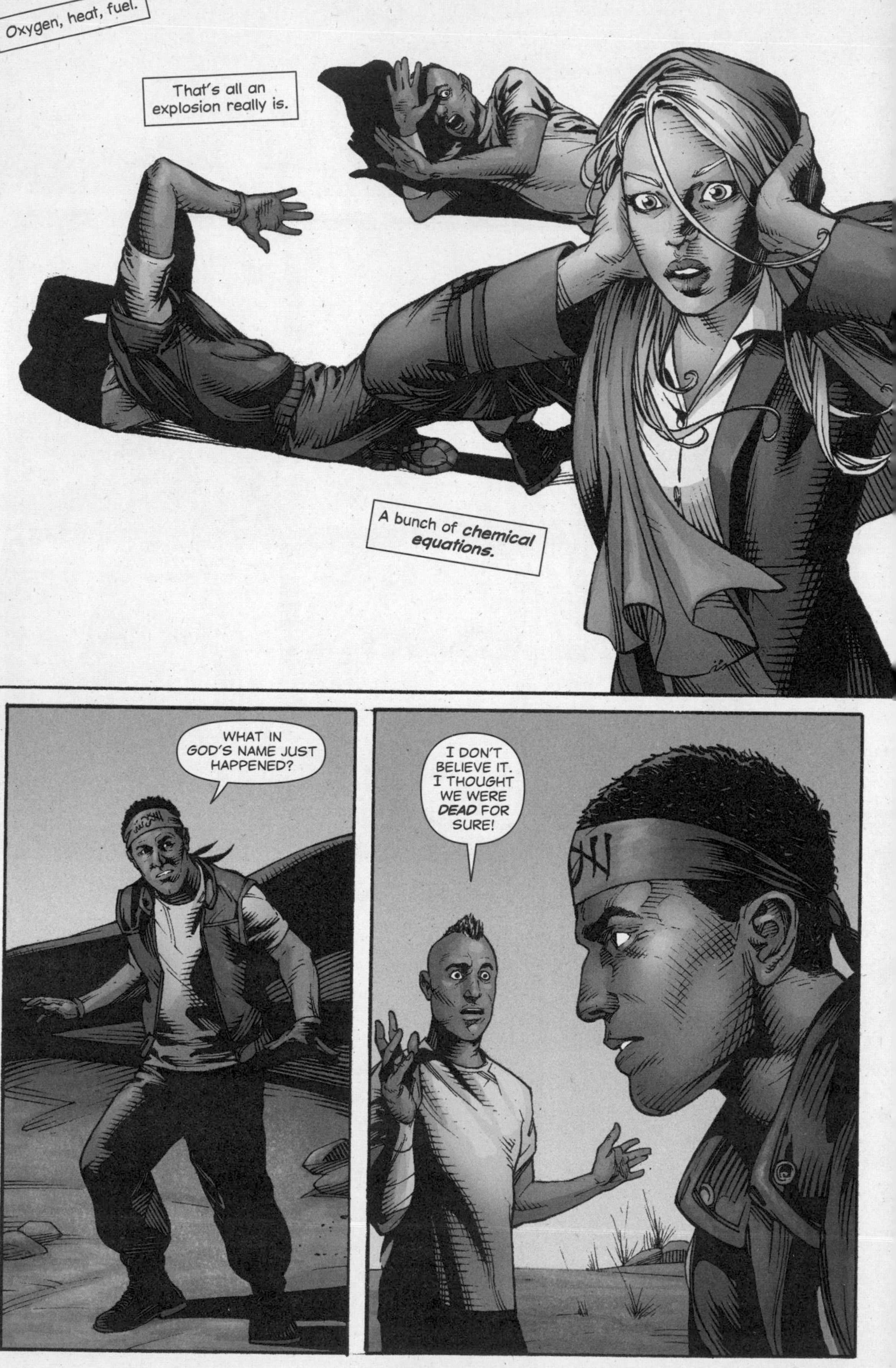

Oxygen, heat, fuel.
That's all an explosion really is.
A bunch of chemical equations.
WHAT IN GOD'S NAME JUST HAPPENED?
I DON'T BELIEVE IT. I THOUGHT WE WERE DEAD FOR SURE!

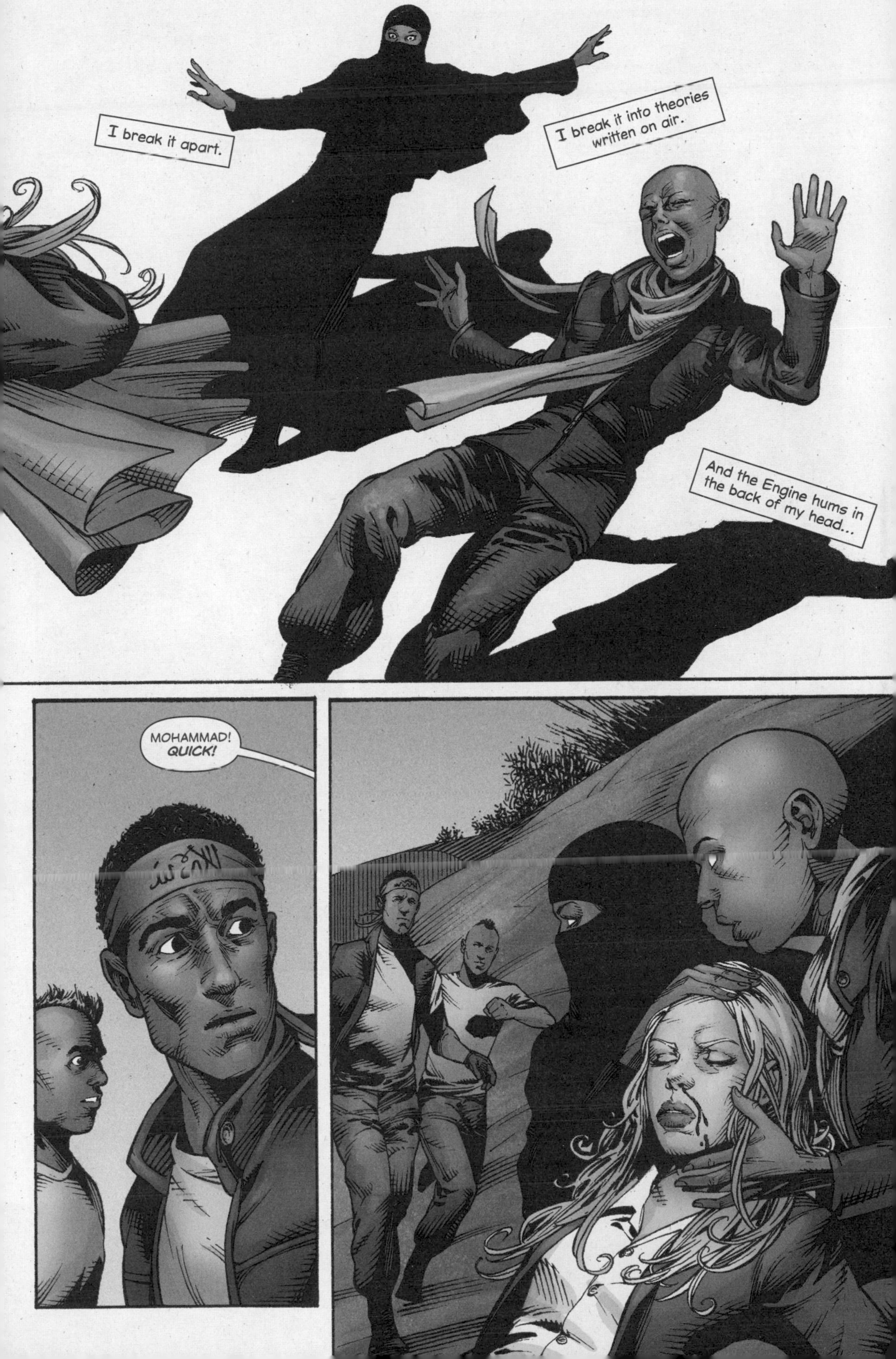
I break it apart.
I break it into theories written on air.
And the Engine hums in the back of my head...
MOHAMMAD! QUICK!

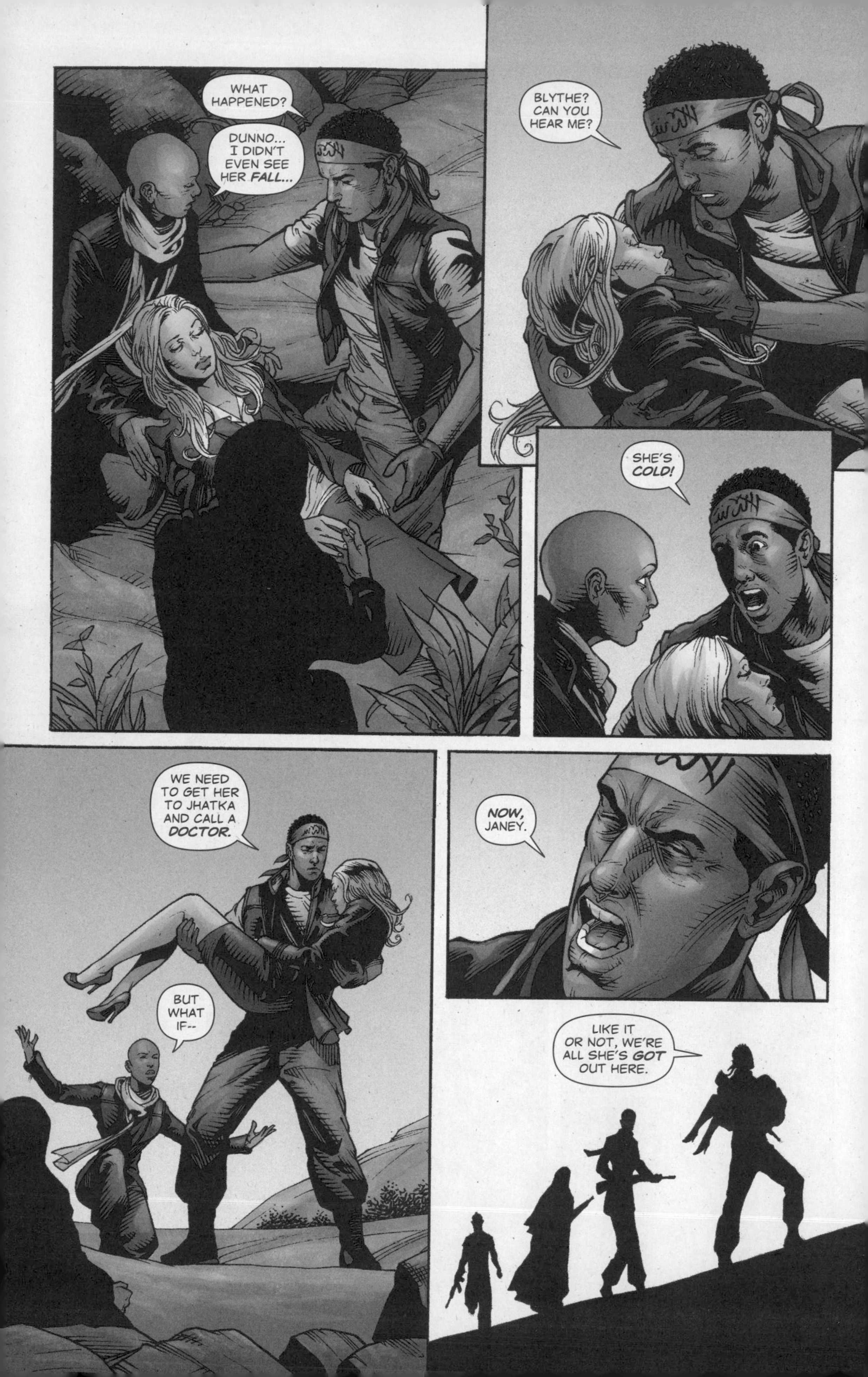
WHAT HAPPENED?
DUNNO... I DIDN'T EVEN SEE HER FALL...
BLYTHE? CAN YOU HEAR ME?
SHE'S COLD!
WE NEED TO GET HER TO JHATKA AND CALL A DOCTOR.
BUT WHAT IF--
NOW, JANEY.
LIKE IT OR NOT, WE'RE ALL SHE'S GOT OUT HERE.

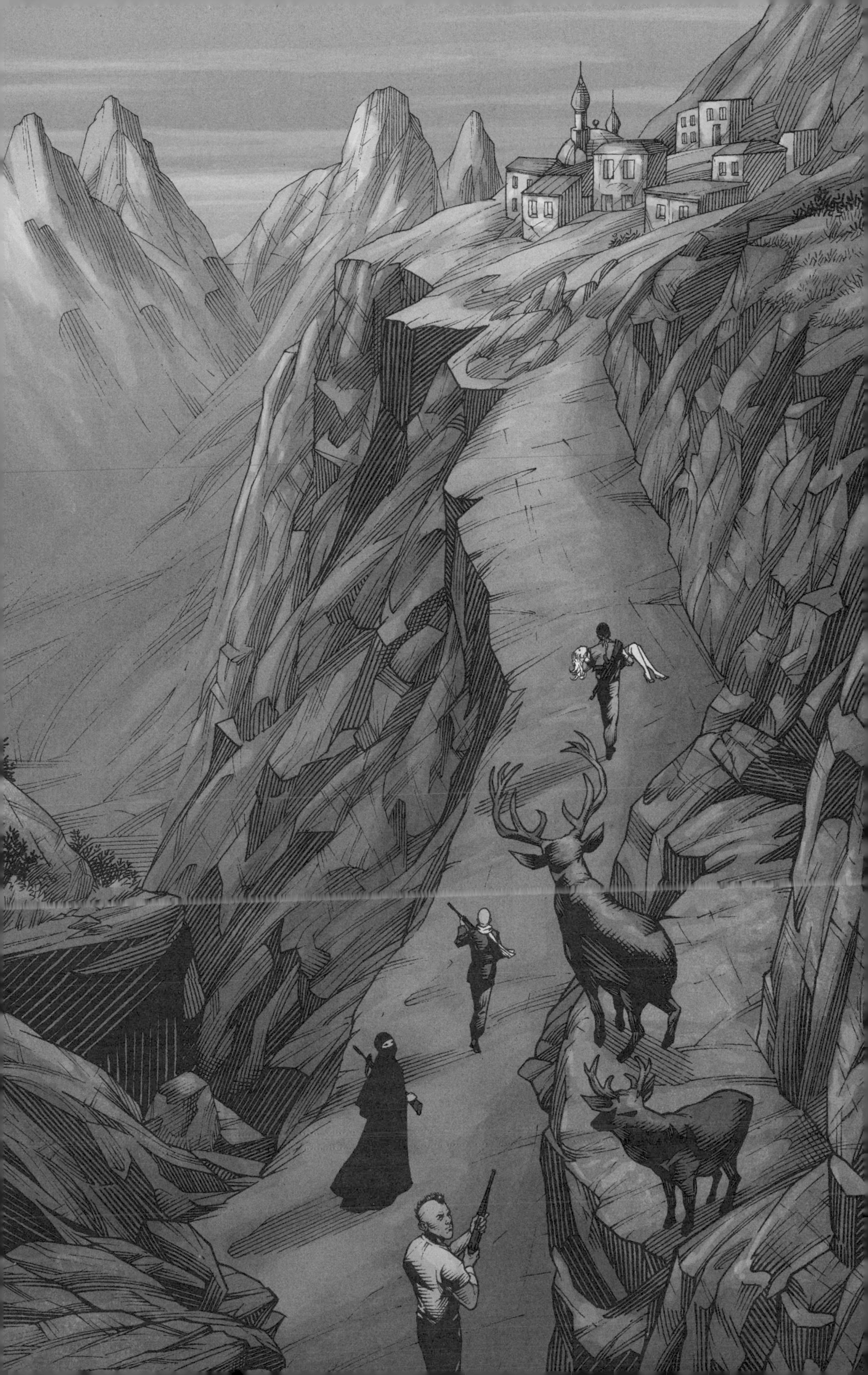

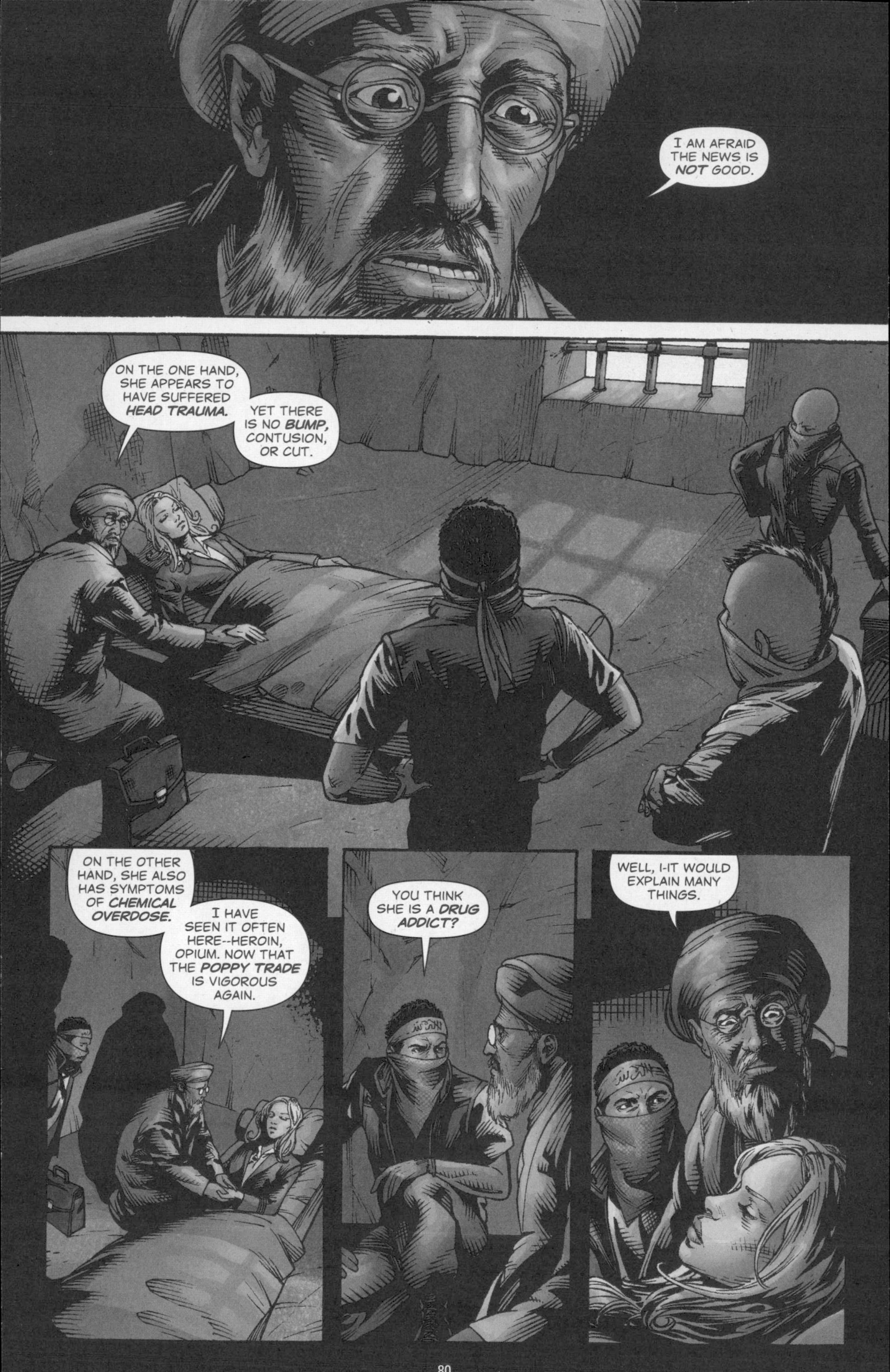
I AM AFRAID THE NEWS IS NOT GOOD.
ON THE ONE HAND, SHE APPEARS TO HAVE SUFFERED HEAD TRAUMA.
YET THERE IS NO BUMP, CONTUSION, OR CUT.
ON THE OTHER HAND, SHE ALSO HAS SYMPTOMS OF CHEMICAL OVERDOSE.
I HAVE SEEN IT OFTEN HERE--HEROIN, OPIUM. NOW THAT THE POPPY TRADE IS VIGOROUS AGAIN.
YOU THINK SHE IS A DRUG ADDICT?
WELL, I-IT WOULD EXPLAIN MANY THINGS.

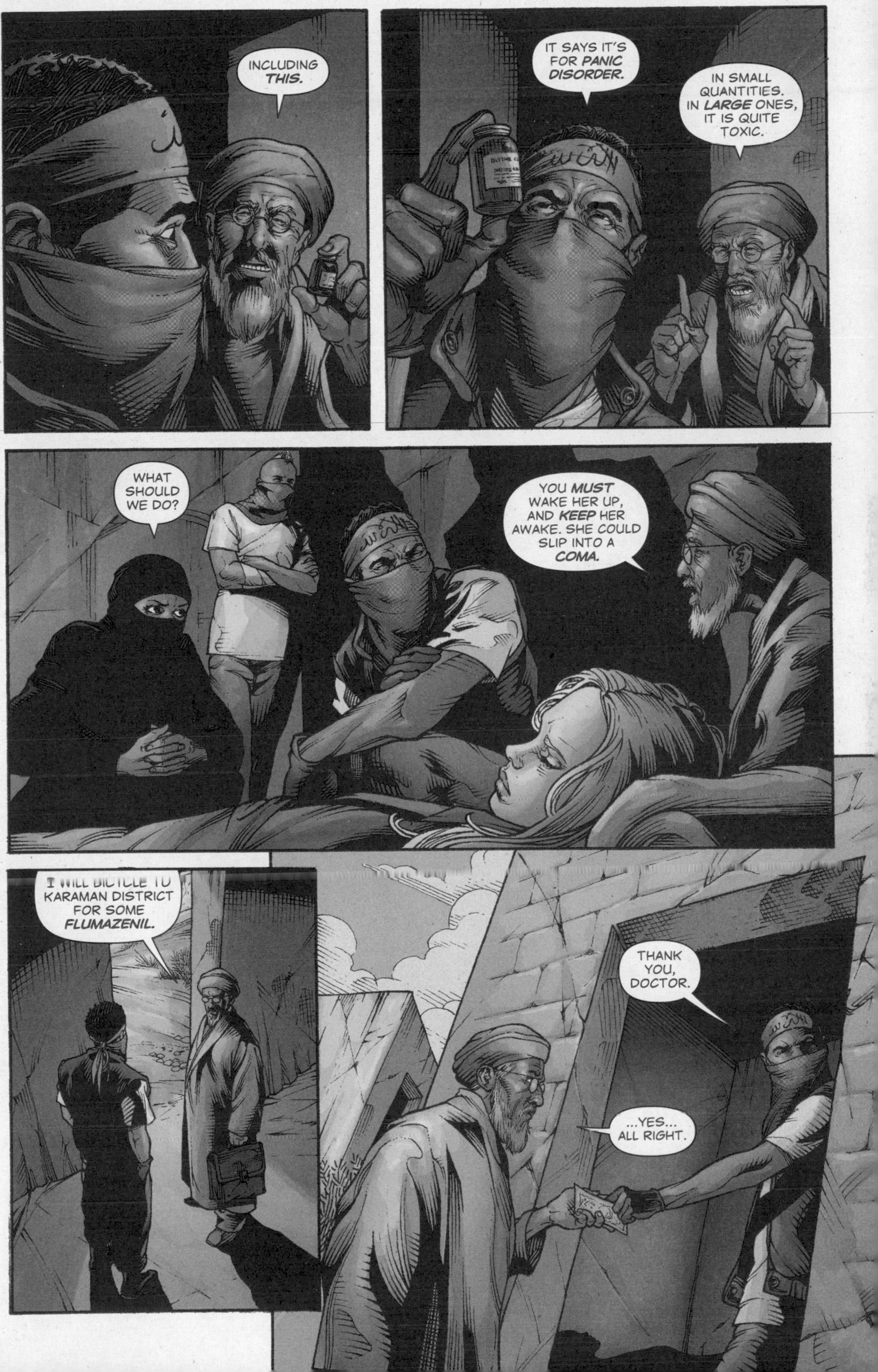
INCLUDING THIS.
IT SAYS IT'S FOR PANIC DISORDER.
IN SMALL QUANTITIES. IN LARGE ONES, IT IS QUITE TOXIC.
WHAT SHOULD WE DO?
YOU MUST WAKE HER UP, AND KEEP HER AWAKE. SHE COULD SLIP INTO A COMA.
I WILL BICYCLE TO KARAMAN DISTRICT FOR SOME FLUMAZENIL.
THANK YOU, DOCTOR.
...YES... ALL RIGHT.

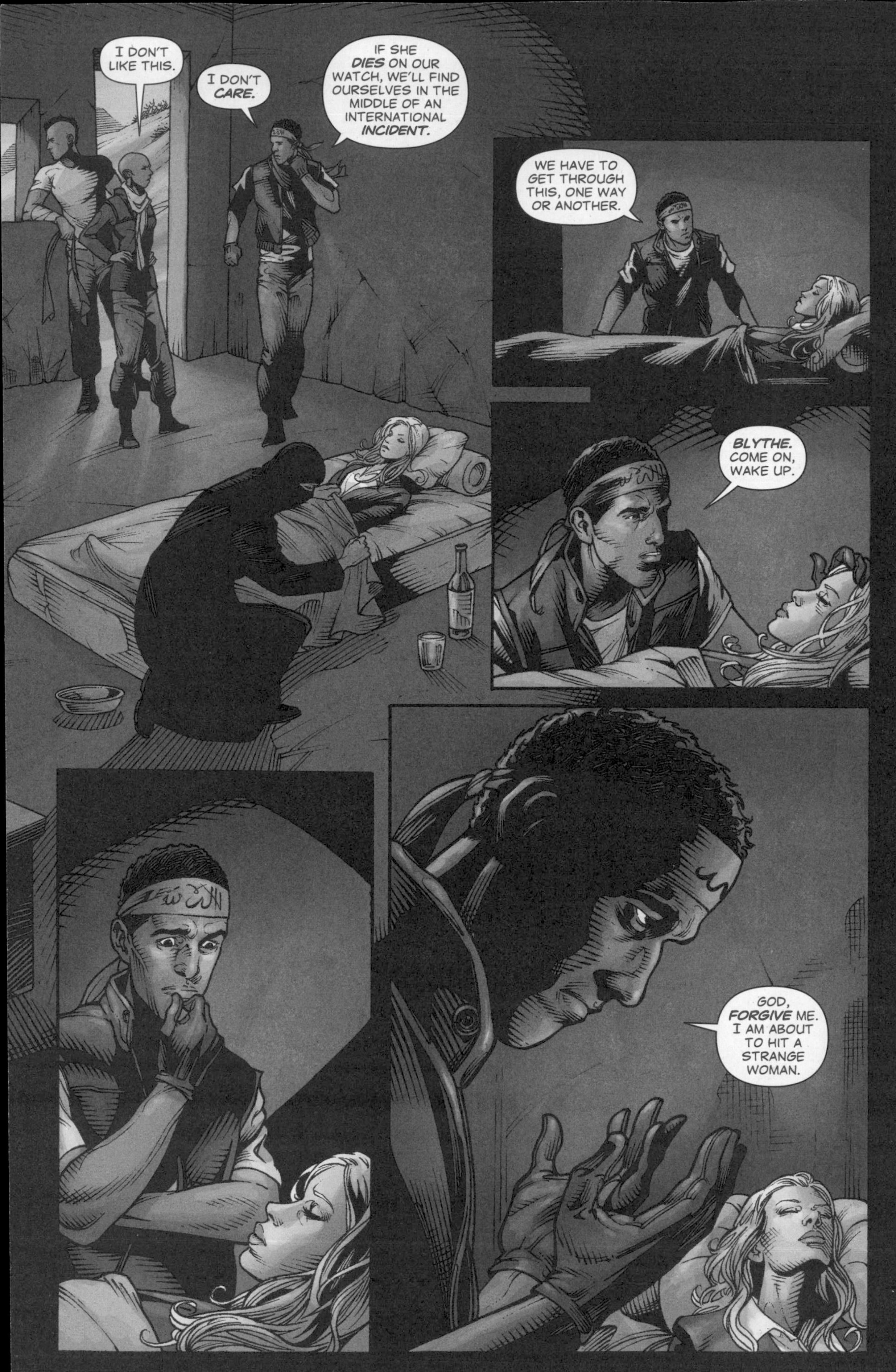
I DON'T LIKE THIS.
I DON'T CARE.
IF SHE DIES ON OUR WATCH, WE'LL FIND OURSELVES IN THE MIDDLE OF AN INTERNATIONAL INCIDENT.
WE HAVE TO GET THROUGH THIS, ONE WAY OR ANOTHER.
BLYTHE. COME ON, WAKE UP.
GOD, FORGIVE ME. I AM ABOUT TO HIT A STRANGE WOMAN.

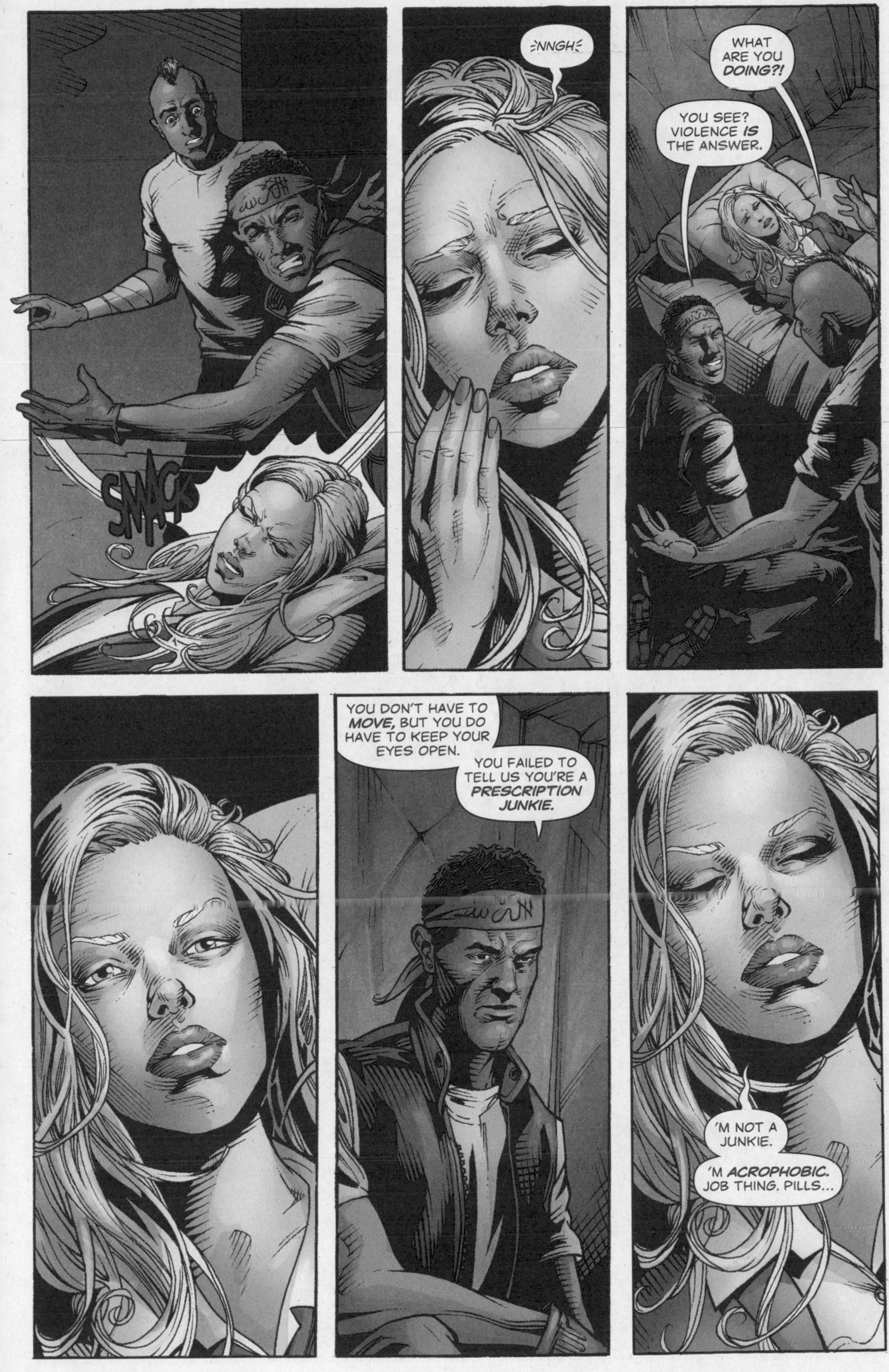
SMACK
NNGH
WHAT ARE YOU DOING?!
YOU SEE? VIOLENCE IS THE ANSWER.
YOU DON'T HAVE TO MOVE, BUT YOU DO HAVE TO KEEP YOUR EYES OPEN.
YOU FAILED TO TELL US YOU'RE A PRESCRIPTION JUNKIE.
'M NOT A JUNKIE.
'M ACROPHOBIC. JOB THING. PILLS...

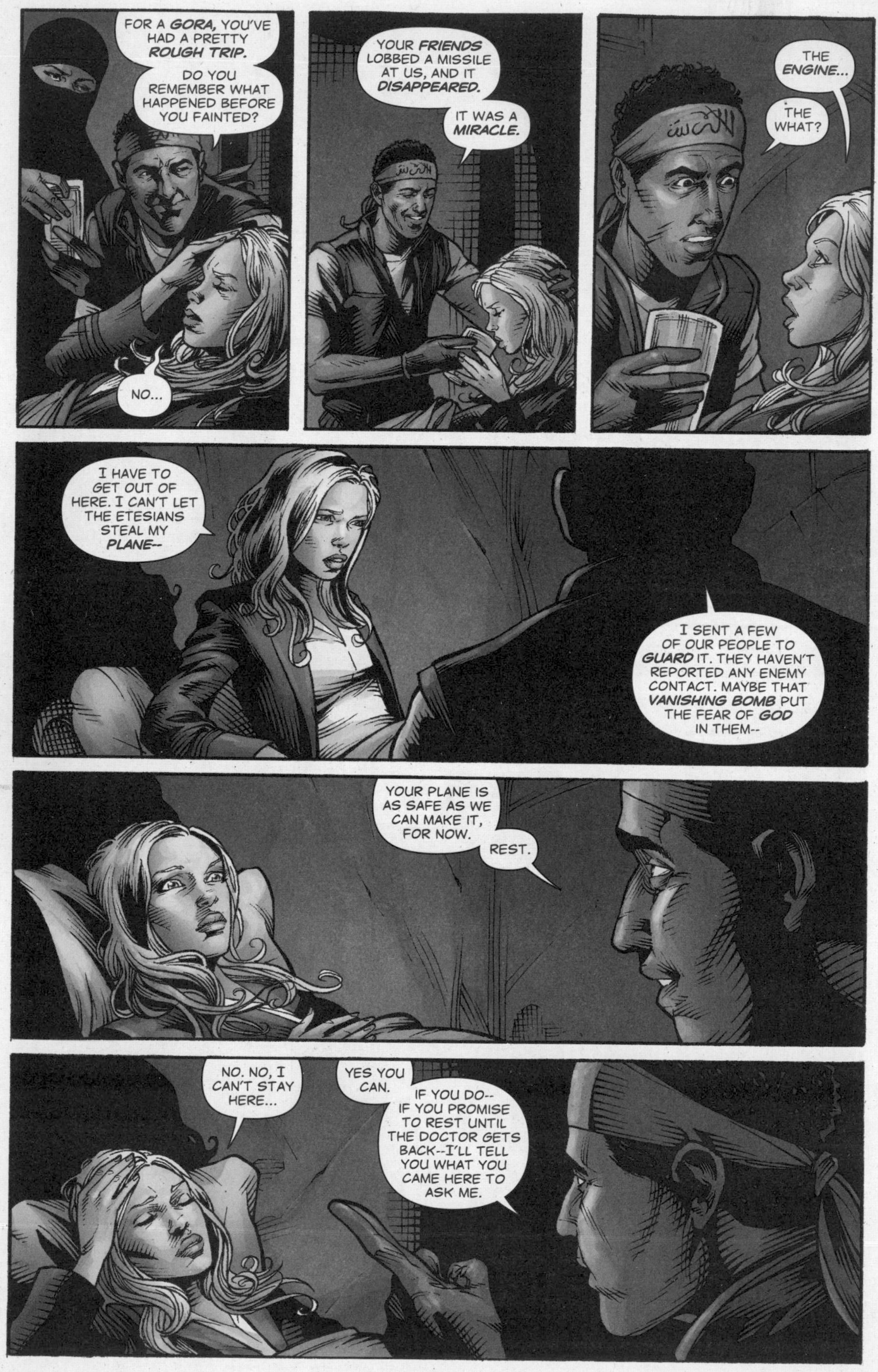

FOR A GORA, YOU'VE HAD A PRETTY ROUGH TRIP.
DO YOU REMEMBER WHAT HAPPENED BEFORE YOU FAINTED?
NO...
YOUR FRIENDS LOBBED A MISSILE AT US, AND IT DISAPPEARED.
IT WAS A MIRACLE.
THE ENGINE...
THE WHAT?
I HAVE TO GET OUT OF HERE. I CAN'T LET THE ETESIANS STEAL MY PLANE--
I SENT A FEW OF OUR PEOPLE TO GUARD IT. THEY HAVEN'T REPORTED ANY ENEMY CONTACT. MAYBE THAT VANISHING BOMB PUT THE FEAR OF GOD IN THEM--
YOUR PLANE IS AS SAFE AS WE CAN MAKE IT, FOR NOW.
REST.
NO. NO, I CAN'T STAY HERE...
YES YOU CAN.
IF YOU DO-- IF YOU PROMISE TO REST UNTIL THE DOCTOR GETS BACK--I'LL TELL YOU WHAT YOU CAME HERE TO ASK ME.

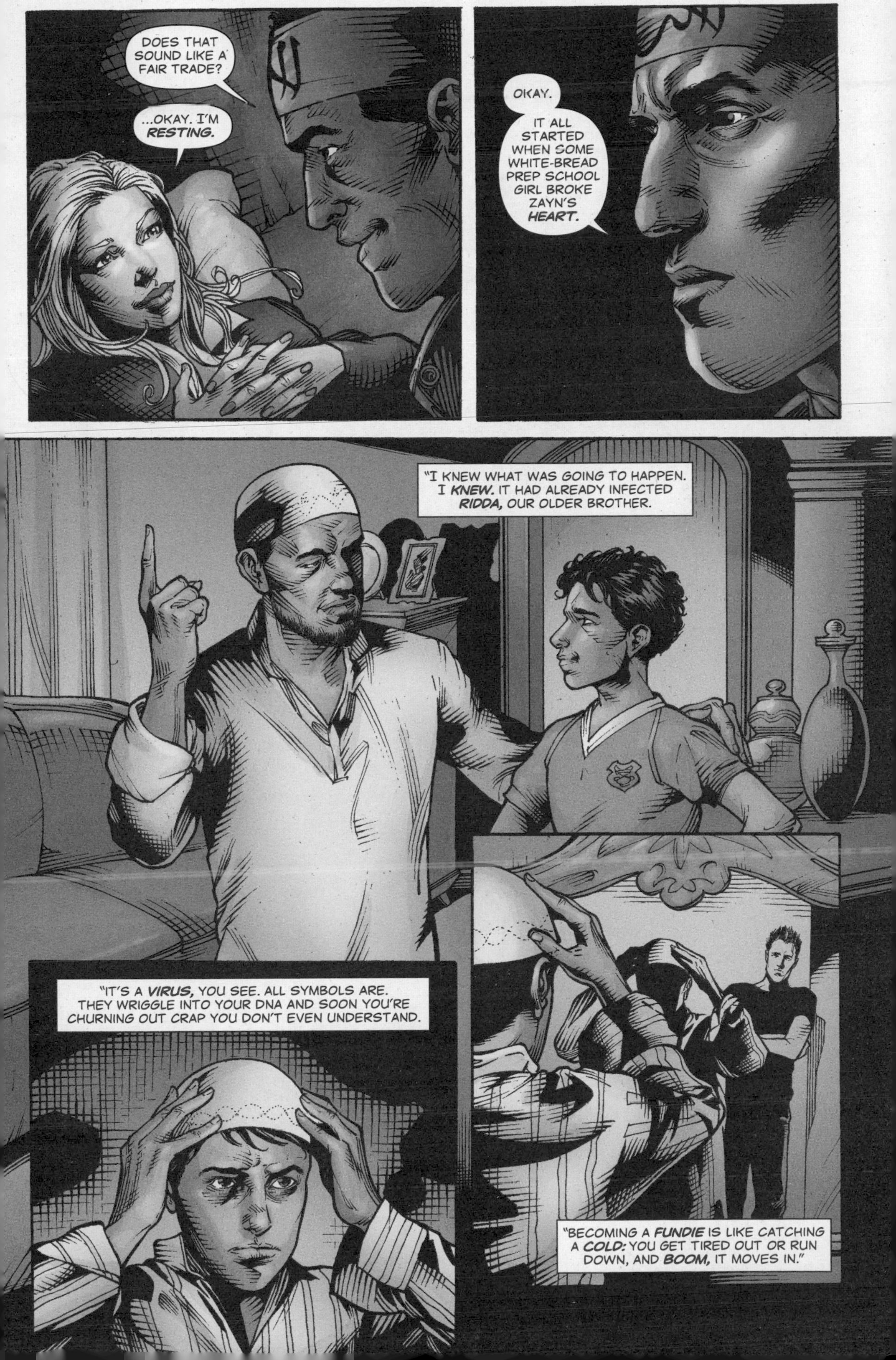
DOES THAT SOUND LIKE A FAIR TRADE?
...OKAY. I'M RESTING.
OKAY.
IT ALL STARTED WHEN SOME WHITE-BREAD PREP SCHOOL GIRL BROKE ZAYN'S HEART.
"I KNEW WHAT WAS GOING TO HAPPEN. I KNEW. IT HAD ALREADY INFECTED RIDDA, OUR OLDER BROTHER.
"IT'S A VIRUS, YOU SEE. ALL SYMBOLS ARE. THEY WRIGGLE INTO YOUR DNA AND SOON YOU'RE CHURNING OUT CRAP YOU DON'T EVEN UNDERSTAND.
"BECOMING A FUNDIE IS LIKE CATCHING A COLD: YOU GET TIRED OUT OR RUN DOWN, AND BOOM, IT MOVES IN."

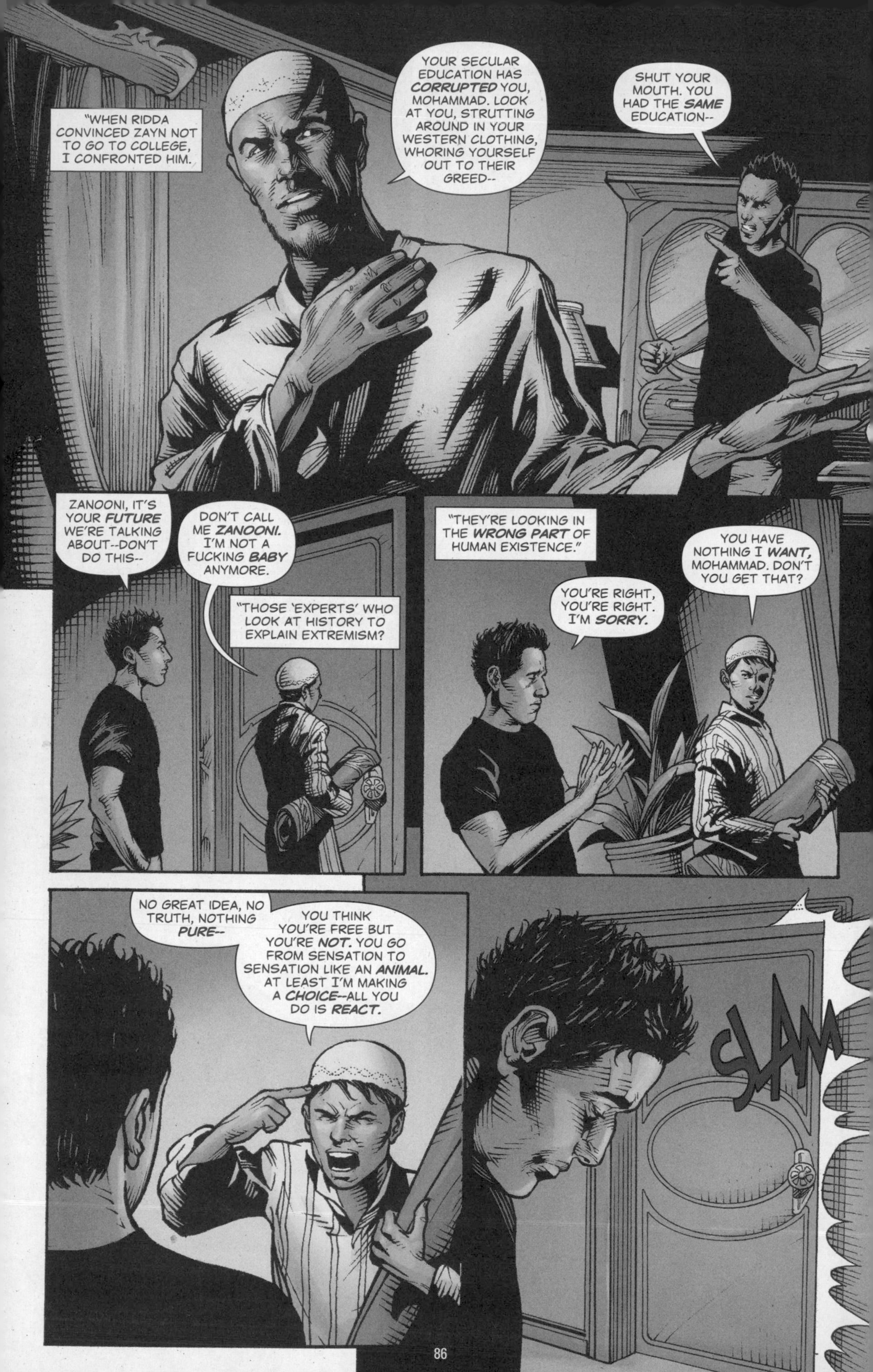
"WHEN RIDDA CONVINCED ZAYN NOT TO GO TO COLLEGE, I CONFRONTED HIM.
YOUR SECULAR EDUCATION HAS CORRUPTED YOU, MOHAMMAD. LOOK AT YOU, STRUTTING AROUND IN YOUR WESTERN CLOTHING, WHORING YOURSELF OUT TO THEIR GREED--
SHUT YOUR MOUTH. YOU HAD THE SAME EDUCATION--
ZANOONI, IT'S YOUR FUTURE WE'RE TALKING ABOUT--DON'T DO THIS--
DON'T CALL ME ZANOONI. I'M NOT A FUCKING BABY ANYMORE.
"THOSE 'EXPERTS' WHO LOOK AT HISTORY TO EXPLAIN EXTREMISM?
"THEY'RE LOOKING IN THE WRONG PART OF HUMAN EXISTENCE."
YOU'RE RIGHT, YOU'RE RIGHT. I'M SORRY.
YOU HAVE NOTHING I WANT, MOHAMMAD. DON'T YOU GET THAT?
NO GREAT IDEA, NO TRUTH, NOTHING PURE--
YOU THINK YOU'RE FREE BUT YOU'RE NOT. YOU GO FROM SENSATION TO SENSATION LIKE AN ANIMAL. AT LEAST I'M MAKING A CHOICE--ALL YOU DO IS REACT.
SLAM

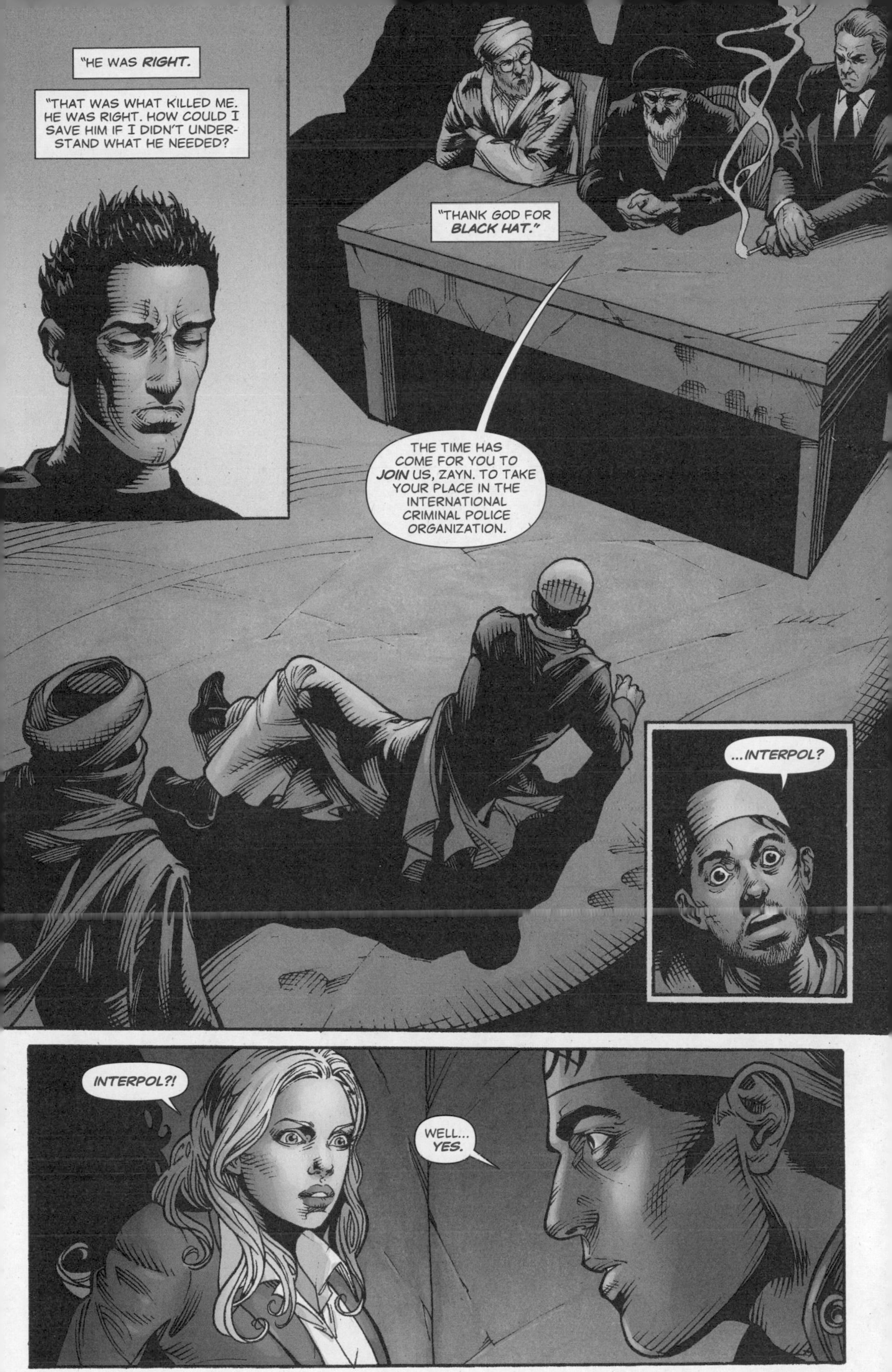
"HE WAS RIGHT.
"THAT WAS WHAT KILLED ME. HE WAS RIGHT. HOW COULD I SAVE HIM IF I DIDN'T UNDERSTAND WHAT HE NEEDED?
"THANK GOD FOR BLACK HAT."
THE TIME HAS COME FOR YOU TO JOIN US, ZAYN. TO TAKE YOUR PLACE IN THE INTERNATIONAL CRIMINAL POLICE ORGANIZATION.
...INTERPOL?
INTERPOL?!
WELL... YES.

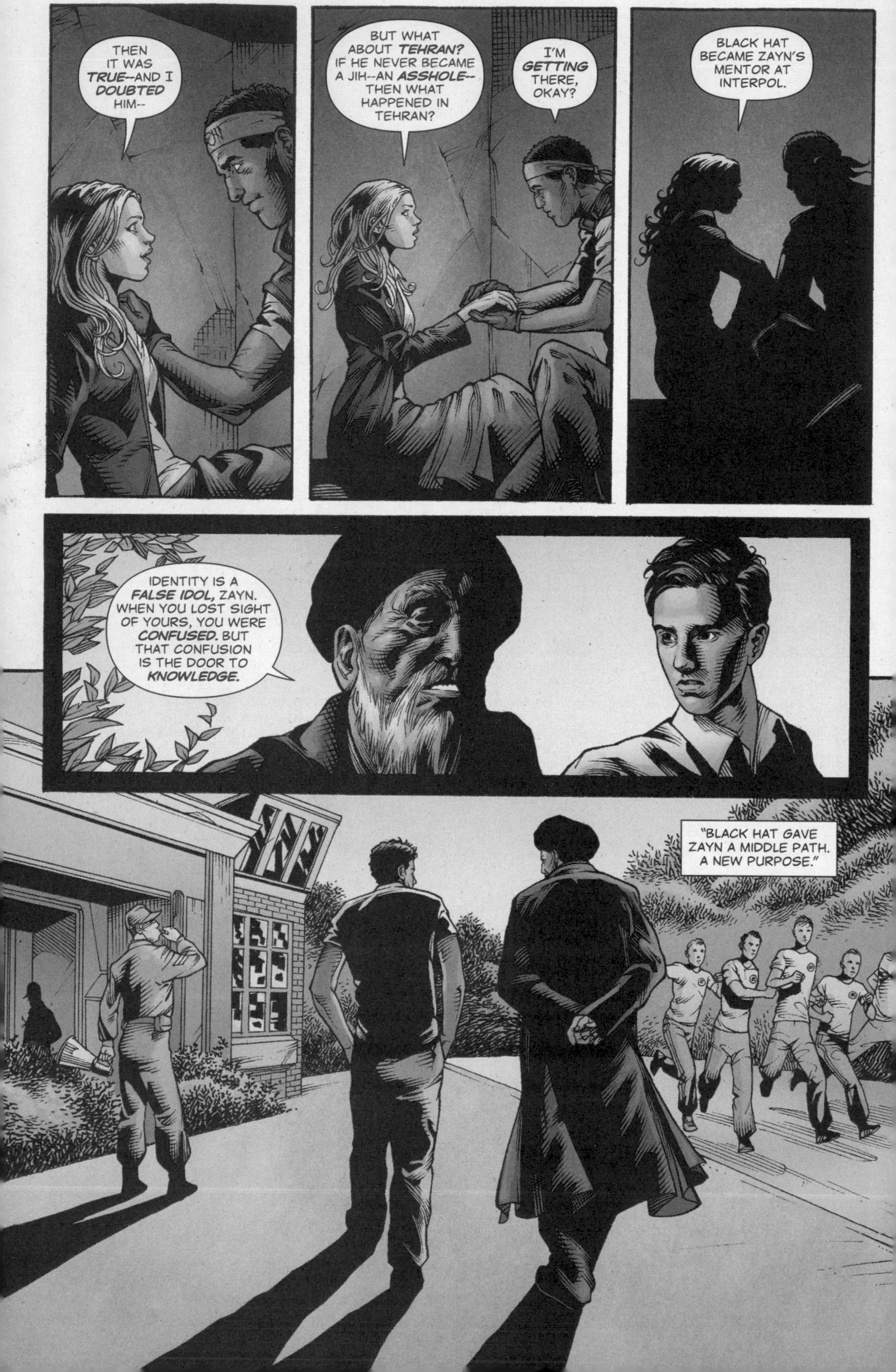
THEN IT WAS TRUE--AND I DOUBTED HIM--
BUT WHAT ABOUT TEHRAN? IF HE NEVER BECAME A JIH--AN ASSHOLE--THEN WHAT HAPPENED IN TEHRAN?
I'M GETTING THERE, OKAY?
BLACK HAT BECAME ZAYN'S MENTOR AT INTERPOL.
IDENTITY IS A FALSE IDOL, ZAYN. WHEN YOU LOST SIGHT OF YOURS, YOU WERE CONFUSED. BUT THAT CONFUSION IS THE DOOR TO KNOWLEDGE.
"BLACK HAT GAVE ZAYN A MIDDLE PATH. A NEW PURPOSE."

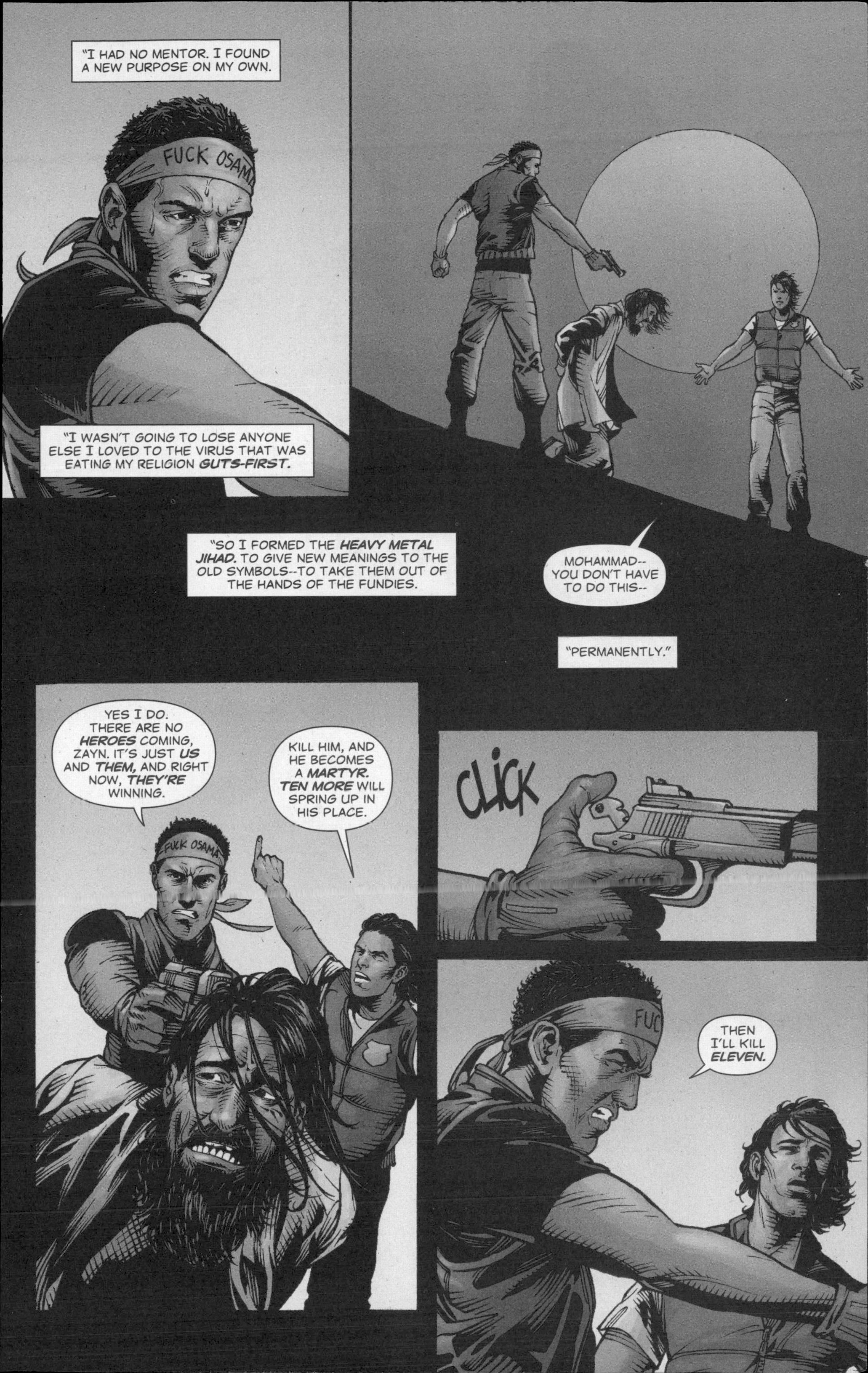
"I HAD NO MENTOR. I FOUND A NEW PURPOSE ON MY OWN.
FUCK OSAMA
"I WASN'T GOING TO LOSE ANYONE ELSE I LOVED TO THE VIRUS THAT WAS EATING MY RELIGION GUTS-FIRST.
"SO I FORMED THE HEAVY METAL JIHAD. TO GIVE NEW MEANINGS TO THE OLD SYMBOLS--TO TAKE THEM OUT OF THE HANDS OF THE FUNDIES.
MOHAMMAD-- YOU DON'T HAVE TO DO THIS--
"PERMANENTLY."
YES I DO. THERE ARE NO HEROES COMING, ZAYN. IT'S JUST US AND THEM, AND RIGHT NOW, THEY'RE WINNING.
KILL HIM, AND HE BECOMES A MARTYR. TEN MORE WILL SPRING UP IN HIS PLACE.
FUCK OSAMA
CLICK
THEN I'LL KILL ELEVEN.

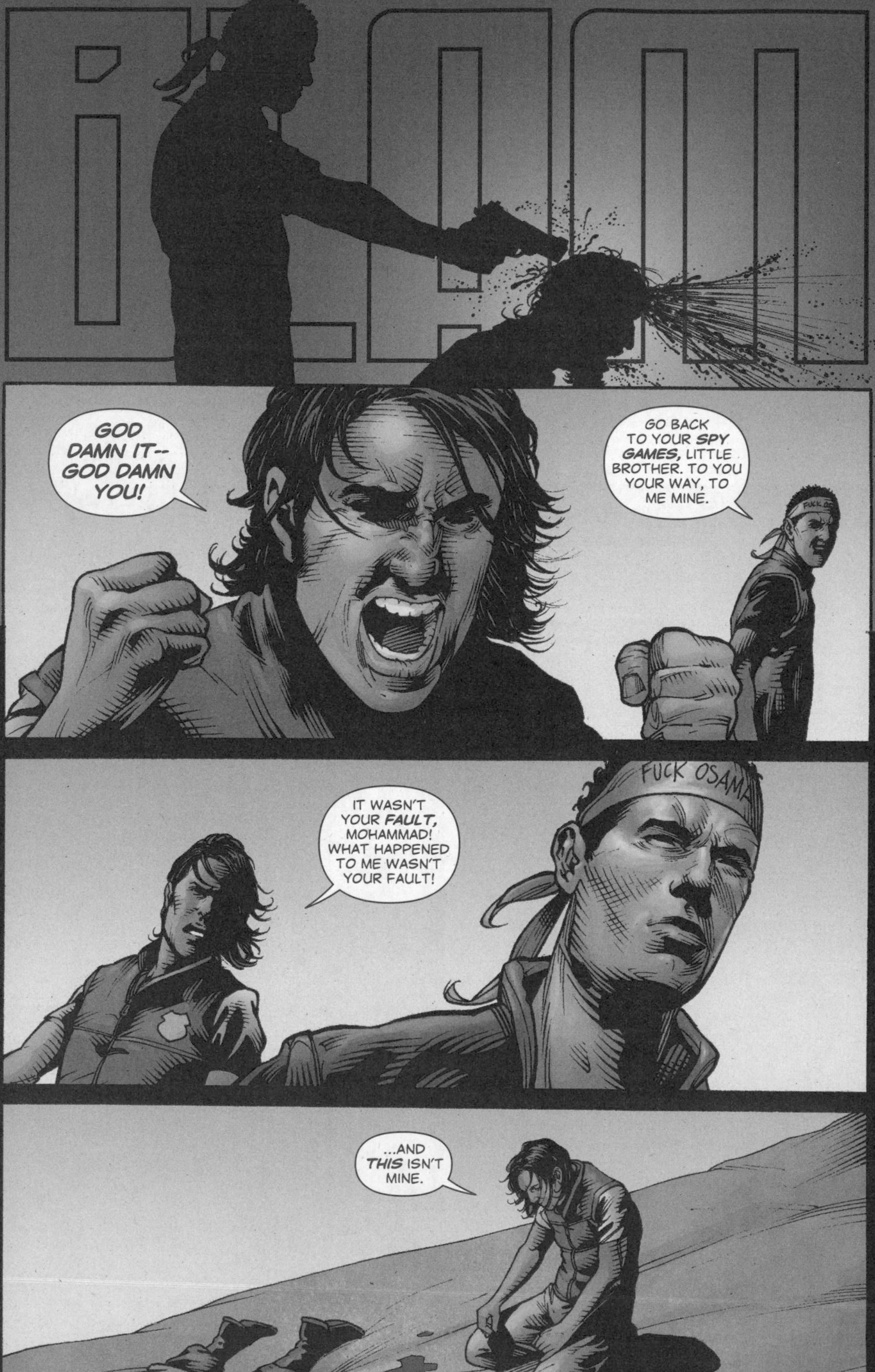
BLAM
GOD DAMN IT-- GOD DAMN YOU!
GO BACK TO YOUR SPY GAMES, LITTLE BROTHER. TO YOU YOUR WAY, TO ME MINE.
FUCK OSAMA
IT WASN'T YOUR FAULT, MOHAMMAD! WHAT HAPPENED TO ME WASN'T YOUR FAULT!
...AND THIS ISN'T MINE.

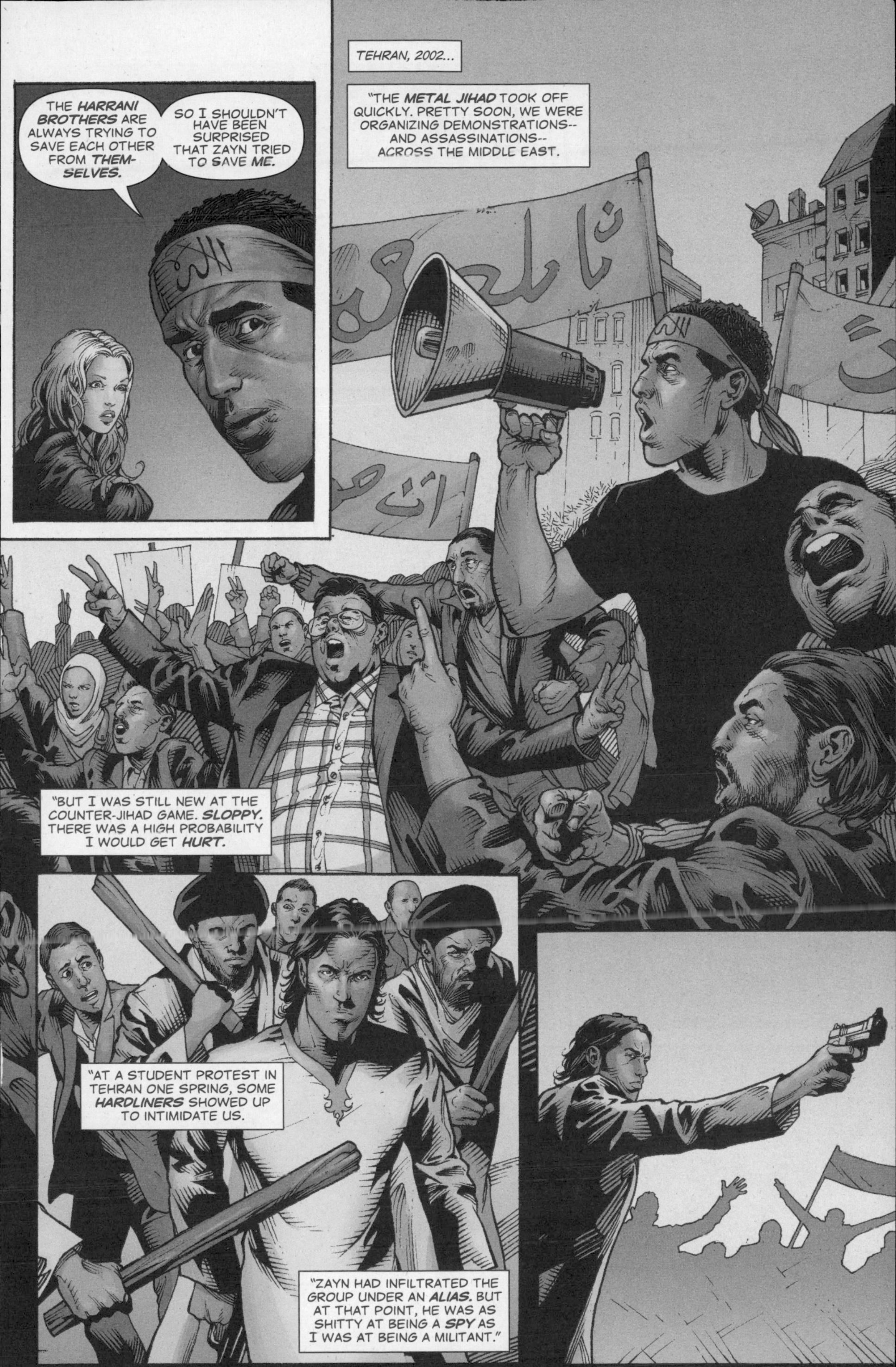
THE HARRANI BROTHERS ARE ALWAYS TRYING TO SAVE EACH OTHER FROM THEM-SELVES.
SO I SHOULDN'T HAVE BEEN SURPRISED THAT ZAYN TRIED TO SAVE ME.
TEHRAN, 2002...
"THE METAL JIHAD TOOK OFF QUICKLY. PRETTY SOON, WE WERE ORGANIZING DEMONSTRATIONS-- AND ASSASSINATIONS-- ACROSS THE MIDDLE EAST.
"BUT I WAS STILL NEW AT THE COUNTER-JIHAD GAME. SLOPPY. THERE WAS A HIGH PROBABILITY I WOULD GET HURT.
"AT A STUDENT PROTEST IN TEHRAN ONE SPRING, SOME HARDLINERS SHOWED UP TO INTIMIDATE US.
"ZAYN HAD INFILTRATED THE GROUP UNDER AN ALIAS. BUT AT THAT POINT, HE WAS AS SHITTY AT BEING A SPY AS I WAS AT BEING A MILITANT."

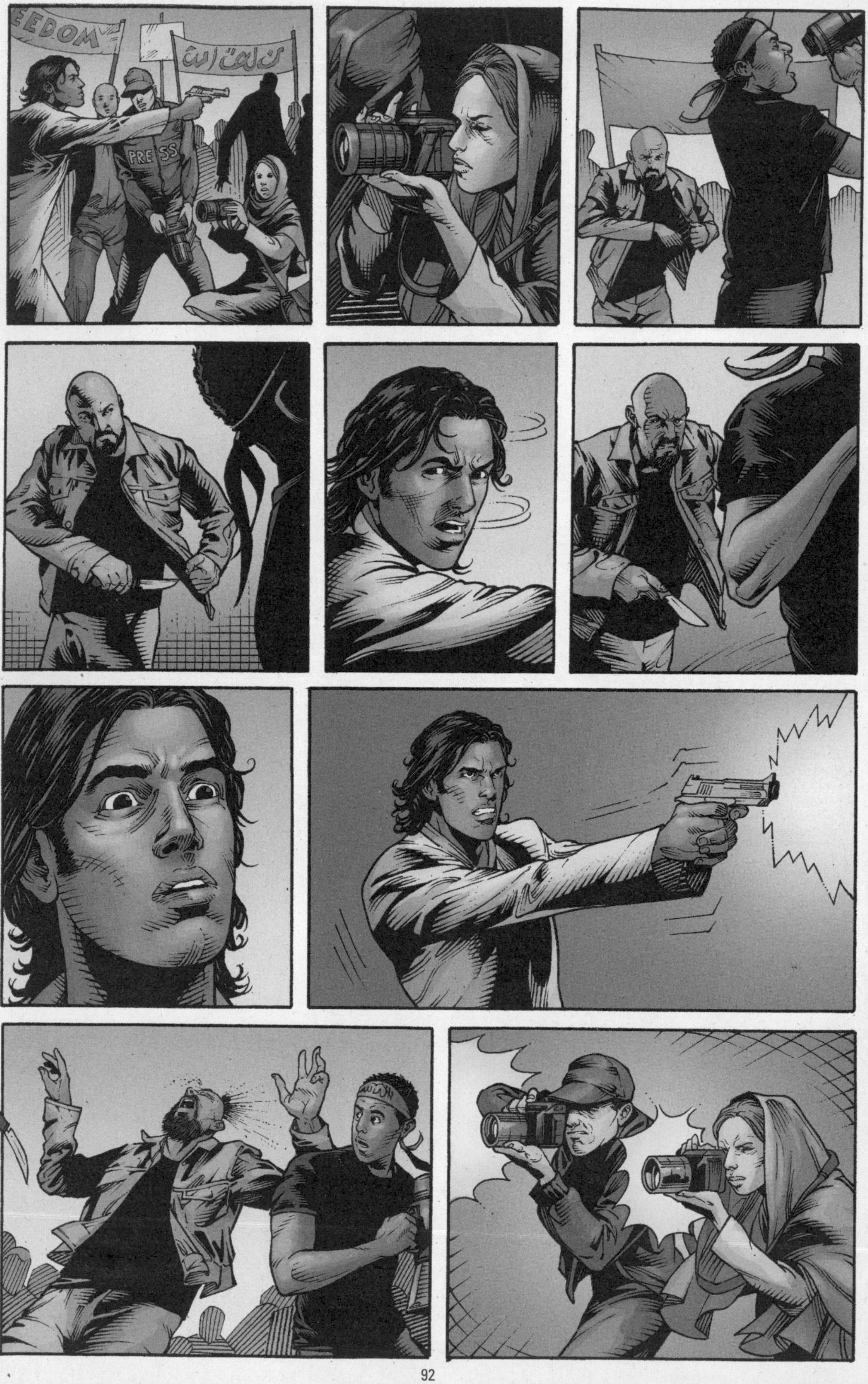
EEDOM
PRESS

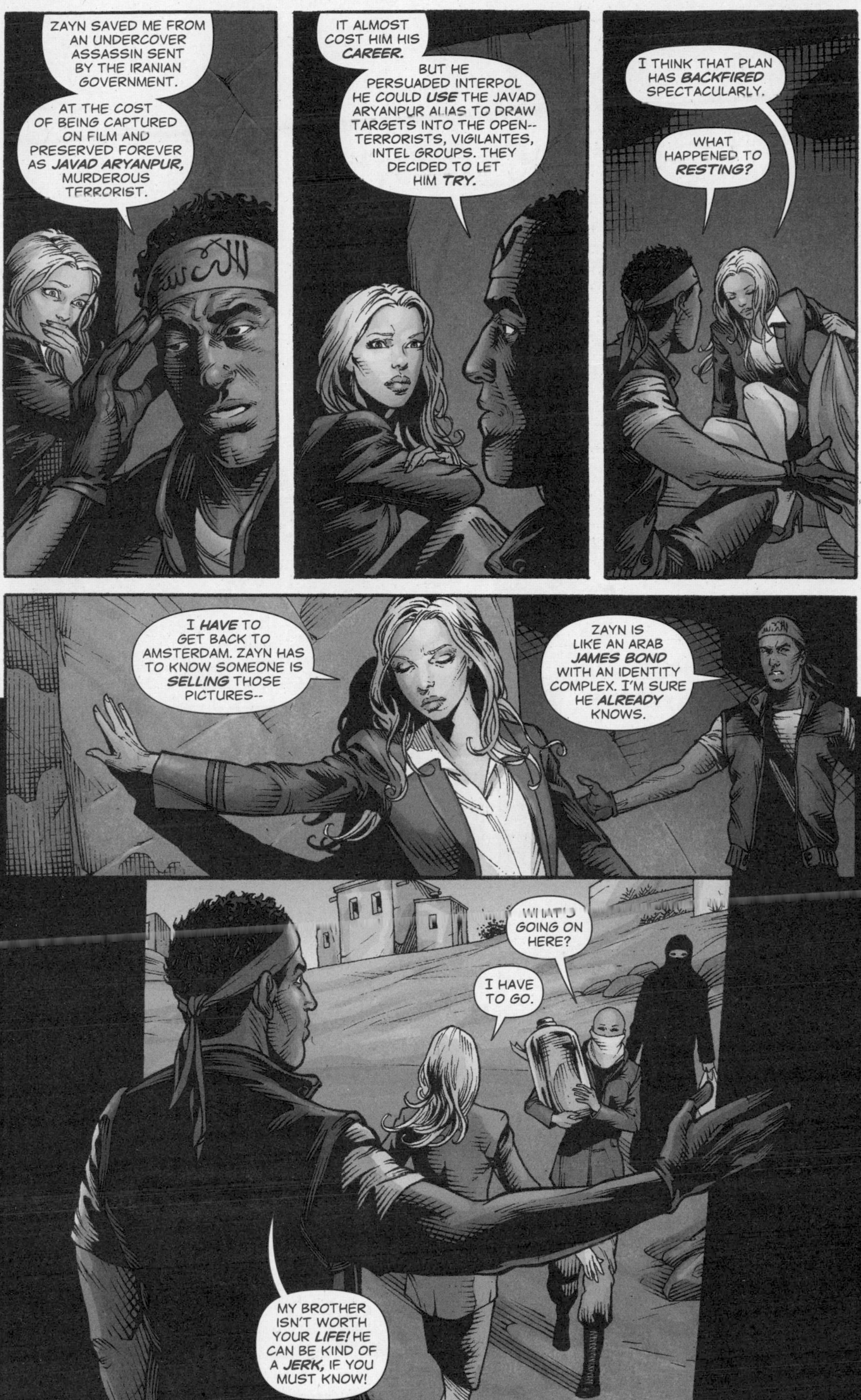
ZAYN SAVED ME FROM AN UNDERCOVER ASSASSIN SENT BY THE IRANIAN GOVERNMENT.
AT THE COST OF BEING CAPTURED ON FILM AND PRESERVED FOREVER AS JAVAD ARYANPUR, MURDEROUS TERRORIST.
IT ALMOST COST HIM HIS CAREER.
BUT HE PERSUADED INTERPOL HE COULD USE THE JAVAD ARYANPUR ALIAS TO DRAW TARGETS INTO THE OPEN-- TERRORISTS, VIGILANTES, INTEL GROUPS. THEY DECIDED TO LET HIM TRY.
I THINK THAT PLAN HAS BACKFIRED SPECTACULARLY.
WHAT HAPPENED TO RESTING?
I HAVE TO GET BACK TO AMSTERDAM. ZAYN HAS TO KNOW SOMEONE IS SELLING THOSE PICTURES--
ZAYN IS LIKE AN ARAB JAMES BOND WITH AN IDENTITY COMPLEX. I'M SURE HE ALREADY KNOWS.
WHAT'S GOING ON HERE?
I HAVE TO GO.
MY BROTHER ISN'T WORTH YOUR LIFE! HE CAN BE KIND OF A JERK, IF YOU MUST KNOW!

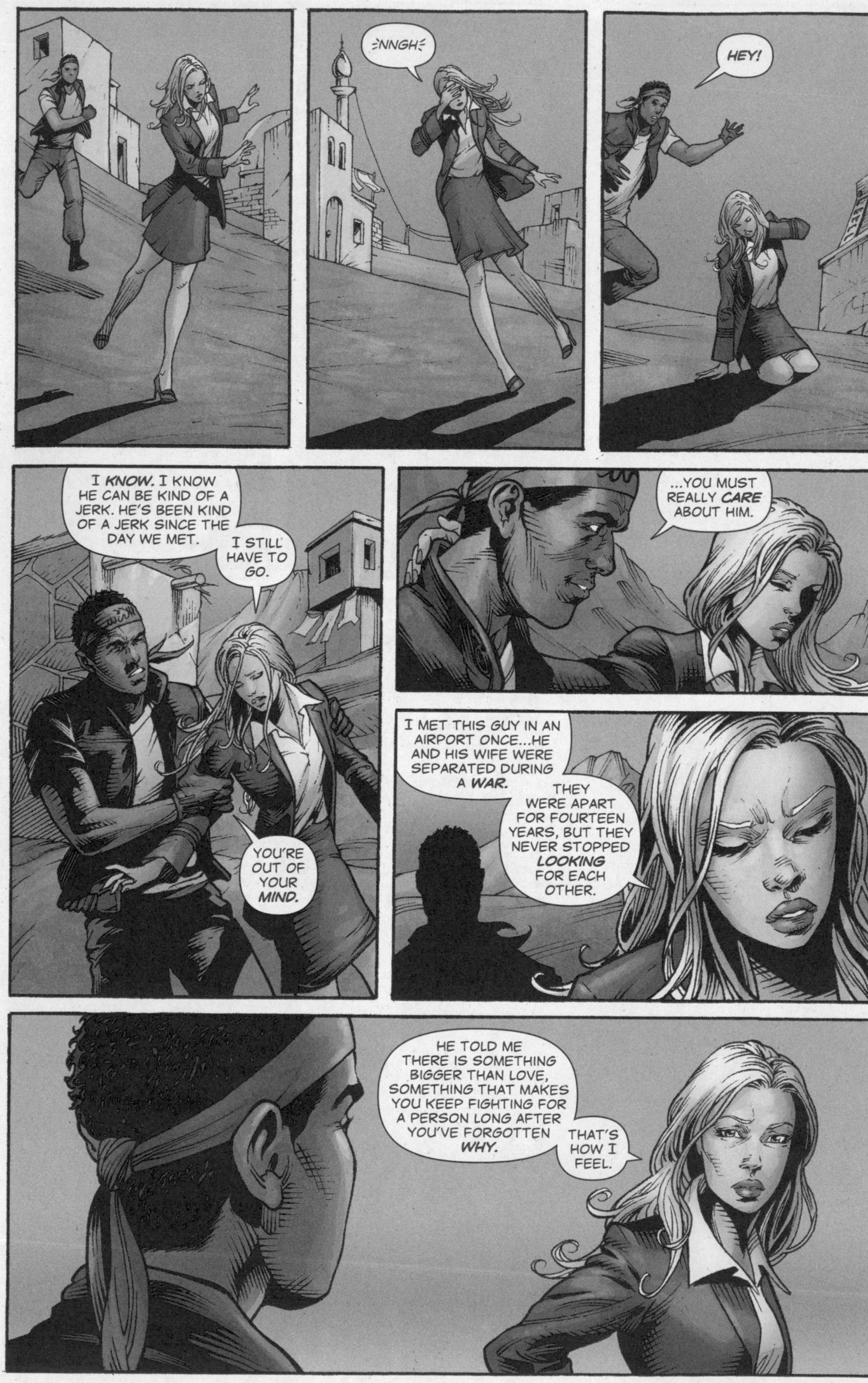

NNGH
HEY!
I KNOW. I KNOW HE CAN BE KIND OF A JERK. HE'S BEEN KIND OF A JERK SINCE THE DAY WE MET.
I STILL HAVE TO GO.
YOU'RE OUT OF YOUR MIND.
...YOU MUST REALLY CARE ABOUT HIM.
I MET THIS GUY IN AN AIRPORT ONCE...HE AND HIS WIFE WERE SEPARATED DURING A WAR.
THEY WERE APART FOR FOURTEEN YEARS, BUT THEY NEVER STOPPED LOOKING FOR EACH OTHER.
HE TOLD ME THERE IS SOMETHING BIGGER THAN LOVE, SOMETHING THAT MAKES YOU KEEP FIGHTING FOR A PERSON LONG AFTER YOU'VE FORGOTTEN WHY.
THAT'S HOW I FEEL.

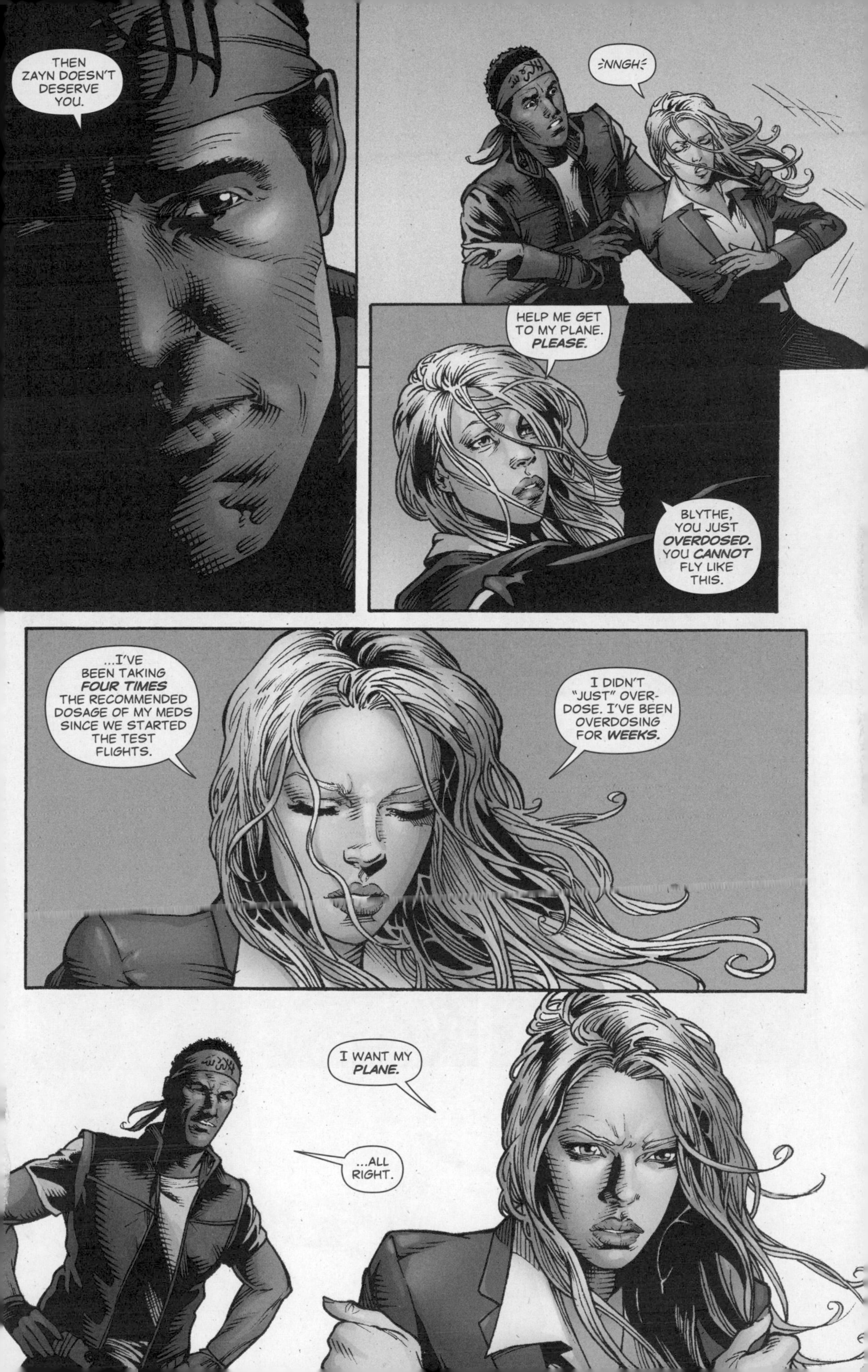
THEN ZAYN DOESN'T DESERVE YOU.
=NNGH=
HELP ME GET TO MY PLANE. PLEASE.
BLYTHE, YOU JUST OVERDOSED. YOU CANNOT FLY LIKE THIS.
I DIDN'T "JUST" OVER-DOSE. I'VE BEEN OVERDOSING FOR WEEKS.
...I'VE BEEN TAKING FOUR TIMES THE RECOMMENDED DOSAGE OF MY MEDS SINCE WE STARTED THE TEST FLIGHTS.
I WANT MY PLANE.
...ALL RIGHT.

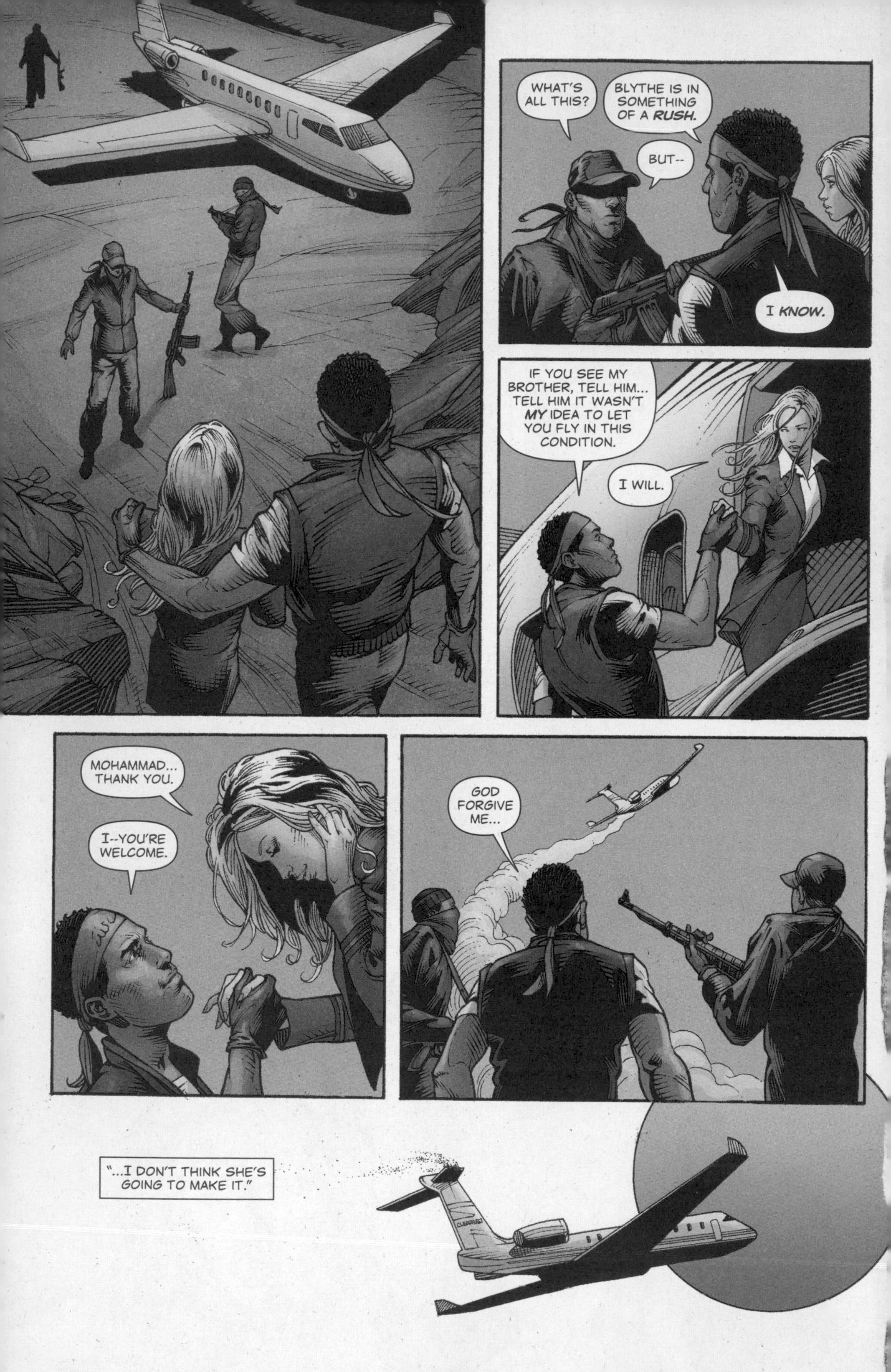
WHAT'S ALL THIS?
BLYTHE IS IN SOMETHING OF A RUSH.
BUT--
I KNOW.
IF YOU SEE MY BROTHER, TELL HIM... TELL HIM IT WASN'T MY IDEA TO LET YOU FLY IN THIS CONDITION.
I WILL.
MOHAMMAD... THANK YOU.
I--YOU'RE WELCOME.
GOD FORGIVE ME...
"...I DON'T THINK SHE'S GOING TO MAKE IT."

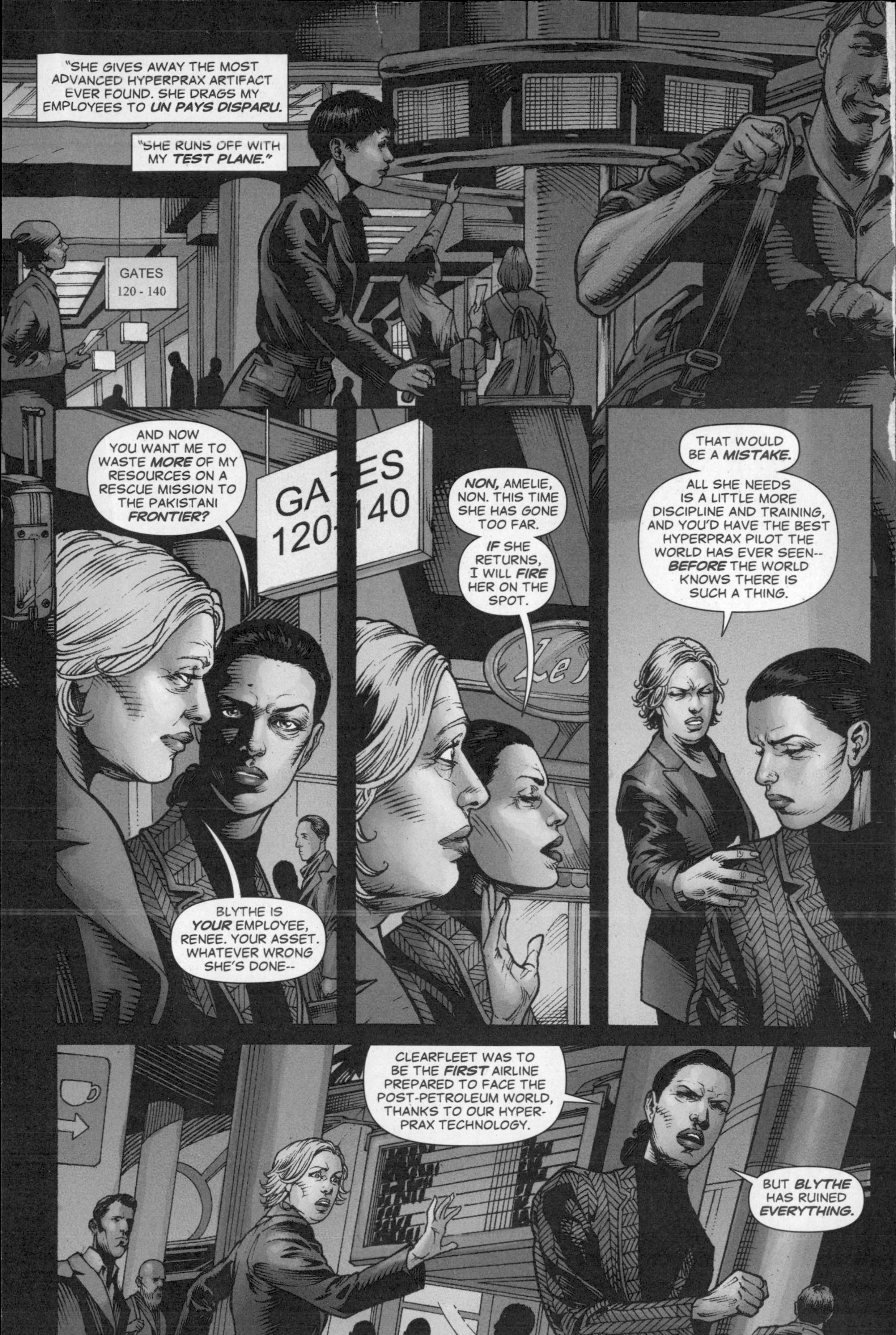
"SHE GIVES AWAY THE MOST ADVANCED HYPERPRAX ARTIFACT EVER FOUND. SHE DRAGS MY EMPLOYEES TO UN PAYS DISPARU.
"SHE RUNS OFF WITH MY TEST PLANE."
GATES 120 - 140
AND NOW YOU WANT ME TO WASTE MORE OF MY RESOURCES ON A RESCUE MISSION TO THE PAKISTANI FRONTIER?
GATES 120-140
BLYTHE IS YOUR EMPLOYEE, RENEE. YOUR ASSET. WHATEVER WRONG SHE'S DONE--
NON, AMELIE, NON. THIS TIME SHE HAS GONE TOO FAR.
IF SHE RETURNS, I WILL FIRE HER ON THE SPOT.
THAT WOULD BE A MISTAKE.
ALL SHE NEEDS IS A LITTLE MORE DISCIPLINE AND TRAINING, AND YOU'D HAVE THE BEST HYPERPRAX PILOT THE WORLD HAS EVER SEEN-- BEFORE THE WORLD KNOWS THERE IS SUCH A THING.
CLEARFLEET WAS TO BE THE FIRST AIRLINE PREPARED TO FACE THE POST-PETROLEUM WORLD, THANKS TO OUR HYPER-PRAX TECHNOLOGY.
BUT BLYTHE HAS RUINED EVERYTHING.

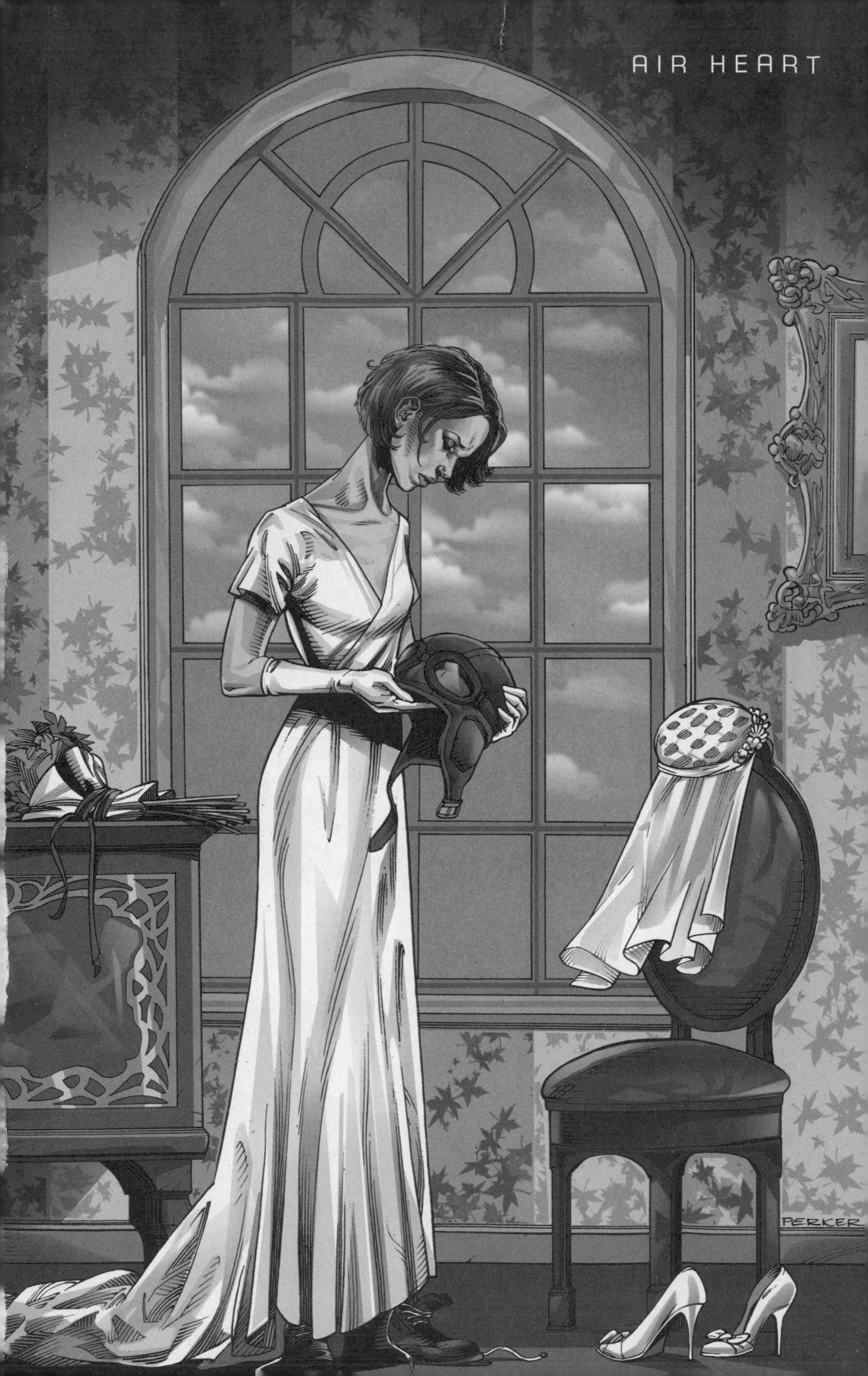
PERKER

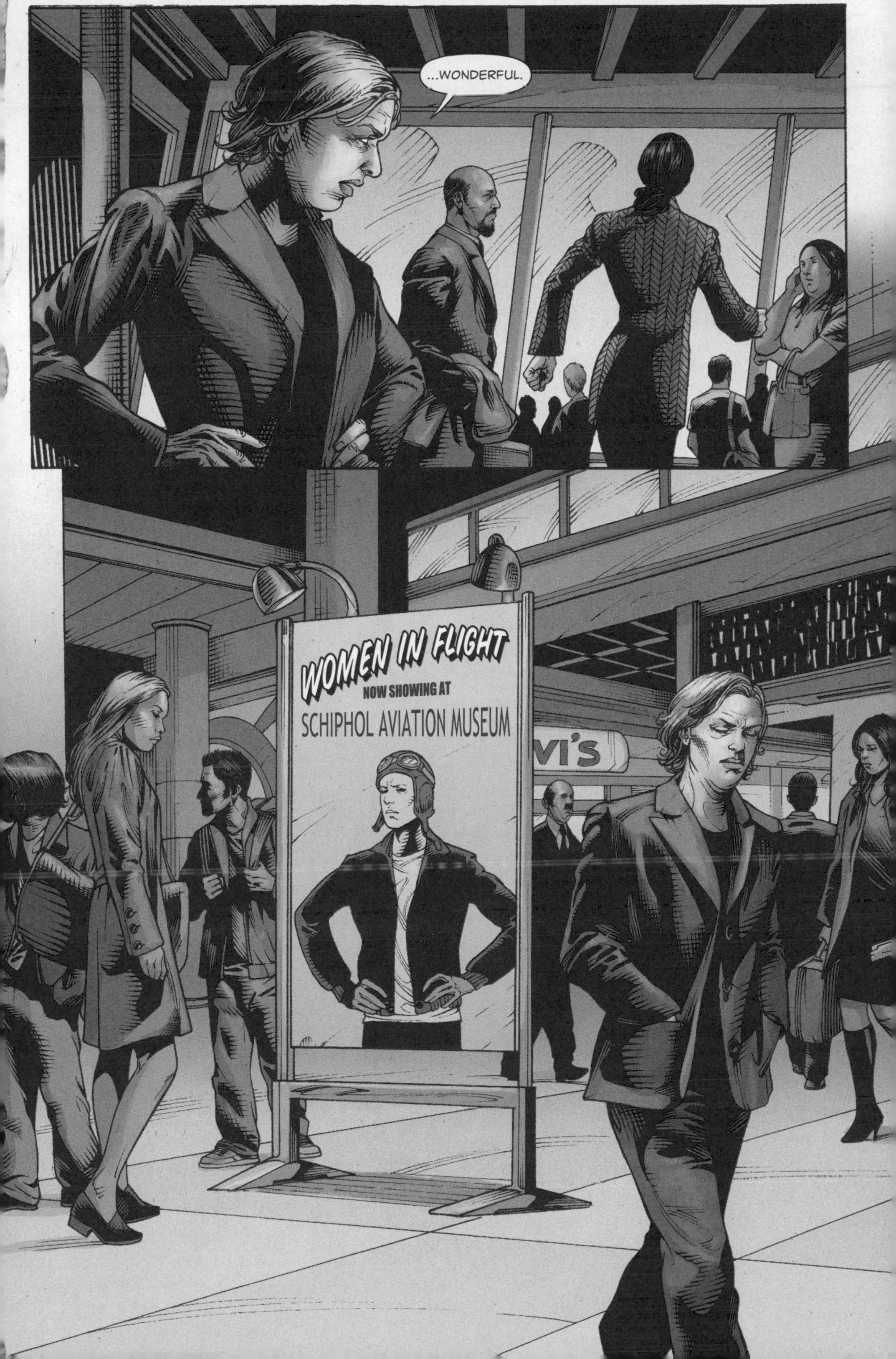
...WONDERFUL.
WOMEN IN FLIGHT
NOW SHOWING AT
SCHIPHOL AVIATION MUSEUM

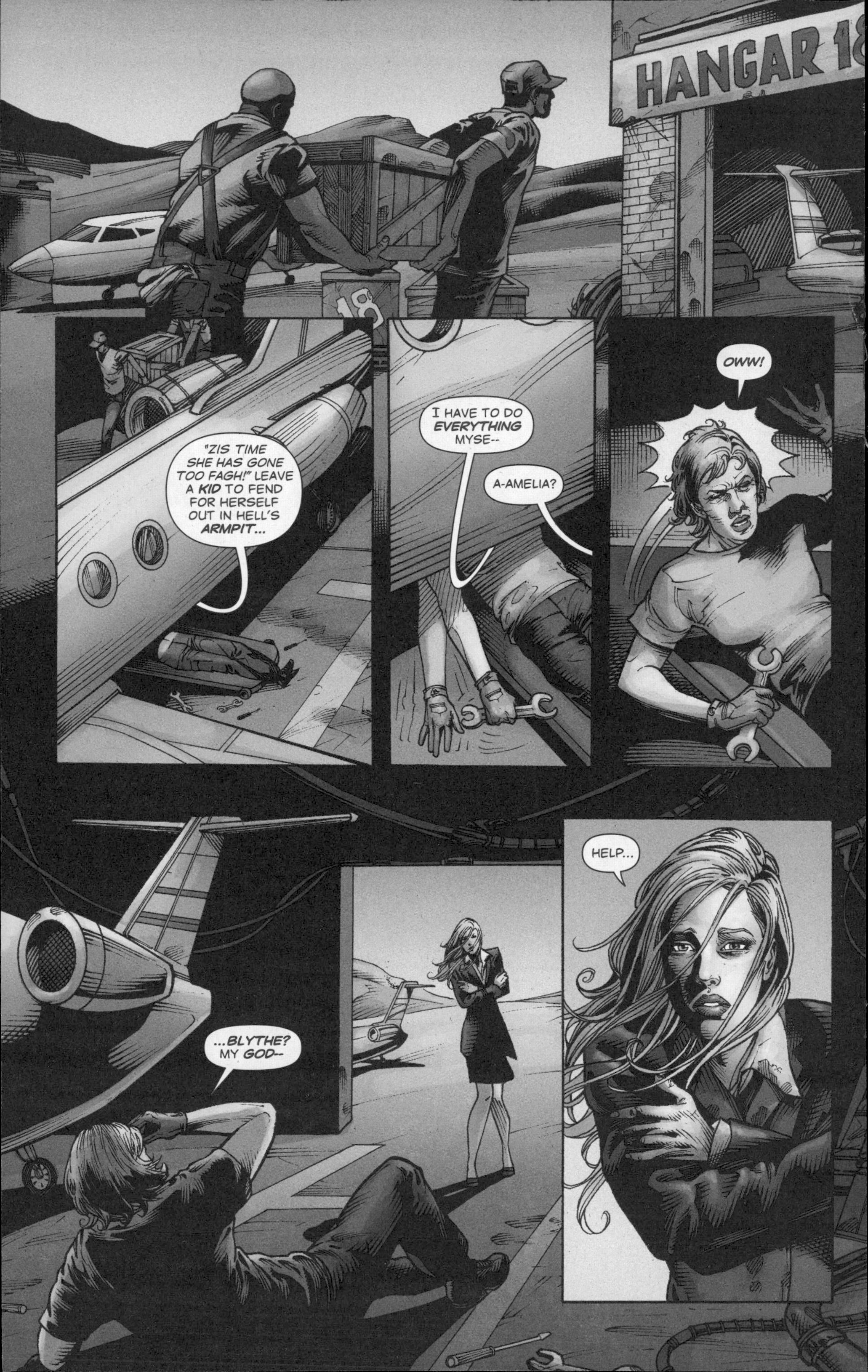
HANGAR 18
"ZIS TIME SHE HAS GONE TOO FAGH!" LEAVE A KID TO FEND FOR HERSELF OUT IN HELL'S ARMPIT...
I HAVE TO DO EVERYTHING MYSE--
A-AMELIA?
OWW!
...BLYTHE? MY GOD--
HELP...

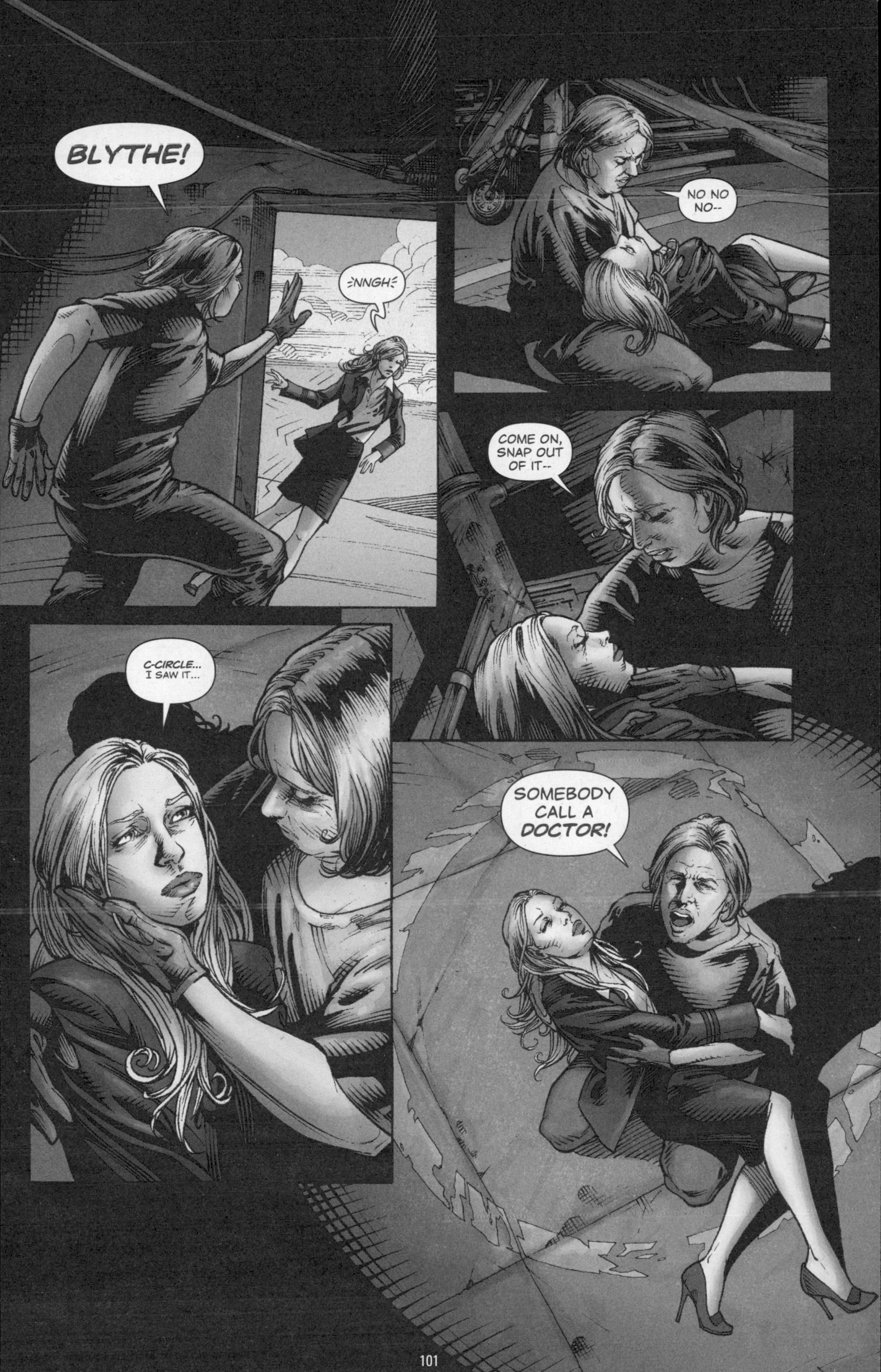
BLYTHE!
NNGH
NO NO NO--
COME ON, SNAP OUT OF IT--
C-CIRCLE... I SAW IT...
SOMEBODY CALL A DOCTOR!

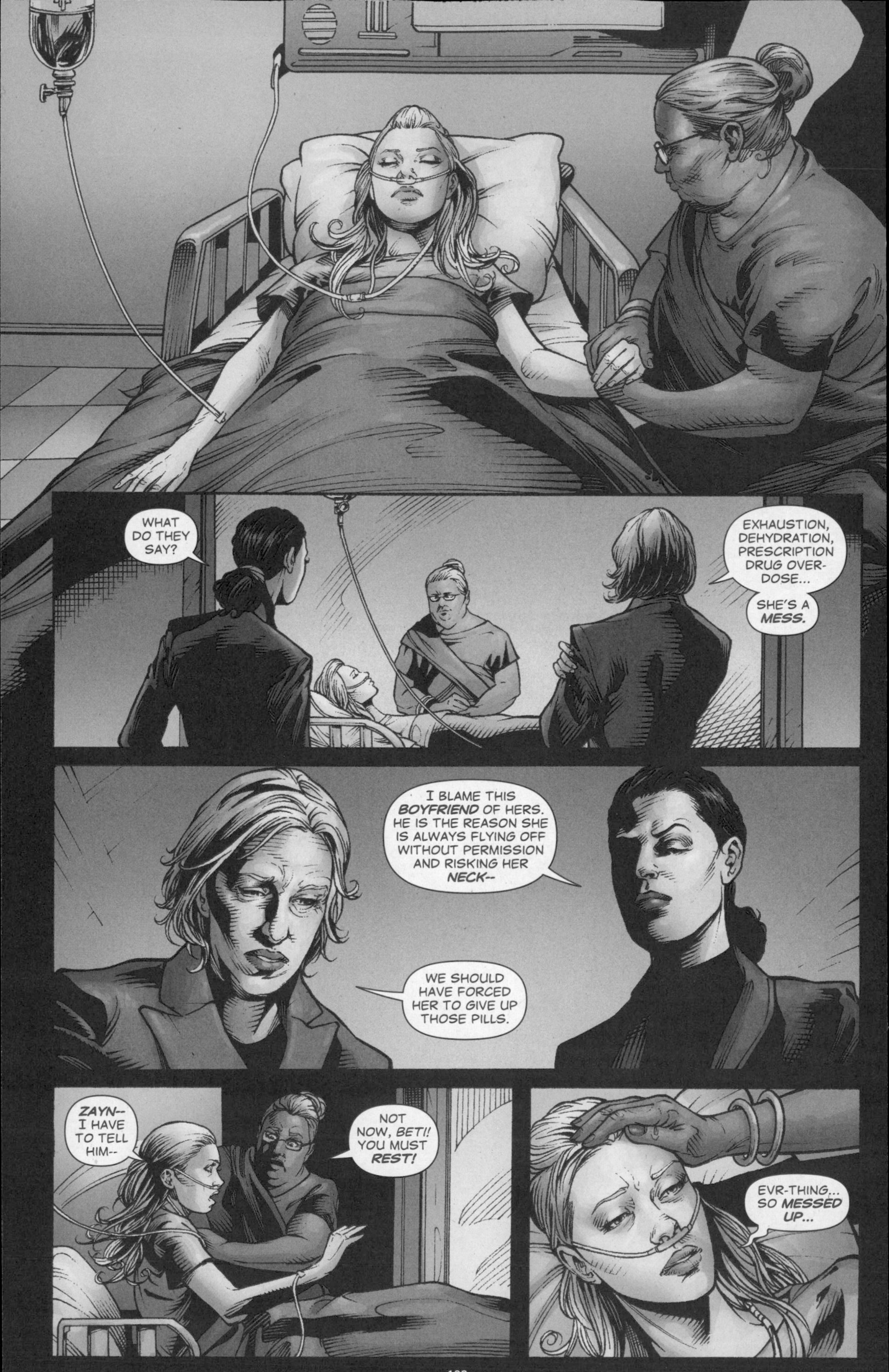
WHAT DO THEY SAY?
EXHAUSTION, DEHYDRATION, PRESCRIPTION DRUG OVER-DOSE...
SHE'S A **MESS.**
I BLAME THIS **BOYFRIEND** OF HERS. HE IS THE REASON SHE IS ALWAYS FLYING OFF WITHOUT PERMISSION AND RISKING HER **NECK--**
WE SHOULD HAVE FORCED HER TO GIVE UP THOSE PILLS.
ZAYN-- I HAVE TO TELL HIM--
NOT NOW, **BETI!** YOU MUST **REST!**
EVR-THING... SO **MESSED UP...**

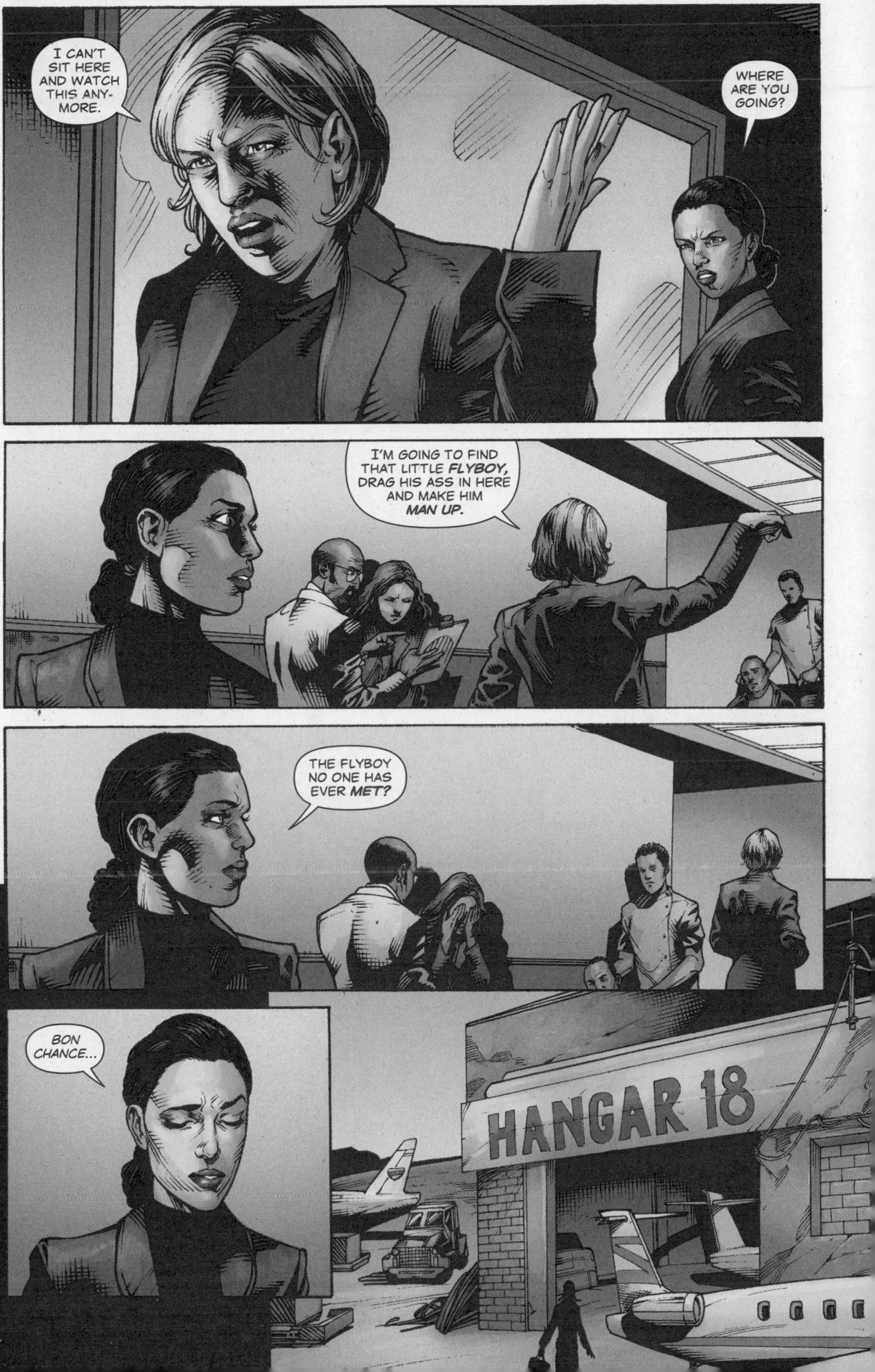
I CAN'T SIT HERE AND WATCH THIS ANY-MORE.
WHERE ARE YOU GOING?
I'M GOING TO FIND THAT LITTLE *FLYBOY*, DRAG HIS ASS IN HERE AND MAKE HIM *MAN UP*.
THE FLYBOY NO ONE HAS EVER *MET*?
BON CHANCE...
HANGAR 18

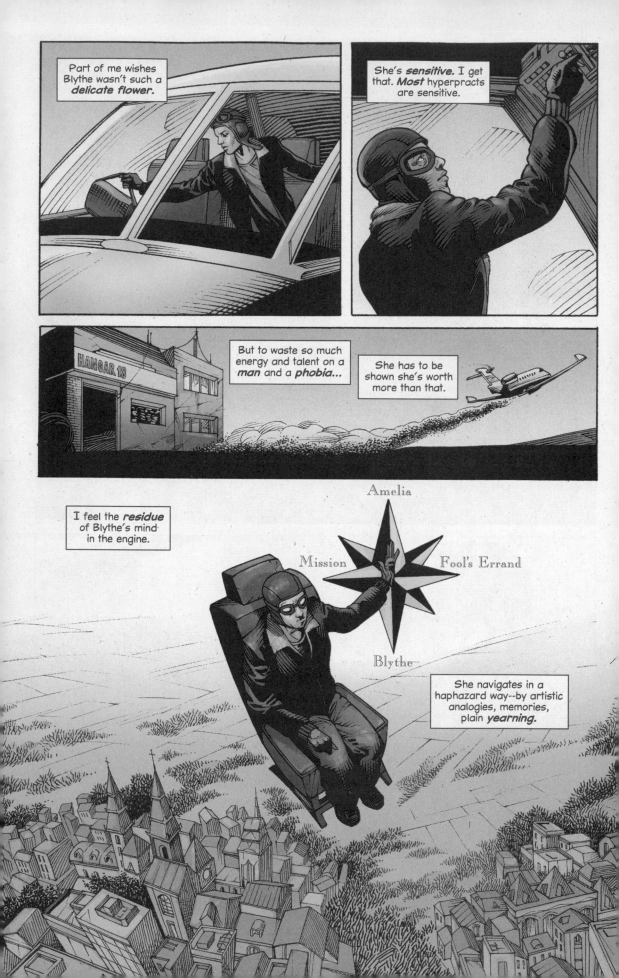

Part of me wishes Blythe wasn't such a *delicate flower*.

She's *sensitive.* I get that. *Most* hyperpracts are sensitive.

HANGAR 18

But to waste so much energy and talent on a *man* and a *phobia...*

She has to be shown she's worth more than that.

I feel the *residue* of Blythe's mind in the engine.

Amelia

Mission   Fool's Errand

Blythe

She navigates in a haphazard way--by artistic analogies, memories, plain *yearning.*

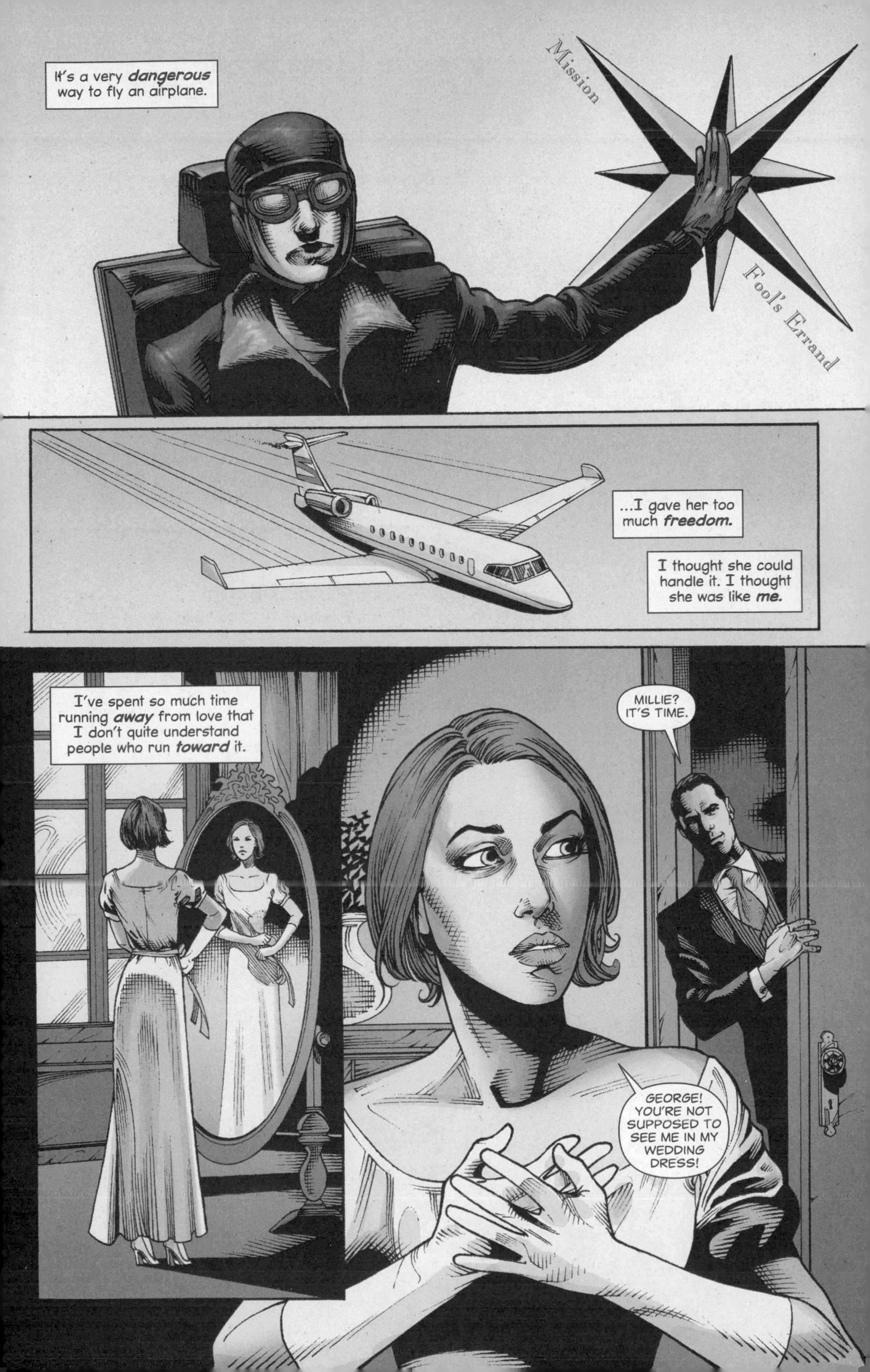
It's a very dangerous way to fly an airplane.
Mission
Fool's Errand
...I gave her too much freedom.
I thought she could handle it. I thought she was like me.
I've spent so much time running away from love that I don't quite understand people who run toward it.
MILLIE? IT'S TIME.
GEORGE! YOU'RE NOT SUPPOSED TO SEE ME IN MY WEDDING DRESS!

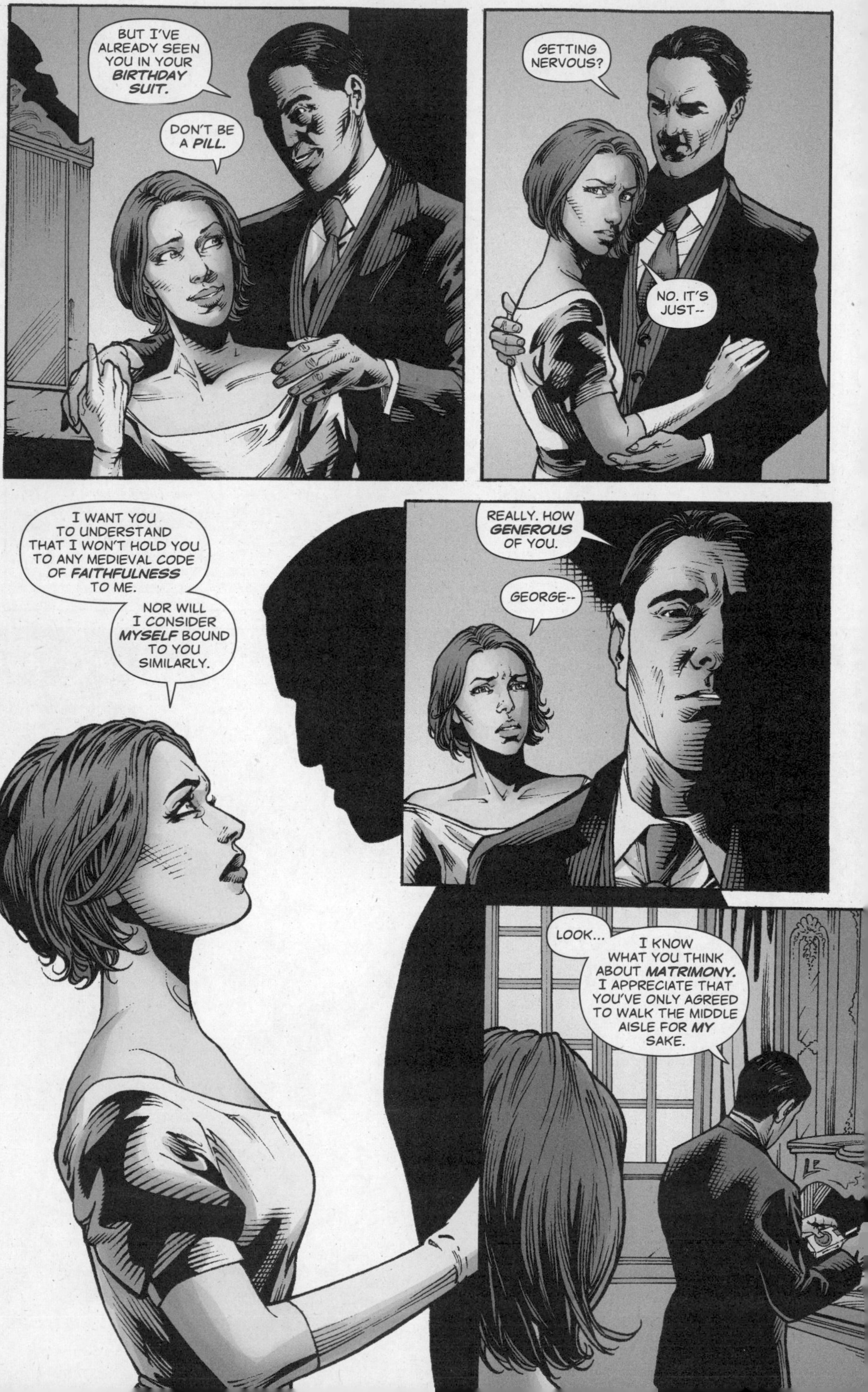
BUT I'VE ALREADY SEEN YOU IN YOUR BIRTHDAY SUIT.
DON'T BE A PILL.
GETTING NERVOUS?
NO. IT'S JUST--
I WANT YOU TO UNDERSTAND THAT I WON'T HOLD YOU TO ANY MEDIEVAL CODE OF FAITHFULNESS TO ME.
NOR WILL I CONSIDER MYSELF BOUND TO YOU SIMILARLY.
REALLY. HOW GENEROUS OF YOU.
GEORGE--
LOOK...
I KNOW WHAT YOU THINK ABOUT MATRIMONY. I APPRECIATE THAT YOU'VE ONLY AGREED TO WALK THE MIDDLE AISLE FOR MY SAKE.

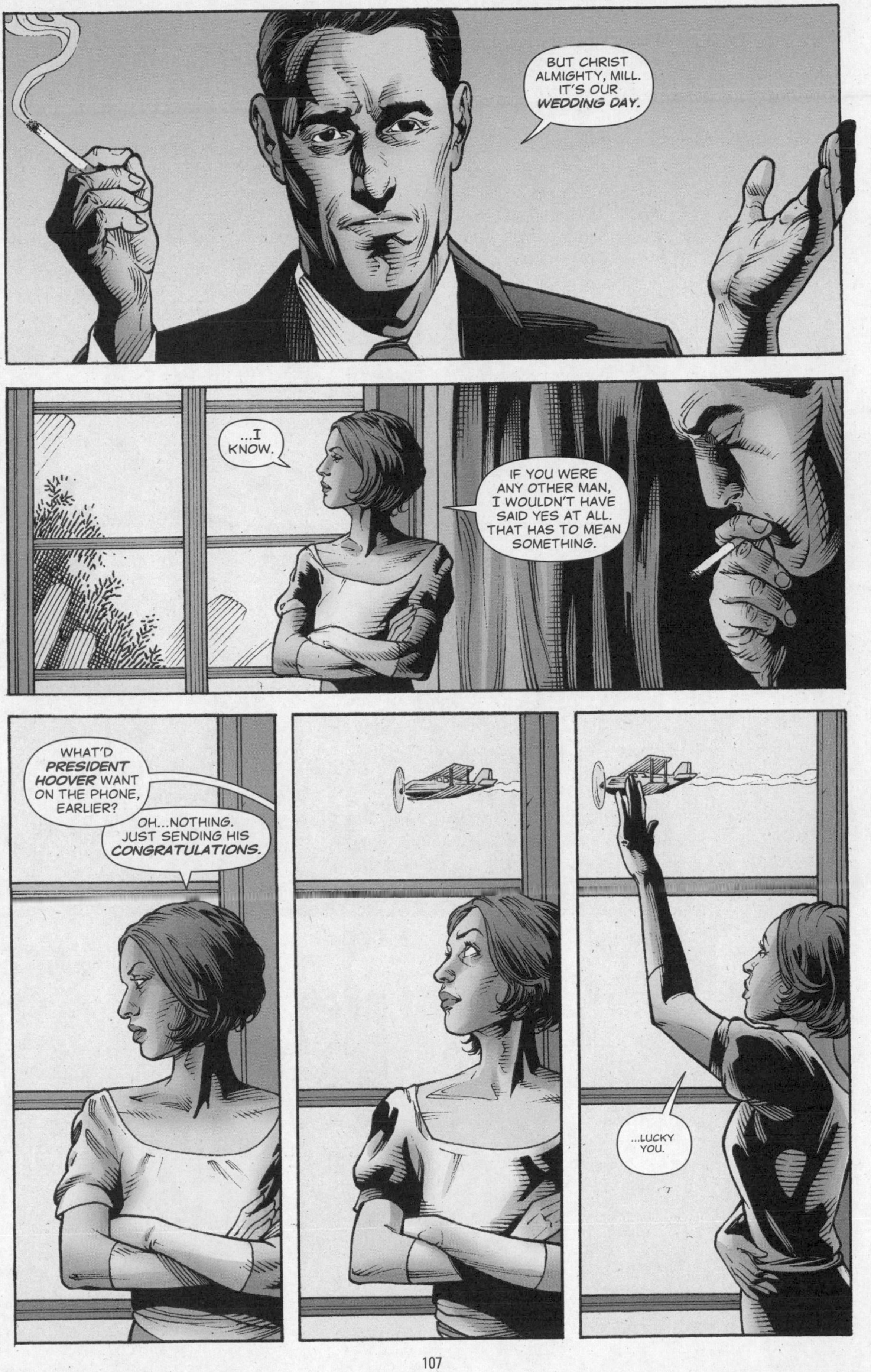
BUT CHRIST ALMIGHTY, MILL. IT'S OUR WEDDING DAY.
...I KNOW.
IF YOU WERE ANY OTHER MAN, I WOULDN'T HAVE SAID YES AT ALL. THAT HAS TO MEAN SOMETHING.
WHAT'D PRESIDENT HOOVER WANT ON THE PHONE, EARLIER?
OH...NOTHING. JUST SENDING HIS CONGRATULATIONS.
...LUCKY YOU.

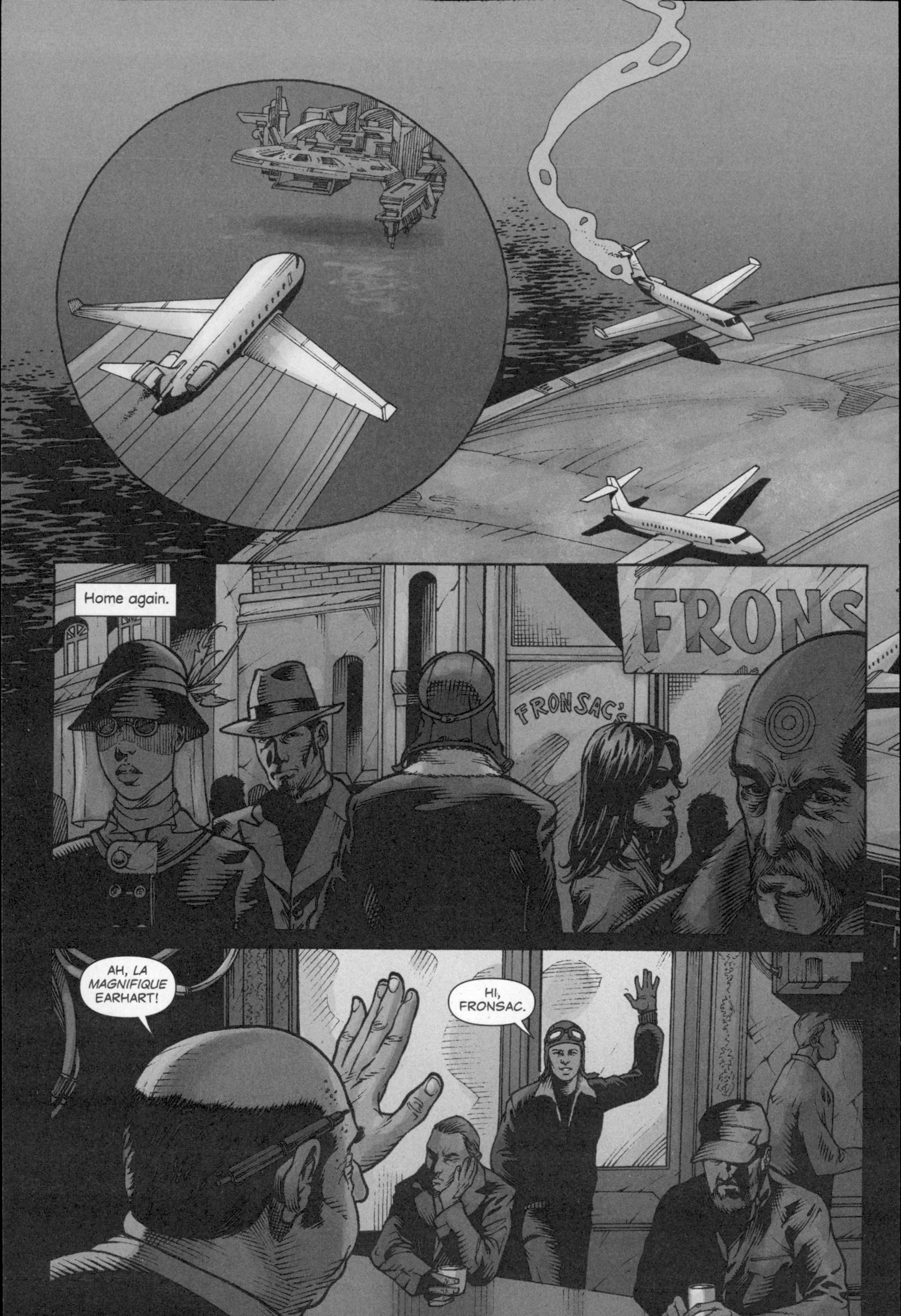

Home again.
FRONS
FRONSAC'S
AH, LA MAGNIFIQUE EARHART!
HI, FRONSAC.

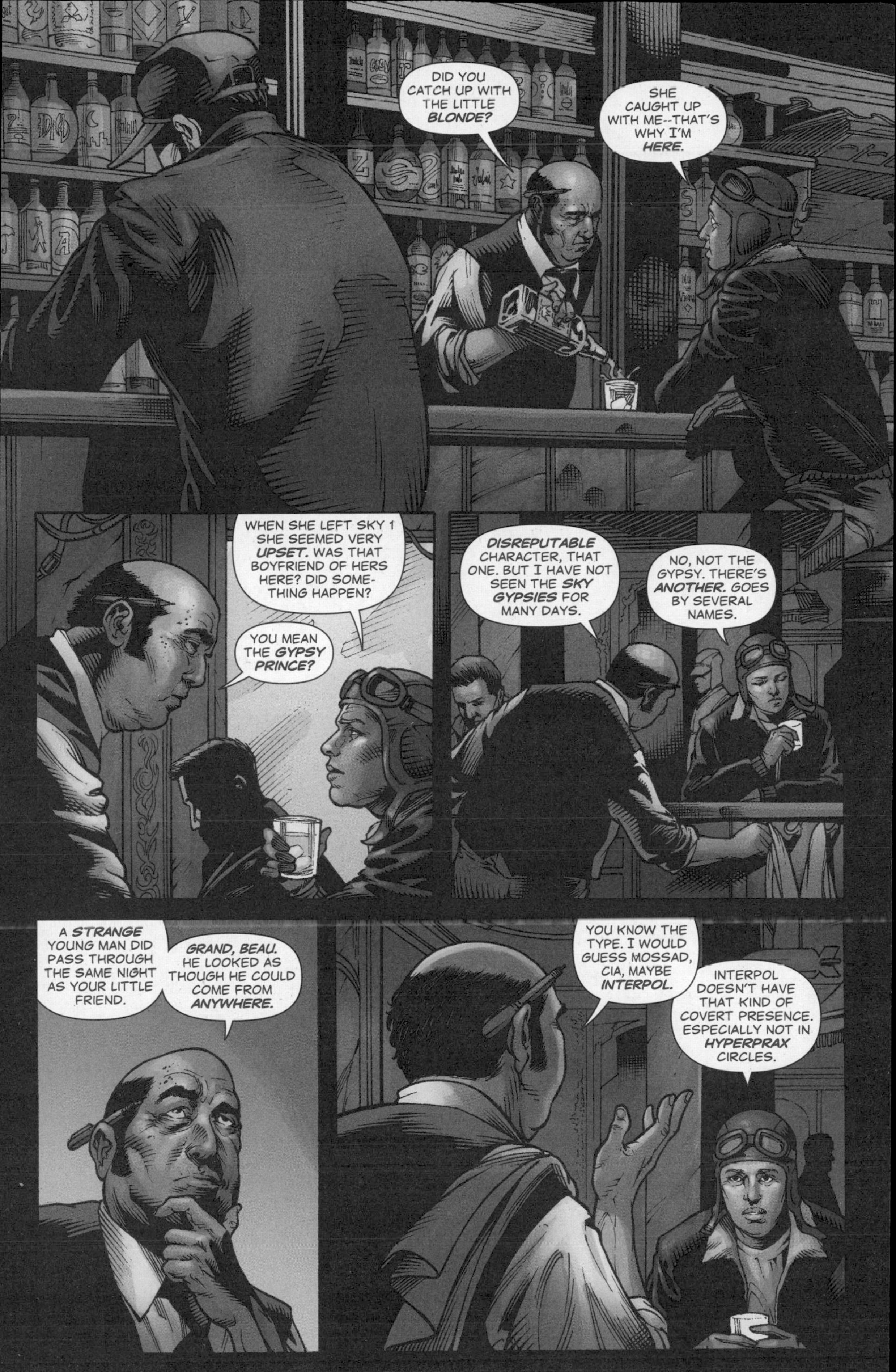

DID YOU CATCH UP WITH THE LITTLE BLONDE?
SHE CAUGHT UP WITH ME--THAT'S WHY I'M HERE.
WHEN SHE LEFT SKY 1 SHE SEEMED VERY UPSET. WAS THAT BOYFRIEND OF HERS HERE? DID SOMETHING HAPPEN?
YOU MEAN THE GYPSY PRINCE?
DISREPUTABLE CHARACTER, THAT ONE. BUT I HAVE NOT SEEN THE SKY GYPSIES FOR MANY DAYS.
NO, NOT THE GYPSY. THERE'S ANOTHER. GOES BY SEVERAL NAMES.
A STRANGE YOUNG MAN DID PASS THROUGH THE SAME NIGHT AS YOUR LITTLE FRIEND.
GRAND, BEAU. HE LOOKED AS THOUGH HE COULD COME FROM ANYWHERE.
YOU KNOW THE TYPE. I WOULD GUESS MOSSAD, CIA, MAYBE INTERPOL.
INTERPOL DOESN'T HAVE THAT KIND OF COVERT PRESENCE. ESPECIALLY NOT IN HYPERPRAX CIRCLES.

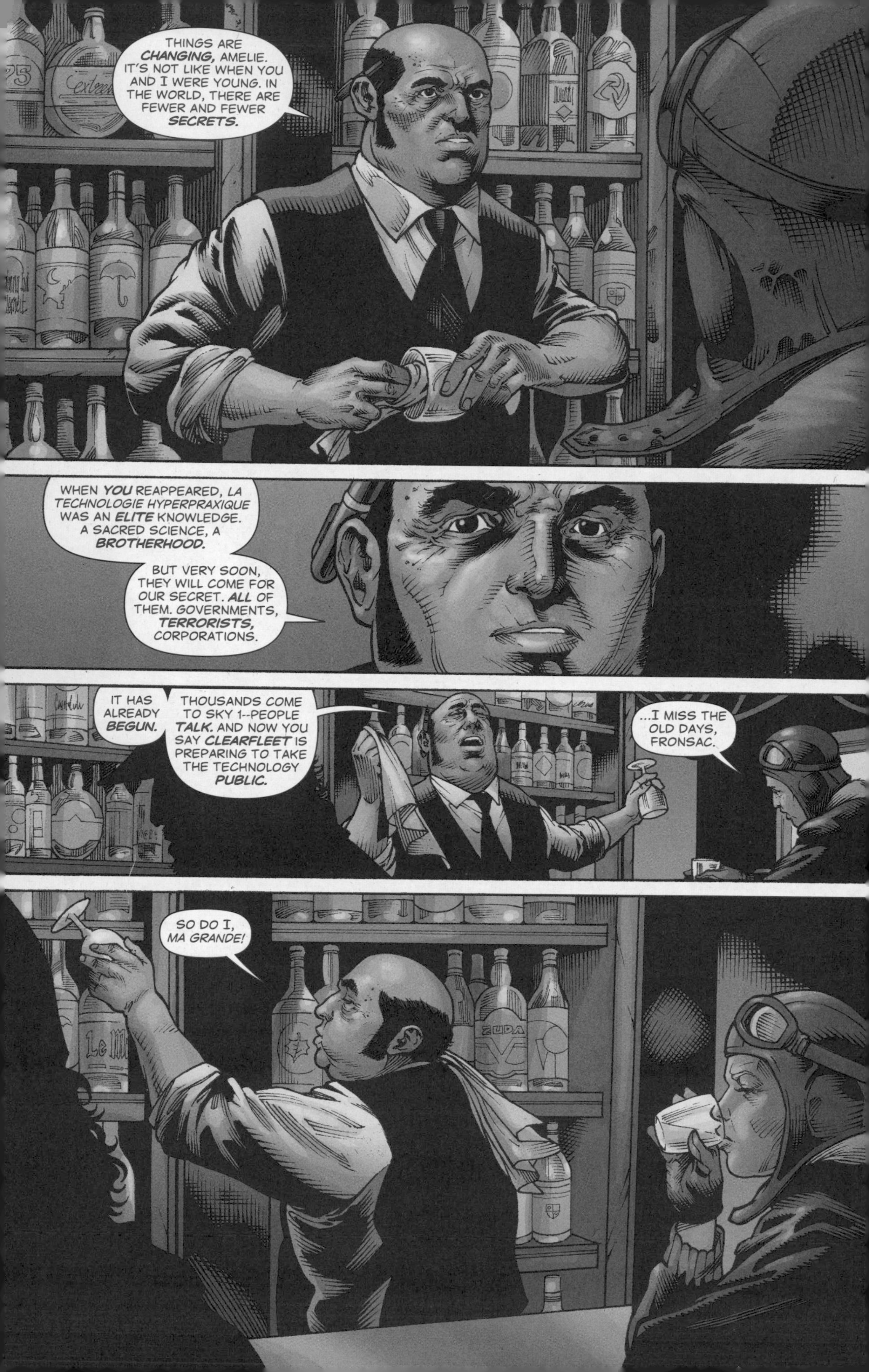
THINGS ARE CHANGING, AMELIE. IT'S NOT LIKE WHEN YOU AND I WERE YOUNG. IN THE WORLD, THERE ARE FEWER AND FEWER SECRETS.
WHEN YOU REAPPEARED, LA TECHNOLOGIE HYPERPRAXIQUE WAS AN ELITE KNOWLEDGE. A SACRED SCIENCE, A BROTHERHOOD.
BUT VERY SOON, THEY WILL COME FOR OUR SECRET. ALL OF THEM. GOVERNMENTS, TERRORISTS, CORPORATIONS.
IT HAS ALREADY BEGUN.
THOUSANDS COME TO SKY 1--PEOPLE TALK. AND NOW YOU SAY CLEARFLEET IS PREPARING TO TAKE THE TECHNOLOGY PUBLIC.
...I MISS THE OLD DAYS, FRONSAC.
SO DO I, MA GRANDE!
ZUDA

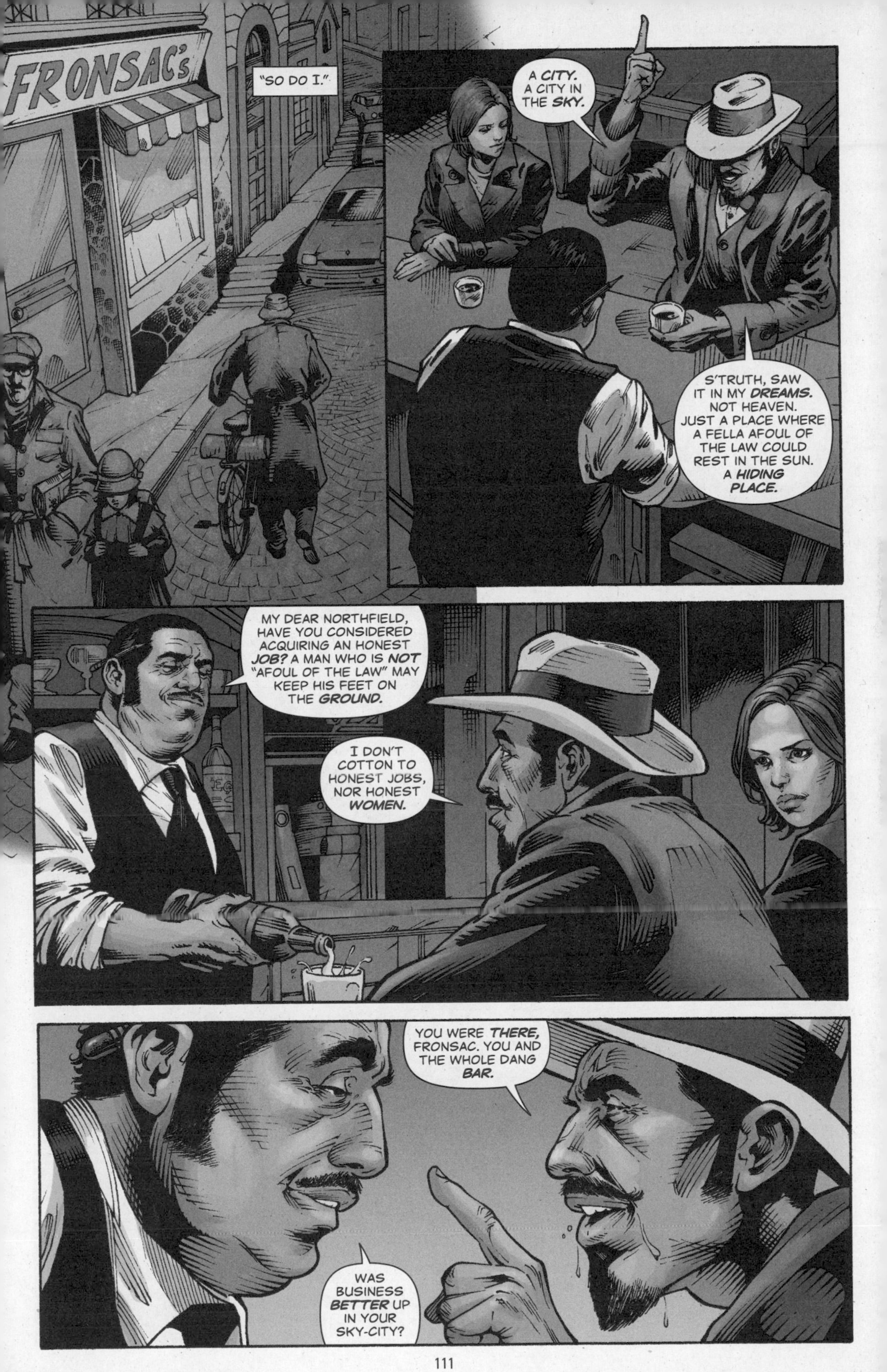
FRONSAC's
"SO DO I."
A CITY. A CITY IN THE SKY.
S'TRUTH, SAW IT IN MY DREAMS. NOT HEAVEN. JUST A PLACE WHERE A FELLA AFOUL OF THE LAW COULD REST IN THE SUN. A HIDING PLACE.
MY DEAR NORTHFIELD, HAVE YOU CONSIDERED ACQUIRING AN HONEST JOB? A MAN WHO IS NOT "AFOUL OF THE LAW" MAY KEEP HIS FEET ON THE GROUND.
I DON'T COTTON TO HONEST JOBS, NOR HONEST WOMEN.
YOU WERE THERE, FRONSAC. YOU AND THE WHOLE DANG BAR.
WAS BUSINESS BETTER UP IN YOUR SKY-CITY?

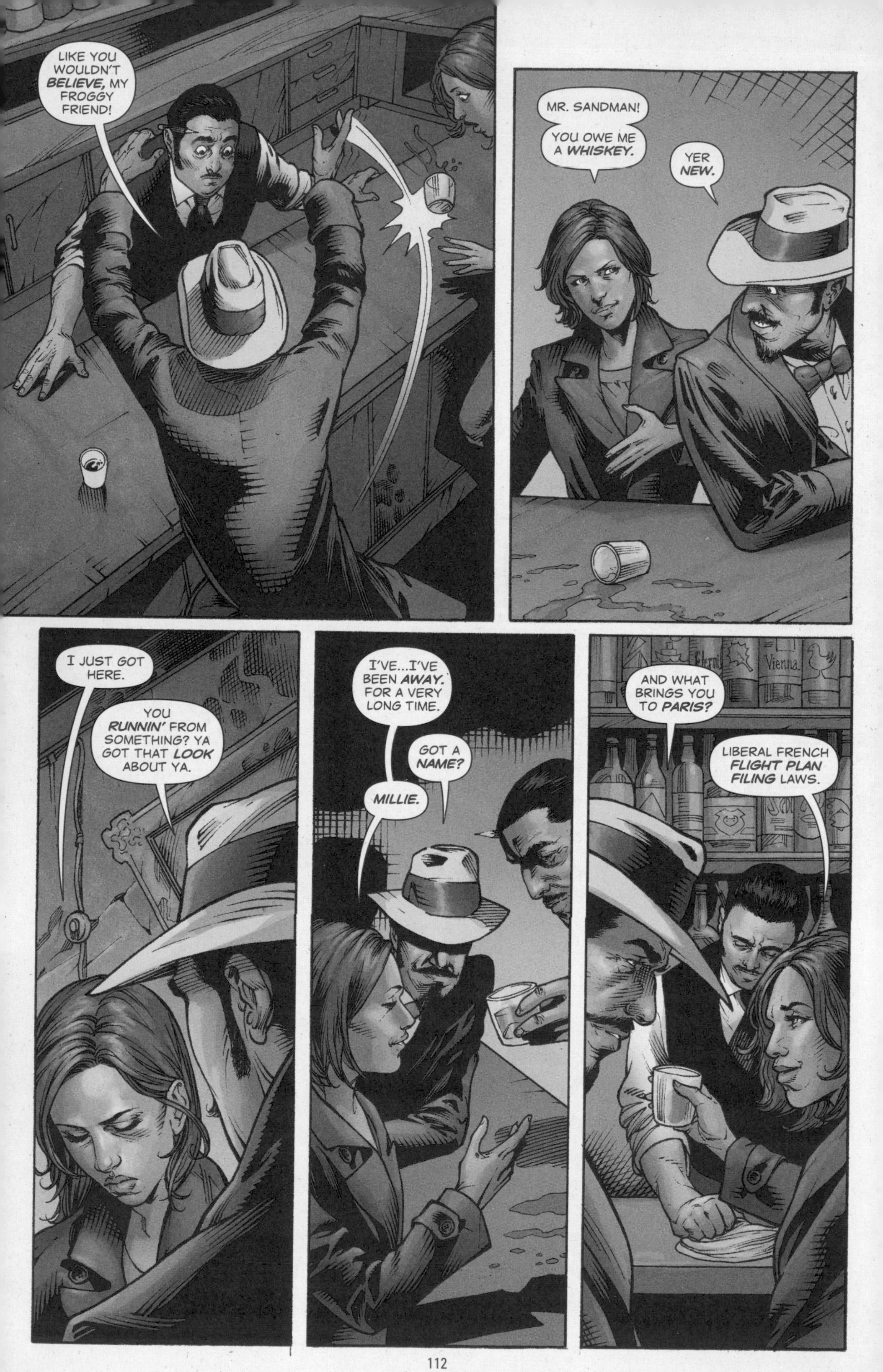

LIKE YOU WOULDN'T BELIEVE, MY FROGGY FRIEND!
MR. SANDMAN!
YOU OWE ME A WHISKEY.
YER NEW.
I JUST GOT HERE.
YOU RUNNIN' FROM SOMETHING? YA GOT THAT LOOK ABOUT YA.
I'VE...I'VE BEEN AWAY. FOR A VERY LONG TIME.
GOT A NAME?
MILLIE.
AND WHAT BRINGS YOU TO PARIS?
LIBERAL FRENCH FLIGHT PLAN FILING LAWS.

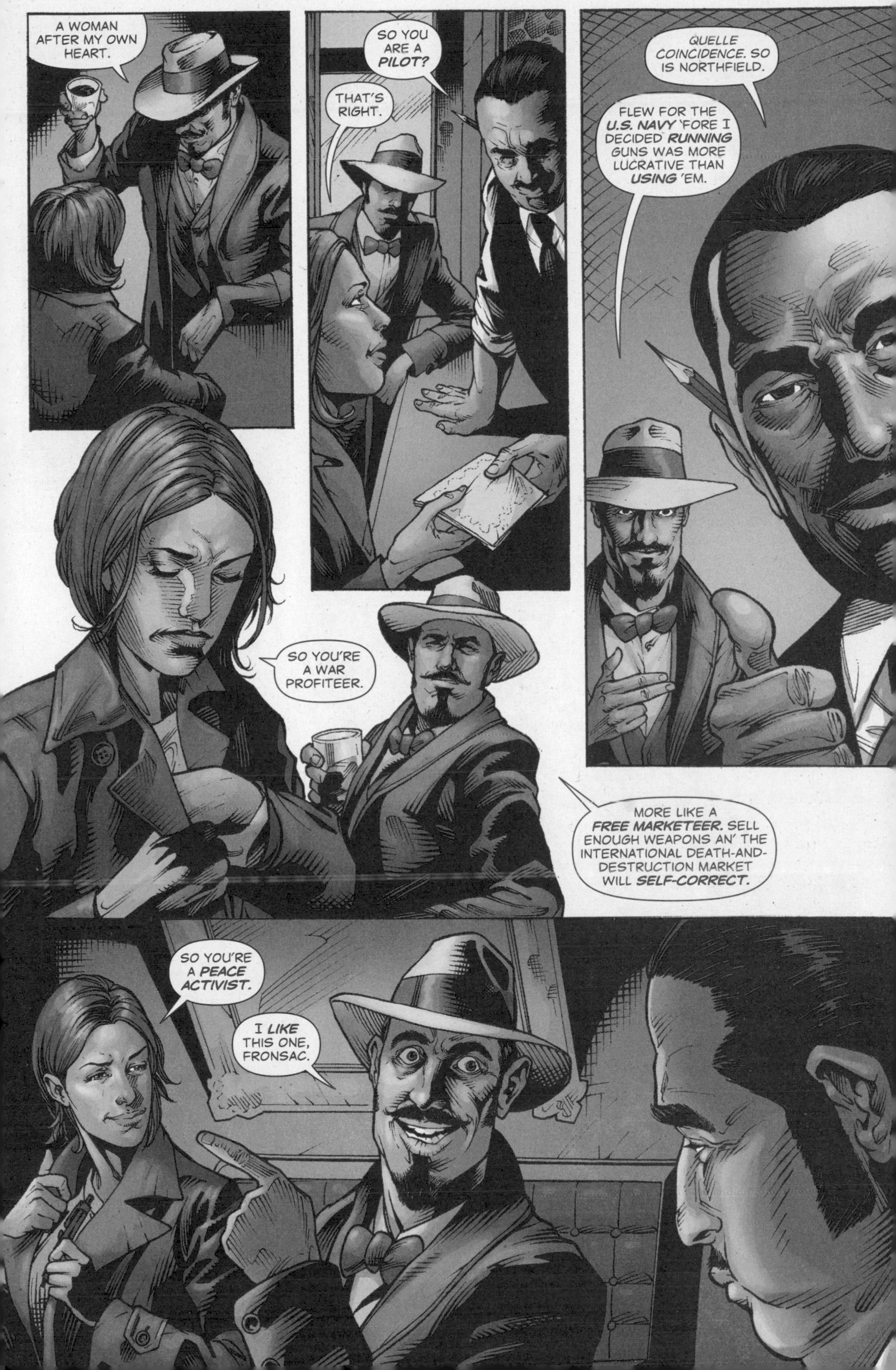
A WOMAN AFTER MY OWN HEART.
SO YOU ARE A PILOT?
THAT'S RIGHT.
QUELLE COINCIDENCE. SO IS NORTHFIELD.
FLEW FOR THE U.S. NAVY 'FORE I DECIDED RUNNING GUNS WAS MORE LUCRATIVE THAN USING 'EM.
SO YOU'RE A WAR PROFITEER.
MORE LIKE A FREE MARKETEER. SELL ENOUGH WEAPONS AN' THE INTERNATIONAL DEATH-AND-DESTRUCTION MARKET WILL SELF-CORRECT.
SO YOU'RE A PEACE ACTIVIST.
I LIKE THIS ONE, FRONSAC.

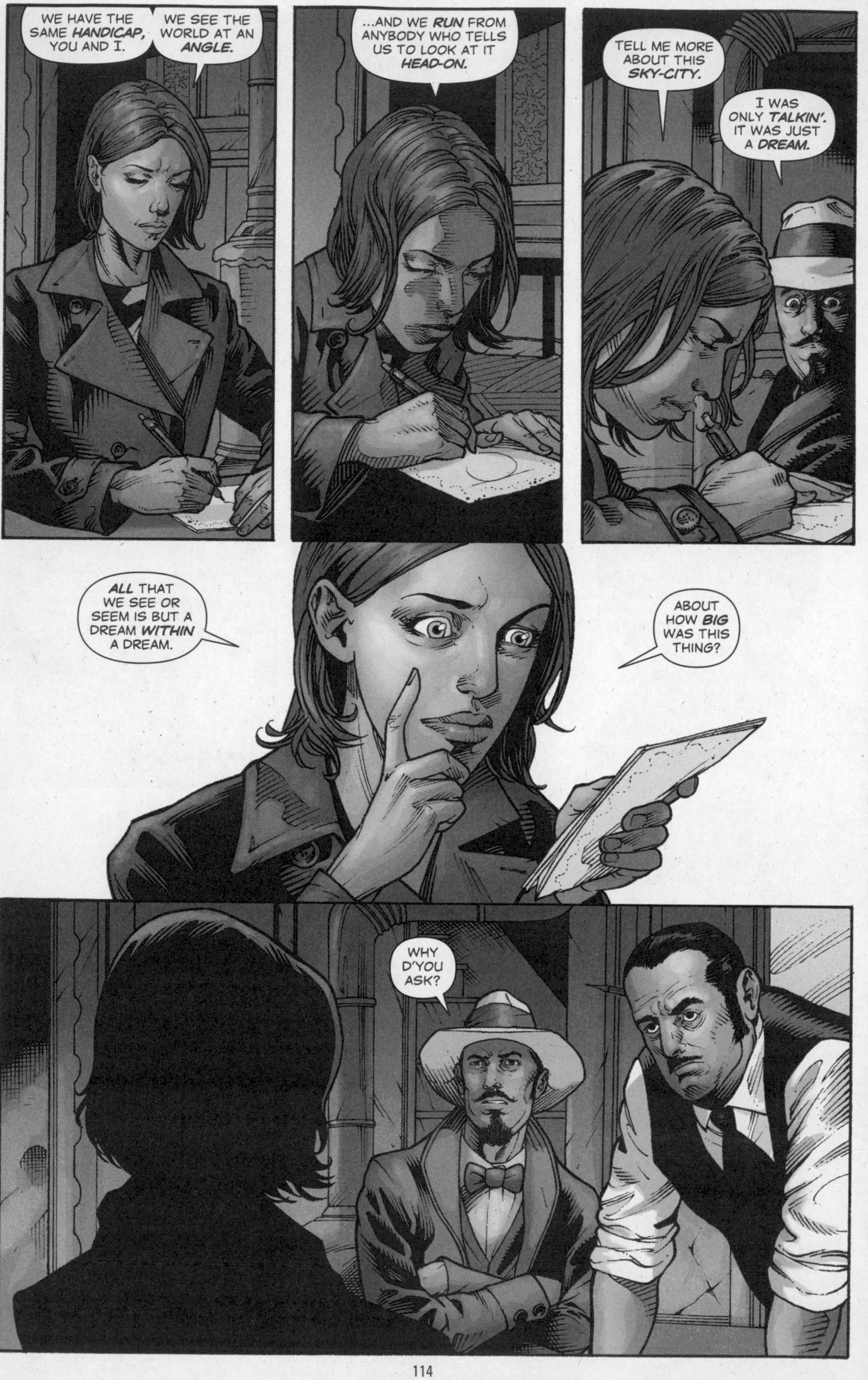
WE HAVE THE SAME HANDICAP, YOU AND I.
WE SEE THE WORLD AT AN ANGLE.
...AND WE RUN FROM ANYBODY WHO TELLS US TO LOOK AT IT HEAD-ON.
TELL ME MORE ABOUT THIS SKY-CITY.
I WAS ONLY TALKIN'. IT WAS JUST A DREAM.
ALL THAT WE SEE OR SEEM IS BUT A DREAM WITHIN A DREAM.
ABOUT HOW BIG WAS THIS THING?
WHY D'YOU ASK?

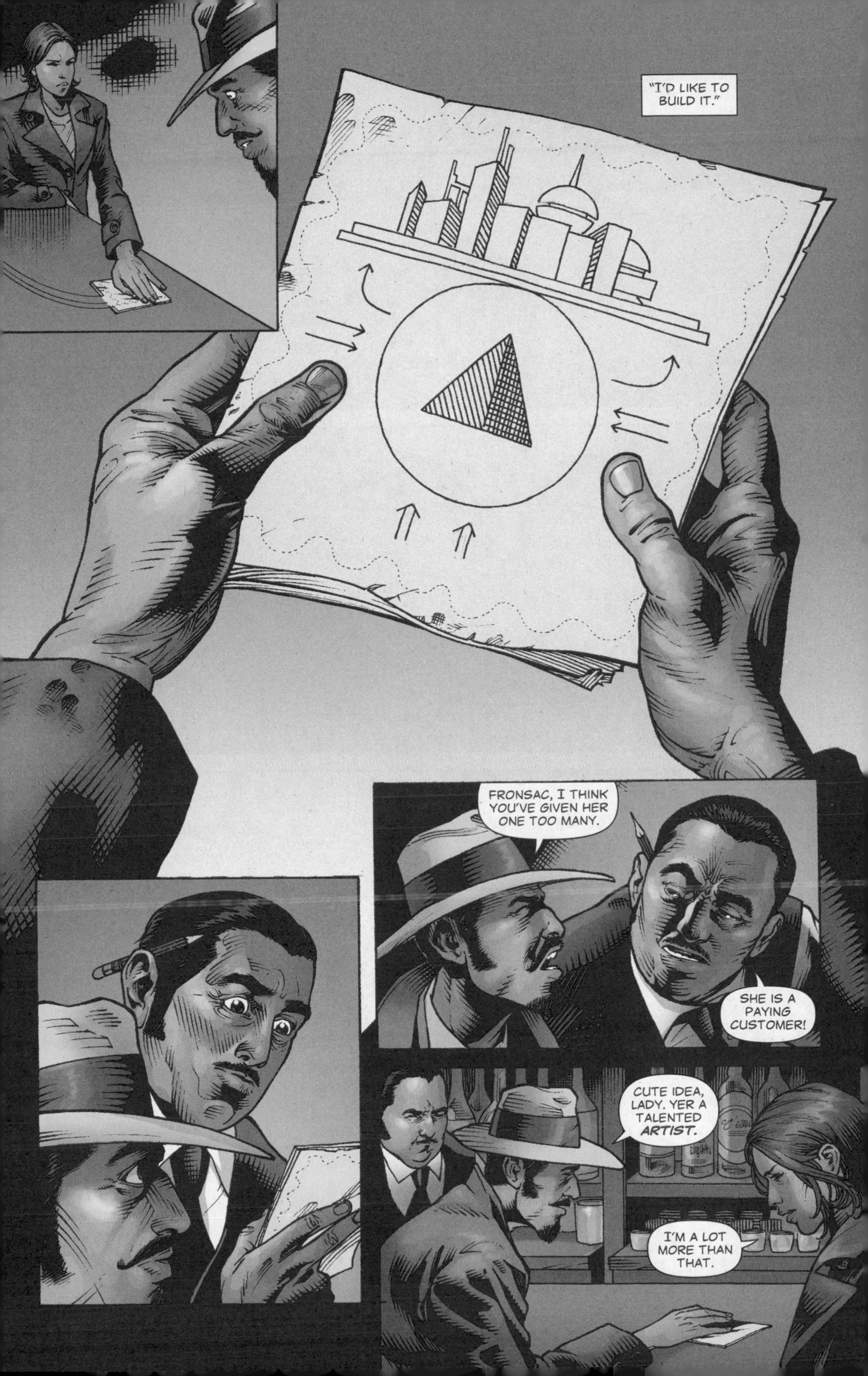
"I'D LIKE TO BUILD IT."
FRONSAC, I THINK YOU'VE GIVEN HER ONE TOO MANY.
SHE IS A PAYING CUSTOMER!
CUTE IDEA, LADY. YER A TALENTED *ARTIST*.
I'M A LOT MORE THAN THAT.

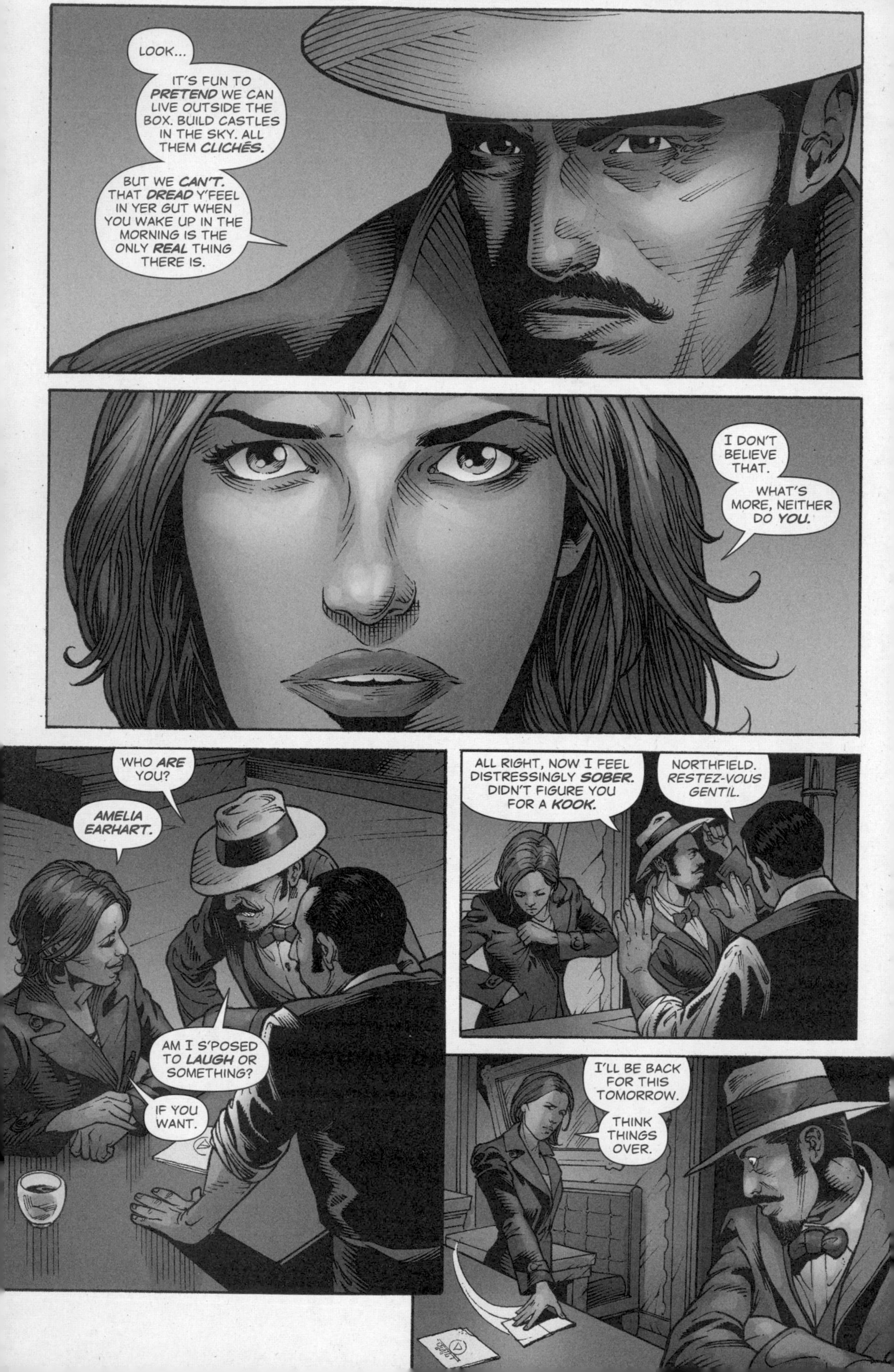
LOOK...
IT'S FUN TO PRETEND WE CAN LIVE OUTSIDE THE BOX. BUILD CASTLES IN THE SKY. ALL THEM CLICHÉS.
BUT WE CAN'T. THAT DREAD Y'FEEL IN YER GUT WHEN YOU WAKE UP IN THE MORNING IS THE ONLY REAL THING THERE IS.
I DON'T BELIEVE THAT.
WHAT'S MORE, NEITHER DO YOU.
WHO ARE YOU?
AMELIA EARHART.
AM I S'POSED TO LAUGH OR SOMETHING?
IF YOU WANT.
ALL RIGHT, NOW I FEEL DISTRESSINGLY SOBER. DIDN'T FIGURE YOU FOR A KOOK.
NORTHFIELD. RESTEZ-VOUS GENTIL.
I'LL BE BACK FOR THIS TOMORROW.
THINK THINGS OVER.

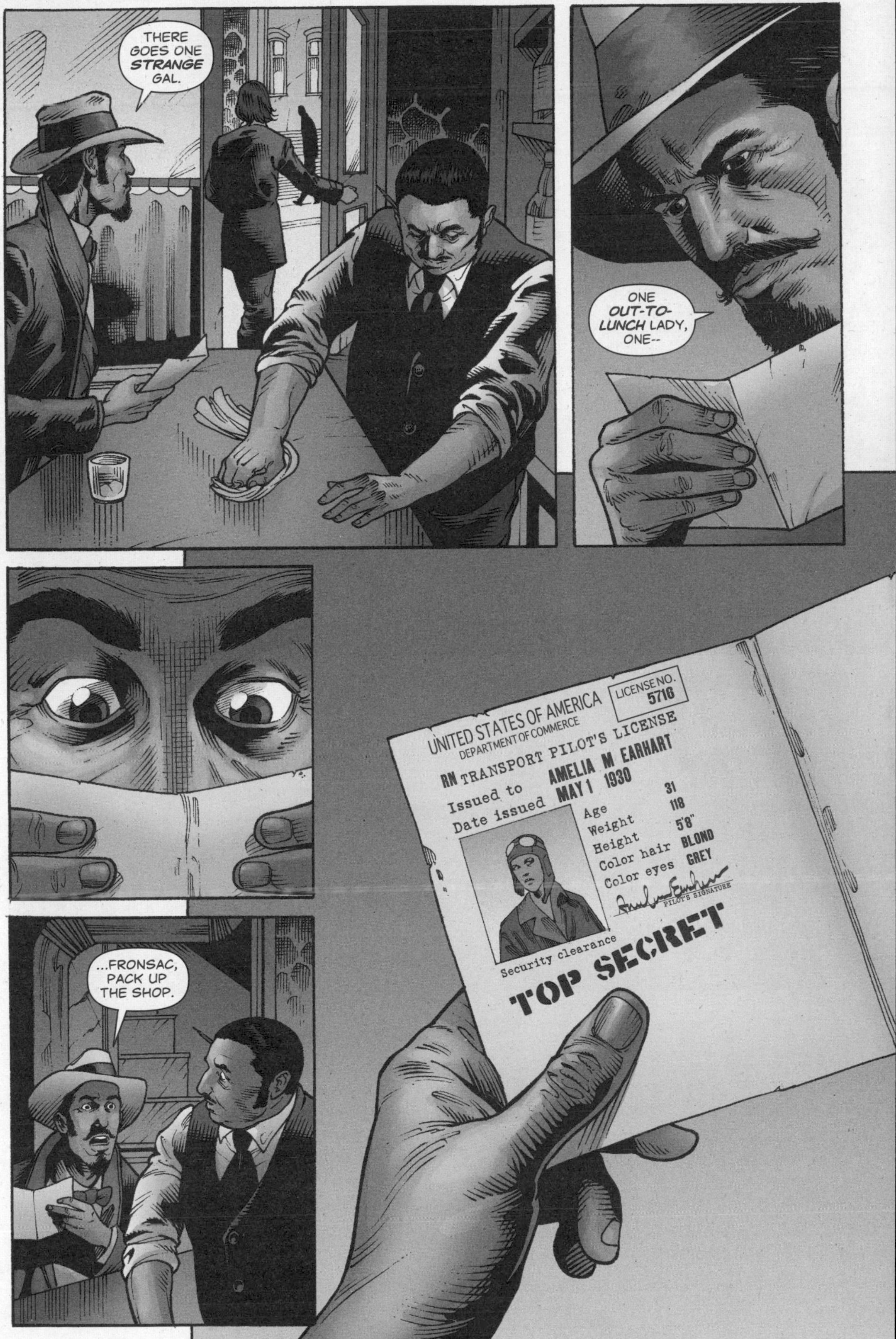
THERE GOES ONE STRANGE GAL.
ONE OUT-TO-LUNCH LADY, ONE--
UNITED STATES OF AMERICA
DEPARTMENT OF COMMERCE
LICENSE NO. 5716
RN TRANSPORT PILOT'S LICENSE
Issued to AMELIA M EARHART
Date issued MAY 1 1930
Age 31
Weight 118
Height 5'8"
Color hair BLOND
Color eyes GREY
PILOT'S SIGNATURE
Security clearance
TOP SECRET
...FRONSAC, PACK UP THE SHOP.

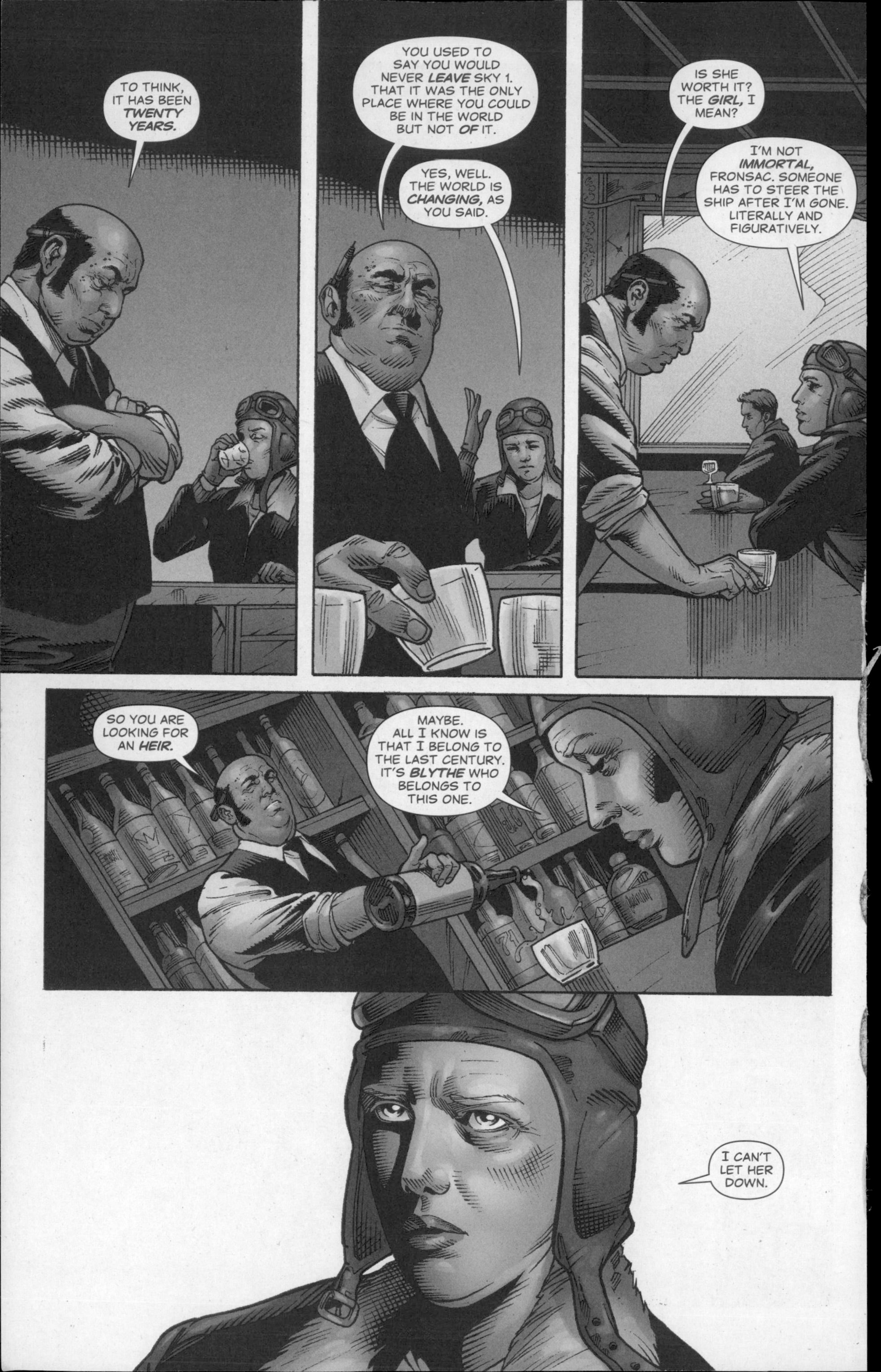

TO THINK, IT HAS BEEN TWENTY YEARS.
YOU USED TO SAY YOU WOULD NEVER LEAVE SKY 1. THAT IT WAS THE ONLY PLACE WHERE YOU COULD BE IN THE WORLD BUT NOT OF IT.
YES, WELL. THE WORLD IS CHANGING, AS YOU SAID.
IS SHE WORTH IT? THE GIRL, I MEAN?
I'M NOT IMMORTAL, FRONSAC. SOMEONE HAS TO STEER THE SHIP AFTER I'M GONE. LITERALLY AND FIGURATIVELY.
SO YOU ARE LOOKING FOR AN HEIR.
MAYBE. ALL I KNOW IS THAT I BELONG TO THE LAST CENTURY. IT'S BLYTHE WHO BELONGS TO THIS ONE.
I CAN'T LET HER DOWN.

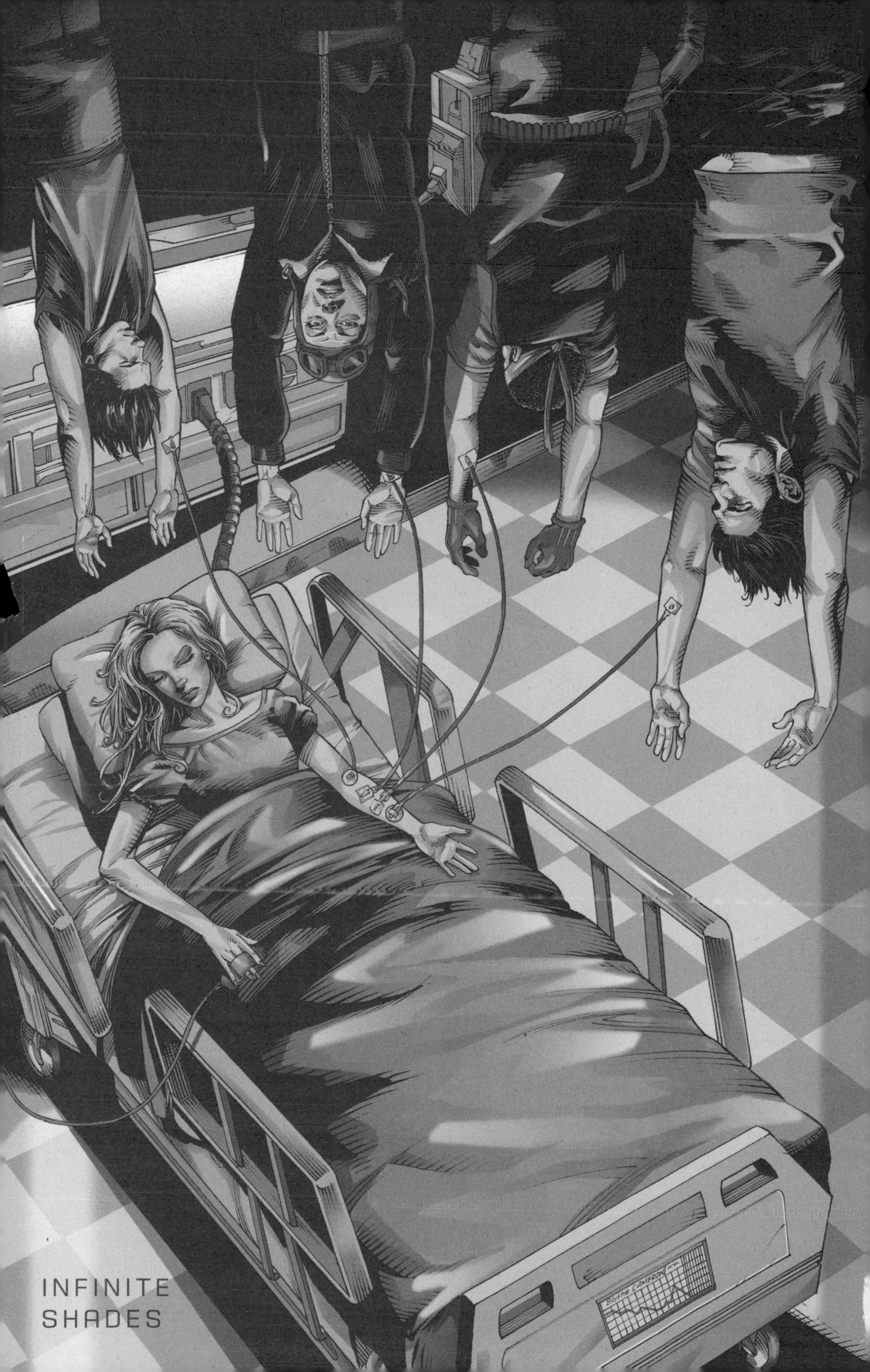
Blythe CAMERON
INFINITE
SHADES

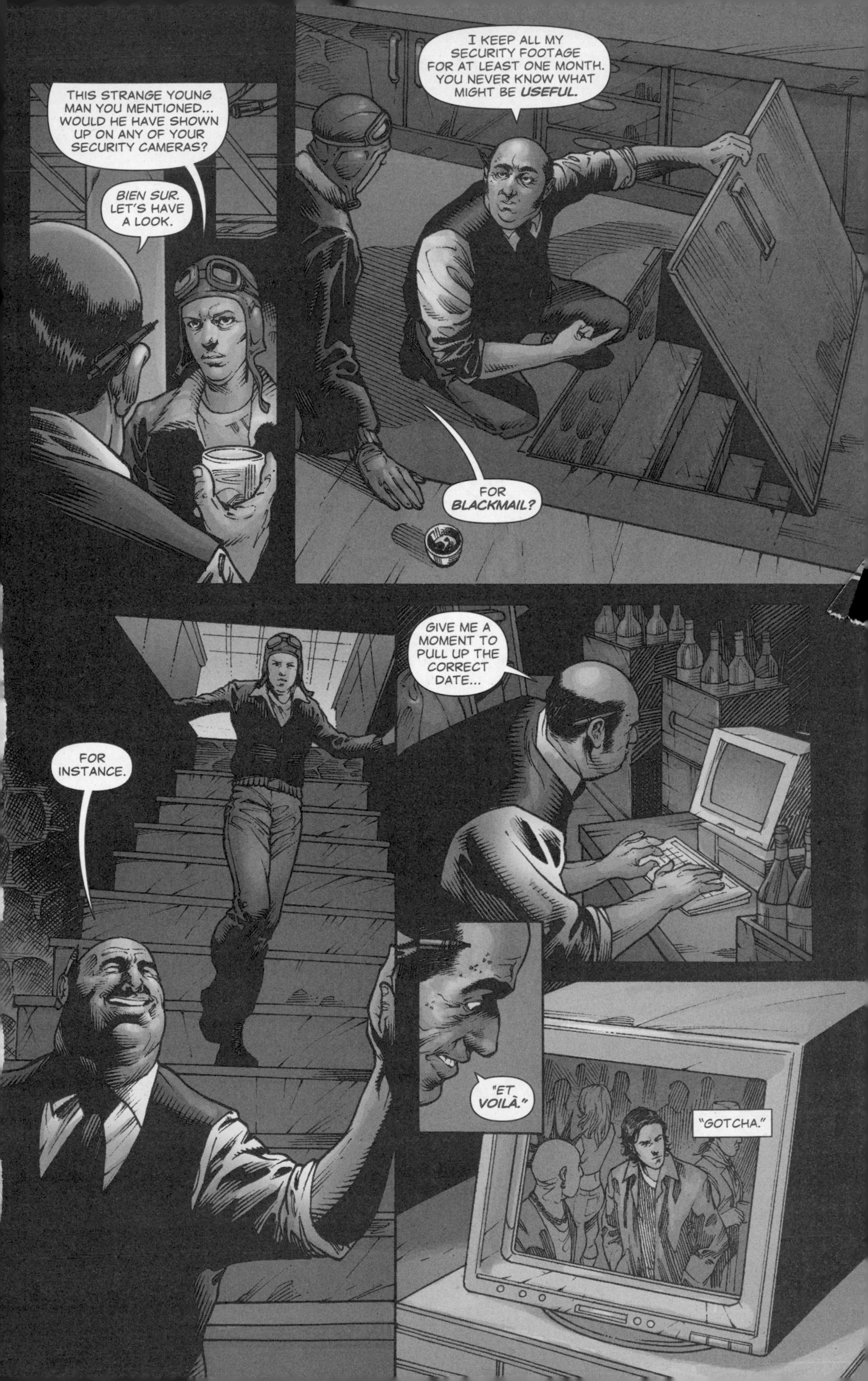
THIS STRANGE YOUNG MAN YOU MENTIONED... WOULD HE HAVE SHOWN UP ON ANY OF YOUR SECURITY CAMERAS?
BIEN SUR. LET'S HAVE A LOOK.
I KEEP ALL MY SECURITY FOOTAGE FOR AT LEAST ONE MONTH. YOU NEVER KNOW WHAT MIGHT BE USEFUL.
FOR BLACKMAIL?
FOR INSTANCE.
GIVE ME A MOMENT TO PULL UP THE CORRECT DATE...
"ET VOILÀ."
"GOTCHA."

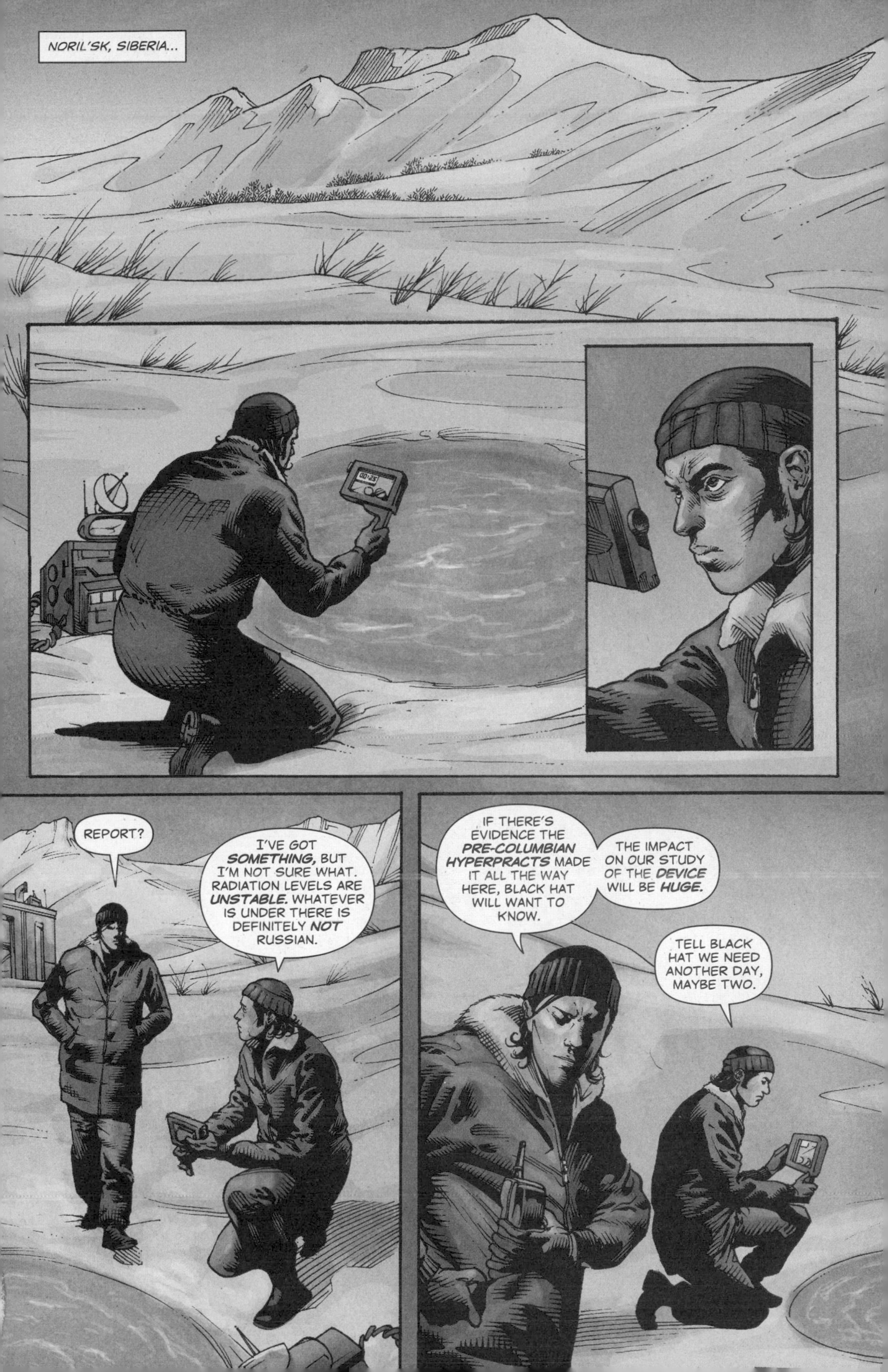
NORIL'SK, SIBERIA...
REPORT?
I'VE GOT SOMETHING, BUT I'M NOT SURE WHAT. RADIATION LEVELS ARE UNSTABLE. WHATEVER IS UNDER THERE IS DEFINITELY NOT RUSSIAN.
IF THERE'S EVIDENCE THE PRE-COLUMBIAN HYPERPRACTS MADE IT ALL THE WAY HERE, BLACK HAT WILL WANT TO KNOW.
THE IMPACT ON OUR STUDY OF THE DEVICE WILL BE HUGE.
TELL BLACK HAT WE NEED ANOTHER DAY, MAYBE TWO.

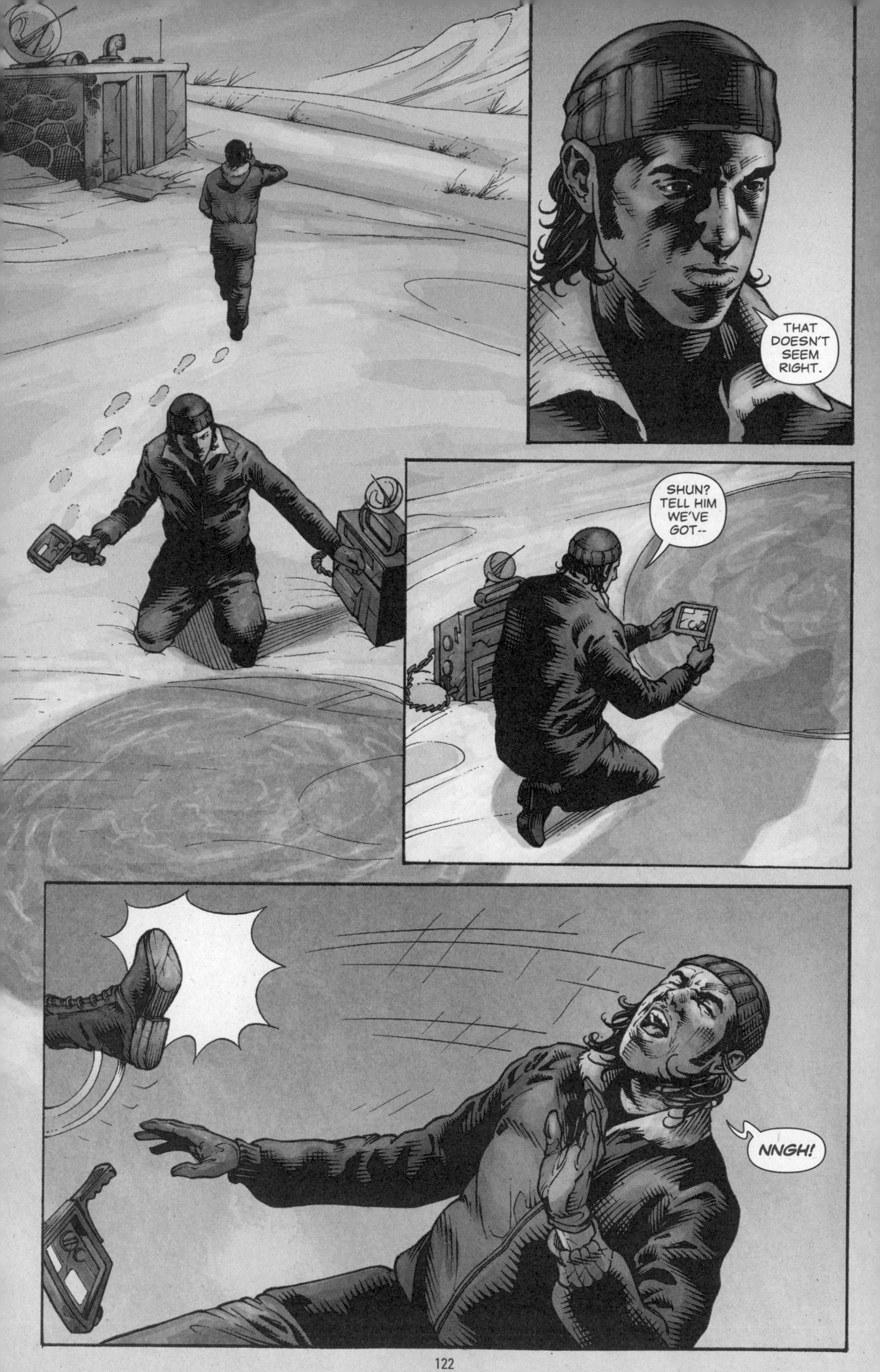
THAT DOESN'T SEEM RIGHT.
SHUN? TELL HIM WE'VE GOT--
NNGH!

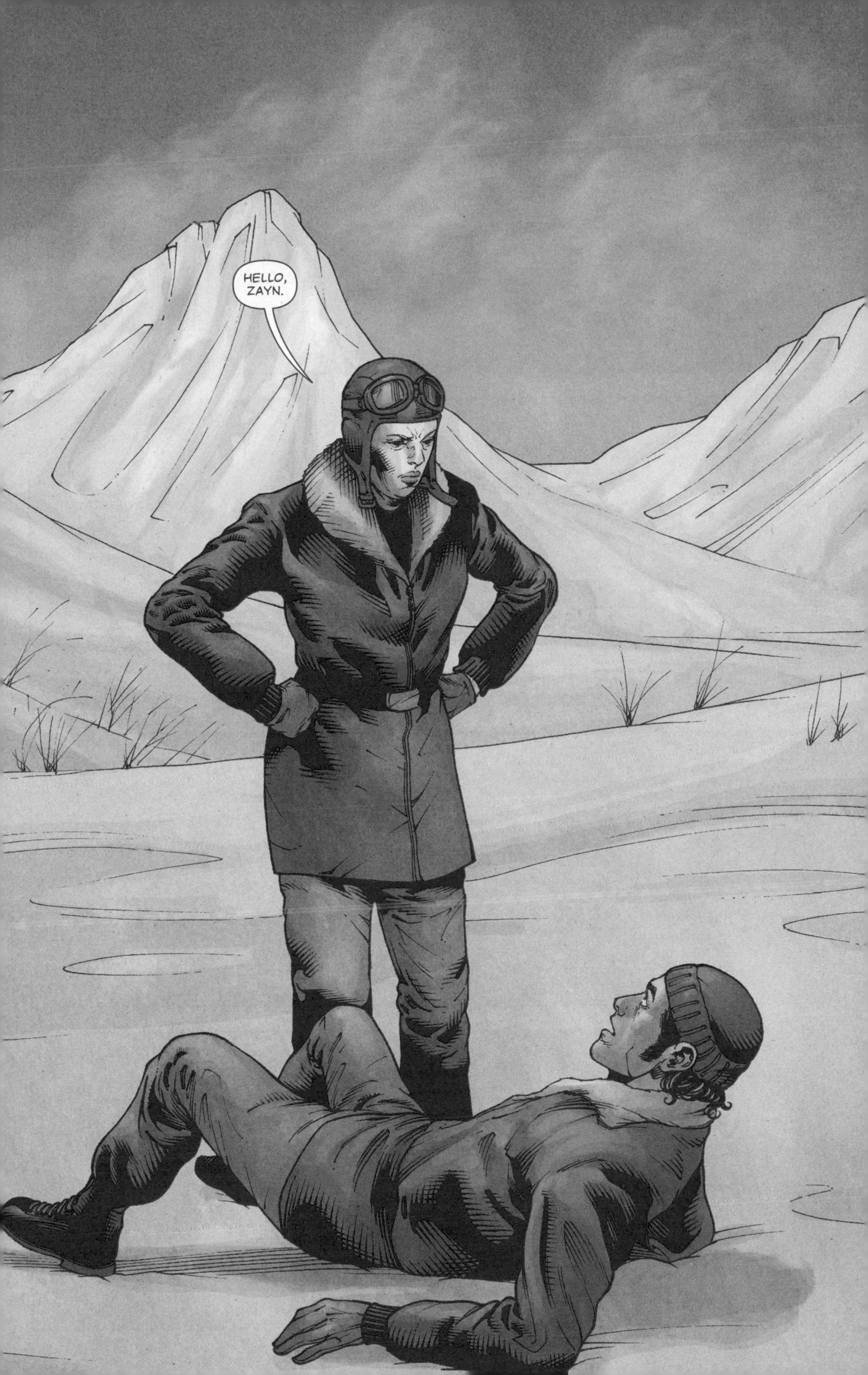
HELLO, ZAYN.

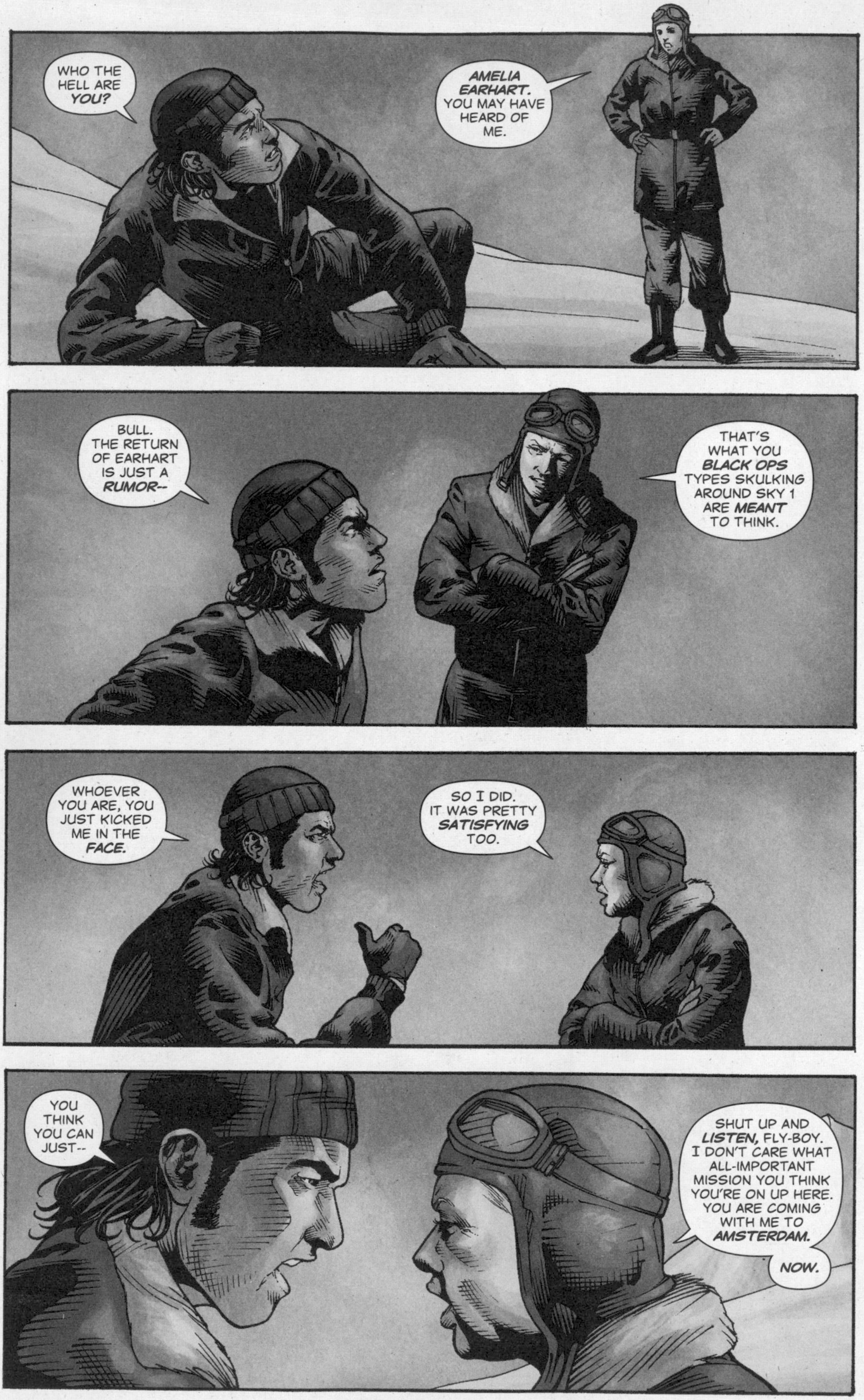
WHO THE HELL ARE *YOU?*
AMELIA EARHART. YOU MAY HAVE HEARD OF ME.
BULL. THE RETURN OF EARHART IS JUST A *RUMOR--*
THAT'S WHAT YOU *BLACK OPS* TYPES SKULKING AROUND SKY 1 ARE *MEANT* TO THINK.
WHOEVER YOU ARE, YOU JUST KICKED ME IN THE *FACE.*
SO I DID. IT WAS PRETTY *SATISFYING* TOO.
YOU THINK YOU CAN JUST--
SHUT UP AND *LISTEN,* FLY-BOY. I DON'T CARE WHAT ALL-IMPORTANT MISSION YOU THINK YOU'RE ON UP HERE. YOU ARE COMING WITH ME TO *AMSTERDAM.*
NOW.

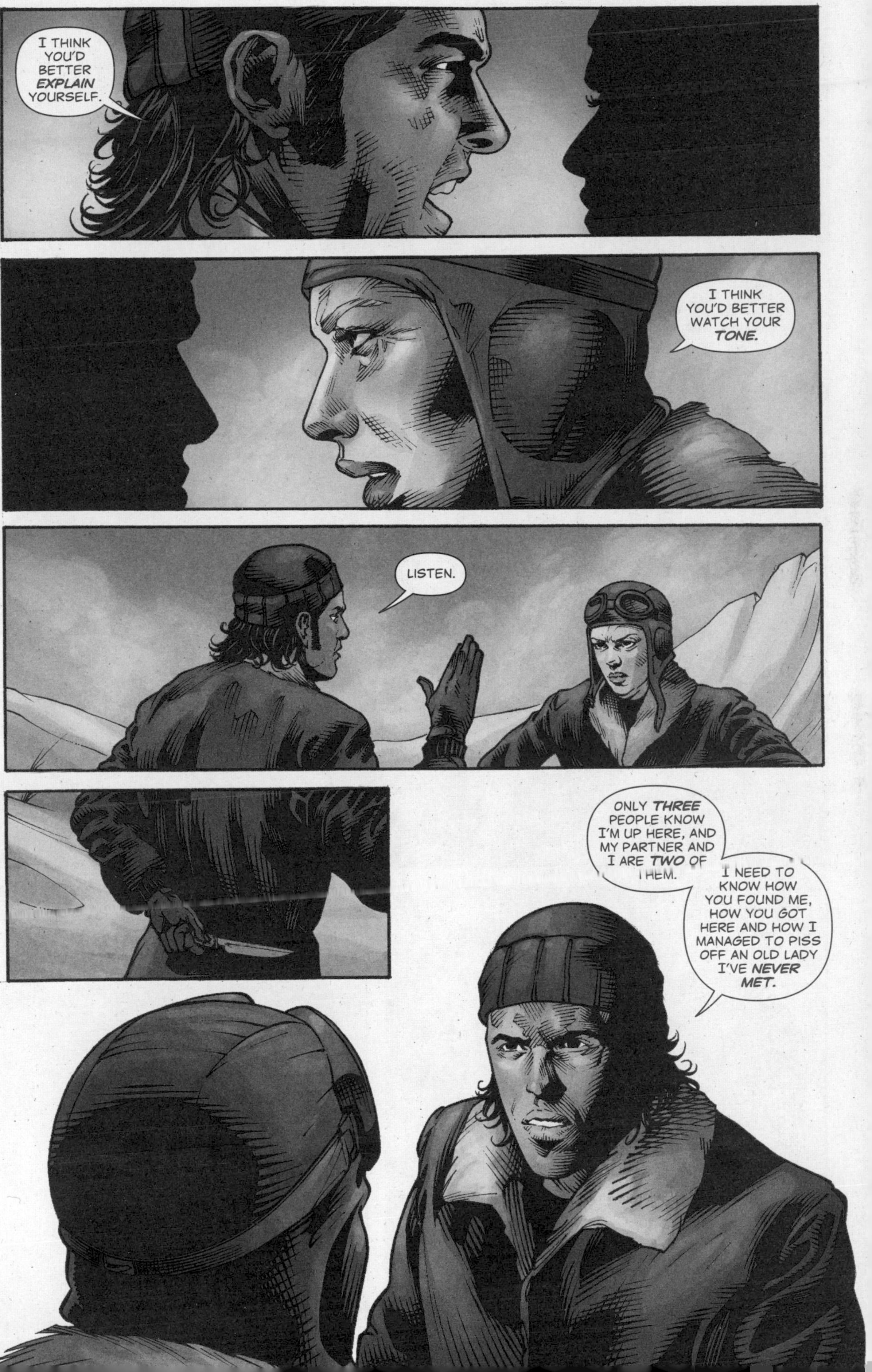
I THINK YOU'D BETTER EXPLAIN YOURSELF.
I THINK YOU'D BETTER WATCH YOUR TONE.
LISTEN.
ONLY THREE PEOPLE KNOW I'M UP HERE, AND MY PARTNER AND I ARE TWO OF THEM.
I NEED TO KNOW HOW YOU FOUND ME, HOW YOU GOT HERE AND HOW I MANAGED TO PISS OFF AN OLD LADY I'VE NEVER MET.

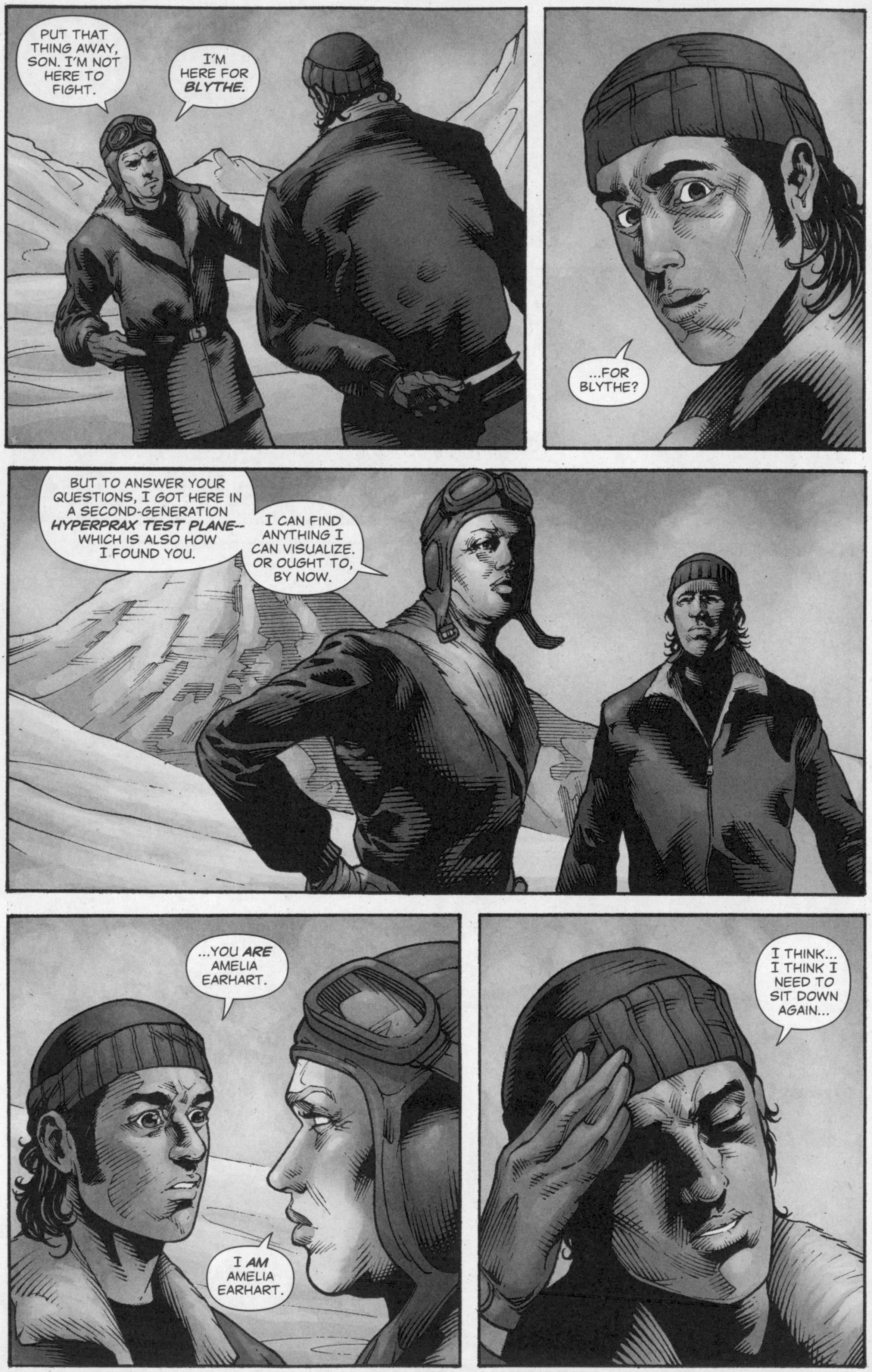
PUT THAT THING AWAY, SON. I'M NOT HERE TO FIGHT.
I'M HERE FOR BLYTHE.
...FOR BLYTHE?
BUT TO ANSWER YOUR QUESTIONS, I GOT HERE IN A SECOND-GENERATION HYPERPRAX TEST PLANE-- WHICH IS ALSO HOW I FOUND YOU.
I CAN FIND ANYTHING I CAN VISUALIZE. OR OUGHT TO, BY NOW.
...YOU ARE AMELIA EARHART.
I AM AMELIA EARHART.
I THINK... I THINK I NEED TO SIT DOWN AGAIN...

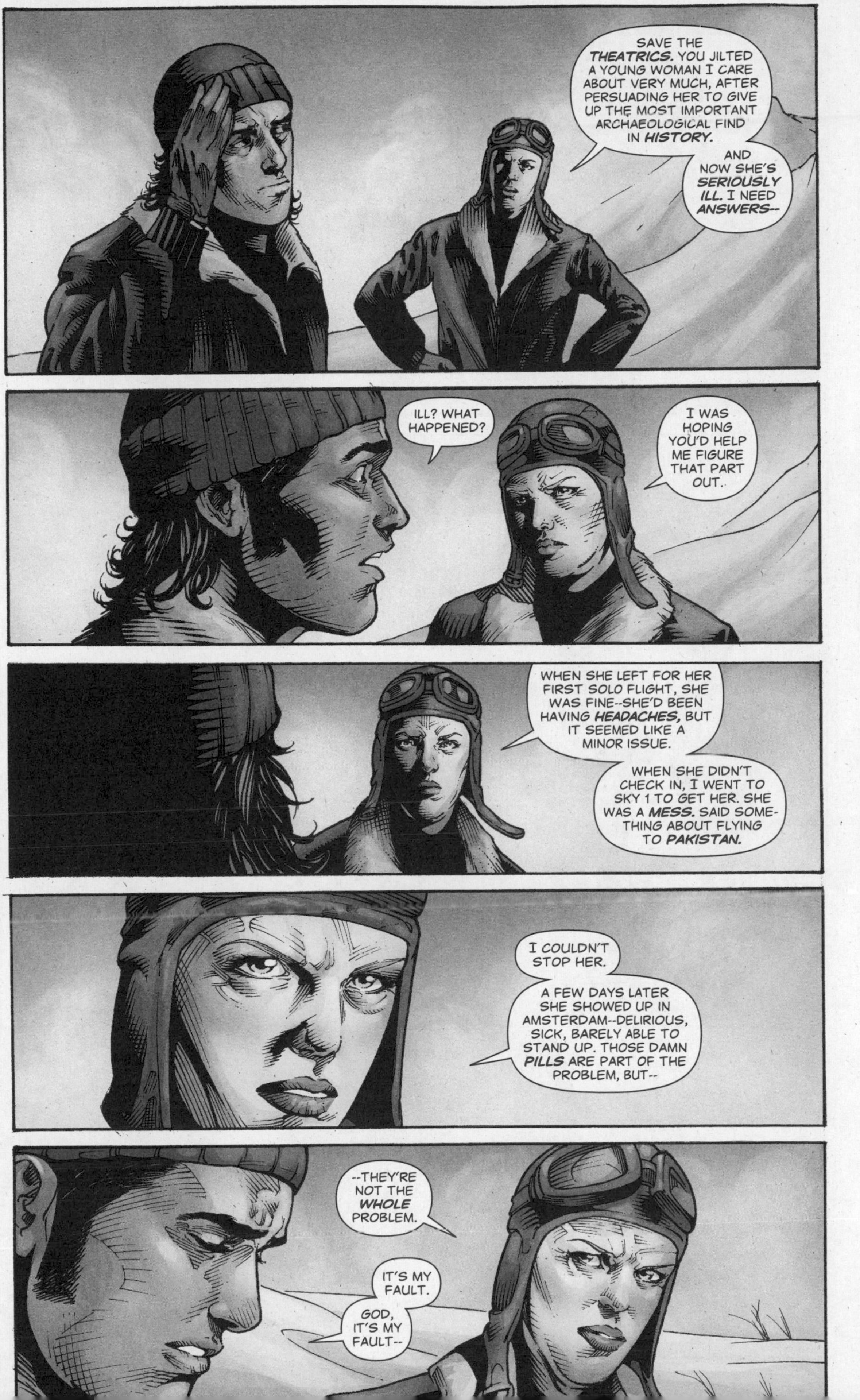
SAVE THE THEATRICS. YOU JILTED A YOUNG WOMAN I CARE ABOUT VERY MUCH, AFTER PERSUADING HER TO GIVE UP THE MOST IMPORTANT ARCHAEOLOGICAL FIND IN HISTORY.
AND NOW SHE'S SERIOUSLY ILL. I NEED ANSWERS--
ILL? WHAT HAPPENED?
I WAS HOPING YOU'D HELP ME FIGURE THAT PART OUT.
WHEN SHE LEFT FOR HER FIRST SOLO FLIGHT, SHE WAS FINE--SHE'D BEEN HAVING HEADACHES, BUT IT SEEMED LIKE A MINOR ISSUE.
WHEN SHE DIDN'T CHECK IN, I WENT TO SKY 1 TO GET HER. SHE WAS A MESS. SAID SOME-THING ABOUT FLYING TO PAKISTAN.
I COULDN'T STOP HER.
A FEW DAYS LATER SHE SHOWED UP IN AMSTERDAM--DELIRIOUS, SICK, BARELY ABLE TO STAND UP. THOSE DAMN PILLS ARE PART OF THE PROBLEM, BUT--
--THEY'RE NOT THE WHOLE PROBLEM.
IT'S MY FAULT.
GOD, IT'S MY FAULT--

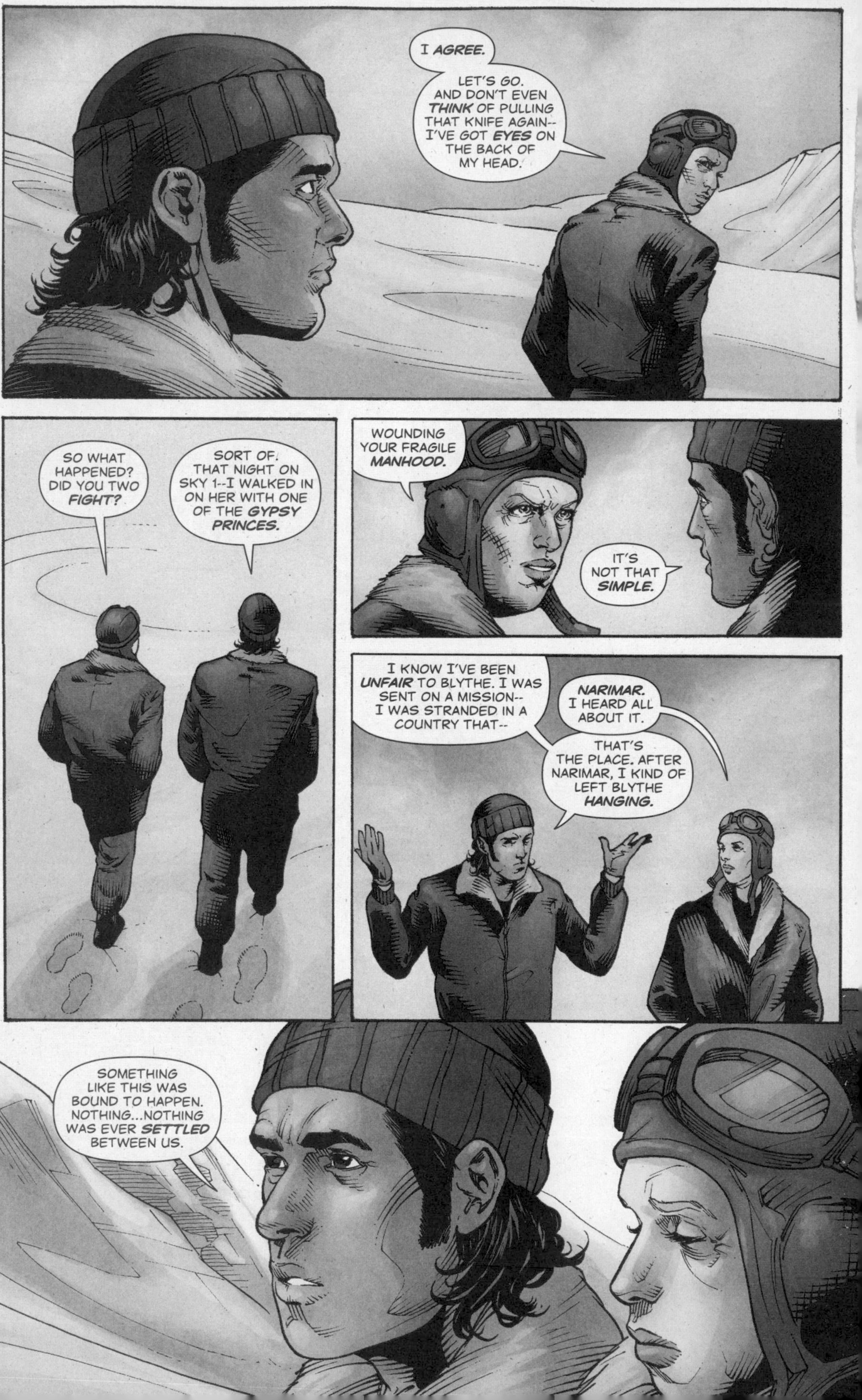
I AGREE.
LET'S GO. AND DON'T EVEN THINK OF PULLING THAT KNIFE AGAIN-- I'VE GOT EYES ON THE BACK OF MY HEAD.
SO WHAT HAPPENED? DID YOU TWO FIGHT?
SORT OF. THAT NIGHT ON SKY 1--I WALKED IN ON HER WITH ONE OF THE GYPSY PRINCES.
WOUNDING YOUR FRAGILE MANHOOD.
IT'S NOT THAT SIMPLE.
I KNOW I'VE BEEN UNFAIR TO BLYTHE. I WAS SENT ON A MISSION-- I WAS STRANDED IN A COUNTRY THAT--
NARIMAR. I HEARD ALL ABOUT IT.
THAT'S THE PLACE. AFTER NARIMAR, I KIND OF LEFT BLYTHE HANGING.
SOMETHING LIKE THIS WAS BOUND TO HAPPEN. NOTHING...NOTHING WAS EVER SETTLED BETWEEN US.

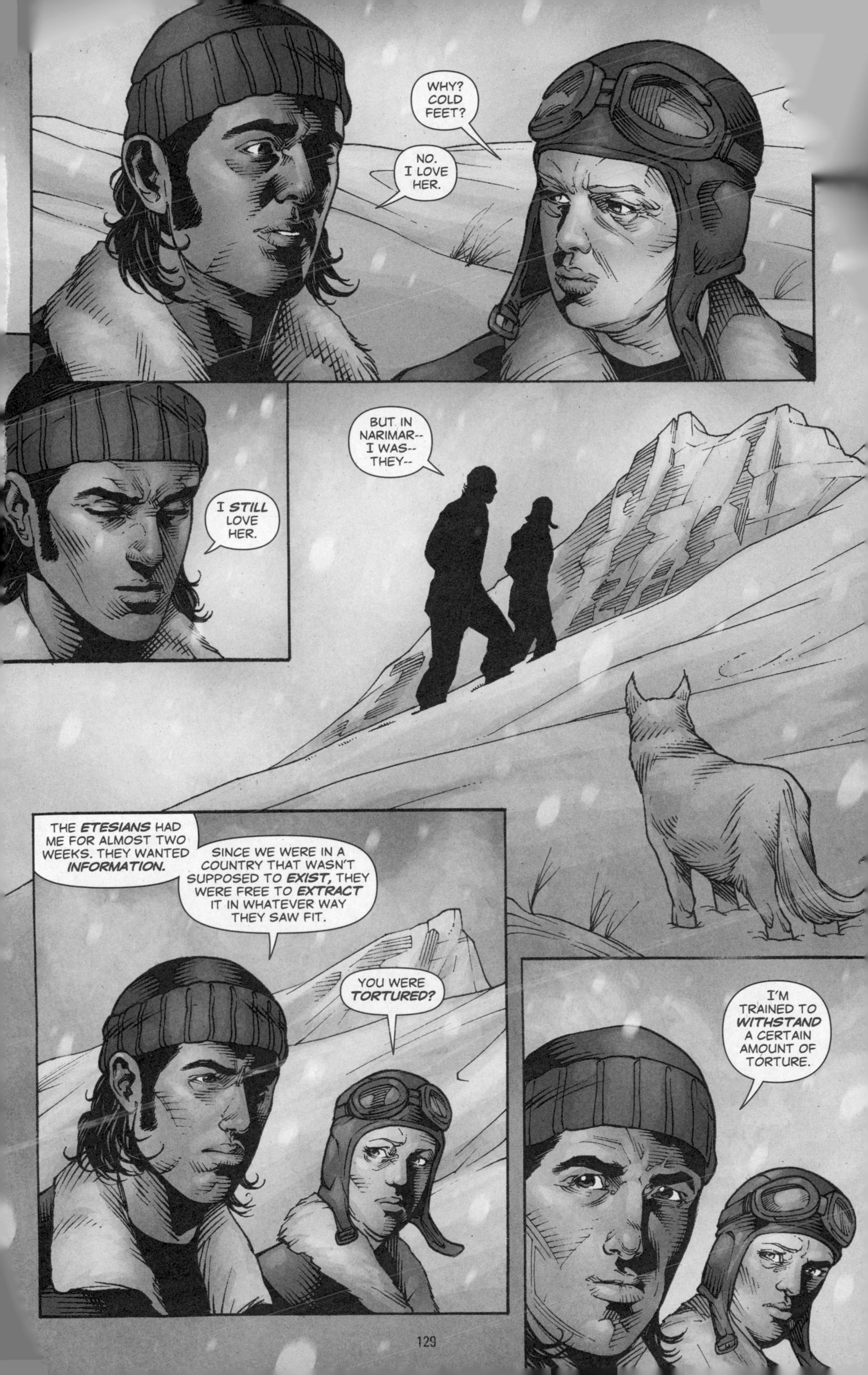
WHY? COLD FEET?
NO. I LOVE HER.
I STILL LOVE HER.
BUT IN NARIMAR-- I WAS-- THEY--
THE ETESIANS HAD ME FOR ALMOST TWO WEEKS. THEY WANTED INFORMATION.
SINCE WE WERE IN A COUNTRY THAT WASN'T SUPPOSED TO EXIST, THEY WERE FREE TO EXTRACT IT IN WHATEVER WAY THEY SAW FIT.
YOU WERE TORTURED?
I'M TRAINED TO WITHSTAND A CERTAIN AMOUNT OF TORTURE.

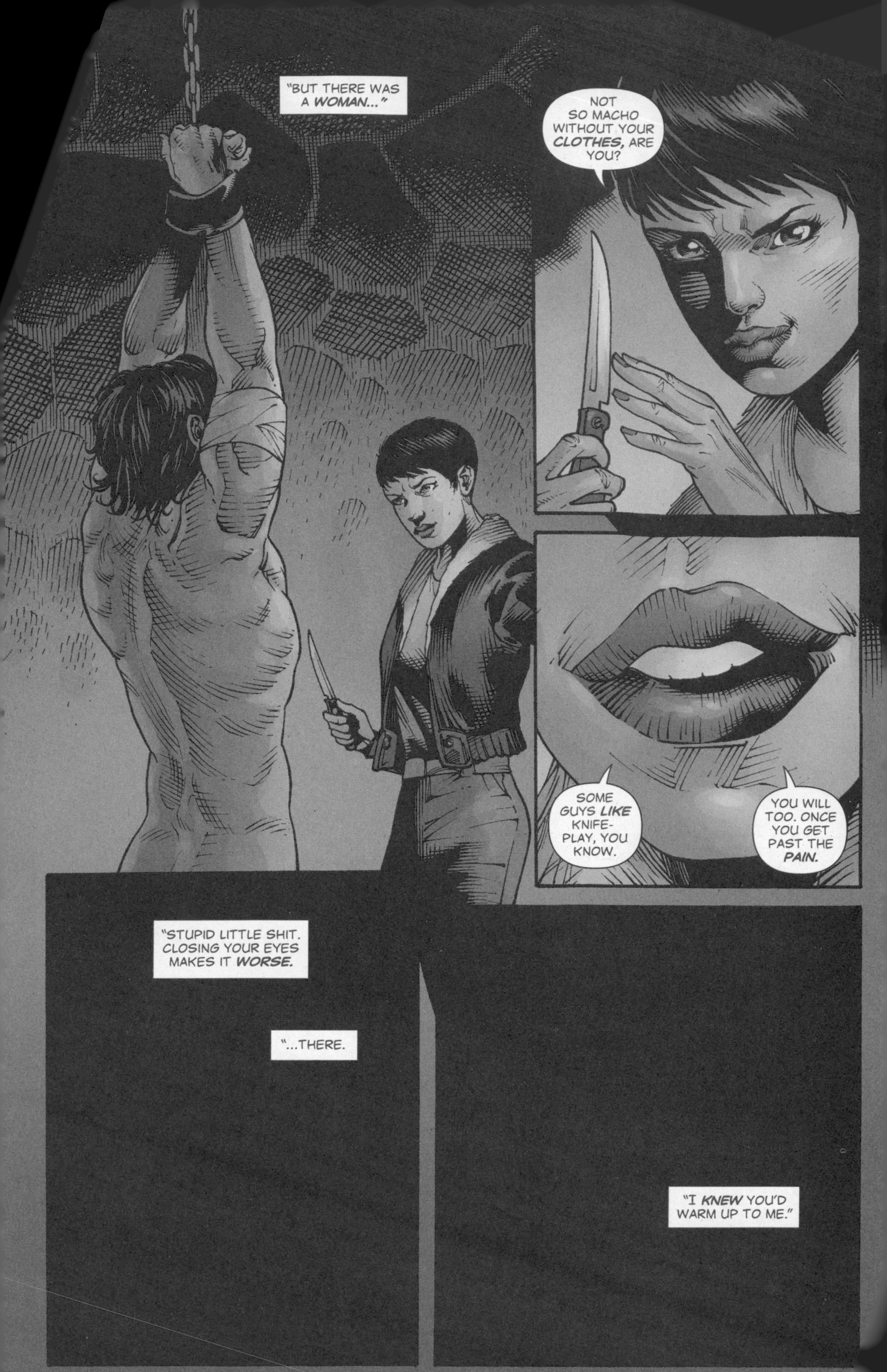

"BUT THERE WAS A WOMAN..."
NOT SO MACHO WITHOUT YOUR CLOTHES, ARE YOU?
SOME GUYS LIKE KNIFE-PLAY, YOU KNOW.
YOU WILL TOO. ONCE YOU GET PAST THE PAIN.
"STUPID LITTLE SHIT. CLOSING YOUR EYES MAKES IT WORSE.
"...THERE.
"I KNEW YOU'D WARM UP TO ME."

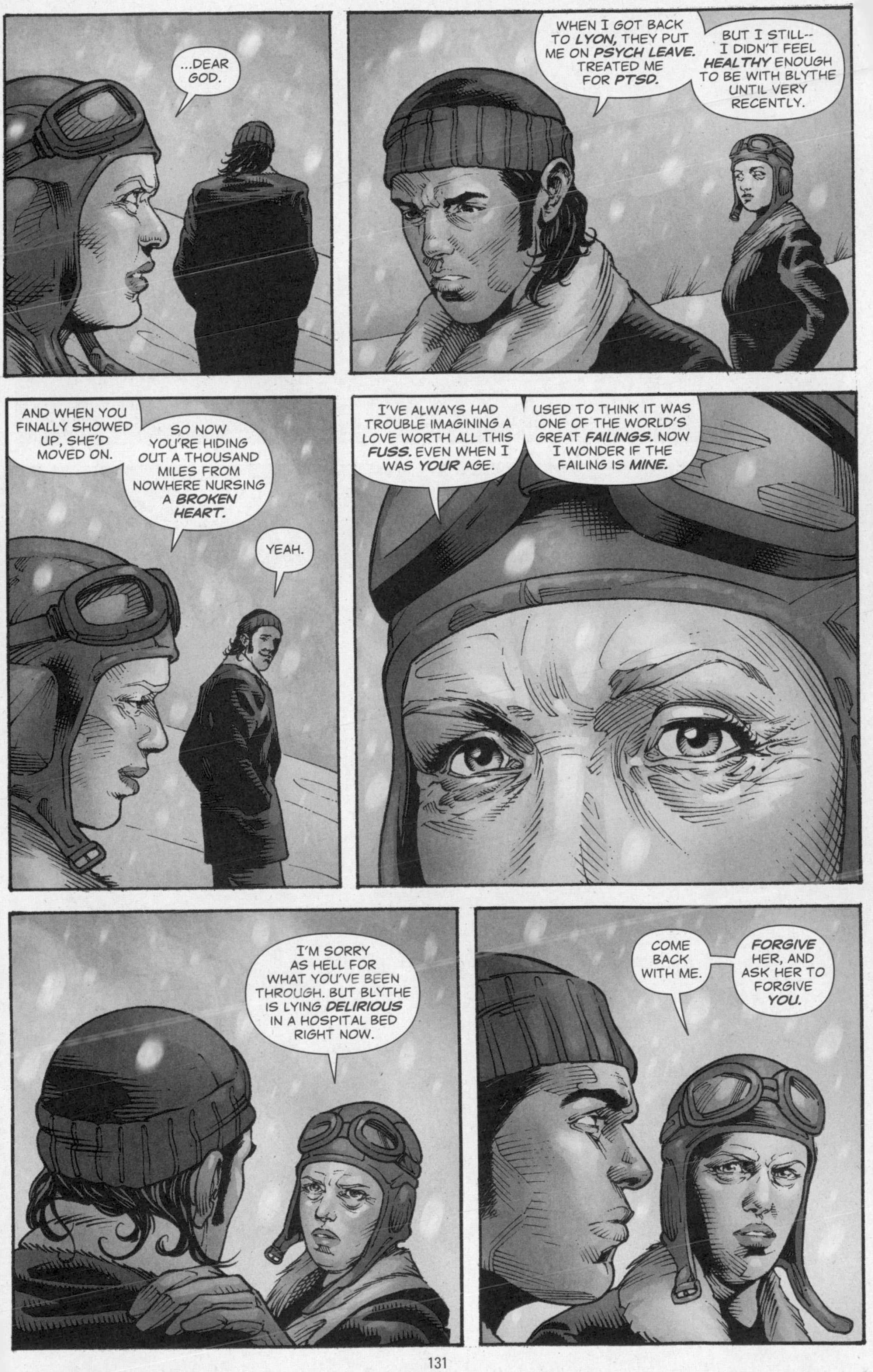
...DEAR GOD.
WHEN I GOT BACK TO LYON, THEY PUT ME ON PSYCH LEAVE. TREATED ME FOR PTSD.
BUT I STILL-- I DIDN'T FEEL HEALTHY ENOUGH TO BE WITH BLYTHE UNTIL VERY RECENTLY.
AND WHEN YOU FINALLY SHOWED UP, SHE'D MOVED ON.
SO NOW YOU'RE HIDING OUT A THOUSAND MILES FROM NOWHERE NURSING A BROKEN HEART.
YEAH.
I'VE ALWAYS HAD TROUBLE IMAGINING A LOVE WORTH ALL THIS FUSS. EVEN WHEN I WAS YOUR AGE.
USED TO THINK IT WAS ONE OF THE WORLD'S GREAT FAILINGS. NOW I WONDER IF THE FAILING IS MINE.
I'M SORRY AS HELL FOR WHAT YOU'VE BEEN THROUGH. BUT BLYTHE IS LYING DELIRIOUS IN A HOSPITAL BED RIGHT NOW.
COME BACK WITH ME.
FORGIVE HER, AND ASK HER TO FORGIVE YOU.

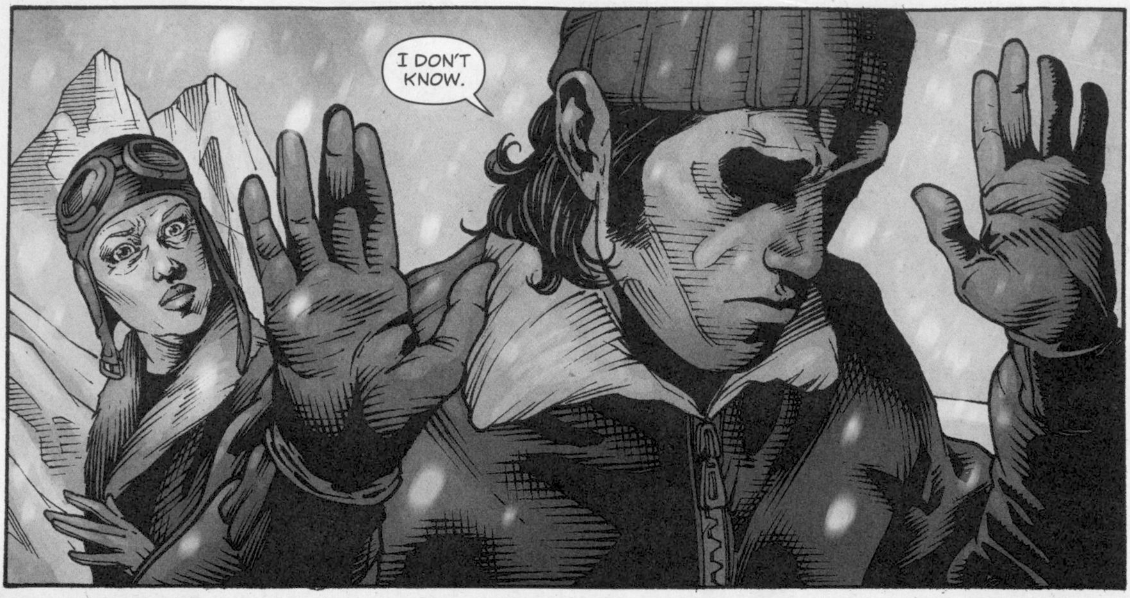
I DON'T KNOW.

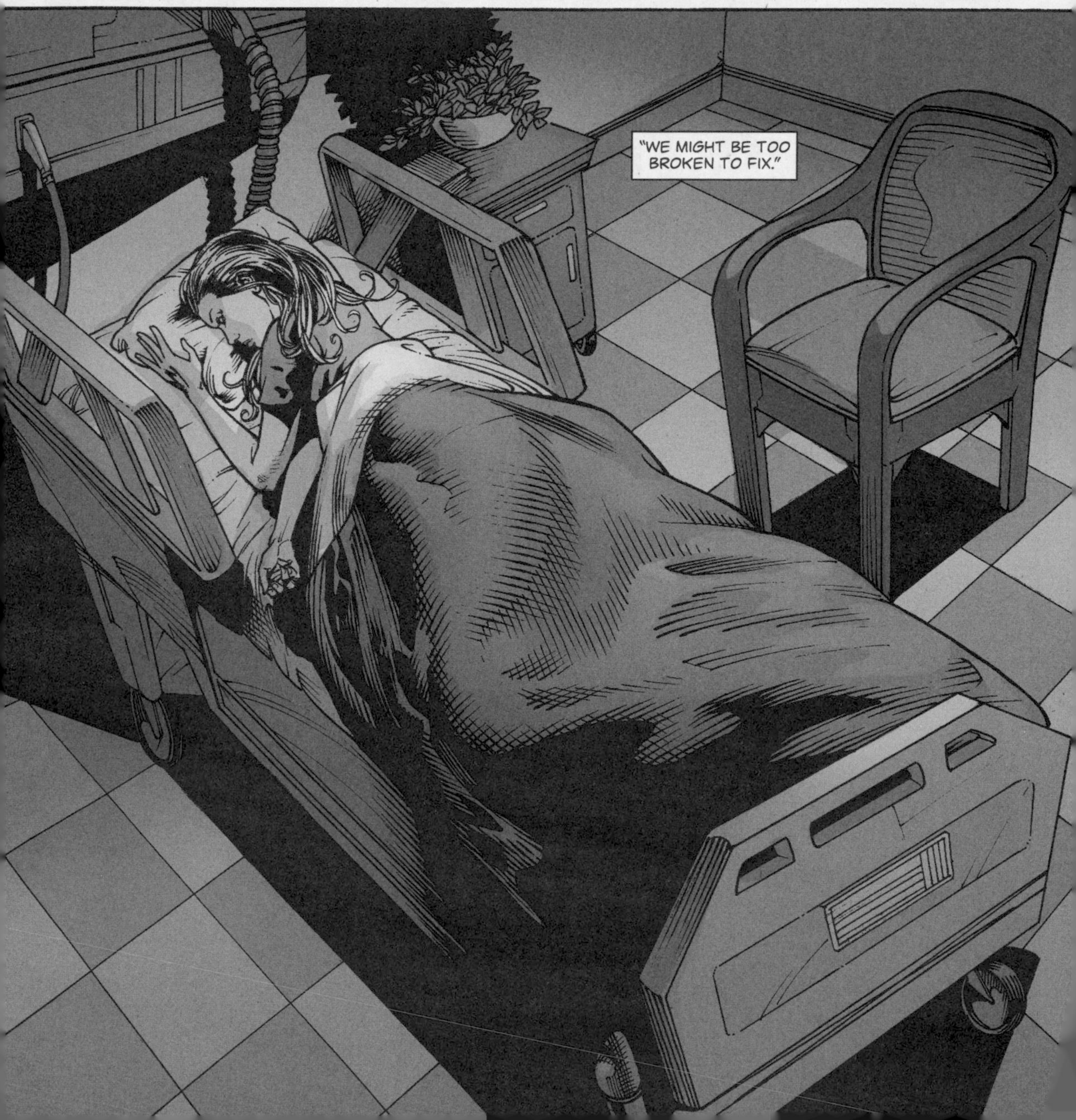
"WE MIGHT BE TOO BROKEN TO FIX."

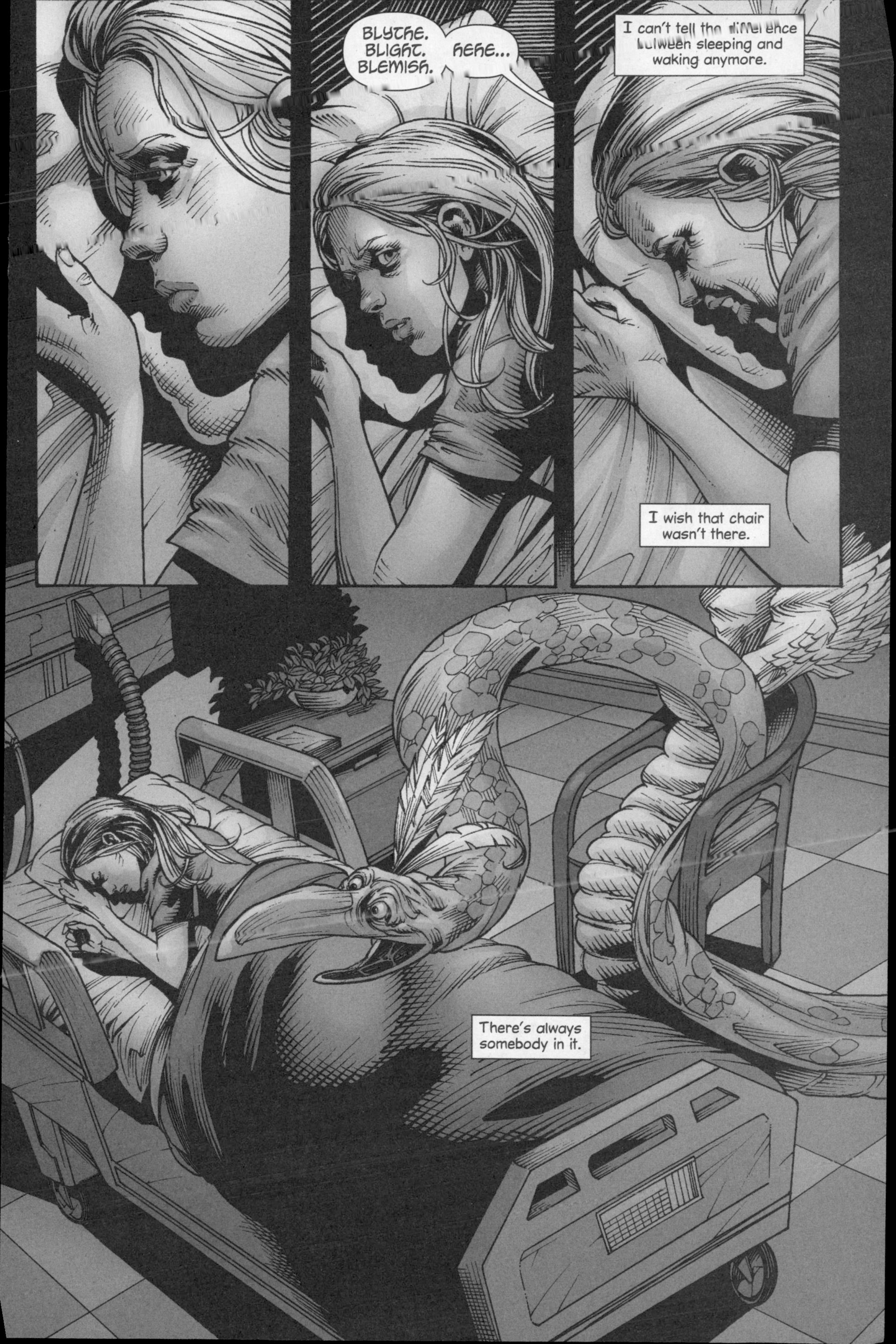
BLYTHE. BLIGHT. BLEMISH.
HERE...
I can't tell the difference between sleeping and waking anymore.
I wish that chair wasn't there.
There's always somebody in it.

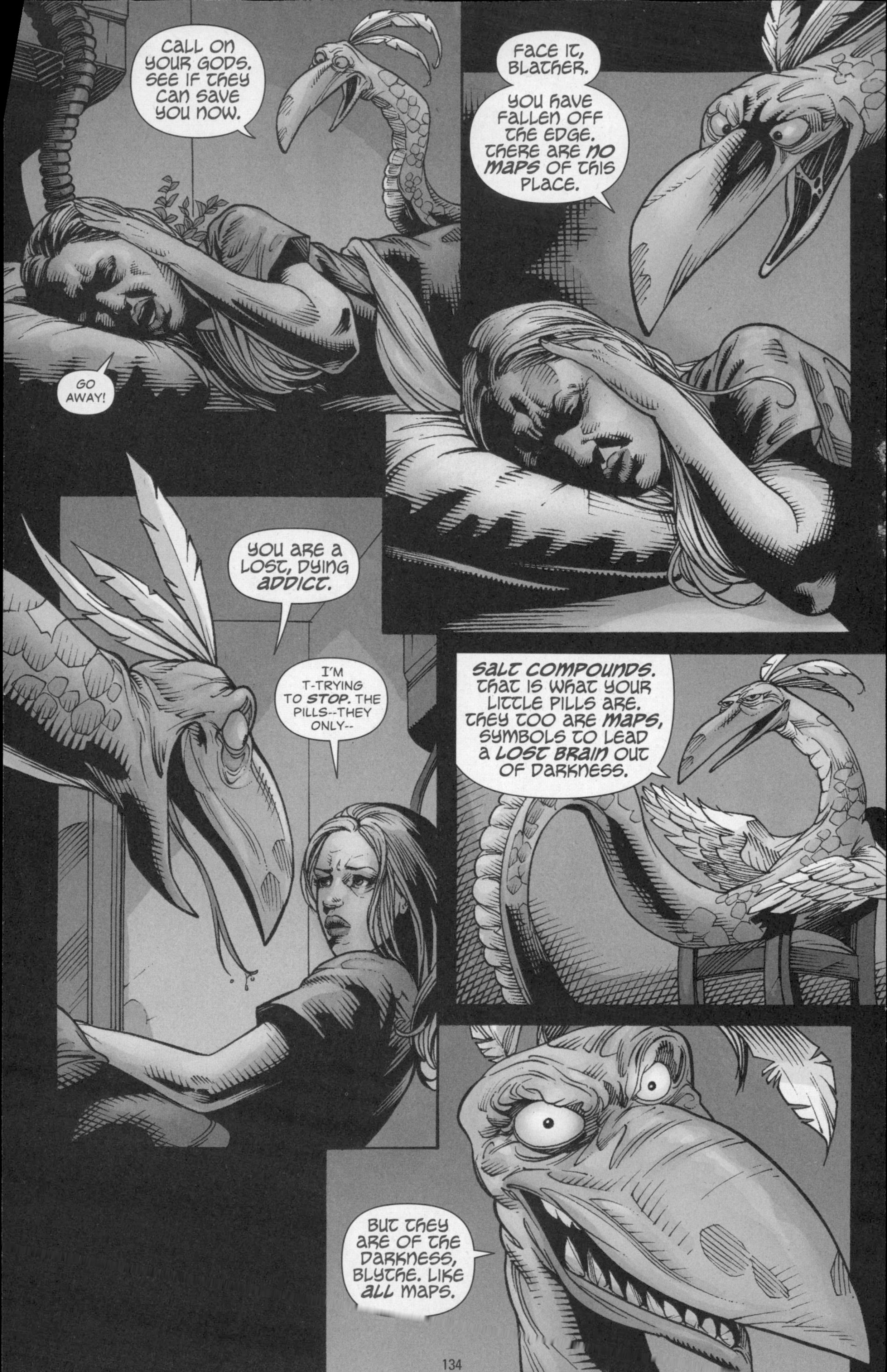
CALL ON YOUR GODS. SEE IF THEY CAN SAVE YOU NOW.
GO AWAY!
FACE IT, BLATHER.
YOU HAVE FALLEN OFF THE EDGE. THERE ARE *NO MAPS* OF THIS PLACE.
YOU ARE A LOST, DYING *ADDICT*.
I'M T-TRYING TO *STOP*. THE PILLS--THEY ONLY--
SALT COMPOUNDS. THAT IS WHAT YOUR LITTLE PILLS ARE. THEY TOO ARE *MAPS*, SYMBOLS TO LEAD A *LOST BRAIN* OUT OF DARKNESS.
BUT THEY ARE OF THE DARKNESS, BLYTHE. LIKE *ALL* MAPS.

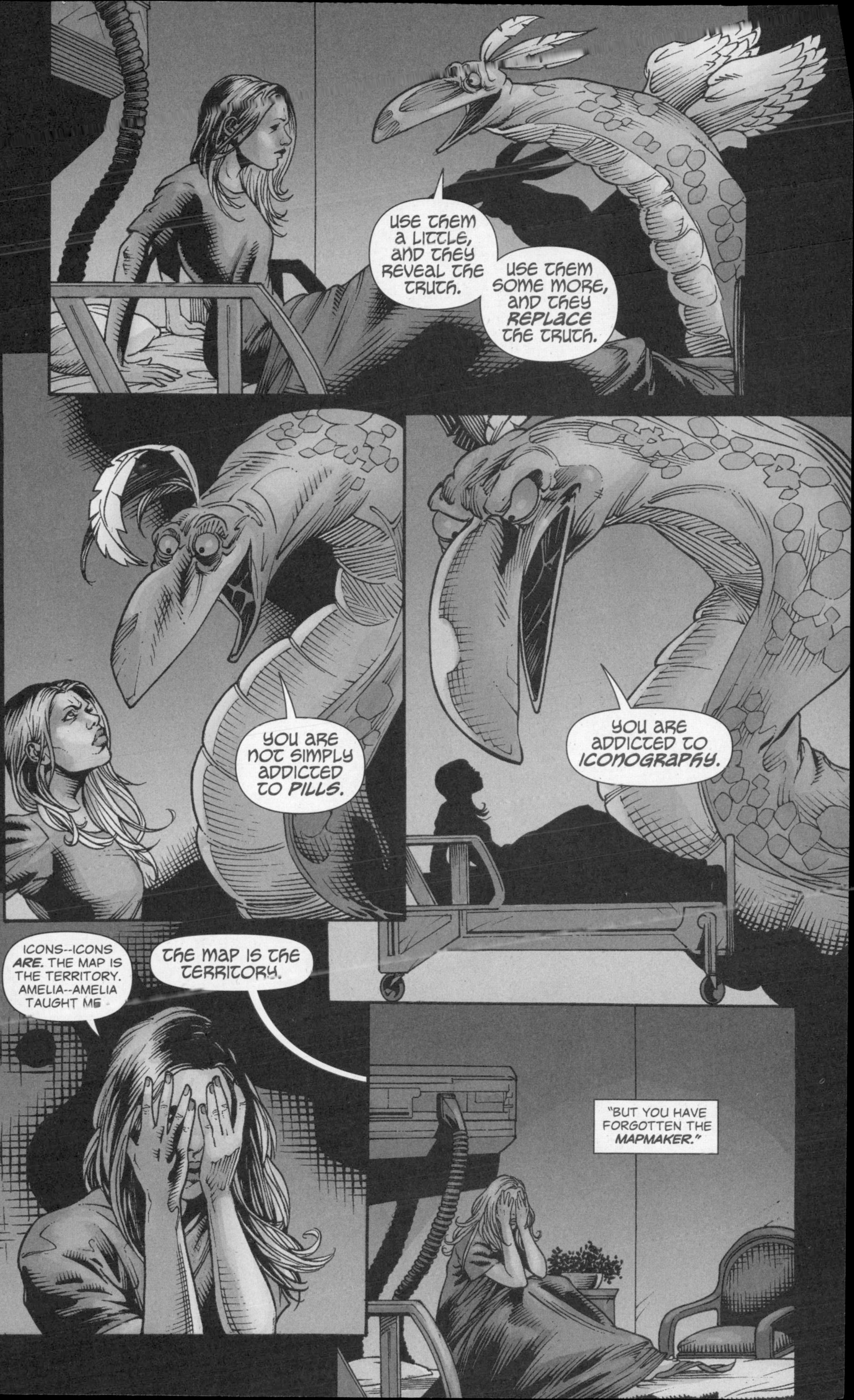
USE THEM A LITTLE, AND THEY REVEAL THE TRUTH.
USE THEM SOME MORE, AND THEY *REPLACE* THE TRUTH.
YOU ARE NOT SIMPLY ADDICTED TO *PILLS*.
YOU ARE ADDICTED TO *ICONOGRAPHY*.
ICONS--ICONS *ARE*. THE MAP IS THE TERRITORY. AMELIA--AMELIA TAUGHT ME
THE MAP IS THE TERRITORY.
"BUT YOU HAVE FORGOTTEN THE *MAPMAKER*."

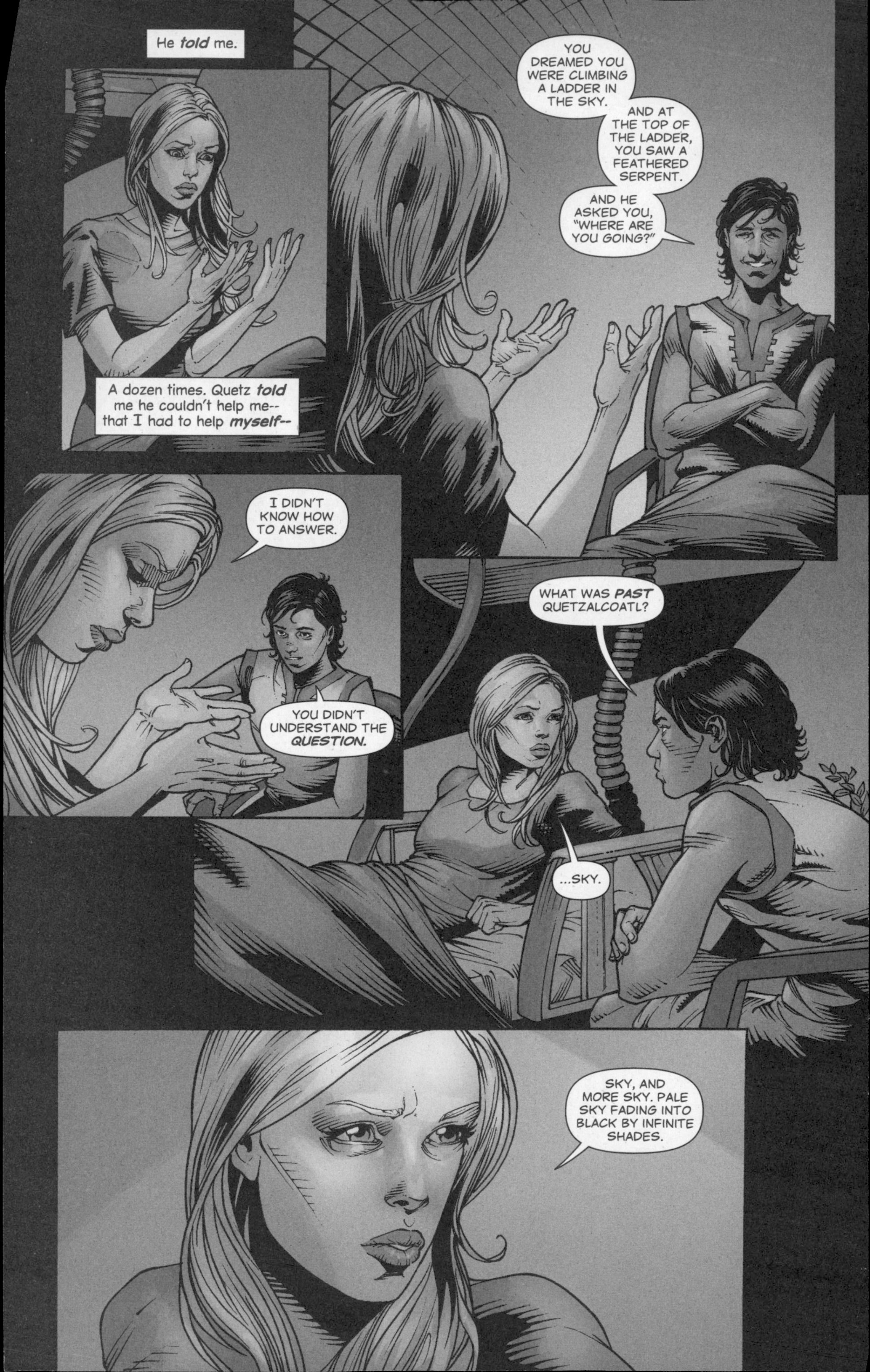

He told me.
A dozen times. Quetz told me he couldn't help me-- that I had to help myself--
YOU DREAMED YOU WERE CLIMBING A LADDER IN THE SKY.
AND AT THE TOP OF THE LADDER, YOU SAW A FEATHERED SERPENT.
AND HE ASKED YOU, "WHERE ARE YOU GOING?"
I DIDN'T KNOW HOW TO ANSWER.
YOU DIDN'T UNDERSTAND THE QUESTION.
WHAT WAS PAST QUETZALCOATL?
...SKY.
SKY, AND MORE SKY. PALE SKY FADING INTO BLACK BY INFINITE SHADES.

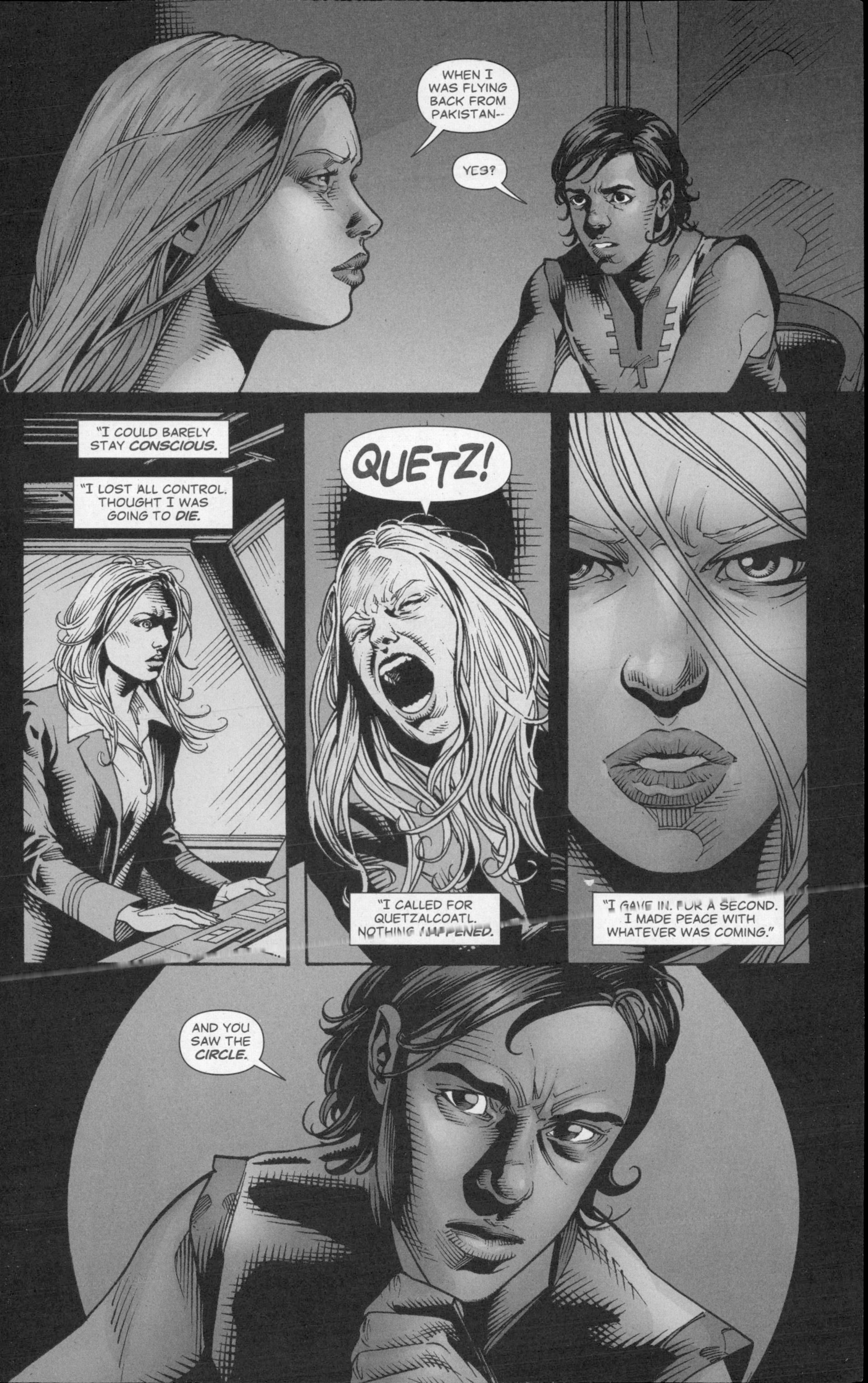
WHEN I WAS FLYING BACK FROM PAKISTAN--
YES?
"I COULD BARELY STAY CONSCIOUS.
"I LOST ALL CONTROL. THOUGHT I WAS GOING TO DIE.
QUETZ!
"I CALLED FOR QUETZALCOATL. NOTHING HAPPENED.
"I GAVE IN. FOR A SECOND. I MADE PEACE WITH WHATEVER WAS COMING."
AND YOU SAW THE CIRCLE.

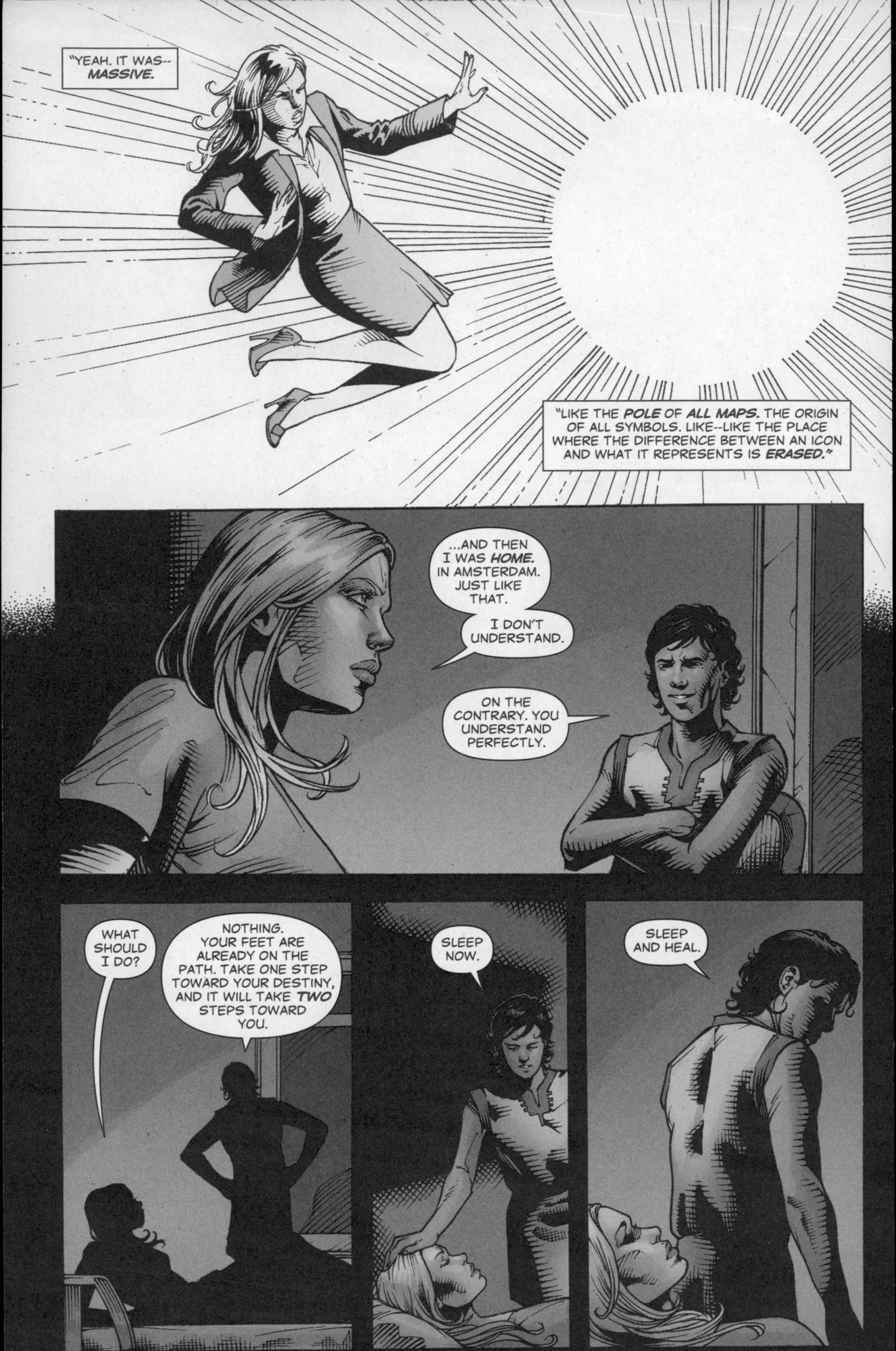
"YEAH. IT WAS-- MASSIVE.
"LIKE THE POLE OF ALL MAPS. THE ORIGIN OF ALL SYMBOLS. LIKE--LIKE THE PLACE WHERE THE DIFFERENCE BETWEEN AN ICON AND WHAT IT REPRESENTS IS ERASED."
...AND THEN I WAS HOME. IN AMSTERDAM. JUST LIKE THAT.
I DON'T UNDERSTAND.
ON THE CONTRARY. YOU UNDERSTAND PERFECTLY.
WHAT SHOULD I DO?
NOTHING. YOUR FEET ARE ALREADY ON THE PATH. TAKE ONE STEP TOWARD YOUR DESTINY, AND IT WILL TAKE TWO STEPS TOWARD YOU.
SLEEP NOW.
SLEEP AND HEAL.

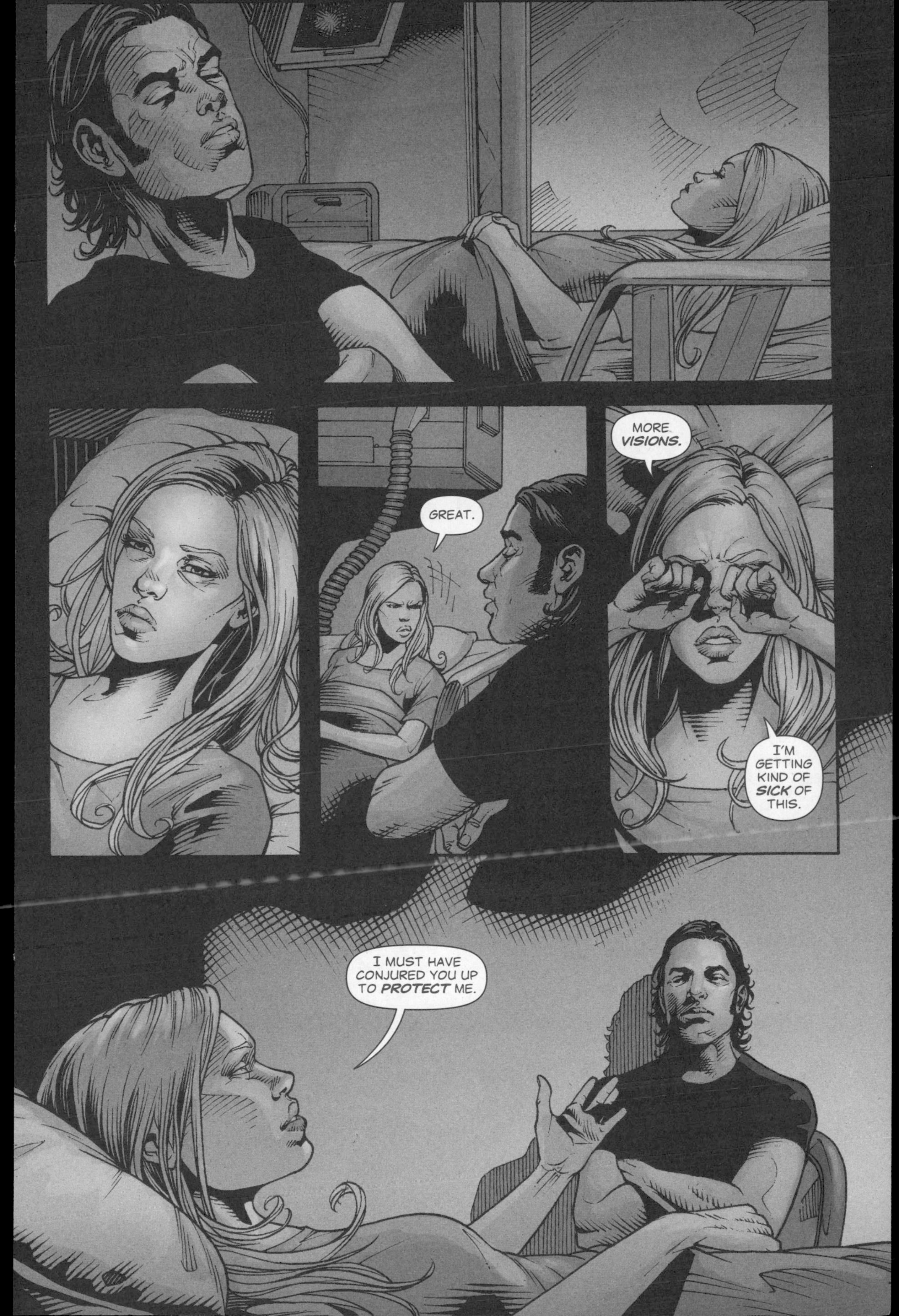
GREAT.
MORE VISIONS.
I'M GETTING KIND OF SICK OF THIS.
I MUST HAVE CONJURED YOU UP TO PROTECT ME.

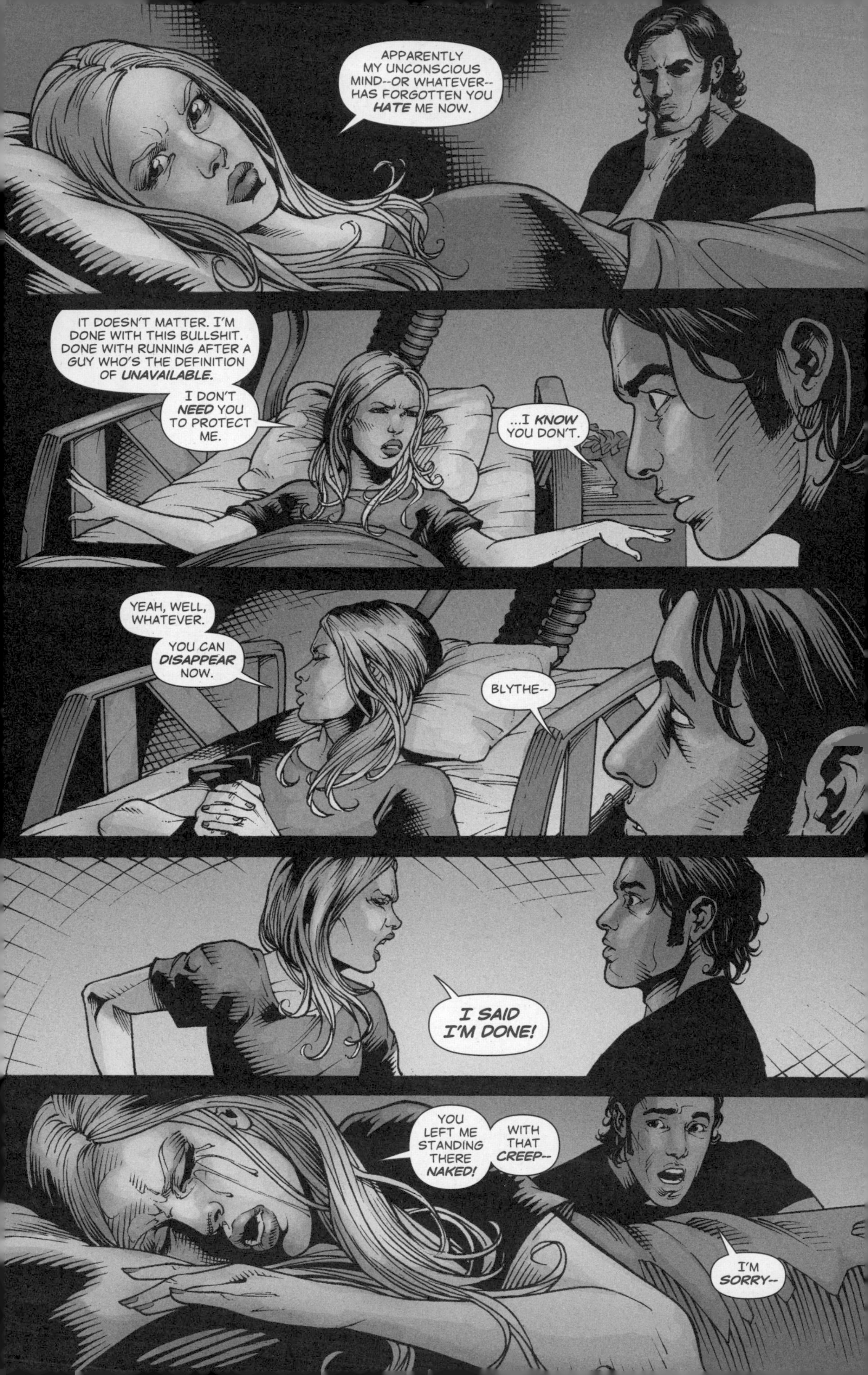
APPARENTLY MY UNCONSCIOUS MIND--OR WHATEVER--HAS FORGOTTEN YOU HATE ME NOW.
IT DOESN'T MATTER. I'M DONE WITH THIS BULLSHIT. DONE WITH RUNNING AFTER A GUY WHO'S THE DEFINITION OF UNAVAILABLE.
I DON'T NEED YOU TO PROTECT ME.
...I KNOW YOU DON'T.
YEAH, WELL, WHATEVER.
YOU CAN DISAPPEAR NOW.
BLYTHE--
I SAID I'M DONE!
YOU LEFT ME STANDING THERE NAKED!
WITH THAT CREEP--
I'M SORRY--

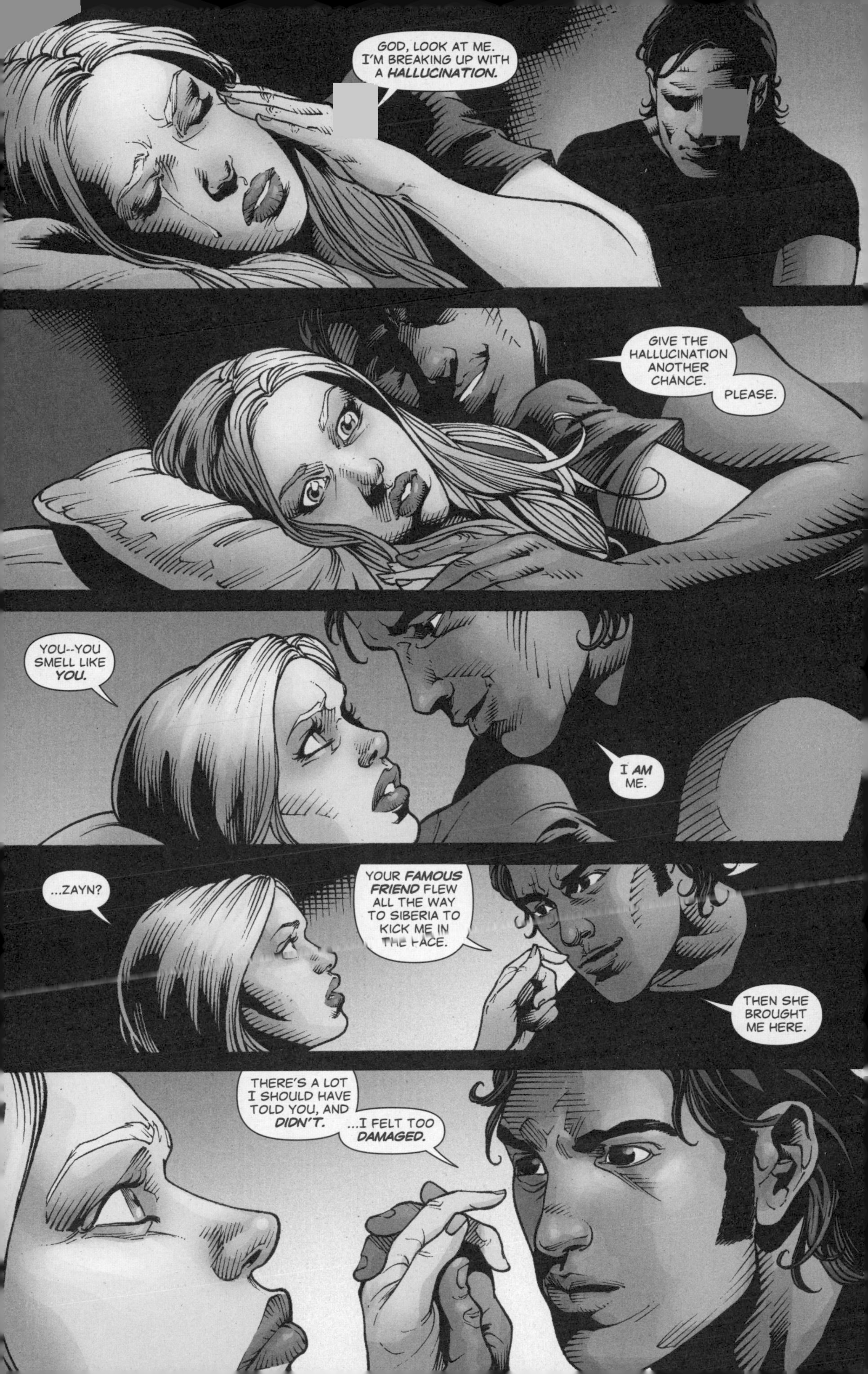
GOD, LOOK AT ME. I'M BREAKING UP WITH A HALLUCINATION.
GIVE THE HALLUCINATION ANOTHER CHANCE.
PLEASE.
YOU--YOU SMELL LIKE YOU.
I AM ME.
...ZAYN?
YOUR FAMOUS FRIEND FLEW ALL THE WAY TO SIBERIA TO KICK ME IN THE FACE.
THEN SHE BROUGHT ME HERE.
THERE'S A LOT I SHOULD HAVE TOLD YOU, AND DIDN'T.
...I FELT TOO DAMAGED.

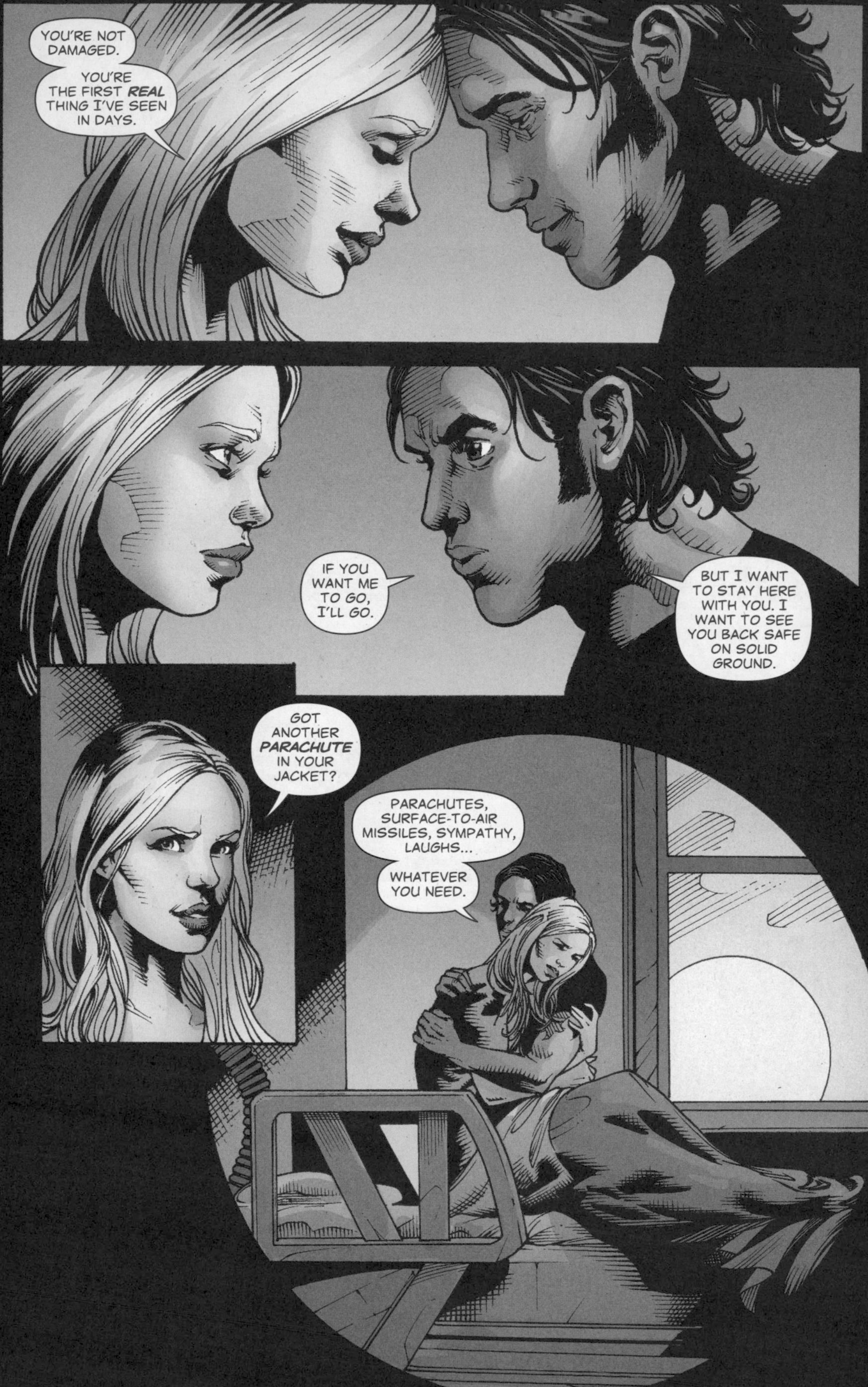
YOU'RE NOT DAMAGED.
YOU'RE THE FIRST ***REAL*** THING I'VE SEEN IN DAYS.
IF YOU WANT ME TO GO, I'LL GO.
BUT I WANT TO STAY HERE WITH YOU. I WANT TO SEE YOU BACK SAFE ON SOLID GROUND.
GOT ANOTHER ***PARACHUTE*** IN YOUR JACKET?
PARACHUTES, SURFACE-TO-AIR MISSILES, SYMPATHY, LAUGHS...
WHATEVER YOU NEED.

THE PICTURE OF BLYTHE ALICE CAMERON

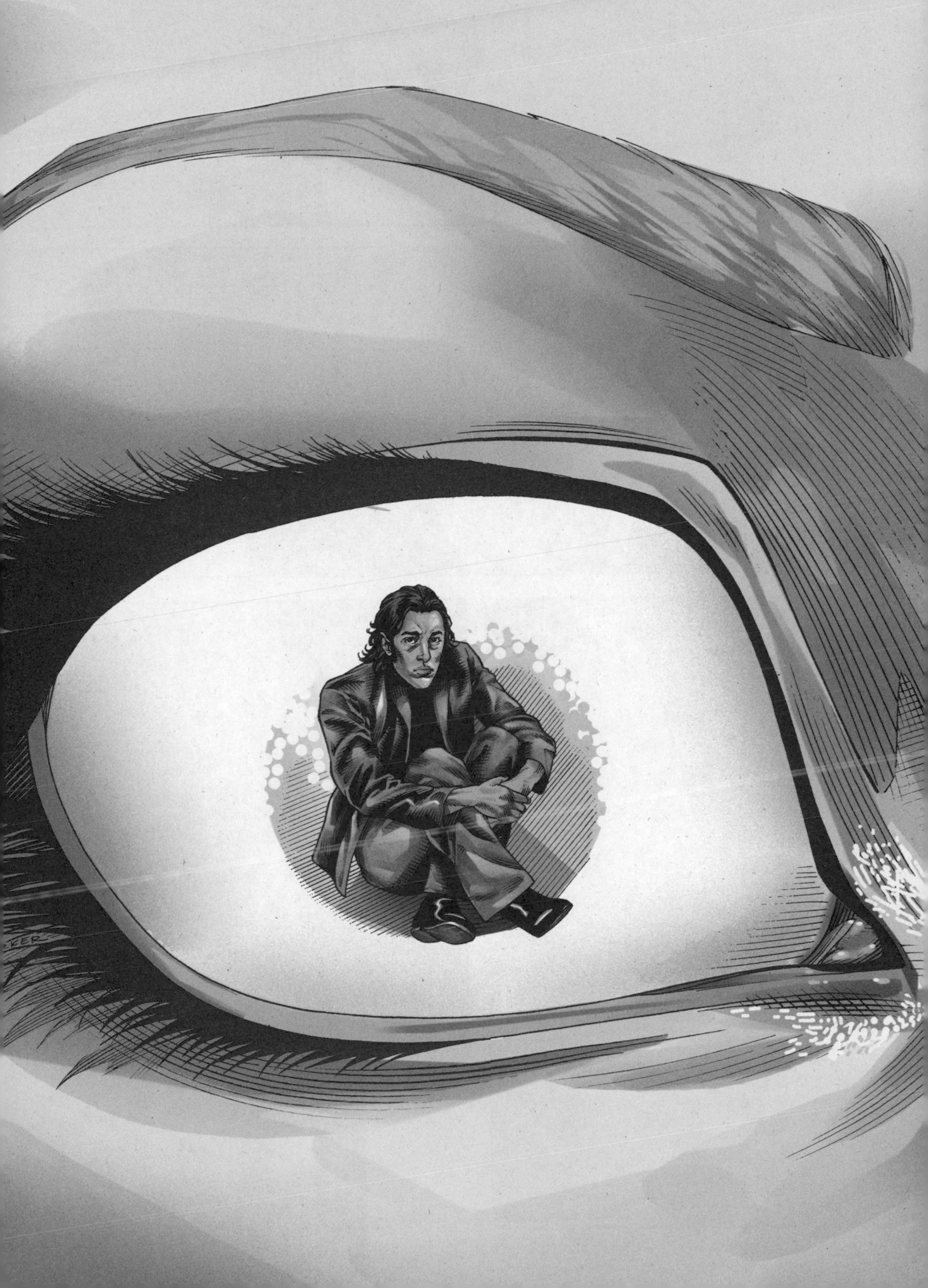

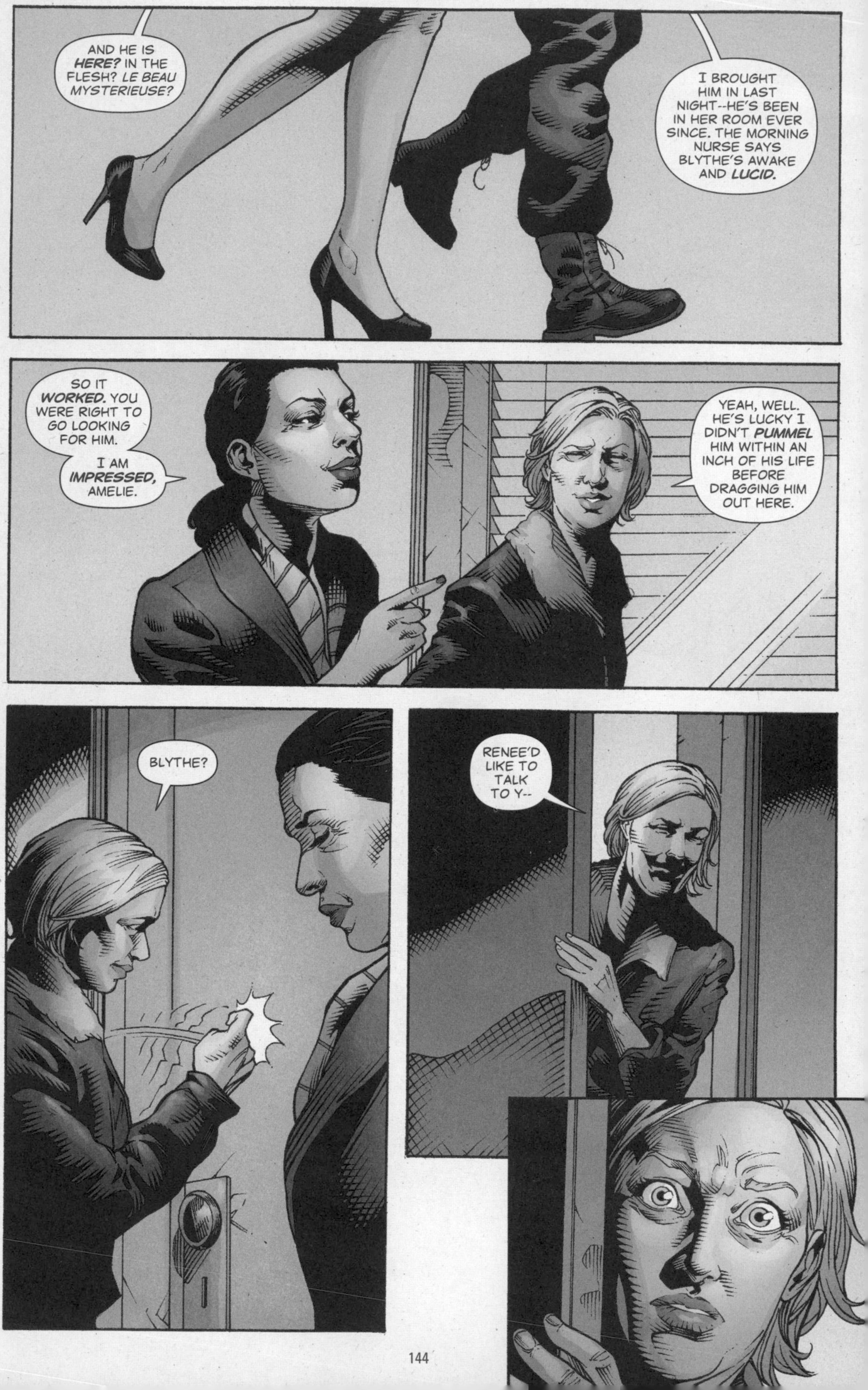
AND HE IS HERE? IN THE FLESH? LE BEAU MYSTERIEUSE?
I BROUGHT HIM IN LAST NIGHT--HE'S BEEN IN HER ROOM EVER SINCE. THE MORNING NURSE SAYS BLYTHE'S AWAKE AND LUCID.
SO IT WORKED. YOU WERE RIGHT TO GO LOOKING FOR HIM.
I AM IMPRESSED, AMELIE.
YEAH, WELL. HE'S LUCKY I DIDN'T PUMMEL HIM WITHIN AN INCH OF HIS LIFE BEFORE DRAGGING HIM OUT HERE.
BLYTHE?
RENEE'D LIKE TO TALK TO Y--

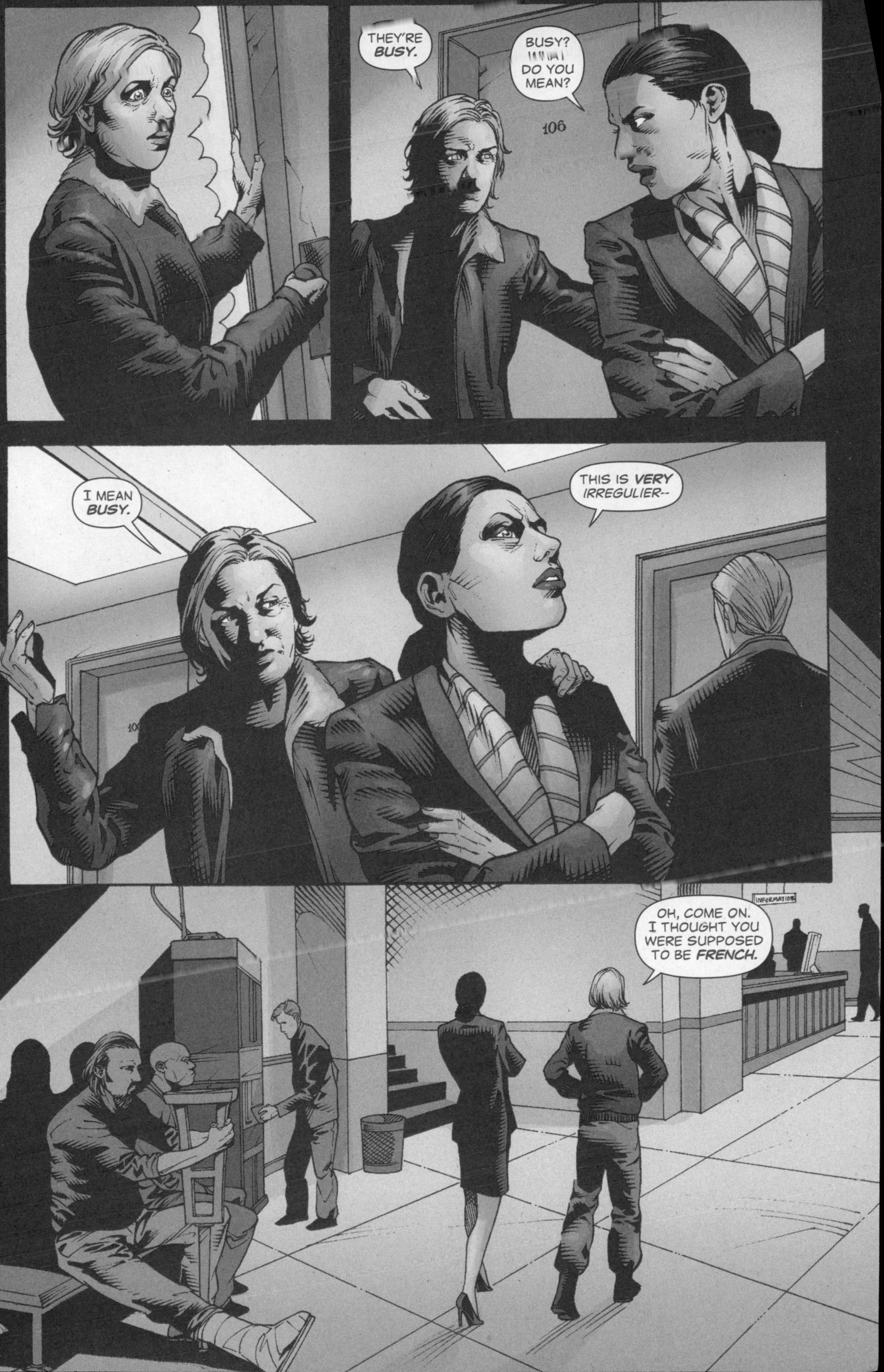
THEY'RE *BUSY.*
BUSY? DO YOU MEAN?
I MEAN *BUSY.*
THIS IS *VERY* IRREGULIER--
INFORMATION
OH, COME ON. I THOUGHT YOU WERE SUPPOSED TO BE *FRENCH.*

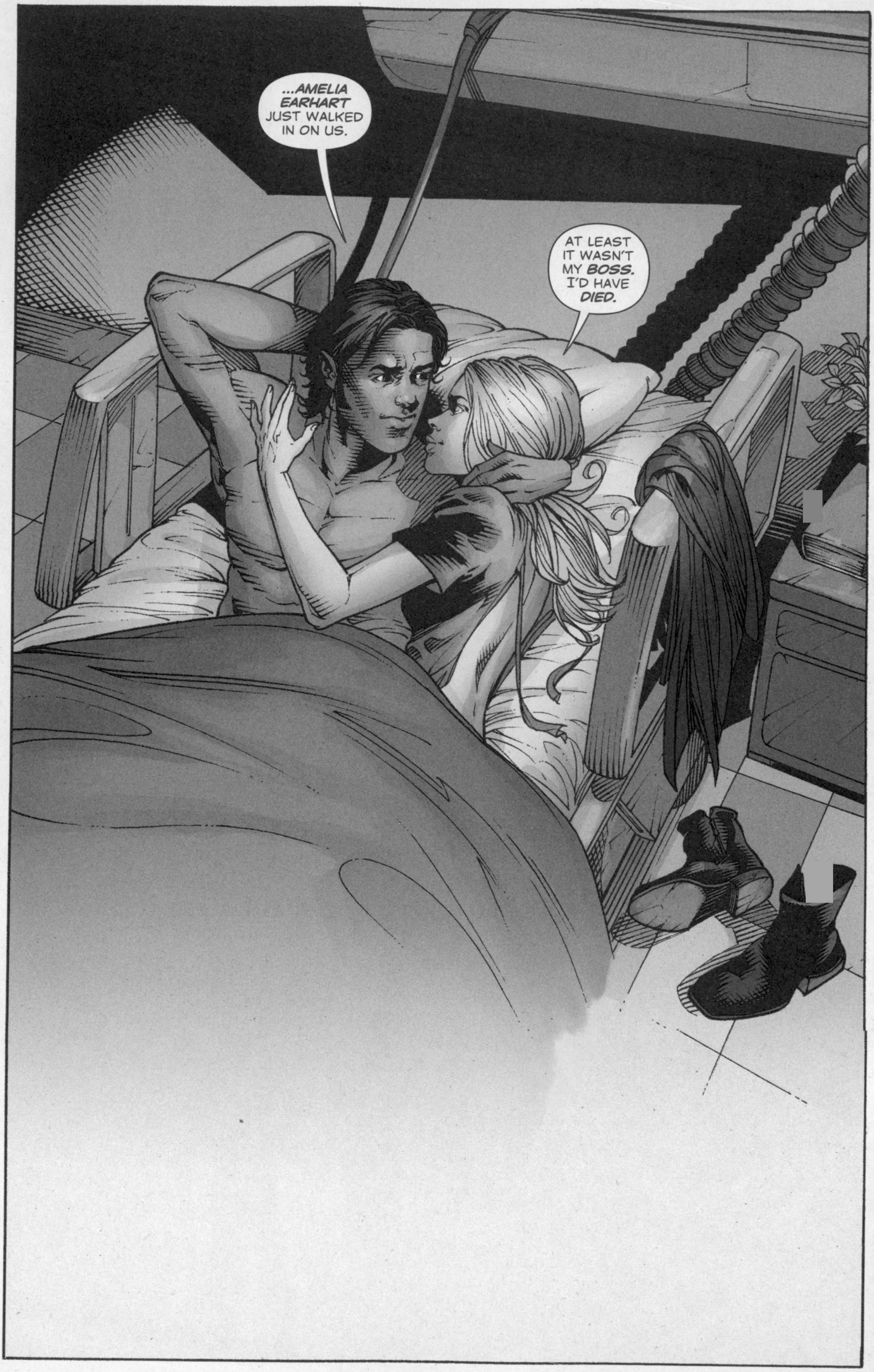
...AMELIA EARHART JUST WALKED IN ON US.
AT LEAST IT WASN'T MY BOSS. I'D HAVE DIED.

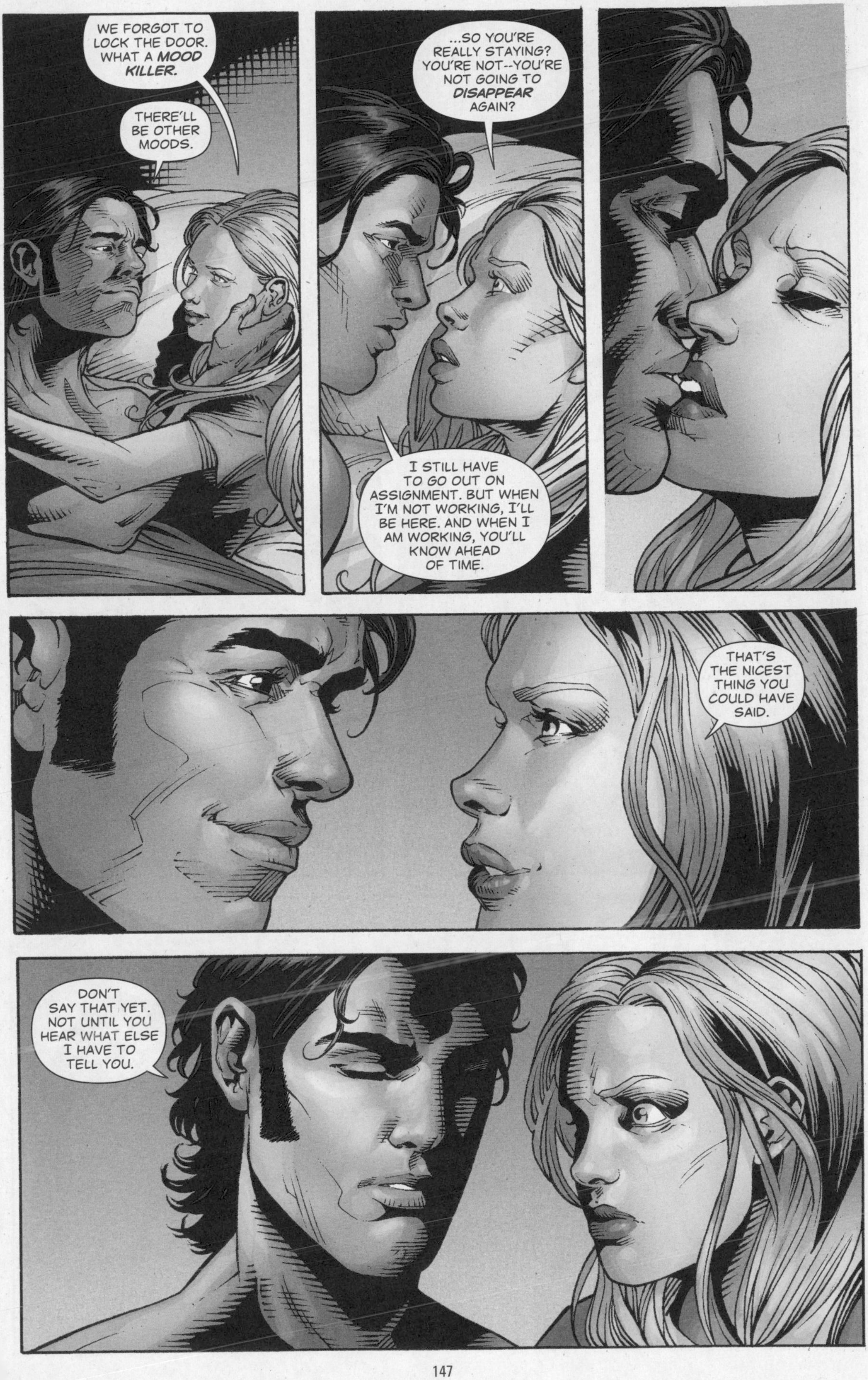
WE FORGOT TO LOCK THE DOOR. WHAT A MOOD KILLER.
THERE'LL BE OTHER MOODS.
...SO YOU'RE REALLY STAYING? YOU'RE NOT--YOU'RE NOT GOING TO DISAPPEAR AGAIN?
I STILL HAVE TO GO OUT ON ASSIGNMENT. BUT WHEN I'M NOT WORKING, I'LL BE HERE. AND WHEN I AM WORKING, YOU'LL KNOW AHEAD OF TIME.
THAT'S THE NICEST THING YOU COULD HAVE SAID.
DON'T SAY THAT YET. NOT UNTIL YOU HEAR WHAT ELSE I HAVE TO TELL YOU.

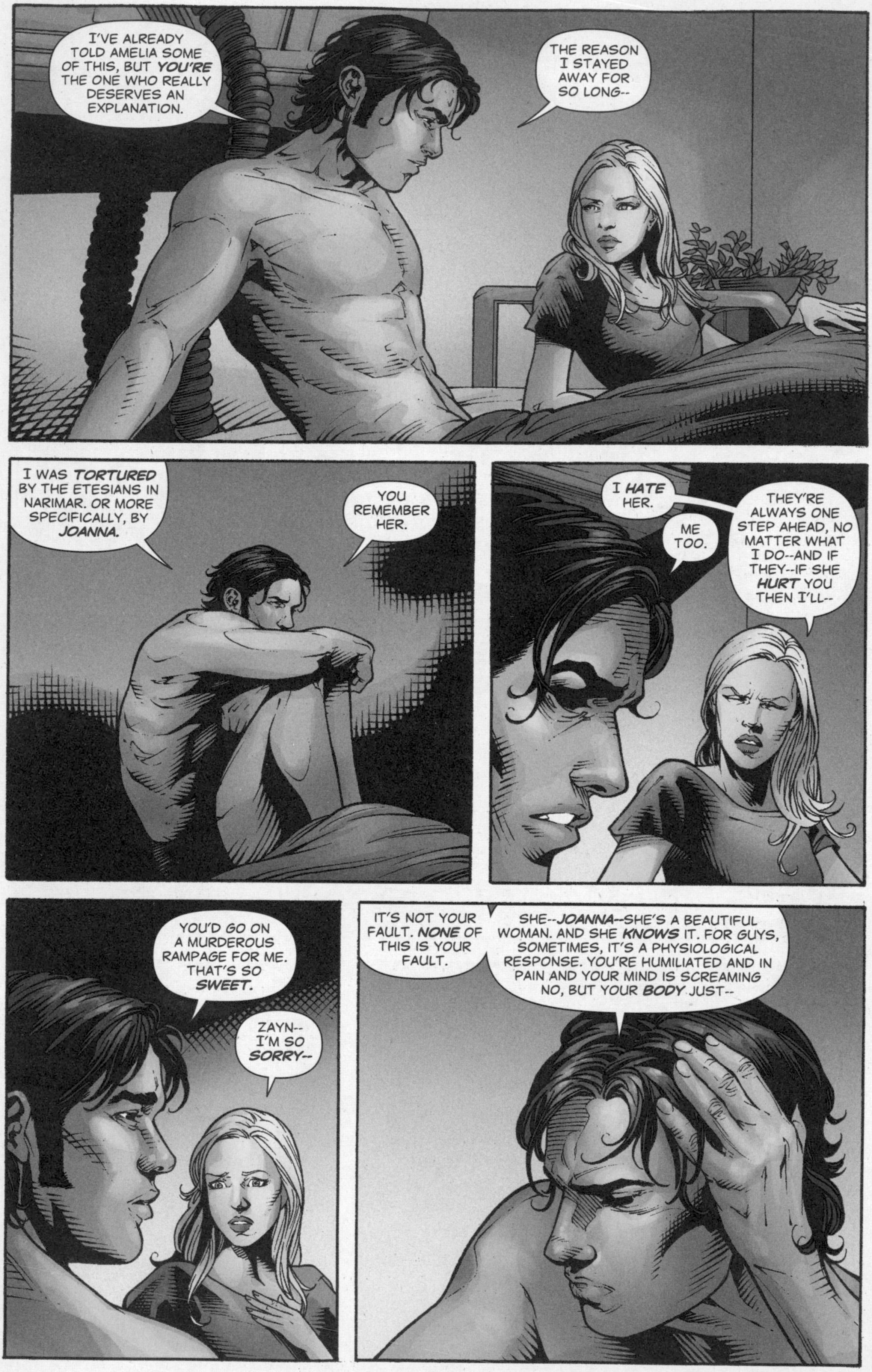
I'VE ALREADY TOLD AMELIA SOME OF THIS, BUT YOU'RE THE ONE WHO REALLY DESERVES AN EXPLANATION.
THE REASON I STAYED AWAY FOR SO LONG--
I WAS TORTURED BY THE ETESIANS IN NARIMAR. OR MORE SPECIFICALLY, BY JOANNA.
YOU REMEMBER HER.
I HATE HER.
ME TOO.
THEY'RE ALWAYS ONE STEP AHEAD, NO MATTER WHAT I DO--AND IF THEY--IF SHE HURT YOU THEN I'LL--
YOU'D GO ON A MURDEROUS RAMPAGE FOR ME. THAT'S SO SWEET.
ZAYN-- I'M SO SORRY--
IT'S NOT YOUR FAULT. NONE OF THIS IS YOUR FAULT.
SHE--JOANNA--SHE'S A BEAUTIFUL WOMAN. AND SHE KNOWS IT. FOR GUYS, SOMETIMES, IT'S A PHYSIOLOGICAL RESPONSE. YOU'RE HUMILIATED AND IN PAIN AND YOUR MIND IS SCREAMING NO, BUT YOUR BODY JUST--

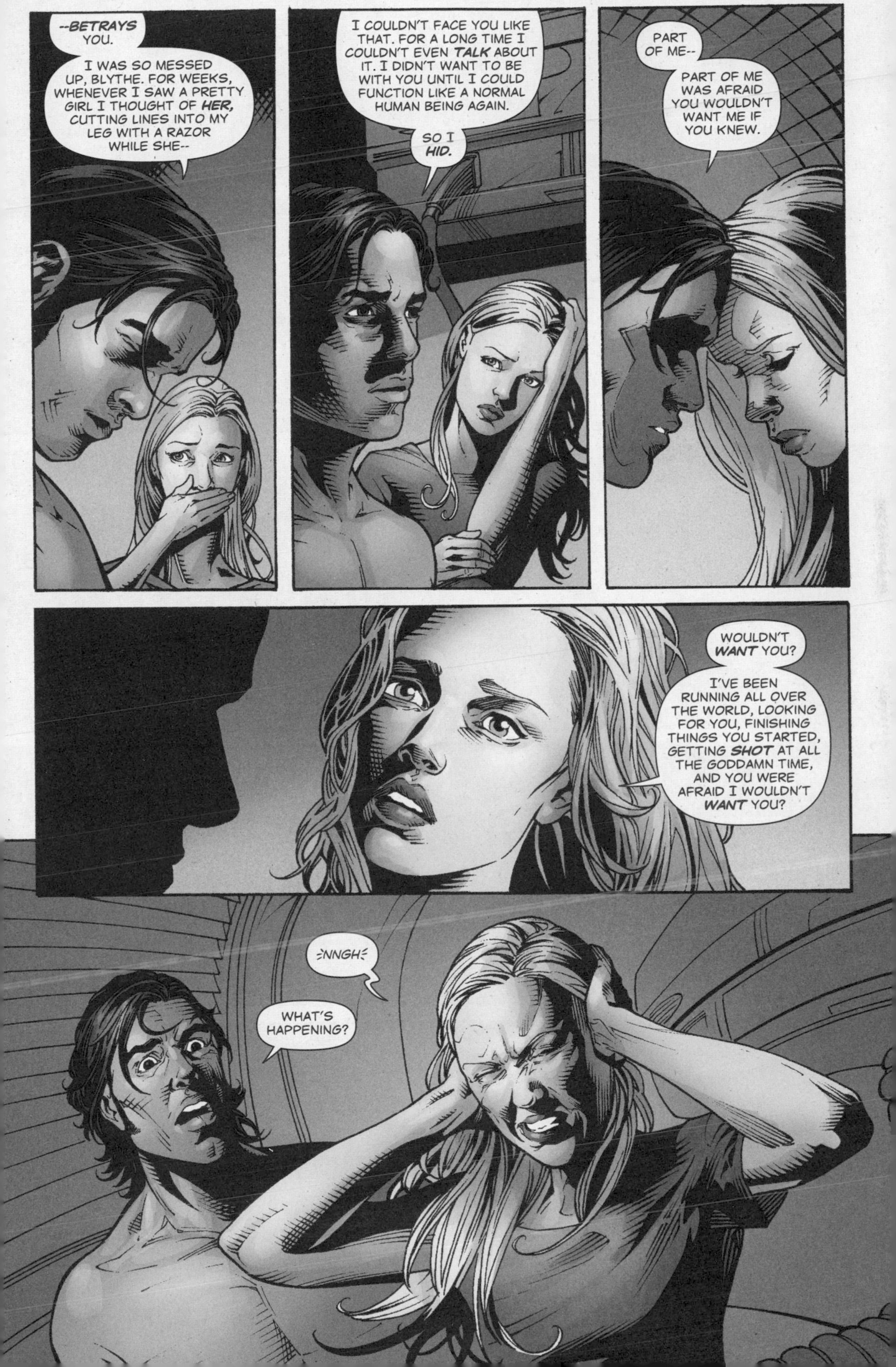
--BETRAYS YOU.
I WAS SO MESSED UP, BLYTHE. FOR WEEKS, WHENEVER I SAW A PRETTY GIRL I THOUGHT OF HER, CUTTING LINES INTO MY LEG WITH A RAZOR WHILE SHE--
I COULDN'T FACE YOU LIKE THAT. FOR A LONG TIME I COULDN'T EVEN TALK ABOUT IT. I DIDN'T WANT TO BE WITH YOU UNTIL I COULD FUNCTION LIKE A NORMAL HUMAN BEING AGAIN.
SO I HID.
PART OF ME--
PART OF ME WAS AFRAID YOU WOULDN'T WANT ME IF YOU KNEW.
WOULDN'T WANT YOU?
I'VE BEEN RUNNING ALL OVER THE WORLD, LOOKING FOR YOU, FINISHING THINGS YOU STARTED, GETTING SHOT AT ALL THE GODDAMN TIME, AND YOU WERE AFRAID I WOULDN'T WANT YOU?
NNGH
WHAT'S HAPPENING?

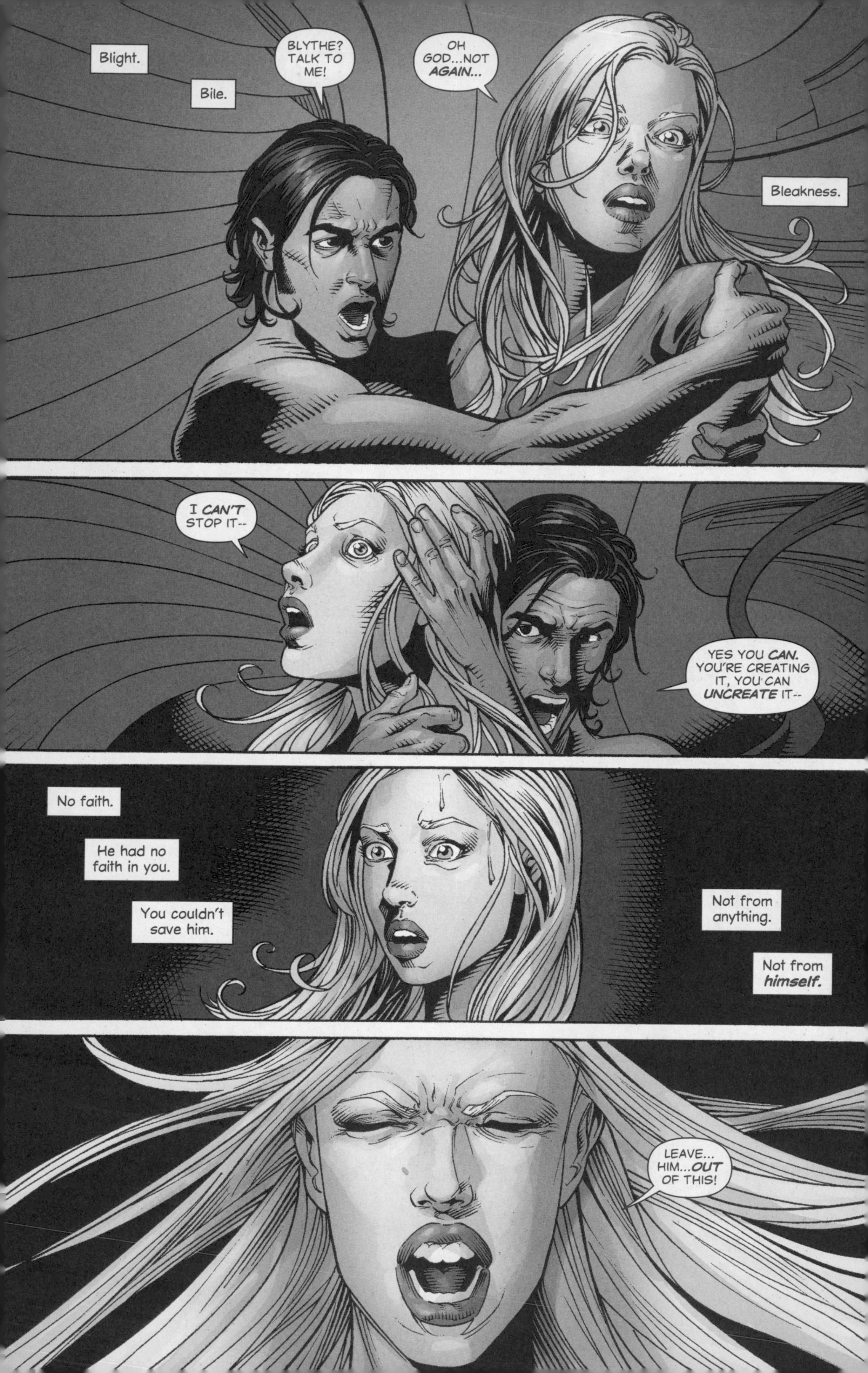
Blight.
Bile.
BLYTHE? TALK TO ME!
OH GOD...NOT AGAIN...
Bleakness.
I CAN'T STOP IT--
YES YOU CAN. YOU'RE CREATING IT, YOU CAN UNCREATE IT--
No faith.
He had no faith in you.
You couldn't save him.
Not from anything.
Not from himself.
LEAVE... HIM...OUT OF THIS!

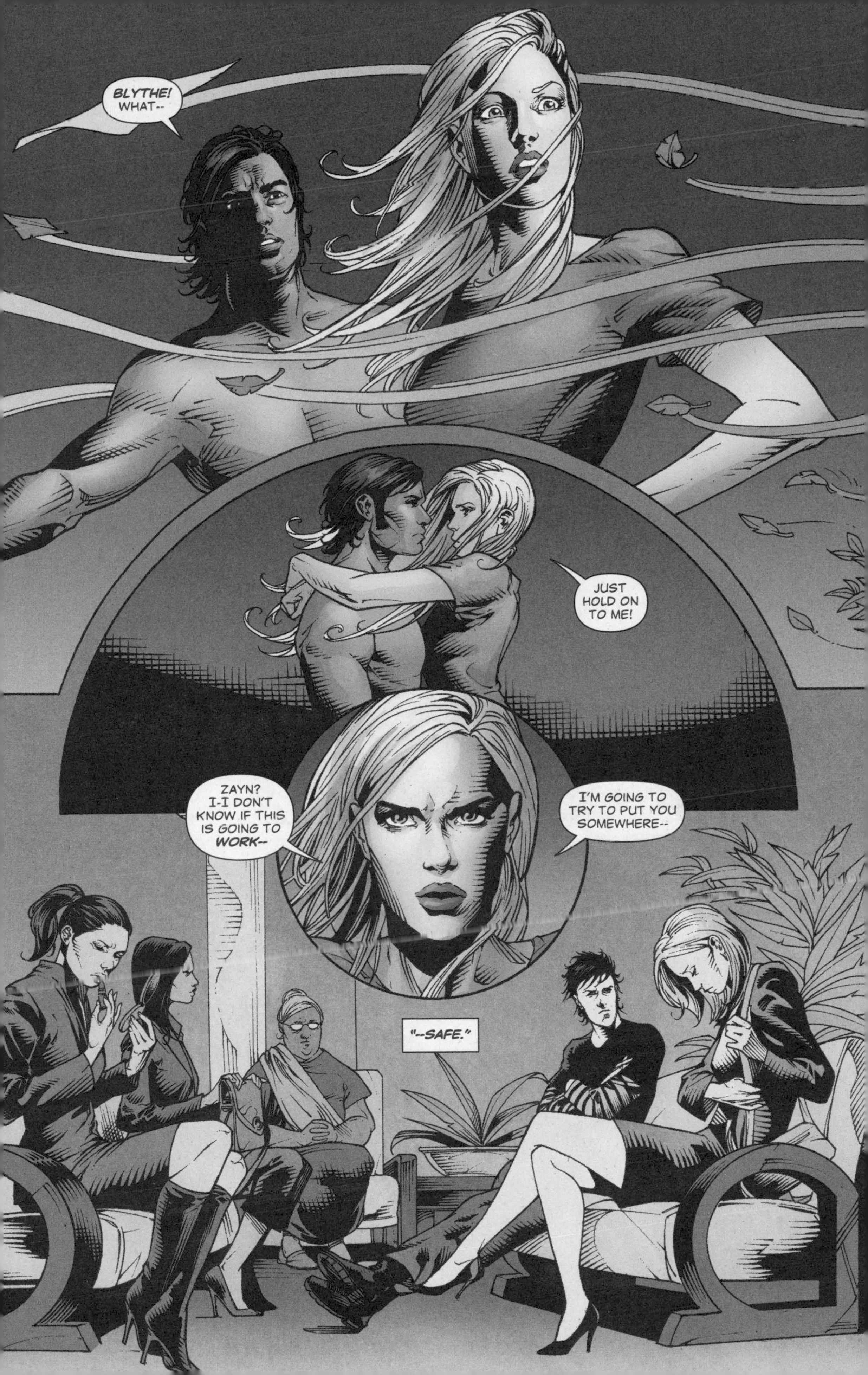
BLYTHE! WHAT--
JUST HOLD ON TO ME!
ZAYN? I-I DON'T KNOW IF THIS IS GOING TO WORK--
I'M GOING TO TRY TO PUT YOU SOMEWHERE--
"--SAFE."

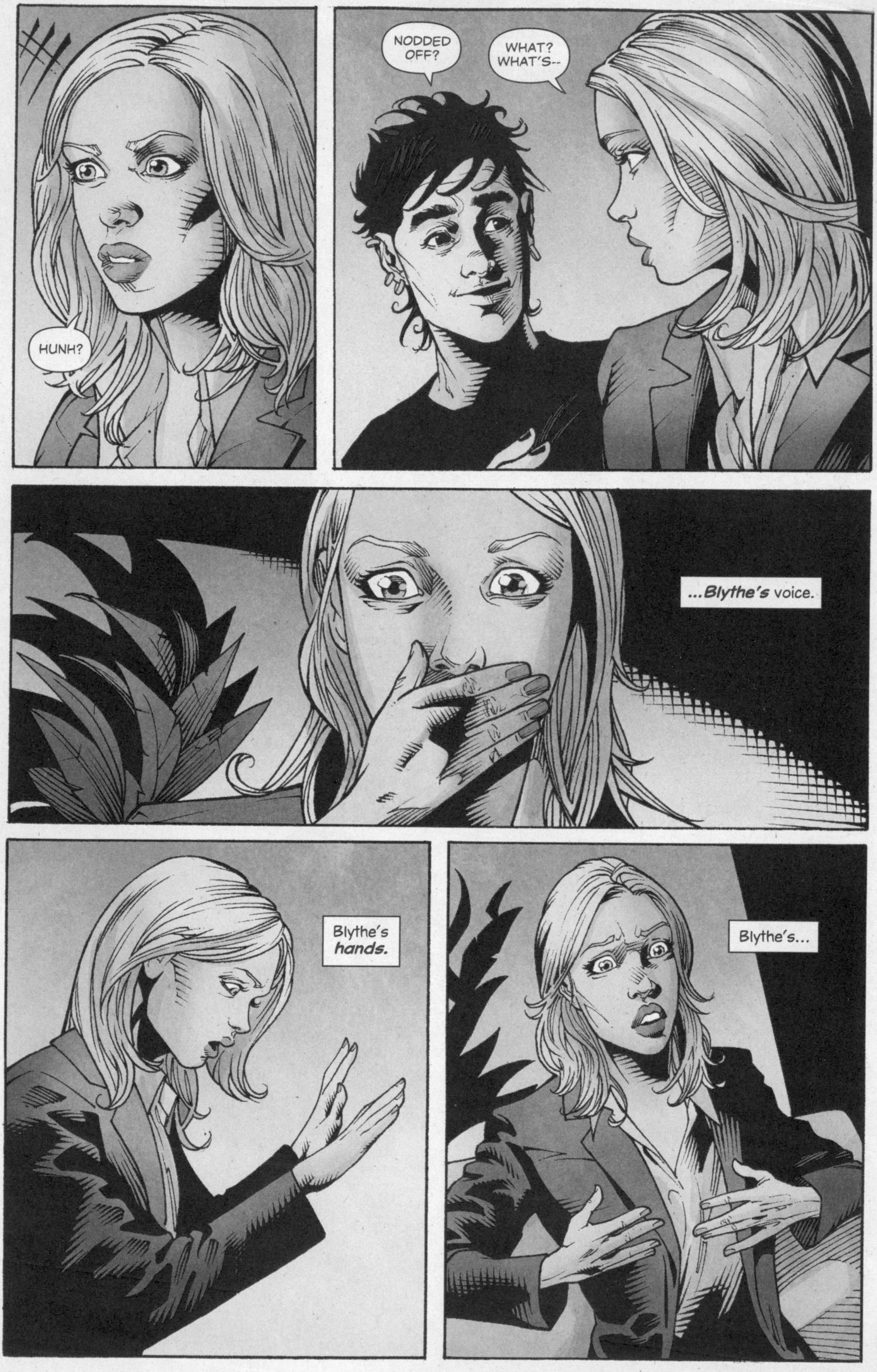
HUNH?
NODDED OFF?
WHAT? WHAT'S--
...*Blythe's* voice.
Blythe's *hands.*
Blythe's...

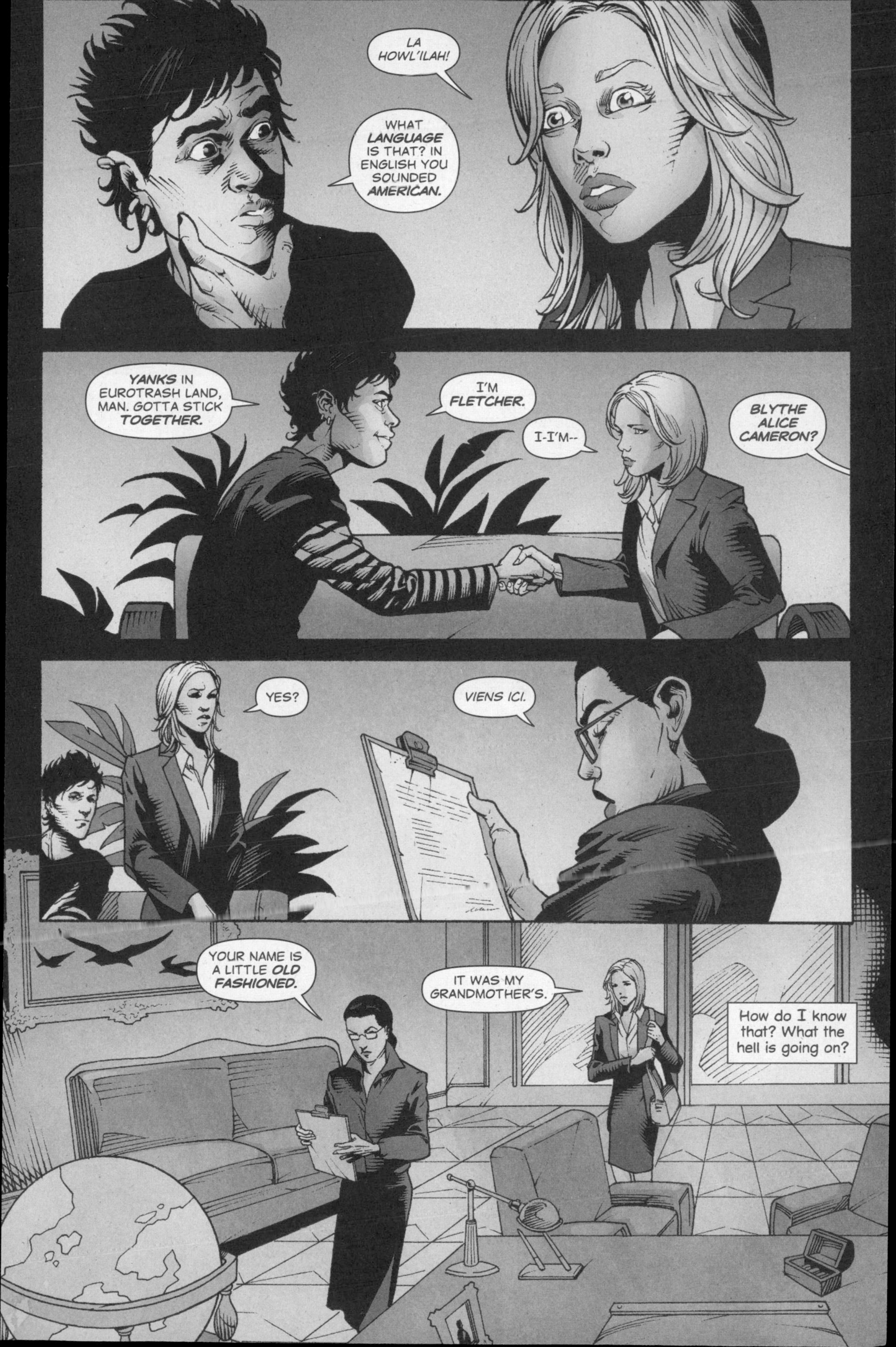
LA HOWL'ILAH!
WHAT LANGUAGE IS THAT? IN ENGLISH YOU SOUNDED AMERICAN.
YANKS IN EUROTRASH LAND, MAN. GOTTA STICK TOGETHER.
I'M FLETCHER.
I-I'M--
BLYTHE ALICE CAMERON?
YES?
VIENS ICI.
YOUR NAME IS A LITTLE OLD FASHIONED.
IT WAS MY GRANDMOTHER'S.
How do I know that? What the hell is going on?

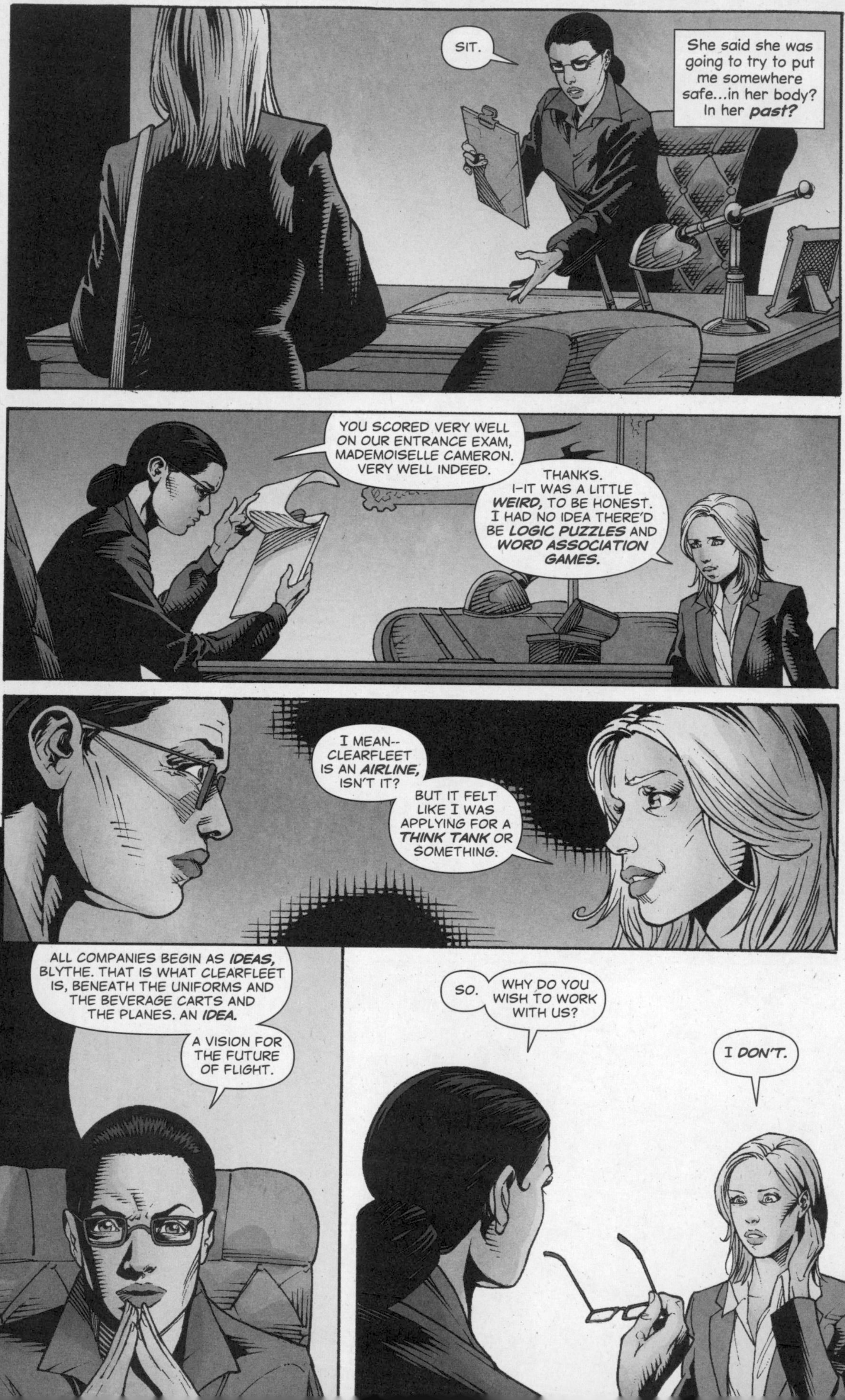
She said she was going to try to put me somewhere safe...in her body? In her *past?*
SIT.
YOU SCORED VERY WELL ON OUR ENTRANCE EXAM, MADEMOISELLE CAMERON. VERY WELL INDEED.
THANKS. I-IT WAS A LITTLE *WEIRD,* TO BE HONEST. I HAD NO IDEA THERE'D BE *LOGIC PUZZLES* AND *WORD ASSOCIATION GAMES.*
I MEAN-- CLEARFLEET IS AN *AIRLINE,* ISN'T IT?
BUT IT FELT LIKE I WAS APPLYING FOR A *THINK TANK* OR SOMETHING.
ALL COMPANIES BEGIN AS *IDEAS,* BLYTHE. THAT IS WHAT CLEARFLEET IS, BENEATH THE UNIFORMS AND THE BEVERAGE CARTS AND THE PLANES. AN *IDEA.*
A VISION FOR THE FUTURE OF FLIGHT.
SO.
WHY DO YOU WISH TO WORK WITH US?
I *DON'T.*

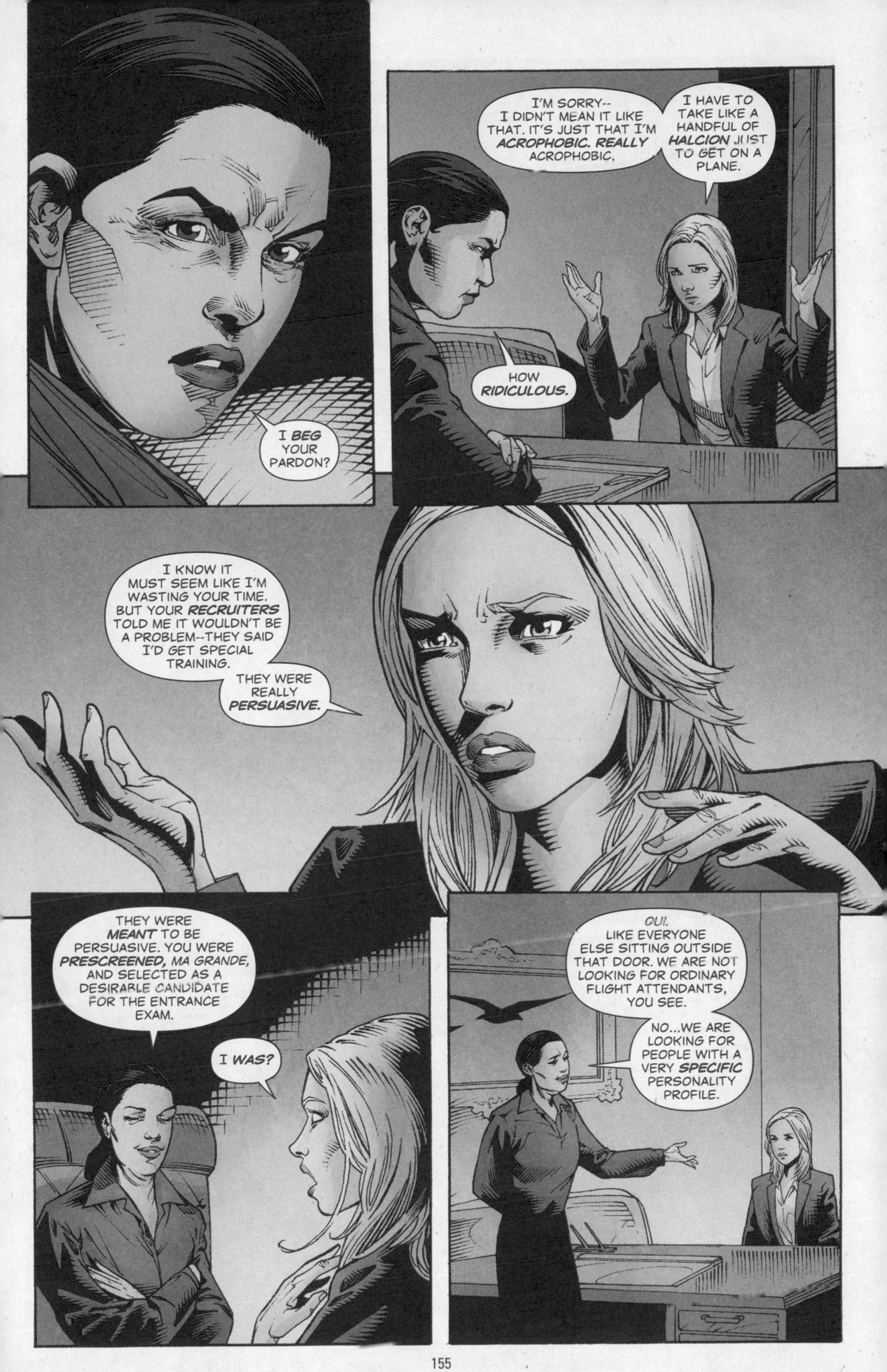
I BEG YOUR PARDON?
I'M SORRY-- I DIDN'T MEAN IT LIKE THAT. IT'S JUST THAT I'M ACROPHOBIC. REALLY ACROPHOBIC.
I HAVE TO TAKE LIKE A HANDFUL OF HALCION JUST TO GET ON A PLANE.
HOW RIDICULOUS.
I KNOW IT MUST SEEM LIKE I'M WASTING YOUR TIME. BUT YOUR RECRUITERS TOLD ME IT WOULDN'T BE A PROBLEM--THEY SAID I'D GET SPECIAL TRAINING.
THEY WERE REALLY PERSUASIVE.
THEY WERE MEANT TO BE PERSUASIVE. YOU WERE PRESCREENED, MA GRANDE, AND SELECTED AS A DESIRABLE CANDIDATE FOR THE ENTRANCE EXAM.
I WAS?
OUI. LIKE EVERYONE ELSE SITTING OUTSIDE THAT DOOR. WE ARE NOT LOOKING FOR ORDINARY FLIGHT ATTENDANTS, YOU SEE.
NO...WE ARE LOOKING FOR PEOPLE WITH A VERY SPECIFIC PERSONALITY PROFILE.

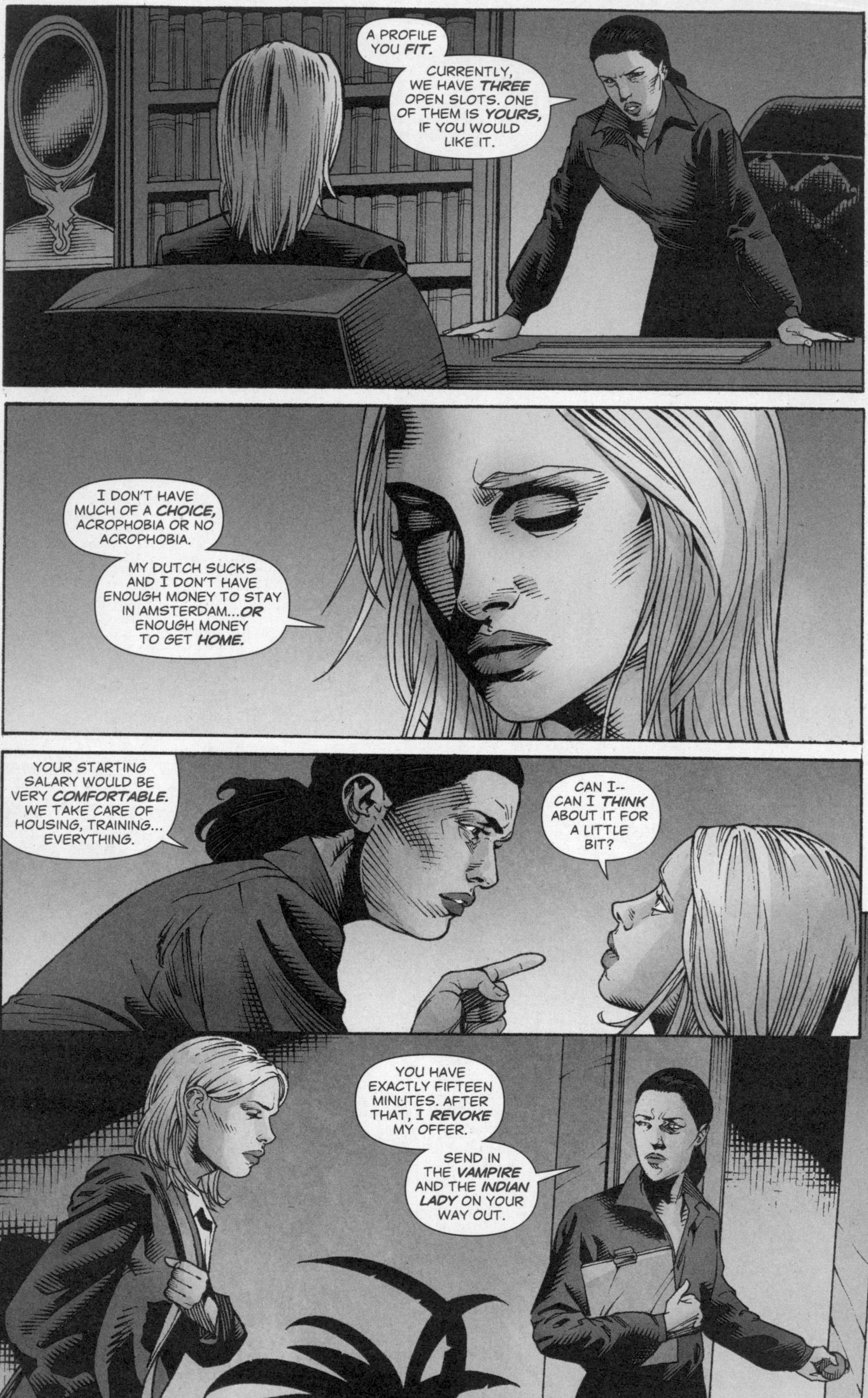
A PROFILE YOU FIT.
CURRENTLY, WE HAVE THREE OPEN SLOTS. ONE OF THEM IS YOURS, IF YOU WOULD LIKE IT.
I DON'T HAVE MUCH OF A CHOICE, ACROPHOBIA OR NO ACROPHOBIA.
MY DUTCH SUCKS AND I DON'T HAVE ENOUGH MONEY TO STAY IN AMSTERDAM...OR ENOUGH MONEY TO GET HOME.
YOUR STARTING SALARY WOULD BE VERY COMFORTABLE. WE TAKE CARE OF HOUSING, TRAINING... EVERYTHING.
CAN I-- CAN I THINK ABOUT IT FOR A LITTLE BIT?
YOU HAVE EXACTLY FIFTEEN MINUTES. AFTER THAT, I REVOKE MY OFFER.
SEND IN THE VAMPIRE AND THE INDIAN LADY ON YOUR WAY OUT.

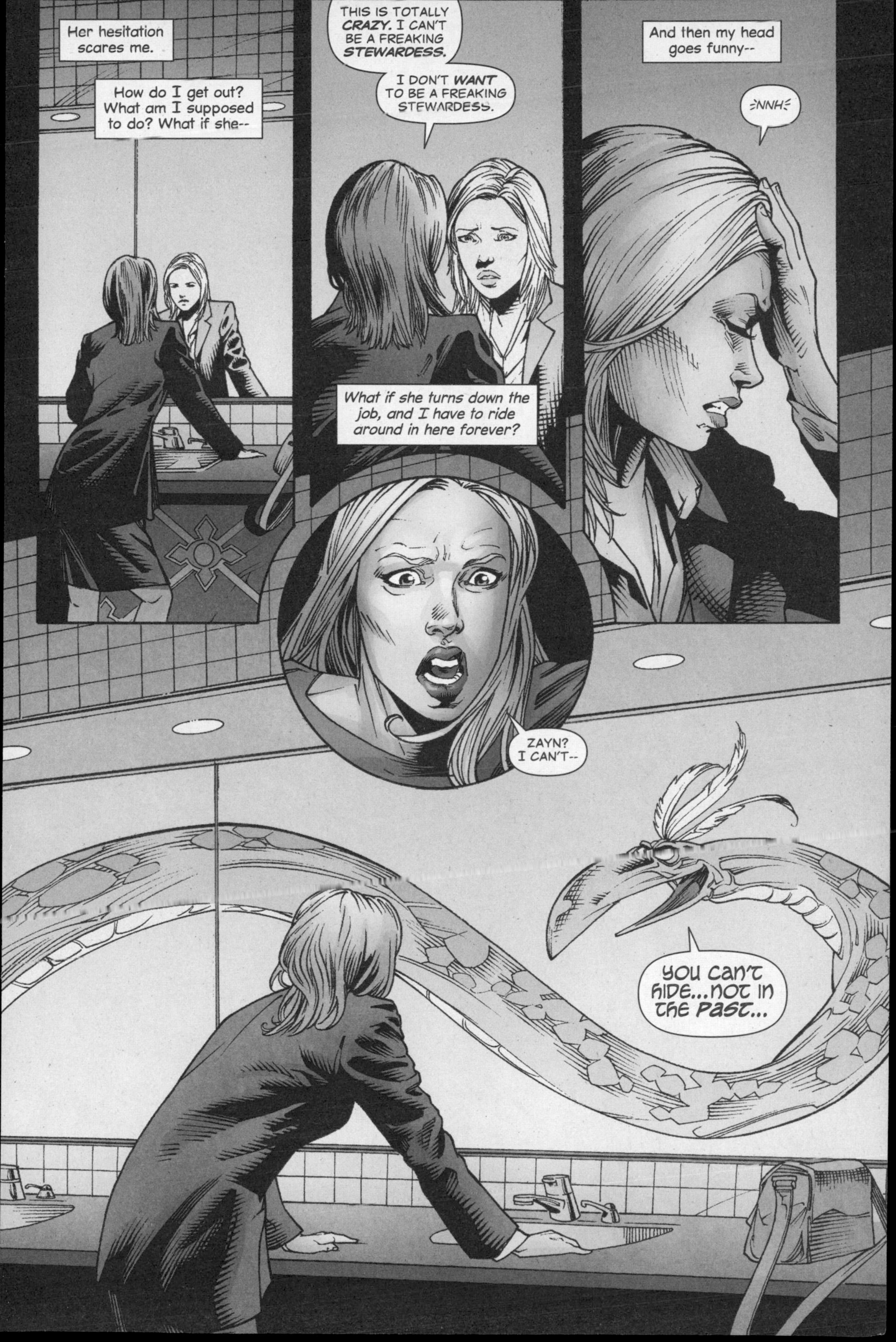

Her hesitation scares me.
How do I get out? What am I supposed to do? What if she--
THIS IS TOTALLY CRAZY. I CAN'T BE A FREAKING STEWARDESS.
I DON'T WANT TO BE A FREAKING STEWARDESS.
What if she turns down the job, and I have to ride around in here forever?
And then my head goes funny--
NNH
ZAYN? I CAN'T--
YOU CAN'T HIDE...NOT IN THE PAST...

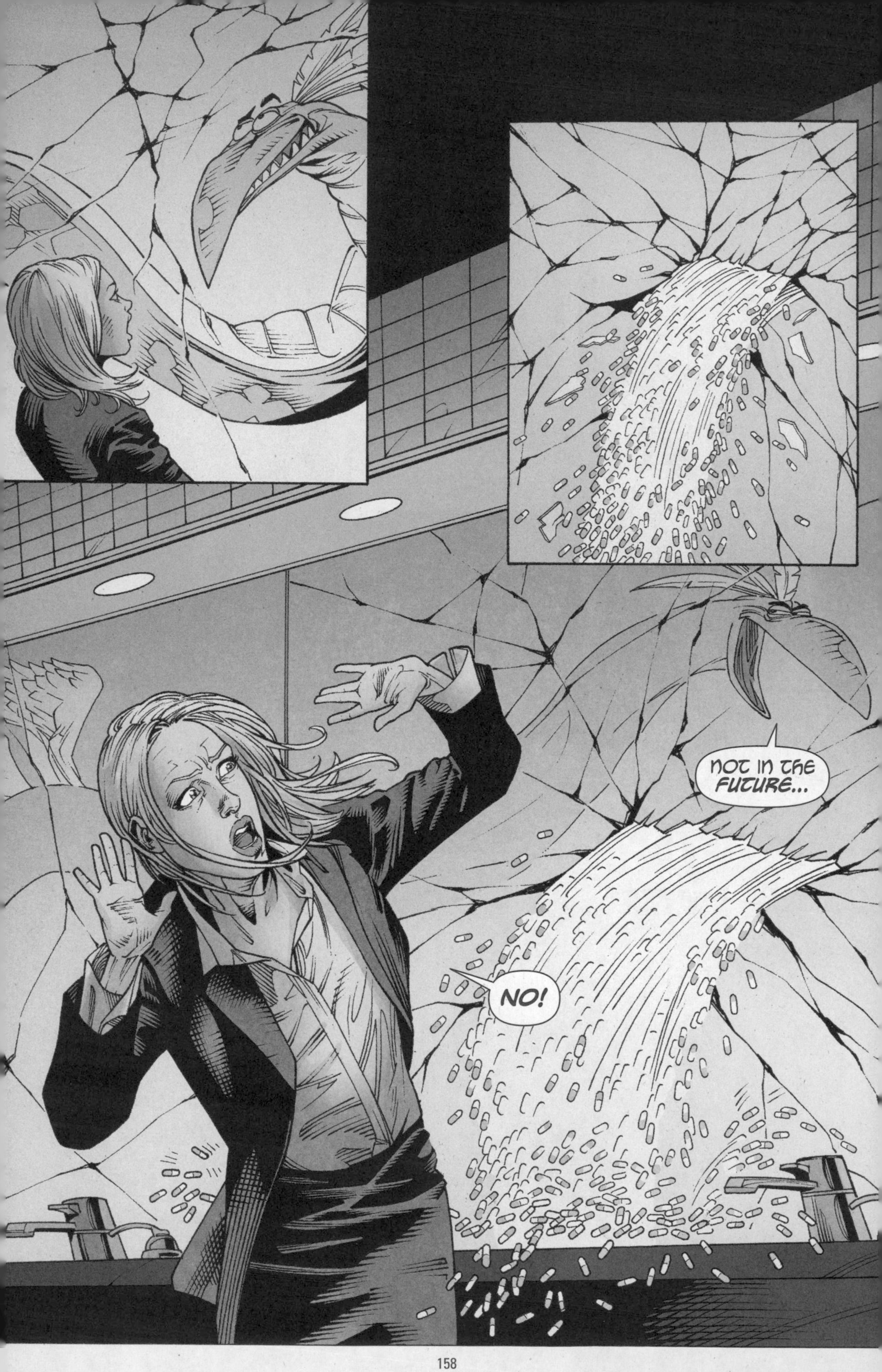
NOT IN THE FUTURE...
NO!

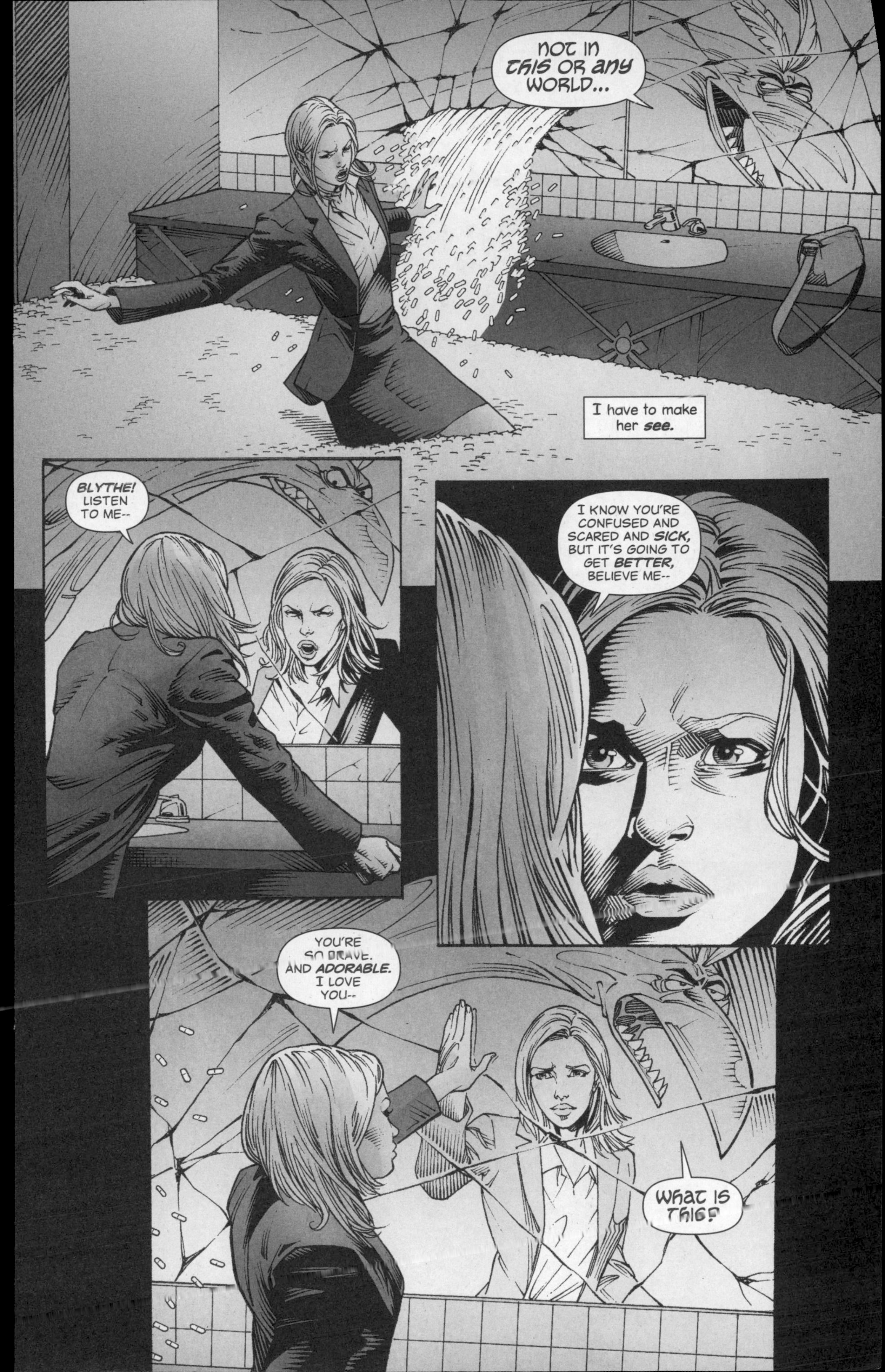
NOT IN THIS OR ANY WORLD...
I have to make her *see.*
BLYTHE! LISTEN TO ME--
I KNOW YOU'RE CONFUSED AND SCARED AND *SICK,* BUT IT'S GOING TO GET *BETTER,* BELIEVE ME--
YOU'RE SO BRAVE. AND *ADORABLE.* I LOVE YOU--
WHAT IS THIS?

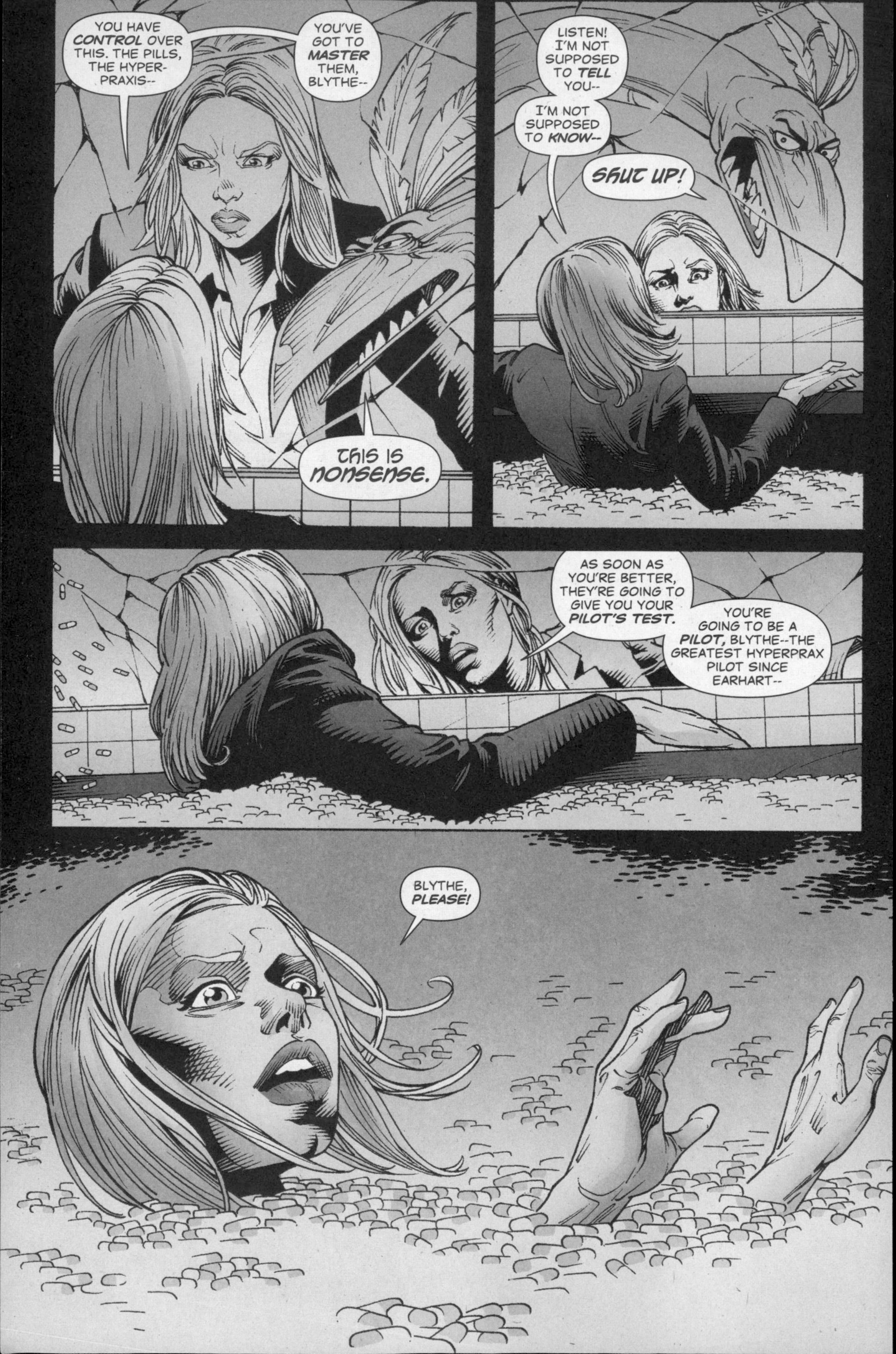

YOU HAVE CONTROL OVER THIS. THE PILLS, THE HYPER-PRAXIS--
YOU'VE GOT TO MASTER THEM, BLYTHE--
THIS IS NONSENSE.
LISTEN! I'M NOT SUPPOSED TO TELL YOU--
I'M NOT SUPPOSED TO KNOW--
SHUT UP!
AS SOON AS YOU'RE BETTER, THEY'RE GOING TO GIVE YOU YOUR PILOT'S TEST.
YOU'RE GOING TO BE A PILOT, BLYTHE--THE GREATEST HYPERPRAX PILOT SINCE EARHART--
BLYTHE, PLEASE!

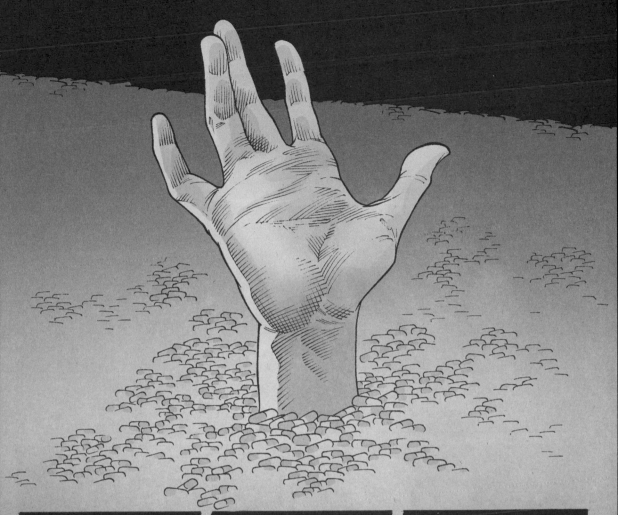

...Zayn?

Can you
hear me?

Yeah. Yeah, I
can hear you.

Why is it
so *dark?*

The *sun's* gone
down. Here--

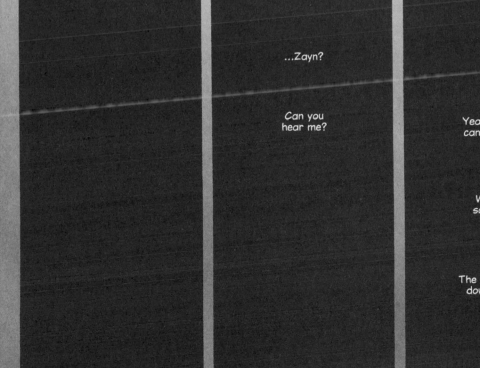

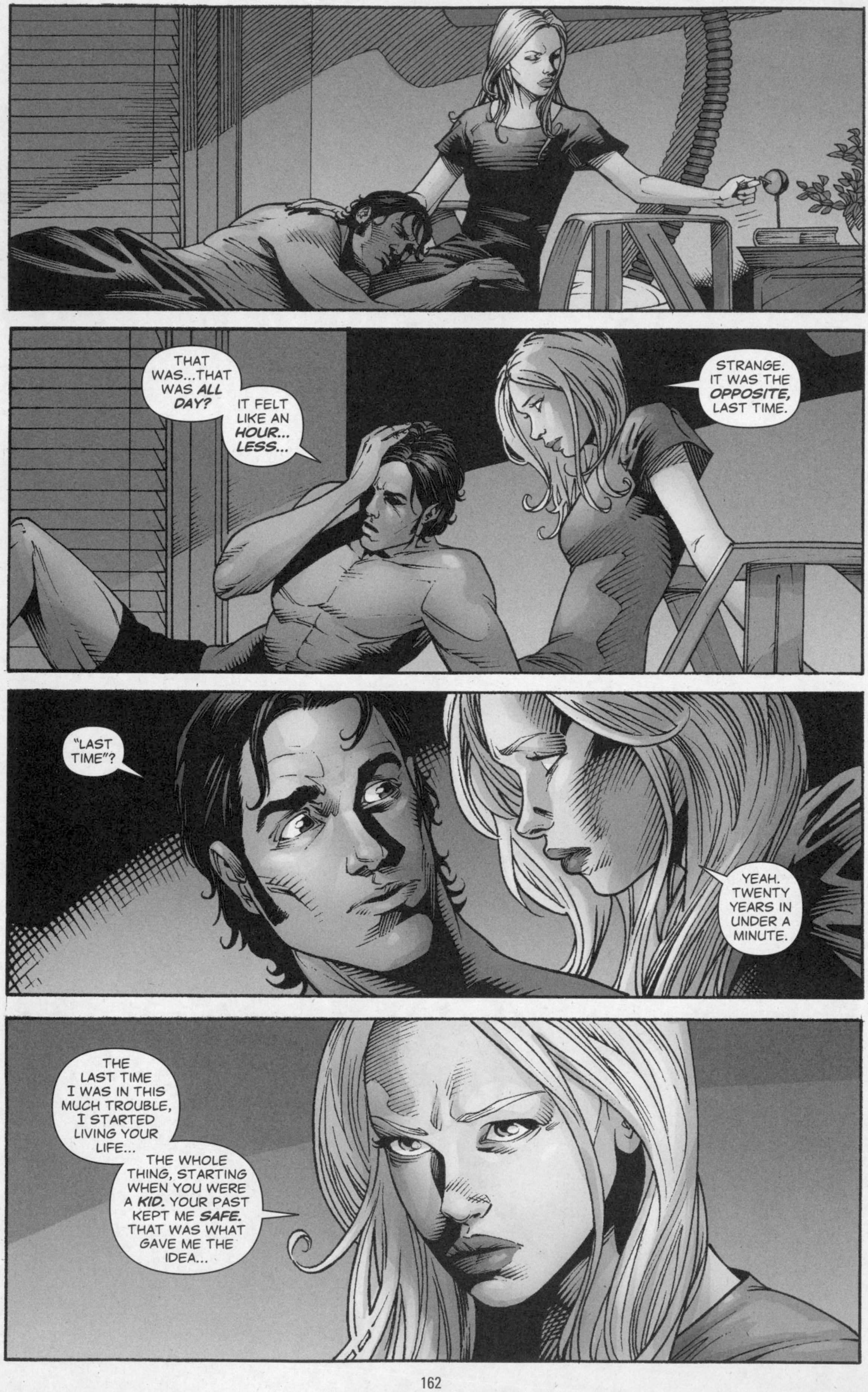

THAT WAS...THAT WAS ALL DAY?
IT FELT LIKE AN HOUR... LESS...
STRANGE. IT WAS THE OPPOSITE, LAST TIME.
"LAST TIME"?
YEAH. TWENTY YEARS IN UNDER A MINUTE.
THE LAST TIME I WAS IN THIS MUCH TROUBLE, I STARTED LIVING YOUR LIFE...
THE WHOLE THING, STARTING WHEN YOU WERE A KID. YOUR PAST KEPT ME SAFE. THAT WAS WHAT GAVE ME THE IDEA...

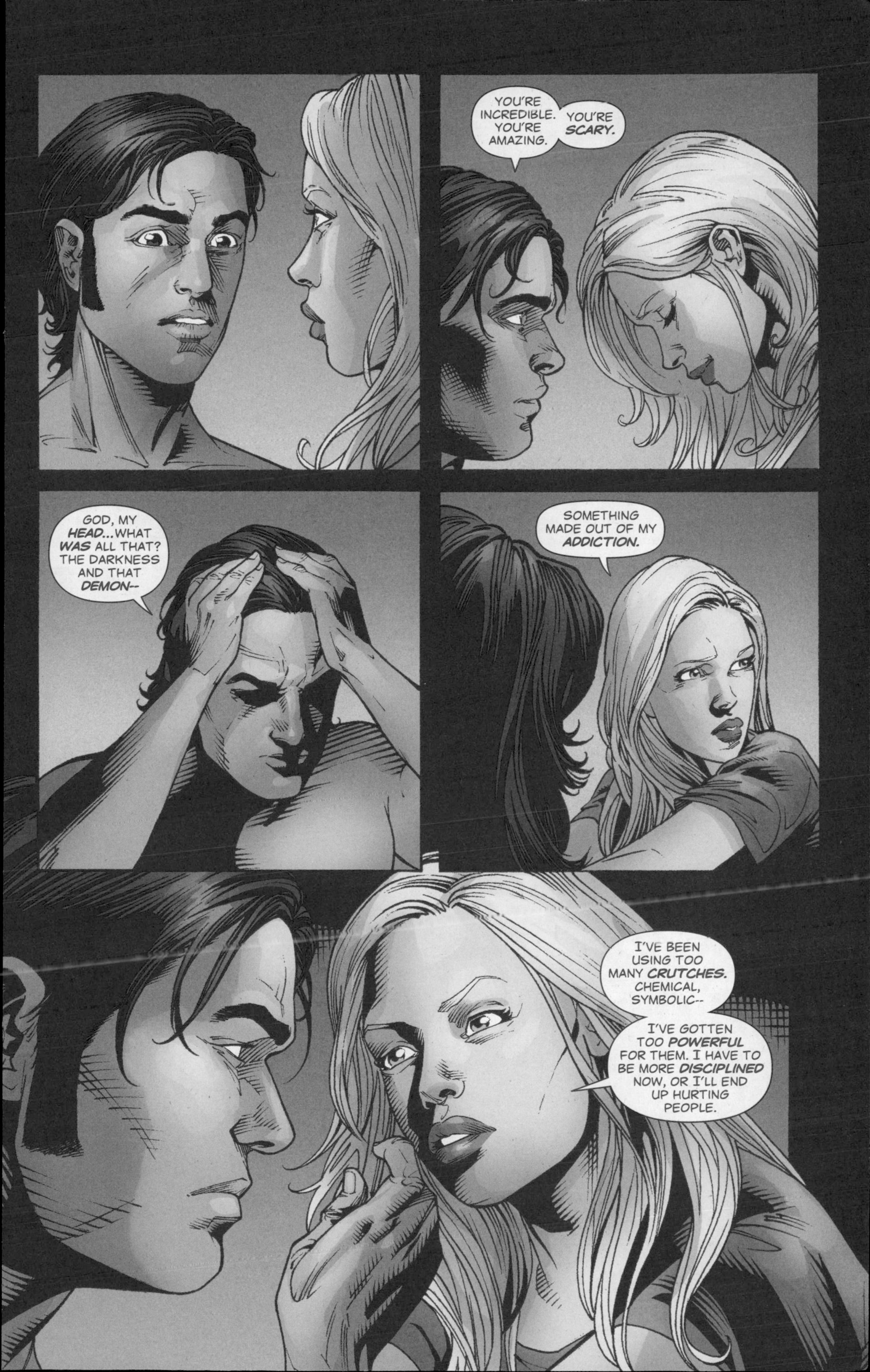
YOU'RE INCREDIBLE. YOU'RE AMAZING.
YOU'RE SCARY.
GOD, MY HEAD...WHAT WAS ALL THAT? THE DARKNESS AND THAT DEMON--
SOMETHING MADE OUT OF MY ADDICTION.
I'VE BEEN USING TOO MANY CRUTCHES. CHEMICAL, SYMBOLIC--
I'VE GOTTEN TOO POWERFUL FOR THEM. I HAVE TO BE MORE DISCIPLINED NOW, OR I'LL END UP HURTING PEOPLE.

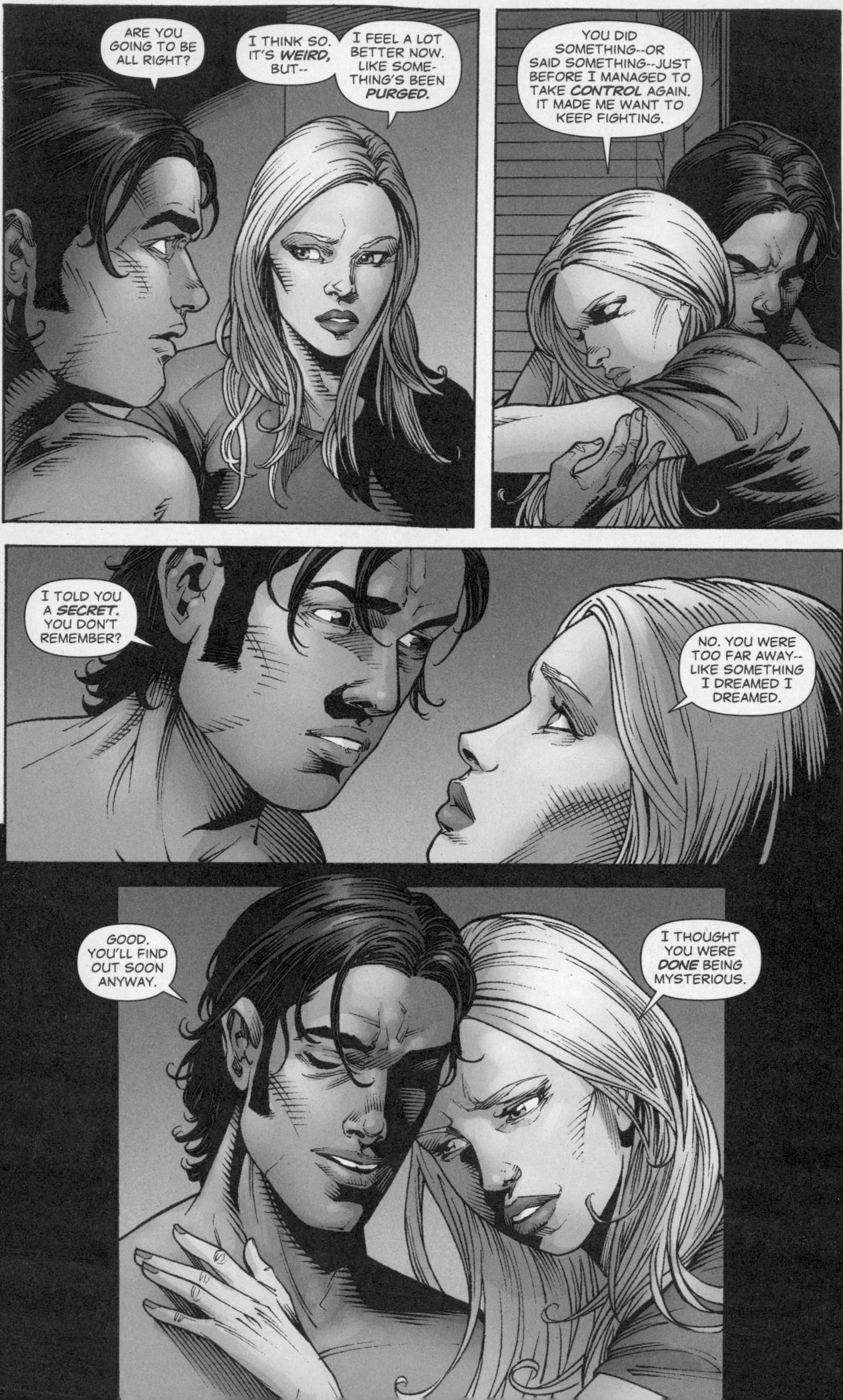

ARE YOU GOING TO BE ALL RIGHT?
I THINK SO. IT'S *WEIRD,* BUT--
I FEEL A LOT BETTER NOW. LIKE SOMETHING'S BEEN *PURGED.*
YOU DID SOMETHING--OR SAID SOMETHING--JUST BEFORE I MANAGED TO TAKE *CONTROL* AGAIN. IT MADE ME WANT TO KEEP FIGHTING.
I TOLD YOU A *SECRET.* YOU DON'T REMEMBER?
NO. YOU WERE TOO FAR AWAY--LIKE SOMETHING I DREAMED I DREAMED.
GOOD. YOU'LL FIND OUT SOON ANYWAY.
I THOUGHT YOU WERE *DONE* BEING MYSTERIOUS.

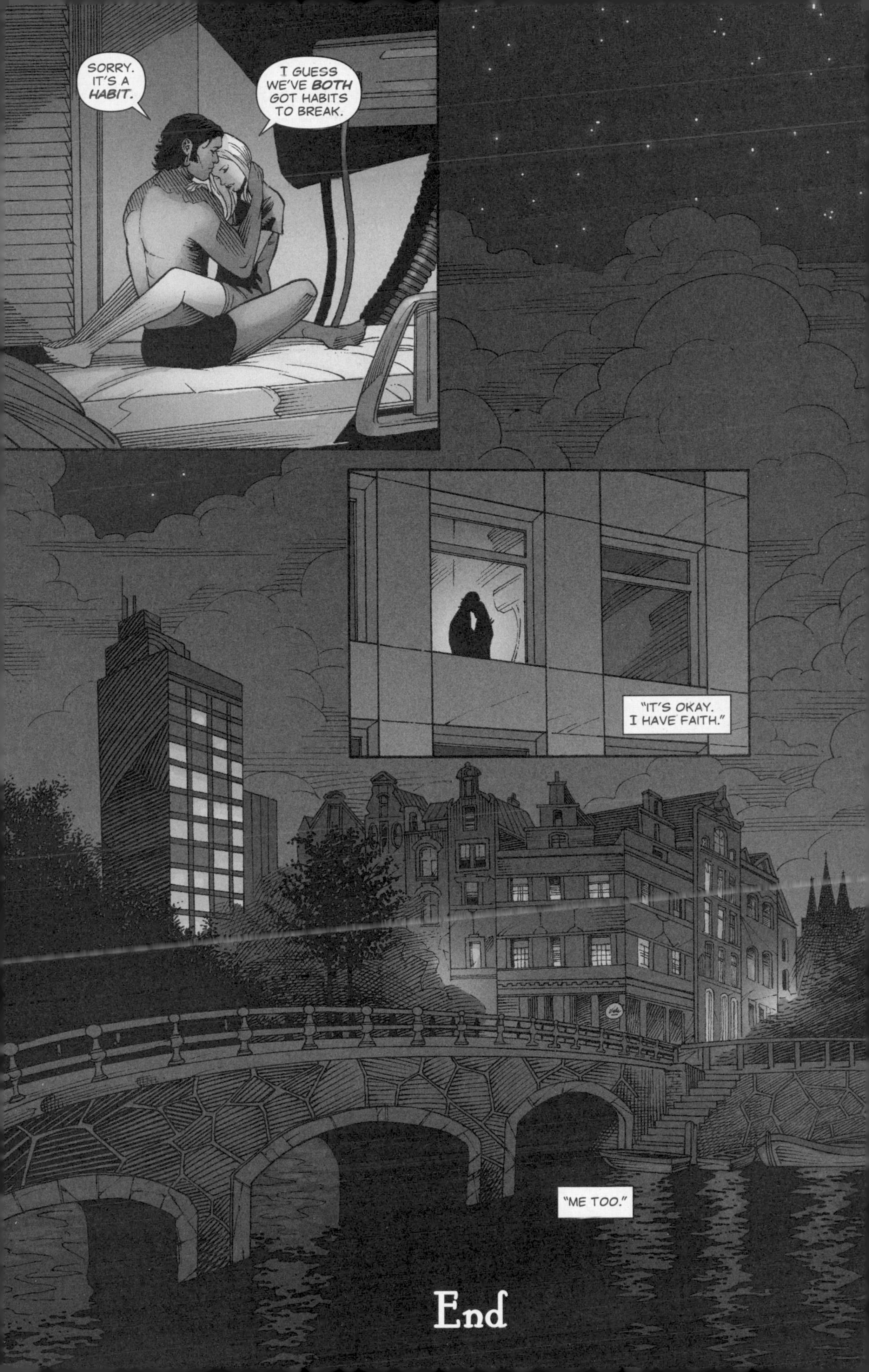
SORRY. IT'S A HABIT.
I GUESS WE'VE BOTH GOT HABITS TO BREAK.
"IT'S OKAY. I HAVE FAITH."
"ME TOO."
End

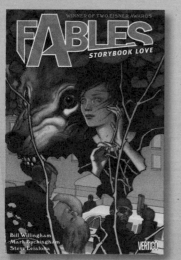